MR. PRESIDENT

An Introduction to American History

by

MAURICE ASHLEY

> Great men are only signposts
> BUDDHA

Biography Index Reprint Series

BOOKS FOR LIBRARIES PRESS
FREEPORT, NEW YORK

First Published 1948 by Jonathan Cape, Limited
Reprinted 1972 by arrangement

Library of Congress Cataloging in Publication Data

Ashley, Maurice Percy.
　Mr. President; an introduction to American history.

　(Biography index reprint series)
　Reprint of the 1948 ed.
　CONTENTS: George Washington.--Thomas Jefferson.--Andrew Jackson. [etc.]
　Includes bibliographies.
　1. Presidents--U. S.--Biography.　I. Title.
E176.1.A8　1972　　　　973'.099　　　　79-38317
ISBN 0-8369-8115-4

PRINTED IN THE UNITED STATES OF AMERICA
BY
NEW WORLD BOOK MANUFACTURING CO., INC.
HALLANDALE, FLORIDA 33009

CONTENTS

I	'MR. PRESIDENT' — INTRODUCTION	9
II	GEORGE WASHINGTON	31
III	THOMAS JEFFERSON	105
IV	ANDREW JACKSON	169
V	ABRAHAM LINCOLN	235
VI	THEODORE ROOSEVELT	311
VII	WOODROW WILSON	369
VIII	EPILOGUE — THE UNITED STATES AND GREAT BRITAIN	433
	INDEX	443

ILLUSTRATIONS

GEORGE WASHINGTON *facing* p. 31
> A bust made from life by Jean Antoine Houdon at Mount Vernon just before Washington's first term as President
> *Reproduced by courtesy of World Wide Photographs*

THOMAS JEFFERSON 105
> Portrait by Rembrandt Peale
> *Reproduced by courtesy of the New York Historical Society*

ANDREW JACKSON 169
> A portrait painted at the White House by Ashel B. Durand during Jackson's second term as President
> *Reproduced by courtesy of the New York Historical Society*

ABRAHAM LINCOLN 235
> A photograph taken by Alexander Gardner four days before the assassination
> *Reproduced by courtesy of Picture Post Library*

THEODORE ROOSEVELT 311
> A photograph taken by H. Havelock Pierce in 1908

WOODROW WILSON 369
> An unfinished portrait by Sir William Orpen capturing his 'rough-and-tumble' look
> *Reproduced by courtesy of Bernard M. Baruch*

MR. PRESIDENT

CHAPTER I

'MR. PRESIDENT'—INTRODUCTION

We are told that when the proposed office of President was originally being examined by the Makers of the Constitution of the United States there was some lively discussion over the manner in which this novel functionary ought to be addressed. The Committee of Detail at the Philadelphia Convention, reporting in August 1787, recommended that he should be called 'your Excellency'. However, in the written Constitution, as it was finally approved by the Convention to be the lodestar of the American people for more than one hundred and sixty years, no such official designation was included. Again the debate raged in the first Senate over the proper mode of address for the President after George Washington had been elected to this position. Should he perhaps be called 'His High Mightiness' after the Dutch style? But it was ultimately determined — and has since become the settled procedure — that the chief executive of the Federal Government should be known simply and with almost studied modesty as 'Mr. President'.

It was a conclusion in harmony with the spirit of the years. For the Presidency of the United States is indeed a unique democratic conception. It epitomizes and embodies much that is most striking in American history, a subject of which all too little is familiar even to educated citizens of other lands. Is it not time that more was known?

In 1944 the author of this book, disguised as a military intelligence officer, paid his first visit to the United States of America. The passage of the North Atlantic by a liner intended for warmer climates took nearly ten days; the ship zigzagged through endless expanses of dismally grey water to evade German submarines; and the sea was so swept by storms that a colonel who had fought with the Eighth Army at El Alamein, with whom I played bridge, turned yellow and then green and finally threw in his hand. I passed much of the time lying in a crowded cabin reading James Truslow Adams's excellent *Epic of America*, one of the few decent

'MR. PRESIDENT'

books in the ship's tatty library. It was a relief and a joy when our faithful vessel chugged up the Hudson River, passed the Statue of Liberty, surprisingly almost as green as the colonel's face had been, and docked amid vivid hooting bustle beneath the superb skyscrapers of New York. A beautiful girl, driving a van somewhat puzzlingly marked 'American Red Cross', took our party to the station, we were settled in armchairs in a Pullman car, and in four hours the train tore over two hundred miles to reach Washington, the federal capital.

I was assured that this journey is one of the dullest in the United States. It was not so then for me, now an acolyte in American history. First, there were the Hackensack Marshes, offering a most extraordinary contrast to the sophisticated charms of New York City, conjuring up thoughts of what the almost empty Atlantic border must have looked like when, four hundred years earlier, there was nothing but vast forest, distant mountains, mud, and Indians. Then one saw on every side the American shacks, each with their verandas, painted porticos, and simple homeliness. Fronting on the railway were samples of the imposing output of American war workers, aeroplanes and tanks and every mechanical device of the Western world. In the area penetrated by this stretch of 'dull' railroad I knew had been enacted many famous episodes in the history of the American people, both at the time of the founding of the Republic and since. New York, Philadelphia, Baltimore, Washington — all were sometime meeting-places of the American Congress. But in so far as American history requires monuments they are to be found in the railroads, the factories, the shacks. The novice in American history will find imagination and a sharp appreciation of more value than the inspection of monuments. The United States must still be a relatively young country. Perhaps its citizens may be wiser for their part, with so many frontiers of the human spirit still open for their conquest, to plan the future than to ponder the past. However, for those of us in the Old World who still grope forward towards the ideal of the good life, an understanding of the American background is more necessary today than it ever was. It is pointless to be supercilious because the American way of life is not ours. One might as well be supercilious about the atom bomb.

INTRODUCTION

At Washington Station, where an excellent 'share the taxi' system then prevailed, so obscure was the suburb for which I was destined that I became an exception to the rule. The taxi carried me a long way through what seemed to be then — and seems to me still in retrospect — one of the most handsome cities in the world. The taxi-driver talked in a friendly informal way and told me that he had a son stationed in England. Every other taxi-driver who subsequently drove me through Washington talked in a friendly informal way and told me that he had a son stationed in England. And from that moment during the weeks I remained in the American capital the social inhibitions, the glacial stares, the neat reticences of London life vanished from my mind. Mr. James Pope-Hennessy, who went to Washington a little later than I did on the same kind of work, named the book in which he wrote of his experiences: *America is an Atmosphere*. Some critics considered that title was puerile. I cannot imagine why. He is right. It has also been said that every man has his little America which he must discover at his own cost or perish. That day I discovered, or thought I had discovered, what America meant — what it has always meant to travellers or immigrants from Europe. And I determined that if the opportunity offered I would look back through the pages of American history and learn what lay behind my elemental discovery, trying to unearth some of its features both for my own benefit and for that of others. This book is the result.

It would have been presumptuous on my part to have attempted to include within the limits of one volume the whole exciting and complicated tale from the struggle for survival among the Pilgrim Fathers to the evolution of the United States as the richest nation on earth. Attracted by the extraordinary institution of the Presidency I have ventured instead to recall and repeat a part of the American story by summarizing the lives of six American Presidents who, it seems to me, are among the fascinating figures of history and trying to gauge their adventures and explain their problems. It is with sorrow that I have had to omit Franklin D. Roosevelt from my list, for the only man to have been four times elected to this strenuous office must long remain an exceptional historical figure; but the omission could not be avoided — the full records are not yet available and the tale is still contemporary (and explosive). Of the other American political leaders who attracted me the most compelling was William Jennings Bryan, the Silver Voice of the West; although, however, like Henry Clay — another regretted exclusion — Bryan stood three times for the Presidency he was never elected and it appeared better to court consistency by limiting my field to men who held the presidential office, where a statesman's conduct can be judged by the most exacting of tests. Thus my choices are George Washington, Thomas Jefferson, Andrew Jackson, Abraham Lincoln, Theodore Roosevelt and Woodrow Wilson. That four of the six were technically southerners and four out of the six of a radical tinge will not, I think, condemn my choice. All were notable men and survive yet not only in their letters and speeches but also in the influence which they still exercise upon American political thought and behaviour. Moreover their lives were all distinct signposts in American history. Washington laid the foundations of the Republic and Jefferson propounded an enduring American political philosophy; Jackson pressed Jefferson's democratic ideals to a severe conclusion. Lincoln preserved the Union which the doctrine of states rights as preached by Jefferson and Jackson (though both had recognized its dangers) had threatened. It was left to Theodore Roosevelt and Woodrow Wilson in their completely different ways to measure the implication for world affairs of the emergence of that unquestionably Great Power which had been welded in the furnace of the Civil War.

What makes the Presidency so remarkable? It is, surely, that it combines many roles performed in other countries by more than one man. The President has to be what the King is in England, what the President is in France, and to a large extent what the Prime Minister is in most nations. Professor C. Perry Patterson has written that 'as a result of more than a century of struggle for supremacy by the President we practically have government by an irresponsible executive'. And yet it is clear beyond vestige of uncertainty that the Framers of the American Constitution never intended that the chief executive should be so compelling a figure. On the contrary, convinced, as they were, that King George III was the villain who had robbed the aspiring

INTRODUCTION

pioneers of their deserved political independence, they were anxious to prevent a ruler with far-reaching executive powers from establishing himself in their midst. Reporting on the atmosphere at the Convention of 1787 Ezra Styles wrote:

> As to the President it appeared to be the opinion of the Convention that he should be a character responsible to the nations [i.e. the States] as well as the federal empire. To this end that as much power should be given him as could be consistent with guarding against all possibility of his ascending in a tract of years or ages to despotism and absolute monarchy... of which all were cautious... accordingly they meant to give considerable weight as supreme executive, but fixed him dependent on the States at large, and at all times impeachable.

Nevertheless, in spite of this careful attitude in the Convention many influential politicians evidently thought that the Constitution went too far even in the limited powers that it conferred on the chief executive: for Alexander Hamilton wrote in *The Federalist* (a series of papers published in defence of the Constitution) of how

> he has been decorated with attributes superior in dignity and splendour to those of a King of Great Britain. He has been shown to us with the diadem sparkling on his brow and the imperial purple flowing in his train....

but pacified his readers by assuring them that the President would be a magistrate and not a king.

In fact the Constitution was intended as a system of checks and balances, bathed in the reflected light of early Whig England, and all rights in it were narrowly restricted so far as mere paper can restrict rights. The prescribed functions of the President may be seen from the following short extracts from Article II:

> Section I. The executive power shall be vested in a President of the United States of America. He shall hold his office during the term of four years....
> Section II. The President shall be Commander-in-Chief of the army and navy of the United States, and of the militia of the several States, when called into the actual service of the United States... He shall have power, by and with the advice of the Senate, to make treaties, provided two-thirds of the Senators present concur....

'MR. PRESIDENT'

Section III. He shall from time to time give to the Congress information of the state of the Union, and recommend to their consideration such measures as he shall judge necessary and expedient . . . he shall take care that the laws be faithfully executed. . . .
Section IV. The President . . . shall be removed from office on impeachment for, and conviction of, treason, bribery, or other high crimes and misdemeanours.

Arguing from this text Alexander Hamilton was at pains to prove that the President was a far weaker vessel than the King of England. The first President was indeed most cautious in his claims to advise Congress. And yet, as Professor Corwin pointed out in his recent invaluable essay, the history of the Presidency 'taken by and large' has been 'a history of aggrandizement', though of intermittent aggrandizement.

How far has this aggrandizement derived from the character of the elected Presidents themselves? In the formative stages of American history it has been denied that this could have been the case. Professor Swisher, writing in 1941, observed: 'It was always possible to find extremely able men in Congress, whereas [up to 1860] with few exceptions the occupants of the presidency were mediocre men as far as executive leadership was concerned.' Lord Bryce in his *American Commonwealth,* published in 1888, could head one of his chapters: 'Why Great Men are not Chosen Presidents.' Professor Woodrow Wilson, himself later to become President, also spoke of the eclipse of the Presidency in the eighteen-eighties. The wheel then turned and Americans of the present generation would agree that there have never been more strong-minded and ambitious Presidents than Woodrow Wilson himself and the two Roosevelts.

But, taking American history as a whole, it is simply untrue to say that great men do not become Presidents. The six Presidents whose biographies are summarized in this book were all great men, and others, with whom I do not deal, such as the two Adams in early times and Cleveland and Taft in later days, were men of outstanding ability. Moreover, as Professor Laski has observed, the institution itself seems to bring out much that is best and most courageous in citizens called to this office. Thirdly — and this probably is the most important point of all — it is not so much any

INTRODUCTION

change in the character of the Presidents but the birth of a complex industrial civilization, conferring responsibilities on the Federal Government that could not possibly have been foreseen by the Framers of the Constitution, that has heightened the stature and significance of the Presidency. Once the railways, the big trusts, the modern banking system and the increase in population and consequent division of labour began to integrate the different parts of the American continent, the Federal Government was compelled to widen its range of authority. And the President, who had been created by the Constitution as the symbol of federal union and had been empowered to see that 'the laws were faithfully executed' had every occasion and chance to employ his powers. Finally, as the United States became a world power, the President's importance as the directing force in foreign policy grew. For did not even Thomas Jefferson, a relatively modest claimant on presidential authority, assert that 'the transaction of business with foreign nations is executive altogether'?

Thus it is fair to say that it was at least in part historical circumstances that brought about the aggrandizement of the presidential office. But admittedly another cause was the character of the famous Presidents who used their opportunities and recognized their broadening responsibilities as the heads of an expanding nation. Indeed each of the six Presidents, whose lives are described in this book, was associated with some particular phase in the development of the office.

George Washington not only consciously fashioned the ceremonial character of the Presidency, but also asserted its independence in the general control of foreign affairs. Ceremonially the President has necessarily to be an aloof figure: he may, as has happened in our own time, hold press conferences and 'jolly' the reporters or address the fireside public in a confidential manner over the wireless, but he is none the less a symbol, the man under the flag, the layer of foundation stones, the shaker of countless hands, the deliverer of appropriate messages to sovereigns and dictators overseas. He must be careful where he goes to dinner and whom he invites home. Although some of the more ardent Republicans criticized Washington's principles of etiquette his extreme scrupulousness on these matters set a pattern that has, on the whole, been followed. But possibly Washington's most telling contribution to the evolution of the office was his decision not to be a mere constitutional monarch, a treasured rubber stamp, relying on Congress for direction. It appears that some of the Framers had in fact intended that the Senate should act as the President's council of state, a plan that might conceivably have worked in those days when the Senate contained only twenty-six members, but the intention, if it existed, was not to be realized. Furthermore, in at least one instance, in relation to foreign policy Washington claimed his right to stick to the letter of his constitutional powers when he refused to lay the papers on the matter before the House of Representatives.

If Washington, the selfless military hero, thus established the Presidency as an influential national institution with the chief executive depending for advice on his own chosen cabinet rather than upon the Senate, Jefferson in contrast further strengthened the institution precisely because he was the acknowledged leader of a party. Though in his first inaugural address Jefferson had spoken as if he conceived of his office in Washington's terms as standing above and outside party, in fact his immense weight and power rested upon his position as the Republican party leader. His cabinet was not, as Washington's had been, at any rate initially, a group of skilled advisers of all shades of opinion, but a party grouping which existed to fulfil the wishes of the leader. Only a majority party leader, who could rely on his supporters in Congress, could have carried through some of Jefferson's policies, notably the Louisiana Purchase. And from Jefferson's time onward the American President has invariably been the chosen leader of a party. Admittedly up to the time when the national party conventions meet there will be competition for the party leadership but once the convention has chosen its presidential candidate, that candidate becomes *ipso facto* the party leader. On the other hand, a party leader, however able, loses virtue if his party splits under him as happened in the cases of Stephen Douglas and Theodore Roosevelt. The Framers of the Constitution evidently conceived of the chief executive as a national leader above party chosen on sheer merit by an elaborately devised system of indirect election. But this ideal was frustrated by solid facts and thus the President acquired a source of strength undreamt of by the Framers.

INTRODUCTION

Andrew Jackson further enlarged the authority of the Presidency by democratic or, as some asserted, by demagogic means: for he laid down the principle that the President is peculiarly the representative of the whole American people. The system of indirect election so painstakingly devised, so carefully praised, had soon collapsed as before a whiff of grapeshot. The presidential electors voted as the majority in the states from which they came desired them to do and the sum of their votes reflected a popular wish. As against this the Senators (only one-third of whom are elected every second year) are never subject to any tidal wave of public feeling. They are there, as James Harrington, their seventeenth-century English sponsor, designed that they should be, to be a safeguard against the excesses of democracy. Moreover, Senators always have special responsibilities to their own states. The House of Representatives is even more than the Senate a conglomeration of local interests. But the President is a national figure and his choice is a national democratic choice. Jackson was the representative not so much of the aspiring western pioneers of middle American history, but, as Professor Schlesinger has shown in his recent book, of the hitherto inarticulate underprivileged of the industrial east. Like Washington, Jackson had a popular appeal as a military hero. 'It is a proud day for the people,' wrote one of his friends at the time of his first election, 'General Jackson is *their own* president.' Indeed so magnetic was Jackson's hold on popular opinion, as he appreciated intuitively what the electors wanted, that he was able to defy a Senate deeply hostile to his policies and in the end he saw the members erase from their own records the vote of censure they had passed upon him. It is no exaggeration to say that almost for the first time in modern history Jackson exemplified the democratically elected leader who became virtually an autocrat with his own selected group of advisers and his own propaganda machine. Though his political programme may not have been entirely wise, he did not abuse his advantages. Yet he was freely accused of dictatorship.

Abraham Lincoln extended the powers of the Presidency by the use he made of the clause in the Constitution which declared that the President should *ex-officio* be: 'Commander-in-chief of the army and navy of the United States, and of the militia of the several States, when called into the actual service of the United States.' Lincoln was elected by a minority of the total votes of the nation and not a single southern state voted in his favour. His election was a signal for civil war. Yet though in consequence it might have seemed that he would have welcomed the aid and counsel of the legislature Lincoln did not at once summon an extraordinary session of Congress (as the Constitution permitted) but of his own authority called up the militia and declared a blockade of the southern ports. Later he suspended writs of habeas corpus and imposed martial law on new categories of citizens. Even his proclamation emancipating the slaves was made in his capacity as Commander-in-Chief. Although condemned on account of his independent conduct of the war for seeking to erect a dictatorship, Lincoln retorted that 'The Executive' had 'found the duty of employing the war power in defence of the Government forced upon him'. In the wars of 1917-18 and 1941-45 President Wilson and President F. D. Roosevelt respectively expanded the application of this 'war power' in particular by creating new organs of administration outside the control of Congress. They too, like Jackson and Lincoln, were accused of being dictators.

After Lincoln's murder there was a quick reaction against presidential 'dictatorship' and the House of Representatives attempted to impeach Lincoln's successor, President Andrew Johnson, before the Senate because he had removed his Secretary of War from office in defiance of an act which forbade him to dismiss any officer appointed by him 'with the advice and consent of the Senate' until a successor had been appointed in the same way. Johnson's impeachment was rejected in the Senate by only one vote. But it was enough that the Presidency had survived the same kind of ordeal that had brought Charles I to the scaffold and transformed the character of the English monarchy.

If Lincoln developed the so-called war power, Theodore Roosevelt took full advantage of Section 3 of Article II of the Constitution which stated that the President should 'from time to time . . . recommend to the consideration of Congress such measures as he shall judge necessary and expedient'. It is perhaps worth observing that such records of the Philadelphia Convention as survive do not suggest that it was in fact at all the intention of

INTRODUCTION

the Framers that the President should announce proposals to Congress in the same way that a British Prime Minister outlines his legislative programme in the King's Speech. In the Committee of Detail the draft section read:

> It shall be his duty to inform the Legislature of the condition of the United States *so far as may respect his Department — to recommend matters to their consideration, etc.*

Of course in practice a modern American President cannot ensure that the legislation he desires will reach the statute book. Even if his party has a majority in both Houses (which of course is not necessarily the case since the House of Representatives is elected every two years together with one-third of the Senate, while the President is elected every four years) the proposals that he places before Congress may be distorted before they become acts. Still it should be remembered that it is only in quite modern times that the President has persistently claimed his right to determine legislation at all. 'The present-day role of the President as policy determiner in the legislative field', writes Professor Corwin, 'is largely the creation of the two Roosevelts and Woodrow Wilson, each of whom came to the Presidency following a notable and successful experience as governor of his home state', and he goes on to quote the first Roosevelt as saying that 'a good executive under the present conditions of American political life must take a very active interest in getting the right kind of legislation, in addition to performing his executive duties with an eye single to the public welfare'. Although an American President seldom or never has a party majority directly bound to his leadership on which he can rely for the passing of bills of the kind that he desires, he does have available many indirect means of bringing pressure to bear on Congress to carry out his policies. In the first place he has the right to veto bills and to explain to the country why he has vetoed them. Most Presidents have used this power and though Congress may override the veto by a two-thirds majority of both Houses it frequently does not do so and the exercise of the veto has come to be regarded not as a tyranny of an autocrat but as the wise caution of a statesman. Secondly, though the influence that the President can exert on individual members of the two Houses through executive patronage tends to be exaggerated and has

'MR. PRESIDENT'

probably diminished in recent years, to compensate for this he now has, through the press and the radio, instruments for bringing his prestige as acknowledged national leader to bear on any question, for in a country where freedom of expression exists public feelings must be regarded. It was Andrew Jackson who first employed the technique of appealing to public opinion over the head of Congress, but it was only as the need for economic and social legislation began to grow in the United States that this technique was exerted in support of legislation inspired by the President. Not only did Theodore Roosevelt try to fashion legislation but he also made the claim that there were special sources of political authority available to the executive power wherever it was not specifically forbidden by the Constitution. 'I did not usurp power,' he said in his autobiography, 'but I did greatly broaden the use of executive power.' In fact Theodore Roosevelt was not responsible for any vast volume of social legislation: an impartial study of his life indicates that his influence was far weightier in the sphere of foreign policy. But his methods were exemplary to his Democratic successors.

In Woodrow Wilson there may be seen to have culminated all the power and authority developed during the terms of his strong predecessors. Like Washington, Wilson was the acknowledged national head of the Union, but of a Union far mightier than in Washington's day. Like Jefferson, he was the chosen leader of an organized political party which at least during his first term looked to him for guidance. Like Andrew Jackson he was carried into office on a wave of revolt against existing economic institutions and could therefore appeal to the people at large to give him moral backing in his reformist policies. Even when in his second term the party majority against him in Congress was hostile, so confident was he of his right to represent the wishes of the people as a whole that he believed that if only he could carry his case to the people, he could overcome the opposition in the Senate — as Jackson had once done. Finally he took over from Abraham Lincoln the bold application of the 'war power' and from Theodore Roosevelt his theory of executive 'stewardship' and legislative leadership to forward his own programmes in war and peace. Franklin D. Roosevelt with all his extraordinary electoral victories and his full three terms of office only adopted much the same

INTRODUCTION

methods for developing presidential influence as had been employed by Woodrow Wilson. To sum up, the modern President is or can be a kind of constitutional monarch, the chief federal executive, the leader of a powerful and often dominant political party, the unique expression of the democratic will, the director of foreign policy, the wielder of vast powers in time of war, and the frequent source of legislative inspiration.

Thus the office of American President has burgeoned from a largely ceremonial institution into one of the most forceful forms of political leadership within the scope of a Western democracy. Though it is true that treaties require the assent of the Senate — and that in one famous instance that assent was withheld — the President's practical control of his country's foreign policy is not challenged; in all internal questions, especially since economic and social matters have become chiefly of an inter-state character, the force of his authority is considerable and an energetic man has many varied means of influencing policy not only by recommending or vetoing legislation but also through administrative action. He is not, like a British Prime Minister, merely the first among equals in his Cabinet, but he *is* the Cabinet, the supreme executive who is in no way obliged to acquiesce in the advice of his chosen ministers. He is secure in office for four years, however the winds of public opinion may blow. And the great American Presidents have proved by their examples that an able man in office can rule in spite of the dead hand of an eighteenth-century written constitution which was designed to ensure a weak central government.

In this brief summary of the roots of presidential power much of the argument has necessarily been left out. But it must again be emphasized that the growth from these roots had not been a continuous process. Every new manifestation of the President's authority has been resisted either by Congress because he was thought to be encroaching on the territory of the Legislature or by the individual states of the Union because he was deemed to be overstepping the bounds of federal authority or by private interests such as the banks, big trusts or corporations, whose activities he attempted to restrain, or by politicians who genuinely feared the rise of autocracy. The constitutional history of the United States is punctuated by a series of *causes célèbres* in the Supreme Court, many of which have been concerned with the limits of presidential power. And even when a position has been won by the chief executive it has not always been held and has even on occasion been voluntarily abandoned.

There are in fact two main theories about the history of the United States as seen in terms of the Presidency. Some say that in the last resort the weight of the Presidency depends on the man who is President. This is a natural, understandable, and human (should one say womanly?) point of view. After a Jackson will come a Van Buren and a W. H. Harrison; after a Lincoln a Johnson and a Grant; after a Wilson a Harding and a Coolidge. Some Presidents assign a higher moral value to their office than others: some regard themselves merely as the chosen leaders of their parties with a well-defined sphere of action — did not Coolidge say that the business of the United States is business? The other theory minimizes the significance of the individual and assures us that while great men become Presidents, Presidents may also become great men. But, the argument continues, there will be a certain swing of the pendulum after the passing of those Presidents who attempt too bold a national leadership: thus a Lincoln, as it were, *produces* a Johnson and a Wilson a Harding. Congress reasserts itself and redresses the balance. A Supreme Court that has perhaps modified earlier constitutional judgments in the light of changed social conditions will revert to a more rigid interpretation of the Constitution. The more ruthless manipulators of private enterprise, formerly driven to take cover from the blasts of public condemnation, will creep out of their hiding-places. Evidently there is truth in both these theories; they are not altogether contradictory; they remind us of the special characteristics and variations to be found in the exercise of the American presidential office.

And yet it is easy to forget them. When Franklin D. Roosevelt held the office many people in England thought of the United States of America purely in terms of his national leadership and were astonished when they visited America to find how virulent was the opposition to his policy. When the author was in Washington early in 1944 he discovered only a barber and a taxi-driver with a word of praise for him: in smart circles it was safer to keep his name out of the conversation. Mr. James Pope-Hennessy was shocked at rejoicing he perceived on Roosevelt's death. On

INTRODUCTION

the other hand, when Mr. Truman succeeded and in 1946 there was a Republican victory in the Congressional elections it was widely thought in England that Mr. Truman would be compelled to resign — though the existence of a President alongside a politically hostile Congress has been no uncommon feature in the history of the United States. But whatever view one holds of this institution no one will deny that it occupies a central place in American history, and therefore this attempt to retell the American story through the lives of six of its presidential leaders is surely not unduly lopsided.

This book ambitiously has three themes. First, it is a broad outline of American history in terms of the lives of six Presidents. Secondly, it attempts to record something of the evolution of a remarkable democratic institution. Thirdly, being written by a British author, it tries incidentally to expound some of the main phases in Anglo-American relations, a delicate and still not wholly explored topic.

The first thing an Englishman writing about the United States has to understand is that he is not in any sense writing about his own country, even though he is concerned with an English-speaking people. Not forty per cent of the population of the United States is of English descent. Up to 1914 two of the principal wars fought by the American people were against Great Britain and every American schoolchild learning his first lesson in political history is taught to loathe the British tyrants who tried to smother the freedom of their country. Suspicion of British motives and never-to-be forgotten tales of Perfidious Albion gnaw deep into the American mind.

Another obstacle to Anglo-American understanding is a singularly uncommon way of life, which we all recognize feelingly when we go to each other's countries. British officials on duty in the United States have often had an unpraiseworthy facility for keeping their noses in the air. Even before the War of Independence Americans were complaining that the conduct of British army officers stationed there resembled that of 'Turkish bashas'. American representatives in England can, for their part, be painfully frank, since our sensitiveness is not pronounced. American officials like to do business by making charming promises over the telephone, committing them to writing as little as possible; British civil servants prefer the tightly drawn loose minute. Many other minor differences of habit and customs from eating and drinking to travelling and smoking, reflect contrasting ways of living. Some of the British lecturers who wrote bright reminiscences of quick short trips round the United States during the last war remarked in innocent amazement on such differences, thus disclosing their own profound ignorance of American history.

Another point that we Englishmen often fail to recognize is that in the social sense the United States is a genuinely egalitarian country. One day I was walking the long distance which it was usually necessary to cover to get from one section of the then War Department building (the 'Pentagon') to another. A workman, struggling with some cardboard contraption, stopped me, saying: 'You're a Britisher, then you must carry a penknife. Lend it me, will you?' I had a penknife and was delayed until the piece of cardboard had been dealt with. Such an incident could scarcely have happened in the British War Office. Americans are equal because Jack has always been as good as his master, save where Jack was a Negro or a defenceless immigrant. That is largely because they have always been a pioneering people. Among pioneers it is the weakest and most foolish who is thrust to the wall: social status does not count any more than it did in the desert island where Sir James Barrie's 'Admirable Crichton' found himself. And since on the frontiers of civilization equality of opportunity is always to be found, Jack is not only as good as his master, but one day expects to be master himself. Out of the thousands of American films I have seen a majority have had the same subject and the same moral: the boy or girl wants to make good, persists, and does make good. To make good is the American dream. It is no doubt a dream here too, but one that hitherto has so seldom been realized as to have been but a rare thread of life. In the land where I write as individuals grow old, ambition recedes and the most they demand is the security of their fireside in the winter and of a hedged garden in the summer. And perhaps an old nation like ours feels much the same — though maybe revolution lies round the corner.

If we turn from domestic themes to questions of foreign policy, we again see how deep is the abyss between British and American

INTRODUCTION

history. No part of the British Isles is far from the sea which has always been our ditch as well as our highway. Our enemies must cross the sea and from the time of King Henry VIII our fate has been interwoven with the prowess of the Royal Navy. Even in 1940, in the age of air power, the Germans recoiled before the idea of invading England while our fleet was in being on the flank of their line of advance. Through her navy Britain became an imperial nation (our critics called us an imperialist nation, although who but cranks speak of an imperialist Rome?) To preserve our independence and safeguard our empire British statesmen have pursued a policy known as that of the Balance of Power. They have not always pursued it consistently and sometimes the power has not in fact been balanced; but broadly it has been so: even the government of King Charles II, who loved the French and disliked the Dutch, had twice to ally itself with Holland against France. The United States, for her part, has, as Mr. Walter Lippmann recently argued, until modern times at any rate, had no foreign policy at all, for it did not need one. America's frontiers were no narrow channels. Her rulers did not need to gaze anxiously eastward across three thousand miles of the Atlantic or westward across three thousand miles of the Pacific. Until 1890 the thoughts of the rulers of the United States were concentrated upon the ever-changing frontiers of their own land — the Appalachians, the Mississippi, the Rockies. In Andrew Jackson's day America was described as 'a vast workshop over the door of which is printed in blazing characters: "No admittance here, except on business." ' Foreign policy could often be summed up in a few words wrongly attributed to President Washington's farewell address: 'No entangling alliances.' It was not until the Cuban war of 1898 that President and Senate had to concern themselves over finding a positive foreign policy — and a big navy. From then on their frontier lay across the oceans and the United States herself appeared to becoming an imperial power. It is because of this early secluded aspect of the history of the United States that in the past some American suggestions about how European affairs should be handled have seemed to us so strikingly out of touch with realities. But equally it must be said, since the United States has shown such genius for absorbing the many different and often antagonistic European immigrants into her civil society, that the impatience of her leaders with Europe's perpetual inability to solve its own nationality problems is understandable.

Today we in Europe are conscious that we are living in a revolutionary and volcanic age. In England we are now taking part in a social and economic transformation, which is hopeful and as yet bloodless. On the European mainland Germany has been torn from the political map, while Russia is a menacing enigma and France torn by dissensions, apparently a wraith of past greatness. But in the United States no sudden change can be prophesied with confidence: the twin institutions of personal freedom (as the old British Whigs understood the meaning of the phrase) and of private property still look sacrosanct. Perhaps the United States now sustains the part in our civilization, as more than one thinker has suggested, that the Roman Empire played in the classical world. In any case because of this contrast between a confused, divided and poverty-stricken Europe surrounded by power kegs of nuclear fuels and a still exuberant American Republic it appears that if a continuous civilization is to survive, if a link, never easily forged, is to couple this old country of ours with the United States, an understanding, or at least a genuine attempt to understand, the American character as shaped by American history is needed. So I wrote this book in the course of teaching myself what I wanted to find out about the main stream of American history of which, though an expensively educated 'doctor' of Oxford University, I had known almost nothing before. I hope the book may entertain and perhaps enlighten others.

London, August 1948

SELECT BIBLIOGRAPHY

HERBERT AGAR: *The People's Choice* (1933).
D. W. BROGAN: *The American Political System* (1943).
JAMES BRYCE: *The American Commonwealth* (1895).
EDWARD S. CORWIN: *The President: Offices and Powers* (1941).
MAX FARRAND: *Records of the Federal Convention* (1937).
(ALEXANDER HAMILTON and JAMES MADISON) *The Federalist* (Home University Library ed. Ashley).
H. J. LASKI: *The American Presidency: an Interpretation* (1940).
C. PERRY PATTERSON: *Presidential Government in the United States* (1947).
THEODORE ROOSEVELT: *Autobiography* (1913).
C. B. SWISHER: *American Constitutional Development* (1943).
ALEXIS DE TOCQUEVILLE: *Democracy in America* (trans. Reeve, 1840).
WOODROW WILSON: *Congressional Government* (1885).

GEORGE WASHINGTON

JEFFERSON
on
WASHINGTON

His mind was great and powerful without being of the very first order . . . It was slow in operation, being little aided by invention or imagination, but sure in conclusion . . . He was incapable of fear . . . Perhaps the strongest feature in his character was prudence . . . His integrity was the most pure, his justice the most inflexible I have ever known, no motives of interest or consanguinity, of friendship or hatred, being able to bias his decision. He was indeed, in every sense of the words, a wise, a good, and a great man. His temper was naturally irritable and high-toned; but reflection and resolution had obtained a firm and habitual ascendancy over it.

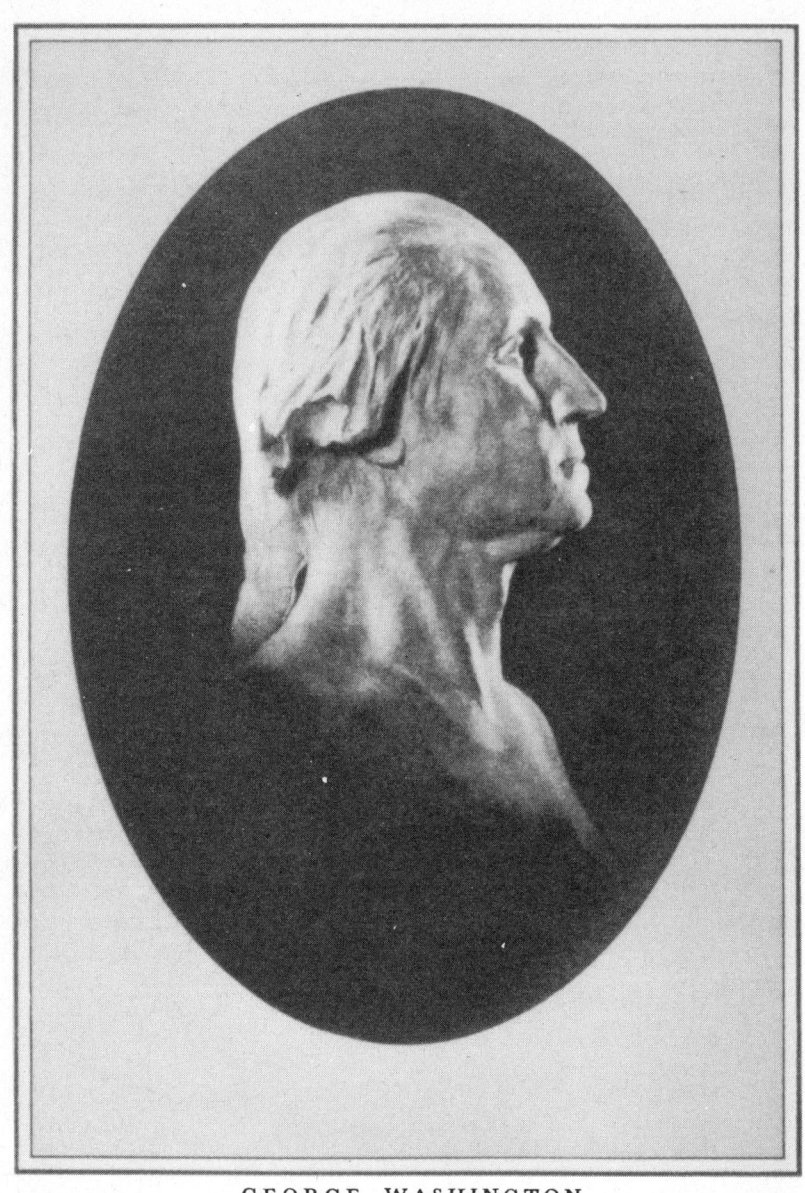

GEORGE WASHINGTON

CHAPTER II

GEORGE WASHINGTON

The character of George Washington, first President of the United States, was full of paradoxes or, let us say, since human beings, properly understood, are seldom really paradoxical, full of contrasts. Reserved in manner, prudent in conduct, and imperturbable to strangers, he had a fierce temper which would on occasions spill out into his letters and his actions. A realist in his handling of men, his approach to women was romantic with all the deference and charm of the eighteenth century. He could be both generous and parsimonious. Though sensitive to a slight and adamant in seeking respect for what he considered were his just rights, he willingly accepted unpaid duties if he was convinced it was necessary for the service of the community.

But the central contrast in Washington's character lay between a habitual slowness in reaching a conclusion and the quick bold resolutions which he sometimes took. Hence he was slow and careful in formulating his view of the presidential office which he undertook sadly. His idea of the Presidency was that it was a position of dignity and limited authority and had nothing to do with party politics. In line with the concept of the separation of powers enshrined in the Constitution he did not attempt to enforce his own opinions on Congress[1] save on foreign affairs and on how to conserve law and order — two spheres which he believed had been assigned to him. If Washington's ultimate view of the office had prevailed, the President might have become a sort of constitutional monarch or, to vary the simile, a Commander-in-Chief obedient to the civil authorities but who inflexibly resists any claim by politicians to dictate how he runs his army. But even in Washington's own lifetime party politics were born through a division of opinion over the respective rights of the Federal Government and the states. And since experience had made him the first and most convinced of the federalists in the end he was compelled to depend on the support of one party. If he had remained in office a third term he would have been irresistibly

[1] Professor C. Perry Patterson points out that he only used the veto power twice.

propelled in the direction taken by his successors — notably by Thomas Jefferson — of becoming a party leader.

The United States owes to Washington a debt for the manner in which he conducted himself as her first President. But apart from that, he earned his place upon an historical pedestal. That is not to say he was not a real man, often harassed and perplexed, and sometimes despairing. Maybe one might not have cared much to meet him on a parade ground or at a presidential party where he would have been frigid and exact. It would have been more entertaining to sample in the splendid isolation of Mount Vernon his dry humour, his streak of romance, even to witness — if one were not its victim — the sharp display of his temper. What a leader to follow into the heart of a battle! What a worker for a worth-while cause! And how fine an American gentleman!

1. THE YOUNG OFFICER AND FARMER
(1732-1758)

The great-great-grandfather of George Washington was a Church of England clergyman who, after having been a Fellow of Brasenose College, Oxford, and the incumbent of a rich living, fell upon hard times during the English Civil War. Sober and loyal but unfortunate, typical offshoot of a respectable county family, he died in 1652 just as Oliver Cromwell was becoming dictator, and his son John shook the dust of a confused and divided England from his boots. Towards the end of the Cromwellian Protectorate John Washington sailed as first mate to an absconding and witch-hunting captain for the colony of Virginia where men were still loyal to the King across the distant waters and land and liberty were there for the seeking of personable young men. John Washington acquired land and a wife who brought him more land and became moreover a colonel of militia repulsing the frontier Indians with a startingly firm hand.

Colonel John Washington's grandson, Augustine, inherited much of this newly found property and prosperity. In old Virginia one had to be a Jack of all trades and 'every farmer was a general, although nobody wanted to be a soldier'. Augustine was a planter, a speculator, a promoter and a sea captain who

THE YOUNG OFFICER AND FARMER

sailed to the homeland and brought convicts back. He was twice married. By his first wife he had two sons who survived him, Lawrence and Augustine. By his second wife he had six children of whom the great George was the eldest. George's mother was born Mary Ball and was known in her youth as the Rose of Epping Forest. She was a lady of strong character and awe-inspiring ways, equally noted for her querulous disposition and high temper, the latter a gift to her famous son. She smoked a pipe constantly, was illiterate and untidy. Augustine, her husband, died in 1743 at the age of forty-nine and evidently it was the mother's character that impressed itself most upon her own children. But Lawrence, the eldest son of Augustine by his first wife, was made guardian to his half-brother George and therefore acted as father as well as eldest brother.

George Washington was born on February 22nd (New Style), 1732 on one of three plantations owned by his father in Virginia named Wakefield. The Wakefield estate of some thousand acres lay between two creeks running out of the Lower Potomac. When George was but three his family moved to another and larger estate, Hunting Creek, further up the Potomac, three hundred miles from its mouth. This lovely estate was to gain world fame as Mount Vernon. But it seems that much of George's childhood was spent on the third estate, Ferry Farm, near the hamlet of Fredericksburg, which his mother inherited and where she lived most of her days, a faded rose, grumbling, smoking and usually disapproving of George.

George's education was scanty but sound as far as it went. He is said to have been first tutored by a convict carried to Virginia by his father and later to have found a schoolmaster and perhaps a school in Fredericksburg. Some of his school exercises survive: they cover geometry, surveying, geography and astronomy. Copies of business forms and legal instruments complete the impression that what he acquired was the three R's and a rudimentary business education. He also wrote some shockingly bad verse. (Most great men do this, but why do they not burn it?) In the end he attained a legible handwriting, some proficiency in the science of surveying, and a conscientious habit of keeping his accounts, delightful to his many biographers. A certain weakness in grammar and spelling was to persist.

GEORGE WASHINGTON

By modern university standards the education of George Washington was defective. An elaborate education is, however, a comparatively rare acquisition of the really famous and even if they have it, they often, like Edward Gibbon, pass it by. In after years they sometimes sigh over what they imagine were missed opportunities and drop a real or a crocodile tear. Do we detect a note of wistfulness in Washington when in later days he advised his stepson to acquire Greek, French and mathematics and added: 'I should think' philosophy was 'a very desirable knowledge for a gentleman'? What George Washington may perhaps have wanted was a grounding in those arts which train quickness of mind.

George Washington always took himself seriously. 'Idleness,' he wrote in his old age, 'is disreputable under any circumstances.' As a boy he must have worked hard and played hard, treating his surveying and accountancy with at least equal attention with that which he gave to dancing and singing, hunting and fishing. 'All Washingtons are born old', his friend, George William Fairfax, is supposed to have said. But only lonely children of serious-minded parents find the pleasures of youth escape them. Old age forgets. Life in Old Virginia was gay and adventurous and for a boy in the lovely vale of the Potomac, with slaves to tend him and brothers to play with, there was bound to be much carefree happiness.

Virginia was the oldest American colony. The original royal grant to the Virginia Company of London covered an area of about five hundred miles of coastline and a hundred miles inland. Inhabited Virginia in Washington's youth was concentrated along the banks of four rivers — the Potomac, the Rapahannock, the York and the James — which emptied into the arm of the Atlantic known as Chesapeake Bay. Ships sailed up these rivers to deliver British goods at the plantation wharves of families dubbed the 'tidewater aristocracy'. Over a hundred miles inland came the Blue Ridge Mountains and beyond them running southward was the Shenandoah Valley to be populated in later times by Scots from Ireland and by German immigrants. Although well watered, much of Virginia was still covered by forests. To lay out new plantations trees had to be felled and Virginia was seldom free from the smell of burning wood.

It was in this land of woods and rivers, where strawberries grew

THE YOUNG OFFICER AND FARMER

and wild turkeys nested, that the first Puritans settled in May 1607. The colonists led by Captain John Smith built Jamestown, thirty miles up the James River and within a dozen years Virginia, named after Queen Elizabeth, had a population of two thousand persons. The first adventurers brought in young girls for wives and Negroes for slaves; and they soon began to grow tobacco. For years tobacco was the main Virginian crop, although in the end it exhausted both the planters' soil and their tempers. The tobacco crop was sold to English or Scottish factors who disposed of it and were also responsible for dispatching from England all the manufactured goods, clothes and luxuries needed by the Virginians.

A loyalist clergyman, who was at one time tutor to Washington's stepson, wrote that a Virginian county was a 'narrow self-centred little world', a 'stratified society'. In the churches families were seated according to their social position, age and estate. At the top of the hierarchy were the rich planter aristocracy, stately gentlemen in many-coloured silk coats who hunted foxes, went racing, attended assembly balls, played cards and drank Madeira (Washington preferred a 'rich oily wine') whilst their overseers, indentured servants and Negro slaves raised the tobacco crop and cultivated the farms. This leisured class did not lack culture and found time to read the works of the seventeenth-century English political philosophers. 'They formed a strange community,' wrote Rupert Hughes, 'these old Virginians with their stately mansions rising here and there in a wilderness as yet unconquered; with their arms and their titles and their carriages, their slaves and their aristocracy set in a jungle of pioneer conditions; with their dances, intrigues, love affairs and bad spelling.' The indentured servants because they had to work off their passage money which they owed to the settlers were serfs, but serfs who could hope for their reward in a small farm of their own and perhaps their own slaves. The demand for labour was never satisfied and ex-convicts and Negroes fetched a high price. In Virginia at this date out of some 300,000 inhabitants over 120,000 were Negroes.

Though Virginian society was thus not classless, it had two characteristics which distinguished it from that of the mother country. The rich man did not draw his income chiefly from rents. For every white man, however poor, might hope to obtain independence and property by staking his claim to a piece of land in the wilderness. There was always land to be had somewhere beyond the western horizon. Next, to be sociable and hospitable was the Virginian's second nature. On the ever advancing frontiers neighbours lent each other a helping hand. In the coastal zones few or no inns existed and planters kept open house. When George Washington was the American Commander-in-Chief he told the cousin whom he left in charge of Mount Vernon: 'Let the hospitality of the house, with respect to the poor, be kept up. Let no one go hungry away.' And for strangers from England southern hospitality was (and still is) lavish. To some visitors — of course there are always such visitors — the life of luxurious ease in the planters' mansions was shocking. One of the Governors of Virginia condemned the wickedness, immorality and profaneness of the people he ruled. But they were not as dissolute as they seemed to such foreigners. Their sense of social responsibility was genuine. When the first Continental Congress met it was remarked that the Virginian representatives were fine fellows 'though very high'. It is no mere coincidence that four of the first five American Presidents came from Virginia.

Two houses in particular stood out in Washington's early life, Mount Vernon and Belvoir, which could be seen from Mount Vernon across the valley of Hunting Creek. Belvoir was the property of the Fairfax family. Old Lord Fairfax, descendant of the Roundhead general, was one of the few English noblemen to take up permanent residence in America. He is said to have owned a small kingdom — five or six million acres of land. His cousin William's daughter, Ann, married Lawrence Washington and the two families were intimate. Mount Vernon rebuilt by Lawrence between 1743 and 1748 for his bride to live in was a modest house for the headquarters of an estate of 2500 acres. The male Washingtons had always loved this estate with its spacious beauty, dry healthy climate, and rich alluvial soil. The aristocracy who lived on these estates in the Upper Potomac, though of necessity they traded with England, had their gaze fixed westward up the river to the promising lands beyond the Blue Ridge Mountains. Here lurked Indians who traded furs for rum or scalped the unwary. And north-west of the Indian hunting grounds were ever encroaching French traders. Other rivals to Virginian prosperity

THE YOUNG OFFICER AND FARMER

were to be found in their neighbours, especially the Pennsylvanians who had a successful knack in dealing with the Indians and the 'crafty' Marylanders whose territory met Virginia to the north of the Potomac River.

When George Washington was sixteen he obtained his first job. His mother at one time thought of sending him to sea, but on learning of the uncongenial prospects had altered her mind. Instead he had completed his training as a surveyor. In February 1748 he went to stay with his half-brother at Mount Vernon (so named after an English admiral under whom Lawrence had served in the West Indies) and in March he set out in company with George William Fairfax, son of William Fairfax, Lawrence's father-in-law, to act as assistant to the local county surveyor and report on the boundaries of the enormous properties of Lord Fairfax in the Shenandoah Valley, which had been invaded by squatters. His trip was an excellent apprenticeship. The two young men stayed with a famous Indian trader at his stockade on the Maryland side of the Potomac where they were fascinated by an Indian war dance, killed the bleak of the early spring days by drinking rum punch, shot turkeys and did a certain amount of work. On the strength of this experience and no doubt with the valuable patronage of the Fairfaxes Washington was a year later appointed surveyor of Culpepper County.

For the next three years George Washington's youth unfolded smoothly and happily. He worked conscientiously at his duties as county surveyor and spent his spare time in hard riding, in playing games, in mild flirtations and occasional trips to neighbouring towns. In the autumn of 1751 he accompanied Lawrence, who had tuberculosis, to Barbados, this being the only occasion in his life when he crossed the sea. In Barbados that winter he was attacked by smallpox, a painful experience that made him a persistent advocate of inoculation. The trip did not cure Lawrence who returned to die on July 28th, 1752, leaving Mount Vernon to his widow and then in succession to his daughter and to George. The daughter died on December 17th, 1754, and George bought out the rights from his sister-in-law.

Soon after his half-brother's death, by one of those wise instances of favouritism that pepper world history, Washington was appointed one of the four adjutants-general of the Virginian militia with the rank of major and pay of £100 a year. His main duties were to raise and train militiamen and search Negro cabins for weapons, but he was always liable to be called out for duty on the frontier. He trained earnestly and in October 1753 was sent on his first expedition to investigate the doings of the French.

The French who occupied Canada had been steadily moving south and south-west in search of the profitable Indian fur trade. They had pressed down from Lake Erie, southernmost of the Great Lakes, along the valley of the Allegheny River where they had built forts and finally came into contact with English traders on the Ohio River. Robert Dinwiddie, a shrewd old Scotsman, who was now the Governor of Virginia, was determined and instructed to resist this French advance which not only threatened the security of the frontier but interfered with the prospects of the newly formed Ohio Company to which both he and Lawrence Washington had subscribed. This company had been given a royal grant to occupy 200,000 acres south of the Ohio, to establish settlements, and to open trade with the Indians. George Washington was ordered to carry a letter to the nearest French commander warning him off Virginian territory and in general to discover French intentions.

Major Washington set off on October 31st, collected a guide and an escort of three Indians, whom he induced to accompany him by a statesmanlike speech and a judicious distribution of gifts. Ultimately he discovered the French commander at a fort (Fort le Bœuf) ten miles south of Lake Erie who received him with the utmost courtesy and made every effort to seduce his Indians. The claims of Virginia on the Ohio were of course politely rebutted. Washington's journey back through never ceasing snowstorms was terrible; the friendly Indians deserted and a less friendly one tried to kill him. The horses on which the party had begun their journey had to be abandoned and a long march made on foot. Washington reported to Dinwiddie that the French had told him over their cups that 'it was their absolute design to take possession of the Ohio and by G—— they would do it'.

Dinwiddie commended Washington for his services and

THE YOUNG OFFICER AND FARMER

ordered him forward to assist in building a fort at a spot known then as the Forks of the Ohio where the Allegheny and Monongahela Rivers merge to form the Ohio. But the French acted more quickly, sailed down the Allegheny in their canoes and seized the fort area while Washington, now promoted lieutenant-colonel and in command of two companies, was still hacking a road through the virgin forest from his base on the Upper Potomac. On learning the news Washington held a council of war and determined to erect a rival fort at Redstone Creek on the Monongahela, some 37 miles south of the Forks of the Ohio. On his way forward he encountered a small French reconnaissance party which with Indian aid he dispatched, killing or taking them all prisoner. This exploit caused much rejoicing in Virginia. Washington was promoted full colonel and received medals for his men and three barrels of rum for the Indians. In a letter home Washington wrote: 'I heard the bullets whistle; and, believe me, there was something charming in the sound.' The letter was printed and found its way to England, where it caused George II to observe: 'He would not say so, if he had been used to hear many.'

Washington certainly spoke too soon; the Indians, having had their fill of scalps and rum, lost interest when retreat was envisaged; expected reinforcements failed to arrive; a larger French force was sent against him; and the Virginians were compelled to withdraw hastily along the Redstone road to a position known as the Great Meadows between two mountain ranges where a makeshift base named Fort Necessity had been constructed. Here a French force of seven hundred caught and outnumbered them. The French commander was brother to a French officer who had been killed in the earlier affray. Taking advantage of the ignorance of Washington's interpreter the Frenchmen made Washington and an English regular officer (who with a few soldiers had joined him) sign a paper confessing that they had 'assassinated' his brother and agreeing to the release of their prisoners. As he signed that unfortunate paper on the dark and rainy morning of July 4th, 1754, Washington learned one of the most melancholy lessons of his brief military career: he had allowed himself to be surrounded by a superior force in an indefensible position. Nevertheless he received the thanks of the Virginian House of Burgesses and his friends consoled him with the thought that even the great Duke of Marlborough had known retreat. After various squabbles with Governor Dinwiddie over questions of pay and rank and impossible orders, Washington, an impatient young man (for he had after all enjoyed his share of luck) resigned his commission in October, though he confessed a little later that his inclinations were still 'strongly bent to arms'.

George Washington was now twenty-two. He had blue-grey eyes, dark brown hair which he wore in a queue, a big nose and a coutnenance which most men found severe and commanding. Six foot two inches tall, 'as straight as an Indian' with wide shoulders, so smartly dressed that some called him a dandy, he was every inch a soldier and a gentleman. His iron physique had proved itself in marches in the snow and he could tell Dinwiddie 'I have a constitution hardy enough to encounter and undergo the severest tests'. The winter of his resignation he moved into his white house at Mount Vernon with its hall and nine rooms and fine view of the river. The estate was perhaps unkempt through neglect since his half-brother had died but he had obtained slaves along with the land from his sister-in-law and could now attend to its reconstruction. Across the way at Belvoir his friend, George William Fairfax had a charming and sympathetic wife, born Sally Cary; another Sally, Fairfax's sister, who was also married, was often at Belvoir too and these ladies with others looked after the young bachelor, lent him recipes for jellies, and had his shirts mended for him. He had other country houses too where he could dine, wine and play cards and taverns where he could find good company. But as soon as the winter was over, he took the first opportunity to become a soldier again.

An experienced British officer of Irish descent but now a ruin of a man, General John Braddock, was sent to the colony in command of two British regiments with orders to march from the Potomac to retake the lost fort at the Forks of the Ohio, which its French conquerors had called Fort Duquesne. Braddock dispatched a courteous letter through one of his aides-de-camp inviting Washington to accompany him on his operation as a volunteer 'member of his military family'. Washington explained that his only object was 'to merit the esteem of his country and the good will of his friends' and gladly accepted.

THE YOUNG OFFICER AND FARMER

Braddock was a strict though scrupulously fair disciplinarian. In carrying out a campaign he stuck rigorously to his book. But he welcomed advice and treated his young American aide almost as an equal. Unluckily for him the advice was not in all respects disinterested. He was under orders to advance on Fort Duquesne by the difficult Redstone road which Washington had twice painfully followed before. This route was chosen largely out of deference to the wishes of shareholders in the Ohio Company; Washington who was personally concerned in the development of the territory along the route had no objections to offer. But the choice of this road proved fatal. From the beginning Braddock had a foreboding of disaster. He suffered from lack of money and supplies, from quarrels between the different colonies, the exactions of the contractors, the unreliability of the militia, the mutinous conduct of his own men, and the desertion of friendly Indians. After many delays the roads were slowly cut through the dark forest and Braddock accepted Washington's advice to push on with a small lightly equipped force of some thirteen hundred men. Washington, who had been ill, joined this force not long before it crossed a ford in the Monongahela River seven miles from Fort Duquesne one July day. Here the straggling column which had emerged from many grim experiences ran into a party of about nine hundred French, Canadians and Indians who had come out to fight them. The Canadians fled but the Indians scattered behind the trees and mowed down Braddock's men as they tried to form into line. Washington described how the regulars panicked, though the Virginians 'fought like heroes and died like men'. Braddock was mortally wounded as he attempted to drive his men forward, but they broke and ran, as Washington saw them, like 'sheep pursued by dogs'. Washington, who had four bullets through his coat and two horses shot under him, is said to have read the funeral service over the commander he had admired and, ascribing his own escape to 'Providence' or 'Luck', helped to withdraw the survivors. On Braddock's Field fought three English officers who were to play a significant part in Washington's later life — Lieutenant-Colonel Thomas Gage, Lieutenant-Colonel Charles Lee and Captain Horatio Gates.

To the searing experiences of this wretched campaign may be attributed some of the considerations that guided Washington's political development. Of old he had taken for granted a primary loyalty to Virginia and a loyalty — more distant — to the mother country. But the cowardice of the regular troops gave him an anti-British feeling (though he praised the British officers) and the disappointments of the campaign convinced him of the utter necessity for a union of the colonies in their own defence. At the same time he was impressed by Braddock's stern sense of discipline, which he was to imitate.

Sick and worried Washington went back to Mount Vernon. On August 2nd, 1755, he wrote a revealing letter to his half-brother Augustine regretting every step he had taken in the last three years of his life — steps that had caused him to 'suffer much in my private fortune, besides impairing one of the best constitutions'. The Governor, however, pleaded with him to take command of the Virginian troops and guard the frontiers now perilously threatened by Indians and white renegades running amok. Washington's mood of self-pity passed. He told his mother that he would be dishonoured were he to refuse. On August 14th he was commissioned Colonel of the Virginia regiment and Commander-in-Chief of all the forces of the colony. He was twenty-three and a half.

Colonel Washington spent the next two years in organizing the defence of the 'cold and barren frontiers' of Virginia which were 350 miles long against the 'incursions of a crafty savage enemy'. He toiled under trying conditions. The Virginian militiamen did not care for being organized, for above everything the frontiersman valued his independence, the right to protect his own family with his own shotgun. 'Discipline,' Washington insisted, 'is the soul of an army', but discipline was harder to enforce than to preach. He did his best. In a letter to one of his captains dated December 28th, 1755, he wrote of the 'continual complaints of the misbehavior of your wife'. 'If she is not immediately sent from the camp,' he threatened, 'I shall take care to drive her out myself and suspend you.' Another captain was admonished, 'not as a superior officer but as a friend' for drinking too much. At twenty-two Washington was not shy.

There were many difficulties with the Governor. Washington felt he had not sufficient troops to man the line of frontier forts and wanted to concentrate on the defence of a few essential positions,

THE YOUNG OFFICER AND FARMER

but Dinwiddie was reluctant to authorize the evacuation of any of the King's forts. The Governor reproved him for taking leave too frequently although he was quickly given leave of absence when he fell ill of dysentry. Public criticisms in the Assembly and in the press of the misbehaviour of his men also perturbed him. For all these reasons he threatened to resign his commission again. In 1757 he was overwhelmingly defeated in standing for the Virginia House of Burgesses. That year was perhaps the least happy in his life, but next year the sun shone.

War had been officially declared by Britain upon France in August 1756 — although unofficial war had existed on the Virginian frontiers ever since Washington had left his letter at Fort le Bœuf three years earlier. William Pitt's assumption of the direction of imperial affairs had at first brought no relief to Virginia, but in the spring of 1758 Major-General John Forbes, a gallant and able officer, arrived at Philadelphia, the capital of Pennsylvania, to plan a fresh expedition to drive the French from Fort Duquesne. Washington hastened to write to friends asking that he be recommended to Forbes as 'distinguished in some measure from the *common run* of provincial officers'. An ambitious young man, his services naturally earned him recognition. He was profuse in his advice to the new commander and tried to induce Forbes to proceed again by the familiar Braddock's road of painful memory. Forbes, after considering the question impartially, decided that another old Indian trail which ran from Raystown (now New Bedford, Pennsylvania) was the more promising as well as the shorter way. Washington protested vigorously and sincerely, although his personal and sentimental interest in Braddock's road made his motives suspect to the general. In August Forbes wrote: 'By a very unguarded letter of Colonel Washington that accidentally fell into my hands I am now at the bottom of their [the Virginian] scheme against the new road, a scheme that I think was a shame for any officer to be concerned in . . .' Forbes warned his second-in-command to be careful how he regarded Washington's advice 'as his conduct about the road was not that of a soldier.' Nevertheless when in September 1758 Washington joined the army at Raystown he was put in charge of the road making and in the final stages of the advance along it he commanded the most forward of three brigades; and although to the end of the campaign he sulked and ascribed the slow progress of the British advance to Pennsylvanian intrigues, he was able to report proudly on November 25th that the French had withdrawn from Fort Duquesne, a Virginian garrison occupied the long contested battleground, the site of modern Pittsburgh.

Brigadier George Washington took no further part in the French war; he retired on these laurels from the active service to marry Martha Custis, a widow, and settle down at Mount Vernon.

Much has been written about the sex life of George Washington. It was abnormal, however, in only one respect, namely that his wife who had borne four children to her first husband had no child by Washington. Hardly any letters between Washington and his wife have survived and so no light can be thrown upon this intimate question. Probably, as with Andrew Jackson and his Rachel, this want of children of their own in no way damaged the reality of the married love of George and Martha Washington; it may indeed have drawn husband and wife closer, as it has many other childless couples. Martha Custis, who was the daughter and widow of Virginians, was a pretty sociable woman, whose life proved her devout and charitable. She was twenty-six when she met Washington in March 1758. They were engaged that May and married on January 6th, 1759. She brought her husband a handsome dowry.

Washington always had a high romantic attitude to women and wrote to them in a florid gallant bantering style that meant courtesy and devotion. From some of his early letters he is seen passing through the normal polygamous state of youth, when 'an agreeable young lady' next door fluttered his heart or memories of distant beauties revived a former passion. Whenever he went on campaign he loved to hear from his lady friends, especially from the young ladies of Belvoir who had mothered him in his illness and cheered the idle hours of a lonely bachelor. Sally Fairfax was his closest confidant to whom he hastened to reveal his engagement to Martha Custis. To Martha he wrote during that happy year of 1758: 'My thoughts have been continually going to you as to another self.' To Sally Fairfax he confessed he had become a 'votary of love'. And so at the age of twenty-seven he declared that he intended to settle down for life with his 'agreeable consort', hoping to 'find more happiness in retirement than I ever experienced amidst a wide and bustling world'. But he could not in fact settle down — his interests were too many, his energy too violent, the call of a growing country too insistent. On February 22nd he took his seat as a member of the House of Burgesses at Williamsburg, the Virginian capital. He also became a Justice of the Peace in the newly built town of Alexandria, nine miles from Mount Vernon. His business interests in England kept him in touch with political events there. As the French and Indian menace receded, new war clouds began to gather, though the first was smaller than a man's hand. And while Washington was through his wife's dowry and his own speculations becoming a wealthy landowner enjoying everything that the life of Virginia had to offer, his experiences had created both a soldier and a frontiersman and both of them were for ever restless.

2. TOWARDS INDEPENDENCE (1758-1777)

George Washington was an aristocrat in the best sense of the phrase; he was to rank in the American story as the Cecils, the Stanleys, the Greys and the Churchills have ranked in English history; men of property and established position who might, if they had wished, have passed their lives pleasantly in cultivating their own souls and estates but who have preferred to expend their lives in public service; men who have had an innate conviction that they were born to rule and yet because material fortune has been kind to them escaped a full sense of the worries and stress of the common man. Such men can often unbend without condescension and give fire to any company by the breadth of their interests and the infectiousness of their ideals; others among them exhibit to outsiders only an icy charm and a sense of hidden strength which sometimes repels. Washington belonged to this latter class. One of his aides went so far as to say that 'he was reserved and austere, better endowed by nature and habit for an Eastern monarch than a republican general'. Silent, cautious in his business affairs, and often stern, he did not have many close friends and few dared to call him George. At public gatherings his modest manner and his determination never to be caught off his guard made a profoundly favourable impression. Was it awareness of a technique or the success of the practice of a lifetime that caused him to advise a nephew in later years: 'Never exceed a decent warmth and submit your sentiments with diffidence'? The statement attributed to Alexander Hamilton that 'his heart was of stone' is surely nonsense. Those who knew him best were aware that beneath that cold exterior fires could burn. They burned so fiercely, however, that they quickly burned out.

In one of his earliest letters Washington speaks of the fire of love as that 'chaste and troublesome passion' and later in a sharply revealing sentence he says that 'in the composition of the human frame there is a good deal of inflammable matter . . . when the torch is put to it, that which is within you may burst into a blaze'. His passions so often suppressed broke through to the surface more freely in his early life. He could write letters of stinging rebuke, to an extravagant nephew who wanted money or to an importunate fellow officer saying 'drunkenness is no excuse for rudeness'. His anger with the carpers, the inefficient or the cowardly lighted up his conduct as Commander-in-Chief. A pleasing account of a conversation during his Presidency survives. General Henry Lee who was visiting him said: 'I saw your portrait the other day, but Stuart says that you have a tremendous temper.' Mrs. Washington: 'Upon my word, Mr. Stuart takes a great deal upon himself to make such a remark.' General Lee: 'But stay, my dear lady, he added that the President had it under wonderful control.' General Washington (with something like a smile): 'He is right.'

Like many aristocrats Washington was a generous friend and patron and a severe master. To the men of the Virginia regiment whom he tried to flog into obedience his charity was extensive. Promising sons of his friends or even acquaintances were helped with their education. His slaves were adequately cared for and allowed sweet tea, broths and a little wine if necessary when they were ill; but, on the whole, their lives were hard. Washington found his slaves unprofitable and would have welcomed the gradual abolition of the institution by legislation. At one time when he had too many slaves for his purposes he said that he could not sell those that he did not need 'because I am principled against this kind of traffic in human spirits'. At another time he

TOWARDS INDEPENDENCE

swore that he never meant 'to possess another slave by purchase'. In his will he gave instructions that all his slaves were to be freed on his wife's death.

During his years of retirement from military service Washington gave much of his time to his stepchildren. Two of Martha's four children had died young. The others were a girl and a boy. The girl Patsy (this was also the name that Washington used for his wife) suffered from epilepsy. Though he tried every conceivable doctor and medicine and sent her to the watering place known as Warm Springs (which he visited himself to obtain relief from dysentery) she died at the age of sixteen, 'a sweet and innocent girl' whom he plainly loved. To console his wife he took the drastic step of inviting his mother-in-law to come and live with them at Mount Vernon. She did not come. Martha found some consolation for her daughter's death in the company of her son's wife. Jacky Custis as a boy loved hunting more than books and girls more than either. Washington showed a conscientious concern over his education, warning his tutor not to let him stay away at night or go rambling in vicious company, and minutely investigating the wisdom of letting him travel abroad. All these precautions were vain, for before he was twenty Jacky fell desperately in love. Washington ordered that he must not marry for three years. Mrs. Washington sided with her son and he soon married the girl of his choice. This is the only recorded instance of a difference of opinion between George and Martha. It did not matter. Jacky had only a few years of happiness, dying from exposure at the siege of Yorktown in 1781. His stepfather, long since mellowed, treated the offspring of this hasty marriage as if they had been his own grandchildren.

One other difference of opinion may possibly have disturbed his otherwise smooth family life. Mrs. Washington was a devout Christian. George Washington was in duty bound a vestryman of the local church and also had a pew at a church in Alexandria. He went to church fairly often; but there were many Sundays when he found more amusing things to do or gravely noted in his diary: 'At home all day alone.' He was not a communicant, he never knelt at prayers, and the word Christ never appears in his letters. Sometimes he speaks of Providence with a Cromwellian fervour as after a successful battle: 'The hand of Providence has been so conspicuous in all this, that he must be worse than an infidel who lacks faith and more than wicked that has not gratitude enough to acknowledge his obligations.' But there was little of the deeply religious man in Washington and the detailed account of his last illness gives no hint that he was a Christian. On the contrary, there is testimony that, like Thomas Jefferson and many other aristocrats in the age of Voltaire and Rousseau, he was not a believer in any established religion.

From 1759 to 1774 Washington's days and months and years moved with the regularity of the sun. In January and February he hunted foxes, shot ducks, and supervised threshing. In March and April he grafted fruit trees, bottled cider, mixed composts, and saw to the ploughing. In May sheep were sheared. In July it was time to cut hay and harvest the summer wheat, while in August and September the winter crops were sown. Then came ditching and finally the killing of pork for the Christmas season. This left time for him to attend the short spring and autumn meetings of the Virginia House of Burgesses to which he was regularly elected.

His taste in amusements was catholic: outdoors besides hunting and shooting there was cockfighting and the Annapolis horse races to follow; indoors were concerts, plays and balls; at home he drank moderately but with enjoyment, liked a game of cards (he came out about even) but seldom smoked.

In the mid-seventeen-sixties he stopped growing tobacco which was fetching poor prices, in favour of wheat and a certain amount of mixed farming. Like most Virginian farmers of his day he suffered from a chronic shortage of cash and though he bought a book on *A Speedy Way to Grow Rich* he does not seem to have learnt the secret. He turned eagerly to land speculation and tried to establish his claim to land on the Ohio through investments in various companies. Much paper, ink and thought were expended on trying to make good his right to a share in 200,000 acres promised to serving soldiers by the Governor of Virginia in 1754. Interminable disputes took place over the validity of this claim, but Washington had hopes. He told his agents to buy up other officers' claims to the 'bounty land' cheap (at £5, or £6 or £7 per thousand acres) on his behalf but in their names 'as a lottery only' (Washington enjoyed lotteries). In 1770 Washington made an

TOWARDS INDEPENDENCE

autumn journey to the Ohio, once again traversing Braddock's road to Pittsburgh, but this time shooting only buffalo, to see what the prospects were. Later he was officially appointed agent for the officers with claims. The association hired a surveyor and the last claim certificates were lodged towards the end of 1773. But so vast was the intrigue, so numerous the claims and counter-claims that by the time the War of Independence began the matter was still unsettled. Another real estate speculation was an investment in a concern with the unpromising title of the Dismal Swamp Company which planned to develop lands between Virginia and North Carolina; he was also trustee in a company to improve navigation on the Potomac River. Washington was neither more nor less scrupulous than other land speculators of his time — he was not above making false entries to avoid inconvenient regulations. But he was no idler content to sell his crops and pocket the returns from London. His thoughts were always turning restlessly towards an expanding America where interest and patriotism joined hands. Washington was at once one of the landed aristocracy and a frontiersman. The call of the west was the call to nationhood. And though the young Washington was first and foremost a Virginian, he was soon to learn of outside events that were giving a new meaning to the word America.

When George Washington was a young man only part of the east coast of the North American continent had been settled by British colonists. The French not only ruled Canada but had advanced along the Mississippi Valley and hoped to pin the English between the Appalachian Mountains and the Atlantic Ocean. In the south Spaniards had established profitable trading posts along the Gulf of Mexico and enterprising Jesuits were headed westward. The war against France which began unofficially when Washington's men first skirmished on the route to the Ohio and in which Washington himself took no further part after the capture of Pittsburgh ended in 1763 with a decisive British victory. British rule replaced French in Canada and Florida and the huge area known as Louisiana which lay to the west of the Mississippi passed into the weaker hand of Spain. To prevent trouble with the Indians and for other less praiseworthy

GEORGE WASHINGTON

reasons the British Government issued a royal proclamation laying down that all further white settlement must stop at the crest of the Appalachian Mountains.

The supremacy of the British settlers in North America was inevitable because whereas the French and Spaniards had developed their territories mainly for trading purposes and had not populated the New World in large numbers the English colonists had come to live there permanently and were out to develop the rich resources of the vast continent and thus grew and flourished. For the same reasons the separation of the thirteen colonies from the mother country was bound to come. The enterprising men and women who had risked their lives and all they had to build new homes in a strange land could not be expected in the long run to submit to government ineffectively administered three thousand miles away, especially at a time when it took ships many weeks to cross the Atlantic. In the northern colonies men of puritan descent with economic worlds to conquer would not consent to their trade and industry being regulated from Whitehall. In Virginia the idea of a free democratic republic arose as naturally as it did in ancient Athens. Like Athens a leisured class subsisted on a basis of slaves and bondsmen who made up about half of the population. The only thing that held back the movement towards independence, the desire for which was always latent, was the disunity of the colonies. And now this lack of unity was disappearing.

The French war created the spirit of American unity and the policy of the British Government enhanced it. Even before the war a colonial congress had met at Albany to discuss measures of common defence against the Indians. Under General Forbes Pennsylvanians, Virginians and Marylanders marched together to the Ohio. After the war the colonists united in opposition to the restrictive and galling frontier proclamation. New measures of economic interference, imposed and actively enforced by London, provoked individual colonies and when, in March 1765, an act introducing stamp duties on all colonial business transactions was passed to raise money for the defence of the colonies, all the American colonies led by Patrick Henry, a young Virginian lawyer, protested and there were riots in New York and Boston. A 'Stamp Act Congress' representing nine colonies met in New

TOWARDS INDEPENDENCE

York. George Washington himself objected to the Stamp Act mainly on practical grounds. An economic depression that followed the end of the war made taxation particularly unwelcome: 'We have not the money', he said tersely, 'to pay for the stamps', while he quoted others for the opinion that the measure was unconstitutional. When after the repeal of the Stamp Act another British Cabinet in May 1767 introduced fresh taxes on American imports (the Townshend duties), Washington advocated retaliation by economic action if possible, by arms if need be. 'At a time', he wrote in April 1769, 'when our lordly masters in Great Britain will be satisfied with nothing less than the deprication of American freedom it seems highly necessary that something should be done to avert the stroke and maintain the liberty which we have derived from our ancestors.' He pressed for a joint agreement by the colonies to boycott British goods. Again the British Government largely gave way and later innocently prepared to do the colonies a good turn by giving the East India Company the right to sell their tea direct to the American consumer at reduced prices. But this Tea Act undercut the American middleman and in any case by the time it was introduced in 1772 American blood had flowed (in riots at Boston) and the union of colonies in resistance to England had been tried and found good. On December 16th, 1773, a group of Bostonians disguised as Indians threw a shipload of tea into the sea. The British Government retorted by closing Boston port and by handing over the government to a military dictator, that Colonel, now Major-General, Gage who had fought with Washington on Braddock's Field. Writing of these 'Coercive Acts' Washington said: 'The Ministry may rely on it that Americans will never be taxed without their own consent that the case of Boston — the despotic measures in respect to it I mean — now is and ever will be considered the cause of America (not that we approve of their conduct in destroying the tea) and that we shall not suffer to be sacrificed by piece meals . . .' He offered to raise a thousand men at his own expense and march them to Boston to fight Gage who, he thought, was behaving like 'a Turkish Bashaw'. 'Shall we', he demanded, 'after this, whine and cry for relief, when we have already tried it in vain? Or shall we supinely sit and see one province after another fall a prey to despotism?'

GEORGE WASHINGTON

After supporting the boycott proposal at the Virginia Assembly, Washington went with Patrick Henry to represent Virginia at the first Continental Congress which met at Philadelphia on September 5th, 1774. A delegate wrote to tell his wife that Washington 'had a hard countenance... a very young look, and an easy soldier-like air and gesture'. Patrick Henry reported that 'Colonel Washington, who had no pretensions to eloquence is a man of more solid judgment and information than any man in the place'. After returning to Virginia where he drilled an independent company of militia he again went to Philadelphia as delegate to the second Continental Congress which met on May 9th, 1775. This time he was dressed in his uniform as a Virginian colonel. Three weeks before Congress met, fighting between Gage's troops and Massachusetts militia began at Concord Bridge and Lexington. Though unhappy in the thought that 'a brother's sword had been sheathed in a brother's breast', Washington had no doubt where his duty lay. Congress decided to raise a continental army and appoint Washington its Commander-in-Chief. The choice of a southerner for this post as a symbol of American support for Massachusetts was necessary; Washington's character, wealth, military experience, soldierlike bearing and buff and blue uniform commended him to the Bostonian leaders. When John Adams proposed his name Washington 'darted with his usual modesty into the library'. In accepting the appointment he deprecated his abilities and refused all pay. Congressmen found him indeed 'a gent... clever and if anything too modest...' but 'discreet and virtuous no harum scarum ranting swearing fellow but sober steady and calm'. 'It was utterly out of my power to refuse the appointment', Washington wrote home to his wife; but to his brother he confessed 'I am now embarked on a tempestuous ocean from whence, perhaps, no safe harbour is to be found... but the partiality of the Congress, added to some political motives, left me without a choice'.

Second-in-command to Washington Congress appointed General Ward, the elderly commander of the Massachusetts militia who accepted his supersession gracefully and soon retired with dignity. A soldier of fortune, Colonel Charles Lee was chosen third-in-command. Lee had been a soldier all his life. He fought with Washington on Braddock's Field and received the

TOWARDS INDEPENDENCE

name of Boiling Water from the Mohawk Indians when he 'married' one of their daughters named White Thunder. He had campaigned in Portugal and Poland and spoke several European languages. A born adventurer, he had a satiric and incautious pen, a fondness for dogs, a facility in swearing, and a charm of manner that enabled him to borrow money without having to pay it back. Another Englishman, who, like Lee, had been at Braddock's Field and retired happily to Virginia was Major Horatio Gates. Gates was 'the son of a housekeeper of the second Duke of Leeds, who, marrying a young husband when she was very old, had this son by him'. Gates's somewhat limited military career might have seemed over when he came back to America in 1772. 'Major Gates', wrote his wife, 'is far from well and I fear I shall have a hard task to support his spirits till the employment we shall have to cultivate . . . rouses him from his present dejection.' Gates, who made friends among the New Englanders, was delighted when he was appointed Brigadier-General and Adjutant-General of the new army. Washington knew both these English officers who had become fellow Virginians and had entertained them at Mount Vernon where Lee had borrowed £15 from him. The other Major-Generals were Philip John Schuyler of New York and Israel Putnam, a Connecticut farmer. Among the Brigadier-Generals was Nathanael Greene, son of a Rhode Island Quaker, who was in due course to become Washington's right hand.

On July 2nd, 1775, Washington reached Cambridge in Massachusetts, three miles from Boston where he took over the command from Ward and lived for a time in the president's house at Harvard University. Washington had an army of some 15,000 to 20,000 effectives, whilst Gage in Boston had some 10,000 regulars. The strategic situation that confronted Washington required the utmost caution. The Americans had no arms factories and depended for muskets and powder on such stores as belonged to the local militia. For heavier weapons they relied upon what they could capture or buy from abroad. The volunteers whose services were enlisted for the army, though often men with experience of Indian fighting, were undisciplined and liked to go home at harvest time. The British for their part were handicapped by being three thousand miles from their base and having very few troops in the whole of the North American continent. Their generals were competent but uninspired regular officers many of whom had friends in America and abhorred the idea of a civil war, as they regarded it. One overwhelming advantage possessed by the British was command of the sea. This enabled their soldiers to be transported from one to another part of the Atlantic seaboard without interference, whereas the Americans had to move their forces by land in a country where there were few good roads except between Baltimore and Boston.

When Washington reached Cambridge he found his camp was like a country fair. Discipline scarcely existed, the men, who often elected their own officers, treated them, according to Washington, like broomsticks. There was a pronounced lack both of powder and of public spirit. Though Washington told his friends of this state of affairs and admitted he was little impressed by the New Englanders, he was careful to avoid giving any public sign of his dissatisfaction. Nevertheless his opinions became known and for once belied his reputation for carefulness. John Adams wrote to a Boston officer: 'Pray tell me, Colonel Knox, does every man to the southward of Hudson's river behave like a hero, and every man to the northward of it like a poltroon or not? . . . I must say that your amiable General gave them much occasion for these reports by his letters. . . .'

Washington struggled to create order out of chaos. He set his troops on building defences every day from four in the morning till eleven at night. He instituted frequent courts martial and punished desertion and other crimes with lashes up to one hundred in number, later asking permission to increase the number to five hundred. His complaints of the 'dearth of public spirit and want of virtue' and 'the dirty mercenary spirit' that prevailed were very bitter. It was his conviction that 'three things prompt men to a regular discharge of their duty in time of action: natural bravery, hope of reward, and fear of punishment'. 'The first two', he said, 'are common to the untutored and the disciplined soldiers; but the latter most obviously distinguish the one from the other. He therefore pressed upon the Congress the need for better terms of service and more lashes. Beyond these immediate cares Washington was worried about his wife's safety. Surely, he wrote home, the Governor of Virginia could not 'act so low and unmanly

TOWARDS INDEPENDENCE

a part as to think of seizing Mrs. Washington by way of revenge upon me?'

The concrete local problem that faced Washington of getting the British troops out of Boston was simplified by the fact that General Sir William Howe, who took over the command from Gage in October 1775, had orders to evacuate at the earliest opportunity. Washington had surprisingly little idea of his enemy's intentions (his intelligence service was never very good) but thought 'the enemy by their not coming out are I suppose, afraid of us'. Boston stands on a peninsula jutting out into the sea and to the north and south of it are the heights known respectively as Bunker Hill and Dorchester Heights. English forces had occupied Bunker Hill by driving the Americans back with a direct assault launched from the sea before Washington took command. This cost them over a thousand killed and wounded and they never tried a frontal assault again. They neglected to occupy Dorchester Heights, probably because they knew the Americans had no cannon which might render it dangerous to them. Washington saw his chance. Whose advice he followed scarcely matters: he was responsible for the decision. He sent Colonel Knox to fetch cannon all the way from the Canadian frontier where it had been captured at the outbreak of the war. Knox, a Boston bookseller, carried out his task of dragging the cannon hundreds of miles in midwinter with great proficiency. At the end of February Washington prepared to take possession of Dorchester Heights 'which will', he said, 'it is generally thought bring on a rumpus between us and the enemy'. On March 4th the Americans occupied the heights, but no rumpus came, for a storm intervened. Generals need luck. Knox's cannon now dominated Boston harbour and on March 17th the British evacuated to Halifax. By tacit understanding Washington did not interfere with the enemy's withdrawal and the British did not destroy the town as they left.

In war strategy is never concerned exclusively with military factors and political considerations are often paramount. In 1776 the British Government still hoped to come to terms with the American colonists without shedding overmuch blood. At the time when the first Continental Congress was meeting Benjamin Franklin, the internationally famous scientist who was the

Massachusetts agent in London, was asked by a friend at the Royal Society if he would like to play a game of chess with a pleasant lady. The lady was Miss Howe, sister to General Sir William Howe and Admiral Lord Howe, a Whig member of parliament who a year later was to command the British Atlantic Fleet. The game of chess was a feeler by the Howes to discover through Franklin if there were any practical means of peaceably ending the dispute between Great Britain and her colonies. And when the Howes sailed to America to direct the campaign they insisted that they should go also as peace commissioners. They planned their strategy with the approval of the British Cabinet, so as to facilitate peace moves. Boston was abandoned because it was an unsuitable base and the natives were unfriendly. Instead they proposed to make New York, which they believed contained many loyalists, into their main strategic centre and thence — but only if their peace moves were disregarded — to invade New England and defeat the American army. At home a secondary campaign was planned with Canada, another loyalist centre, as the base. Washington realized all this — indeed the Howes on their arrival in Boston hastened to approach him under the ambiguous title of 'George Washington Esquire etc. etc.' and the American commander remarked how 'Lord Howe takes pains to throw out, upon every occasion that he is the Messenger of Peace'. It followed that Washington recognized that New York was a danger spot and as early as January he dispatched the eccentric Major-General Lee from Boston to supervise the strengthening of its defences. During the previous autumn he had approved a campaign against Canada directed by General Schuyler and carried out by two able young officers, Brigadier-General Richard Montgomery and Colonel Benedict Arnold, and had detached a thousand men from his own meagre resources for their support. Montgomery actually took Montreal in November and Washington had large hopes. On December 5th he wrote to Benedict Arnold: 'It is not in the power of any man to command success; but you have done more — you have deserved it, and before this, I hope, have met with the laurels which are due to your toils, in the possession of Quebec.' But on the last day of the year the Americans were defeated in attempting to storm Quebec, Montgomery was killed, and Arnold was left to draw off a

TOWARDS INDEPENDENCE

shattered force to rot in the blizzards of a Canadian winter. Nevertheless this campaign delayed British preparations for an offensive based on Canada.

The American strategic problem was also influenced by several non-military factors. Until they could build up supplies and find allies they could not undertake a large-scale offensive. Washington therefore favoured a defensive war 'avoiding a general action on all occasions' and was ready to abandon and burn New York if necessary. Time in fact was on his side. Outwardly serene, however, he was inwardly appalled by the magnitude of the difficulties before him in fashioning a disciplined and well-supplied army capable of acting on the offensive.

In April 1776 Washington arrived in New York to direct its defence against the expected assault from the sea. It was at this time that Washington finally decided in his own mind that complete independence must be their aim. He had read Tom Paine's incisive pamphlet *Common Sense* published that January and found his arguments unanswerable. On May 15th the Virginia Assembly declared itself in favour of independence and Washington expressed his delight, condemning some members of the Congress who were 'still feeding themselves upon the dainty food of reconciliation'. Washington's mind was a practical one. He recognized that the war had cut the knots, never firmly tied, that bound the wealthy and vigorous communities of the New World to London, that it was ludicrous to continue speaking of the British army in America, as he had been doing, as the 'Ministerial' (and not the King's) troops, and that the Howes had not been empowered to discuss terms but only to grant pardons. On July 2nd Congress resolved upon independence and on July 10th the American Declaration of Independence was read to the troops defending New York.

On the same day that the decisive resolution had been approved by Congress the British Messengers of Peace began to land their men and guns on Staten Island to the south of New York City. By the middle of August the British had four hundred transports, thirty-two warships and twenty-seven smaller craft off New York. Sir William Howe's land forces alone numbered 34,000, while Washington had only between fifteen and twenty thousand men. On August 22nd the British landed on Long Island, east of New York and four days later by a perfectly concerted manœuvre outflanked the left of the American line. With the British commanding the sea and the Americans not owning the means to block the entrance to the East River, which separates New York from Long Island, Washington had no alternative but to withdraw. He took personal charge of the operation. He is reported to have said: 'If I see any man turn his back today I will shoot him through; I have two pistols loaded; but I will not ask any man to go further than I do; I will fight as long as I have a leg or an arm.' The withdrawal was completed on August 28th, Washington having been in the saddle for forty-eight hours and never having once closed his eyes. Again he had some degree of luck as Howe, unnecessarily frightened by what he believed to be the strength of the American fortifications on Brooklyn Heights, failed to follow up his initial success and a foggy night hid the withdrawal. On the other hand, Major-General Greene who had been in charge of the defences was taken desperately ill at the crucial moment and the waters were stormy when the boats ferried the men across to Manhattan Island. The Battle of Long Island was not a major engagement, for the withdrawal was inevitable once the British landed in force and the American losses in men and materials were not significant. Far more serious was the loss of New York itself which followed. Again command of the sea and superior numbers gave the British every advantage. They landed on September 15th at Kipps Bay on the Manhattan shore four miles from Washington's headquarters at Harlem. The forces responsible for guarding this sector panicked and Washington again appeared on the scene, losing his temper so completely that it almost cost him his life. Next day calm followed the storm and he rallied his men to repulse the British and their Hessian mercenaries.

On October 20th after Howe had threatened to cut the American line of retreat Washington withdrew his main forces from Manhattan Island and occupied a defensive position at the village of White Plains on the Bronx River. Eight days later he was attacked. Thus the British commander had managed to split the American forces, the major part under Washington retiring to New Jersey while some three thousand men left under Greene to deny the passage of the Hudson River, were isolated on Manhattan Island. Greene had not been given positive orders to evacuate by Washington and by the time he had gone there himself and found it was untenable he had left it too late. On November 16th Howe's troops stormed the fort and five days later they captured the cannon and stores on the fort opposite (Fort Lee) on the New Jersey shore of the Hudson River. Washington had only himself to blame for these misfortunes. General Greene, the man on the spot, could advise but could not be expected to make the final decision on a question which involved overall strategy.

General Washington was deeply distressed by this campaign. He spoke of the affair at Kipps Bay as having been 'most shameful and disgraceful running away ... without firing a single gun'. To his intimates he confided that £50,000 would not induce him to go through it all again. Such moods are common to defeated generals. The first Duke of Marlborough adopted much the same tone during his less successful campaigns, but this did not prevent his organizing victory. For it is in the apparently hopeless days that great men disclose themselves. George Washington too was no 'sunshine patriot'. In so far as one man at one time can determine events, Washington in December 1776 was to save the American Revolution.

Washington's heroic stature was to be seen in the afterglow of events. But at that time those who stood nearest to him regarded him as an incompetent muddler. Major-General Charles Lee who, after repelling a small British force at Charleston, South Carolina, had returned with his green trousers and his litter of dogs to join the main army in New York, was the leader of the critics. To him Joseph Reed, who had been Washington's secretary and had now become his Adjutant-General, wrote after the fall of Fort Washington and Fort Lee, complaining of his chief's fatal lack of decision: 'I have no doubt had you been here the garrison at Mount [Fort] Washington would now have composed a part of this army.' His words fell on receptive ground. Lee replied: 'I ... lament with you that fatal indecision of mind which in war is a much greater disqualification than stupidity or even want of personal courage — accident may put a decisive blunderer in the right — but eternal defeat and miscarriage must attend the man of the best parts if cursed with indecision.' Lee's letter accidentally fell into Washington's hands; he returned it with magnificent courtesy to Reed, apologized for opening it by mistake and conveyed his best respects to Mrs. Reed.

General Lee and his friend, Horatio Gates, who had also been promoted Major-General did not lack decision; they knew what they wanted to do and were convinced that they could do it much better than George Washington. When Washington after the defeats at New York had withdrawn across the Hudson pursued by the British General Cornwallis he had left Lee in charge of a powerful rearguard in the area of White Plains. In order to gain a respite and reorganize his forces, many of whom, being only enlisted up to the end of the year, were about to desert him, Washington had slowly retired south through Newark and New Brunswick to Trenton and thence on December 8th across the broad Delaware River. In November and early December he wrote a series of letters requesting (but not ordering) Lee to join him. Lee did not intend to comply if he could avoid doing so. For he thought he could do far better on his own: 'I am in hopes here to reconquer the Jerseys,' he boasted to Gates on December 13th, *entre nous* a certain great man is most damnably deficient . . . he has thrown me into a situation where I have my choice of difficulties.' Lee's own problems were soon solved. For as he was at last beginning a leisurely move to join Washington, he allowed himself to be taken prisoner by a British detachment and his troops were ultimately led to Washington by his second-in-command, Major-General Sullivan. General Gates who had just returned from the northern front was also begged by Washington to join him and if he could not bring his troops at least give him the benefit of his advice. Gates answered that he felt much too ill to do this and hurried off to find Congress and to press upon the members the need to put him in supreme command in the north. So Washington had to manage as best he could without this precious pair; he did pretty well.

Cornwallis, on Howe's orders, had only followed Washington's retreating army across New Jersey as far as New Brunswick. Howe thought that he had done more than enough for glory and after all it was winter when fighting always stopped. Cornwallis

TOWARDS INDEPENDENCE

too had outrun his line of communications from New York and was in difficulties for food. He fixed winter cantonments as far as the west side of the Delaware at Trenton and set off to go home to England on leave. Washington was determined not to bow to the exigencies of the season. His plan was to take up his winter quarters at Morristown, some twenty-five miles west of New York, in an excellent defensive situation, mountainous but well supplied. He organized the troops that he had now collected amounting with those brought down by Sullivan to about six thousand men into three divisions and prepared to recross the Delaware, attack the British detachments first at Trenton and then in Princeton (half-way between Trenton and New Brunswick) and then march to Morristown, raiding New Brunswick on the way. The first stage of this bold operation was the most risky. He had to cross a broad river by night in face of an entrenched enemy (consisting of some fourteen hundred Hessians) at a time of year when the weather was sure to be unfavourable. Christmas Day was selected for the enterprise, a day when the Germans might be drinking and dreaming of home, and the chosen password was 'Victory or Death'. The Delaware was so storm-swept that two out of his three divisions failed to make the crossing. The division of which he took personal command alone got across although it arrived much later than he had intended some hours after dawn. Complete surprise was achieved: 868 prisoners were taken for the loss of but four wounded. This action helped restore the morale of the whole American army. The British reacted violently. Howe recalled Cornwallis from his leave and he came pounding south through the mud into the New Jersey winter. Washington had been compelled to draw back after his first success, but on December 29th he crossed the Delaware in force and the two sides met at a bridge to the north of Trenton on January 2nd, 1777. Cornwallis's men outnumbered those of Washington and exclaiming 'I have the old fox in a trap' he went to bed. But Washington, who stayed awake, decided to pursue his original scheme. That night after a council of war he lit fires to deceive the enemy and pushing round Cornwallis's left flank made for Princeton. Here he found only a small party of British who fought gallantly but were overwhelmed, losing some four hundred casualties. Washington then decided rather reluctantly not to delay by raiding New Brunswick, site of the British war chest, but to thrust on to the safety of Morristown, where he arrived on January 7th. The British withdrew from the greater part of New Jersey and in distant London it was confessed that Washington's 'march through our lines' was 'a prodigy of generalship'.

The importance of the victories at Trenton and Princeton was out of all proportion to their scale. Nicholas Cresswell, an American loyalist, wrote on January 5th, 1777: 'The minds of people are much altered. A few days ago they had given up their cause for lost. Their late successes have turned the scale and now they are all liberty mad again.' Washington had triumphed over almost insurmountable difficulties. His men were nearly all on short-term enlistments and he had written: 'Our only dependence now is upon the steady enlistment of a new army. If this fails, I think the game will be pretty well up.' Again and again he emphasized to Congress the impossibility of fashioning a disciplined force out of continental soldiers on a year's contract and out of militia who were always likely to melt away at the call of home and harvest. 'I am clearly of the opinion', he said in one letter, 'that if 40,000 men had been kept in constant pay since the first commencement of hostilities and the militia had been excused doing duty during the period the Continent would have saved money.' On December 20th he wrote to Congress saying that 'ten days more will put an end to the existence of our Army' and begged for fuller power — 'desperate diseases required desperate remedies'. The day after his victory at Trenton Congress responded by giving him 'full, ample and complete powers' to raise new forces and requisition property. These were granted at a time when Congress in fright had left Philadelphia for Baltimore, and were limited to a period of six months. It is an exaggeration to say that Washington was made a dictator; he was given authority which ought to have been exercised by a competently run War Department but which Congress had failed to exercise effectively.

One of Washington's modern critics made much play with the fact that while he complained of the failure of Congress to raise an adequate army he made no positive proposals for overcoming the difficulties peculiar to a loose experimental federation of states. But surely the point is that the Commander-in-Chief ought never to have been expected to concern himself with raising his forces as well as leading them? The resolution of Congress in December 1777 was a measure of their own failure to organize victory, and, let it be said, their own confidence in George Washington.

These winter days were indeed a turning point in Washington's life. It is true that in November he had shown, as his critics and some of his friends had said, a want of decision. His orders to his commanders had been indefinite and almost timorous. With a beaten and dissolving force to lead, he had experienced the depths of uncertainty and despair. Yet it was at that very moment that he had aroused himself to take his most daring resolutions. He induced some of his men to stay with him to fight for independence by offering them a ten-dollar bounty; he determined upon a counter-offensive with a beaten army in the midst of winter; and he chose one of the greatest of all military hazards, a flank march across the line of a superior enemy. He accepted every risk and won. Then he retired to Morristown to create a new army.

3. TOWARDS VICTORY (1777-1783)

Encamped at Morristown in the winter of 1776-77 George Washington was gloomy and perplexed. He did not look back on the past campaign with any degree of satisfaction. 'The misfortune of short enlistments and an unhappy dependence upon militia', he wrote to his stepson on January 28th, 1777, 'have shown their baneful influence at every period ... At no time, nor upon no occasion, were they ever more exemplified than since Christmas; for if we could but have got in the militia in time or prevailed upon those troops whose times expired (as they generally did) on the first of this instant to have continued ... we might, I am persuaded, have cleared the Jerseys entirely of the enemy. Instead of this all movements have been made with inferior numbers and with a mixed motley crew who were here today, gone tomorrow, without assigning a reason, or even apprizing you of it'. He felt that these circumstances had given his enemies a most favourable opportunity and was astonished (as were also some of Sir William Howe's British critics) that Howe did not attack him while he was perforce creating a new army. But Howe thought the Morristown position too formidable and was indeed disturbed by harassing raids. For two months, the British complained in February, they were 'boxed in' in New Jersey, their forage parties beaten up and any movement between posts made dangerous. In April Washington was able to tell his brother 'to my great surprise we are still in a calm'.

Congress had decided that the states should raise eighty-eight battalions for the new campaign and that Washington should enlist sixteen. Although high bounties were paid the recruits came in slowly, so slowly that the General was afraid he might be left without any men at all before his replacements arrived. And so numerous were the deserters that he thought he might have to 'detach one half of the army to bring back the other'. In contradistinction to Oliver Cromwell, Washington said they 'should take none but gentlemen'. The attractions of army life were not marked: hunger and sickness prevailed in the ranks and little grog or warm clothing was available. The American money with which the soldiers were paid had depreciated, while true discipline was unknown. For this the Commander-in-Chief received some blame, for it was said that the discipline of the northern army was superior while that of his own men did not improve until he acquired a first-class Inspector-General from Europe the following year.

That spring Washington found an able twenty-year-old aide in Alexander Hamilton, a lawyer turned artilleryman, who had been born out of wedlock in the West Indies and was soon known as the 'little lion' because of his smallness and aggressiveness. Later in the year he was joined by another very young man, the lank red-haired Marquis de Lafayette who arrived from Paris to seek fame and adventure. Usually Washington distrusted the volunteer soldiers from Europe who were now flocking to the American side all demanding to be made at least major-generals. But he took a fancy to the charm and youthful enthusiasm of Lafayette whose friendship was to add a touch of warmth to his cold dignity. 'We should be embarrassed to show ourselves before an officer who has just left the French troops', said Washington as he greeted the new arrival. 'I have come to learn and not to teach', was the apt reply. Both Alexander Hamilton and Lafayette were to be real influences in Washington's life.

The British plan of campaign for 1777 was conspicuous for muddle. A force headed by 'Gentleman Johnny' Burgoyne was to advance south from Canada to Albany on the Hudson River with the object of cutting off New England from the rest of the colonies and the commander was told to aim at 'a most speedy junction' of his army with that of Howe. In New York Howe lacking clear orders from England planned, on the contrary, not to await Burgoyne, of whom he seems to have been jealous, but instead to capture Philadelphia, the 'rebel capital'. After all, in a European campaign the occupation of the enemy's capital always ended the war. George Washington was not unnaturally mystified by Howe's proceedings, for he wrote in July that Howe's only 'rational end in view' must be to link with Burgoyne. After striking at two points in Washington's line (Washington claimed that the British were given 'a pretty good peppering') Howe withdrew from New Jersey and on July 23rd embarked his troops and after ploughing the seas for three weeks landed at the Head of Elk in Chesapeake Bay with the evident intention of advancing on Philadelphia. Congress at once clamoured for protection and although later critics say that he ought to have attacked the weakened British forces in New York, Washington had no alternative but to do as he was told. He marched his army of some 15,000 men in the summer heat through Philadelphia to Wilmington in Virginia and decided to stop Howe at the fords across the Brandywine Creek.

At the battle of Brandywine the British succeeded in outflanking the American right, partly owing to inadequate reconnaissance by Washington's forces. The day was saved from disaster by the bold soldierlike action of General Greene who commanded in the centre and prevented an enemy break-through. Afterwards Howe outmanœuvred Washington and on September 26th the British entered Philadelphia. Brandywine had not been a severe defeat; Washington reported his losses lower than those of the enemy and said his troops were in good spirits. Howe established his headquarters at Germantown to the north of Philadelphia and for a week the two sides licked their wounds. Then with the support of his loyal lieutenants the American Commander-in-Chief produced a daring plan — a repetition of the battle of Trenton on a vaster scale. By a night march in four columns he would overwhelm Howe. The operation proved too difficult for the relatively untrained American troops. Yet Washington achieved the first principle of good offensive generalship by surprising his foe. If a dense fog had not accentuated the semi-darkness of the dawn assault he might have won a resounding victory; indeed he told Congress that his men retreated when the prize was within their grasp. A stone house transformed into a temporary blockhouse by an alert British colonel held up the initial stages of the attack and in the fog two American divisions fired on each other. The Americans suffered a thousand casualties and had to retire into winter quarters twenty-five miles north of Philadelphia to a place that was to become unenviably notorious, Valley Forge.

Whilst Washington fought his unavailing campaign to save Philadelphia, City of Brotherly Love, Major-General Gates was winning a reputation on the northern front.

The northern command, which covered the route from Montreal in Canada down via Lake Champlain and Lake George to the Hudson through New York State and Vermont, was always considered a separate command not under the direct control of the Commander-in-Chief. Washington insisted that he must be kept fully informed of operations in this theatre and that he had the right to offer advice to the commanding general there, but accepted it as being outside the area of his jurisdiction. In 1776, after the defeat of the American attempt to take Quebec the British had gone over to the offensive, but after they had made considerable progress southward they had, to the amazement of everyone, withdrawn again. According to some accounts the withdrawal was partly due to a remarkable miniature naval battle which Colonel Benedict Arnold had waged by Valcour Island in Lake Champlain. During this campaign Gates had been in command of the defence of Fort Ticonderoga a strategic point on the route south, but came under the orders of Major-General Schuyler, who was in charge of New York State. At the end of this campaign, Gates, as we have seen, refusing Washington's plea for his

TOWARDS VICTORY

valuable advice in New Jersey, had felt sick and gone off to Congress to seek the supreme command on the northern front.

At the beginning of 1777 Gates resumed his post of Adjutant-General to the continental army. His biographer says: 'Everybody in Congress who knew what was going on, realized that the continental army needed a stronger hand than Washington's . . . it simply had to have Gates or it would have gone shimmering to utter ruin.' Be that as it may, it is evident that the Commander-in-Chief did not find his Adjutant-General, who, it was said, had the inherited manners of an upper class servant, at all congenial. 'I discovered very early in the war symptoms of coldness and constraint in General Gates's behaviour to me', Washington was to write. We may imagine that the coldness and constraint were not altogether on one side.

Meanwhile General Burgoyne had started his campaign to capture Albany. On July 10th, 1777, he took Fort Ticonderoga, much to Washington's consternation: he wrote to one of his friends that: 'Had not Congress considered this as a separate department, etc.' he would have ordered an inquiry. Congress at once made honourable amends by inviting Washington to nominate a commander to replace Schuyler. But Washington refused and Congress not unnaturally appointed Gates. By the date that Gates took over the command Burgoyne had outrun his communications and his depleted overladen force was getting into difficulties. Gates, on the other hand, steadied his troops since he had replaced a general who had become despondent and unpopular. After two battles, in which the military genius of Benedict Arnold shone, Burgoyne surrendered to Gates at Saratoga on October 17th. 'If old England is not by this lesson taught humility', observed Gates with pardonable self-satisfaction, 'then she is an obstinate old slut, bent on her ruin.'

Gates did not report this fine success to Washington but dispatched his adjutant, Wilkinson, to Congress with the news, although, as it happened, Washington was first to hear about it. On his way Wilkinson lingered at Reading in Pennsylvania for a drinking bout with a friend of Washington's named General Stirling. Over his cups Wilkinson confided to Stirling how an Irish-born French officer, Brigadier-General Conway, who was serving under Washington, had been writing letters to Gates criticizing the Commander-in-Chief. One of these letters (Wilkinson asserted) said: 'Heaven had been determined to save your country, or a weak General and his counsellors would have ruined it.' Stirling hastened to pass on this illuminating item of gossip to Washington, and the fat was in the fire.

Washington had never cared for Conway, any more than he had for Gates. In both cases it was a clash of personalities. Conway, though a competent officer, was boastful and ambitious and Washington put a premium on modesty and unselfish devotion to the cause. On the very day that the convention of Saratoga was signed, Washington had been writing to a friend in Congress expressing the hope that Conway would not be promoted Major-General. Conway's merit, he said caustically, 'was more in his own imagination than in reality: for it is a maxim with him to leave no service of his own untold, nor to want anything which is to be obtained by importunity'. When he received Stirling's letter the Commander-in-Chief saw red. Without stopping to verify if the story were true, he wrote to Conway asking for an explanation. Conway wrote to Gates asking how his private letter had got into the wrong hands and tendered his resignation. The ink flew in every direction. Gates protested to Washington and required to know where he had obtained the letter. Conway announced that in Europe nothing was more common than for officers to criticize their superiors. Washington retorted by refusing Conway's resignation and telling Gates exactly how he had heard of the letter — through the indiscretion of his own adjutant. Back came Gates saying that of course the letter was a forgery. In fact the offending sentence was not exactly what Conway had written. What he really wrote was: 'What a pity there is but one Gates! but the more I see of this [Washington's] army the less I think it fit for general action under its actual chiefs and actual discipline. I speak you sincerely and freely and wish I could serve under you.' If this was not saying much the same thing, it was at any rate sufficiently offensive.

Gates and Conway have not lacked defenders. But only one sound line of defence is open. Gates had sent copies of Conway's critical letters to Congress. By doing so, he was clearly trying to have Washington removed from his command. No doubt he thought, just as his friend Major-General Charles Lee thought,

TOWARDS VICTORY

that Washington was an 'arrogant and vindictive knave' and an incompetent to boot. Washington, when struck, defended himself; he was not without friends. But in the winter of 1777 his ground was not too sure. He had lost Philadelphia and Gates was the hero of Saratoga. In November Congress decided to establish a new Board of War to which Washington would be responsible. It made Gates the president of the Board and promoted Conway at the same time appointing him Inspector-General with power to reorganize the discipline of the army. The measures in themselves were wise and necessary, but the appointments were well calculated to infuriate the Commander-in-Chief. No wonder he wrote to the President of Congress saying that 'a malignant faction had for some time been forming to my prejudice'. No wonder he greeted Conway coolly, more especially as the Irishman had written him a sneering letter comparing him to 'the great Frederick'. But soon Washington's temper burned out. He told Gates that the subject was closed and at the end of February 1778 he informed a friend: 'I have a good deal of reason to believe that the machinations of the Junto will recoil upon their own heads.' And he was right. Nine of his brigadiers protested at Conway's appointment and the boastful Irishman was never allowed to take up his duties; instead he was given a command that failed to materialize, was wounded in a duel, apologized to Washington under the impression that he was on his death bed, and returned to France with the gratuity he had solicited. As for Gates, his singularly inept handling of a campaign in the south in 1779 was to sow the suspicion that the victor of Saratoga owed more to the ability of his subordinates and to the mistakes of his enemies than to his own untutored genius.

Was there a 'Conway Cabal' in the sense that there was an organized plot by a group of men to remove the Commander-in-Chief? It would have been natural enough if in the winter of 1777-78 Congressmen had thought of doing so, but there is virtually no evidence for it. It was also to be expected that army officers — especially ex-British officers like Gates and Lee — should have imagined that they could have done very much better in Washington's place. Much of the true story centred upon personal antagonisms and misunderstandings without any broad historical significance and upon a definition of terms. Probably Washington and his immediate circle of friends exaggerated when they described the half-hearted intrigues of a few disgruntled individuals as a 'Junto'. And in that sense the 'Conway Cabal' is one of the major historical myths.

Washington had chosen Valley Forge as his winter quarters as a compromise between two points of view. He himself would have preferred to spend the winter at Wilmington; but Congress and the Pennsylvanians had insisted that he should encamp where he could not only watch over the capital but also where he would be in touch with New Jersey. Valley Forge lay twenty-five miles up the Schuykill River north-west of Philadelphia; the encampment was in front of two hills which formed one side of the valley that gave the forge its name. A road ran between these two hills to the valley creek on which stood the forge. Washington's headquarters in the stone house of Deborah Howe were in the valley; the army's huts were on the south-east side of the hills, one of which ironically bore the name of Mount Joy. Washington and his staff did not experience much discomfort, but the men lacked shoes and clothes, straw to sleep upon and forage for the horses. The Commander-in-Chief described the conditions during the early part of the winter in these words: 'Without arrogance ... it may be said that no History now extant can furnish an instance of an Army's suffering such uncommon hardships as ours have done, and bearing them with such patience and fortitude. To see men without clothes to cover their nakedness; without blankets to lay on; without shoes, by which their marches might be traced in blood from their feet; marching through frost and snow; and at Christmas taking up their winter quarters within a day's march of the enemy, without a house or hut to cover them, till they could be built, and submitting to it without a murmur, is a mark of patience and obedience which in my opinion, can scarcely be paralleled.' Thousands of men were unfit for duty because of the lack of shoes and clothing and the hospitals could not cope with the emergency. Three out of four men were either sick or absent without leave. Washington did his utmost. He ordered inoculations and divine services each Sunday; but he pitied 'those miseries which it is neither in my power to relieve or prevent'. In February Martha arrived to nurse and knit for the soldiers. It was not too bad for the officers: there were dances and theatricals; the General played 'rounders' or 'cricket' with his aides. Conditions gradually improved, but they did not favour the creation of a brand-new army.

To Valley Forge came Baron von Steuben with his music-loving Italian greyhound Azor to teach the American soldier discipline. Steuben had little English except for a fair flow of swear-words, but he impressed Washington more than most foreigners especially as he was willing to remain a mere brigadier-general until he had proved his value. While Steuben was trying to instil discipline into a force where (he said) it did not exist and thereby causing some displeasure to the American officers, the Commander-in-Chief was having an embarrassing time with another eminent foreigner, Lafayette. Lafayette had been invited by the new Board of War, headed by Horatio Gates, to lead an expedition to the conquest of Canada in midwinter without being given adequate troops or financial resources. Lafayette had earned his major-generalship, which at first had been a purely honorary rank, by his bravery at Brandywine where he had been wounded and by a youthful fervour that had endeared him to all. In his disappointment over the Canadian expedition he was soothed by Washington, who could excel himself in a gracious letter, and returned to Valley Forge in time to share in the rejoicing at the news that the French Government, which had long been helping the Americans with supplies, had now officially declared war upon Great Britain. Washington ordered a gill of rum for his troops and told his officers and men to celebrate the event by wearing nosegays in their hats. The Fabian tactics of the Commander-in-Chief had proved their worth. The long winter of their discontent was over and victory was assured.

While the American army thus suffered and rejoiced at Valley Forge, the British had passed a very comfortable winter in Philadelphia. A season of gambling and love-making culminated in a fancy dress ball of medieval splendour. Then Howe, who had asked leave to resign his command, left the city after handing over to Sir Henry Clinton; and Clinton had orders to withdraw and return to New York overland.

Washington soon guessed his enemy's intention, but sent Lafayette on reconnaissance to make certain. Overruled by his council of war when he proposed to attack the British before they retired, Washington instead followed the retreating army, planning to take it at a disadvantage on the march. An advance force was sent ahead to assault the British rear under the command of Major-General Charles Lee, who had been exchanged and rejoined the troops that spring in an uneven temper. First Lee had refused, then changed his mind, and finally peremptorily demanded the new command.

The Americans were now in excellent spirits. They knew of the French alliance; they had been well drilled by Steuben; and at long last the officers had been promised half-pay at the close of the war. Clinton withdrew slowly, strengthened his rearguard, altered his route and paused two days to rest his men, while the Americans were moving along a parallel line only ten miles north-west of him. Lee emerged, as he had been ordered, at a convenient point to attack the British rear, but not liking the reaction of the British infantry drew off. Washington rode up on a white horse and demanded of Lee the reason for the confusion and retreat. Meanwhile the encouraged British had turned to do battle. Washington reinforced Lee's men on the left and threw another force to the right and thrust himself into the thick of the battle. As at Trenton and Germantown, his blood was up. 'I never saw the General to so much advantage,' wrote Alexander Hamilton, who was there, 'his coolness and firmness were admirable. He instantly took measures for checking the enemy's advance and giving time to the [main] army which was very near to form and make a proper disposition ... America owes a great deal to General Washington for this day's work ... He did not hug himself at a distance and leave an Arnold to win his laurels for him.' It was a battle, wrote Washington himself, 'which from an unfortunate and bad beginning turned out a glorious and happy day. We drove the enemy back ... recovered the field of battle and possessed numbers of their dead, but as they retreated behind a morass ... and had both flanks secured with thick woods, it was found impracticable with our men fainting with fatigue, heat and want of water to do anything more that night.' And at midnight the British stole off 'as silent as the grave'.

According to an unconfirmed account Washington had sworn at Lee 'till the leaves shook in the trees'. Whether he swore or

TOWARDS VICTORY

not, Lee knew well how he felt, for next day the Major-General demanded with a fine bluster what 'misinformation' or 'very wicked person' had caused Washington to make use of such 'very singular expressions' to him. Washington had Lee arrested and a court martial found him guilty of disobedience and insubordination. He retired to his estates to engage in vituperative pamphleteering and to die forgotten.

After the battle of Monmouth Courthouse (as it was called) on June 28th the rest of 1778 was spent by Washington in planning how the Americans could best co-operate with their French allies. On July 14th he wrote to congratulate Admiral d'Estaing who had arrived safely with twelve warships. Lafayette played a useful part as a liaison officer and Washington proposed through him that they should undertake a joint attack on New York or Rhode Island. It was found that the French vessels could not get across the bar in New York harbour and the Rhode Island plan failed, d'Estaing having to draw off to Boston to get his ships repaired because of damage done to them by a storm when they were trying to pursue an inferior fleet under Lord Howe. Washington confessed to his brother that this had 'blasted in one moment the fairest hopes that were ever conceived', but with statesmanlike vigour gave his officers strong orders against recriminations. Lafayette discussed plans for fresh operations with d'Estaing ranging as far afield as Canada and the West Indies, but Washington advised his young friend to go home on furlough to see his wife and children, while recommending Congress on military as well as political grounds not to pursue the idea of a Franco-American expedition to Canada. The Commander-in-Chief and his young French friend then took an affectionate leave of each other. 'I think myself happy', wrote Washington, 'in being linked with you in bonds of strictest friendship.' Lafayette left for France in January 1779. He was to return in time to take part in the greatest stroke of the war.

George Washington spent the winter of 1778-79 more pleasantly than most: his troops were encamped at Middle Brook in New Jersey whence they could watch the activities of Sir Henry Clinton's garrison in New York; and the Commander-in-Chief was able to meet his wife in gay Philadelphia, now comfortably reoccupied by Congress. Here he discussed the next campaign; he realized that now the French had come into the war, the wisest policy was to act upon the defensive until a sizable French fleet appeared and gave the allies at least local command of the sea. For until that time Clinton would have the advantage — hitherto always possessed by the British — of being able to send out a force by sea to attack any point in the colonies before Washington could gather and dispatch troops overland for its defence. Among the projects considered by Congress were of course an attack on New York and another attempt to take the British naval base at Newport, Rhode Island. An expedition to Niagara on the Canadian frontier was also examined. In a letter of January 13th to a committee of Congress Washington pointed out with melancholy dryness that 26,000 men would be needed to attack New York and Rhode Island, a force 'very difficult, if not impossible, to raise', while 20,000 men would be required for Niagara, which would only leave him 13,000 to watch New York. Instead of Niagara he proposed 'some operations on a smaller scale against the savages and those people who have infested the frontier during the previous campaign'. He offered the command of this expedition (which was to be directed against the Indian tribes known as the Six Nations) first to his 'inveterate enemy' Major-General Gates. Gates declined on the ground that he was too old at fifty to face the wilderness and, according to his biographer, because his shrewish wife did not fancy it and in any case because it demeaned the conqueror of Burgoyne to be ordered to chase Indians. So General Sullivan was sent instead with instructions from Washington not merely to overrun but to destroy the Indian settlements. Sullivan carried out his task so thoroughly that Indian chiefs in later years told Washington: 'To this day when your name is heard our women look behind them and turn pale and our children cling close to the necks of their mothers.'

The only other military events of this year were small well-organized assaults on two British forts on the Hudson River and an amphibious expedition, supported by Admiral d'Estaing's warships to Savannah in Georgia. Washington supervised the Hudson attacks but did not take part in them. So far as Savannah was concerned all he could do was write a consoling

TOWARDS VICTORY

letter to Major-General Benjamin Lincoln, the American commander, after he suffered a bloody repulse on October 9th.

It was not surprising that under these circumstances of comparative military inactivity a note of gloom crept into Washington's private correspondence. That summer he wrote of the 'rapid decay of our currency, the extinction of public spirit, the increasing rapacity of the times, the want of harmony in our counsels, the declining zeal of the people, the discontents and distresses of the officers of the army . . .' In a letter to his brother he added severely: 'This is no time for slumbering and sleeping.'

Another trying winter for his army, this time spent at Morristown, where it had previously encamped four years earlier, did not improve Washington's mood. Again desertions and mutinies took place and the usual effort was necessary to bribe recruits for the continental army. Conditions might have been as bad as at Valley Forge had not General Greene been given permission to requisition supplies. The ordinary administration of the commissariat was made impossible by the depreciation of the currency. The officers were bitter and even Washington complained about the log cabins in which he and Martha were lodged. In March he expressed dissatisfaction over the complete stagnation of public affairs. What worried him more than anything else was his feeling that leading American statesmen still appeared to have no adequate idea of the importance of national union for winning the war. In a significant letter to Joseph Jones, the Virginian Congressman, he said: 'Certain I am that unless Congress speaks in a more decisive tone; unless they are vested with powers by the several States competent to the great purposes of war or assume them as a matter of right; and they, and the States respectively act with more energy than they hitherto have done, our cause is lost.' When in June 1780 Clinton returned to New York from a victorious campaign in the south, during which his troops occupied Charleston in South Carolina, hitherto considered impregnable, Washington said: 'I hope the period is not arrived that will convince the different States, by fatal experience, that some of them have mistaken the true situation of the country.' He emphasized in his correspondence with Congress that without effective assistance from the states it was impossible for the continental army to co-operate with the French and he told the Governor of his own Virginia that though it might be threatened by the British his army was far too small to lend any help. He insisted that what was needed to save America and win the war was a carefully planned operation by a well-trained continental army and not a series of piecemeal defensive campaigns in the individual states; but he saw only inefficiency and chaos as Congress let its powers slip back into the hands of the state governments. The patriot government was indeed pictured by him as 'a many-headed monster, a heterogeneous mass, that never will or can steer to the same point'. The American people, he believed, had allowed themselves to be lulled into a false sense of security, trusting that peace was always just around the corner and, because of doctrinaire fears of a standing army, refusing to create an effective fighting force. 'We may rely upon it', he concluded, 'that we shall never have peace till the enemy are convinced that we are in a position to carry on the war.' All that Congress did, however, was to recall the egregious Major-General Gates from his retirement and send him to take over the command on the southern front.

A gleam of hope shone upon the Commander-in-Chief when in May the Marquis de Lafayette (having sadly abandoned the idea that he might take part in a glorious invasion of England from France) returned to his 'dear General' with the excellent news that another French admiral together with Lieutenant-General the Count of Rochambeau was on his way to America with a naval and land force to succour the Americans.

The new French force landed in Newport, which Clinton had evacuated before he set out on his southern expedition; but no sooner had the French arrived than they were blockaded by the British. Rochambeau, who was a somewhat tetchy gentleman, demanded a personal interview with Washington; but at the interview it was agreed that nothing could be done until both sides had received reinforcements. Then came two disasters. General Gates suffered defeat at the hands of General Cornwallis whom Clinton had left in command in South Carolina. After the battle of Camden (August 16th) Gates, according to Alexander Hamilton, 'showed that age and the long labours and fatigues of military life had not in the least impaired his activity, for in three days and a half he reached Hillsborough one hundred and eight miles from the scene of action, leaving all his troops to take care of themselves, and get out of the scrape as well as they could'. It was not as bad as that. Gates had to retire quickly to preserve the remnants of his continental troops. Washington wrote him a polite letter. But 'the heat of the southern climate ... blasted the laurels which were thought in their splendour to be ever green'.

The other disaster was the treachery of Benedict Arnold. Arnold, like Lafayette and Hamilton, had been one of Washington's favourite young men. When his promotion had been delayed Washington soothed him and when Congress had demanded his court martial for alleged peculation in 1779 the Commander-in-Chief had shown the closest solicitude over his treatment. Though acquitted except on a minor charge, the iron entered into Arnold's soul. He had fallen in love with a girl of loyalist connections and he disapproved of the alliance with Roman Catholic France. Above all ambition tempted him and though his plot to betray West Point, his command post on the Hudson, to the British was frustrated, he escaped to be a thorn in Washington's side for the rest of the war. Washington insisted that the English Major John André, who had acted as go-between with Arnold and was arrested in plain clothes, should be hanged as a spy (October 2nd). And so 1780 ended for Washington in wretchedness and impotence without plans, without supplies, without money, almost without men, and left him scarcely knowing whom he dared trust.

We are indebted to a Swedish nobleman, aide-de-camp to Count Rochambeau, for an impression of Washington in the autumn of 1780. 'His handsome and majestic, while at the same time mild and open, countenance perfectly reflects his moral qualities; he looks the hero; he is very cold; speaks little, but is courteous and frank. A shade of sadness overshadows his countenance, which is not unbecoming and gives him an interesting air.' The American doctor, James Thacher, carried away very much the same recollections from a dinner party in the previous year, only he had detected in Washington's face 'a placid smile', though a loud laugh, he heard, 'seldom, if ever, escapes him'.

Thacher also noted that Washington was 'feared even when silent'. Mrs. Washington, he found, had a 'pleasing affability', but possessed 'no striking marks of beauty'.

By this date Great Britain was at war with half the world. In June 1779 the Spanish King had plucked up courage to join the alliance and in the Mediterranean the British possessions of Gibraltar and Minorca were besieged, while a Franco-Spanish fleet threatened the English Channel and the island of Jersey. Russia, Sweden and Holland proclaimed an armed neutrality and afforded protection and hospitality to merchant ships succouring the foes of England. In December 1780 the defiant British Government declared war on Holland and thus added a third navy to its enemies. Sea warfare was waged in the Channel, the North Sea, the Mediterranean and the Atlantic. But the British sailor held his own. The invasion of England was frustrated. Gibraltar was relieved; a Spanish squadron was destroyed near Cape Trafalgar; a French fleet was crippled off the West Indies; and the lucrative Dutch West Indian islands were occupied by the veteran Admiral Rodney. With their responsibilities thus scattered, the British could never maintain a fully adequate naval force in the West Atlantic. And Sir Henry Clinton therefore committed a fatal mistake when in 1781, counting on a delusive naval superiority, he divided his limited land forces into three parts, sending one to fight in the southern states, one to harass Virginia, and keeping his main strength in New York.

As we have said, the ultimate achievement of American independence was — granted the historical conditions — as certain as any political event can be. Even had the British Government been able to concentrate its full military resources upon holding down the former colonies American independence would have come some day and would have left behind a longer trail of hate than it did. As things were, with a world war to fight, the British Government soon resigned itself to the painful but unavoidable decision of separation.

George Washington did not of course see matters in this light. His was necessarily a parochial view. All he knew was that the French fleets were never there when he wanted them; that American political unity had not been realized, for even when at last on March 1st, 1781, all thirteen states ratified the Articles of

TOWARDS VICTORY

Confederation only a loose and weak league was created; and this league would never allow him to command a strong, well-disciplined and truly national army. In January 1781 the Pennsylvania line — that portion of his troops raised by Pennsylvania — mutinied and marched across New Jersey homewards clamouring for better treatment. This outbreak was amicably disposed of, but when a New Jersey contingent followed suit, Washington was adamant. One of his major-generals was ordered 'to compel the mutineers to unconditional submission and execute on the spot a few of the principal incendiaries'. Two ringleaders were in fact hanged and later Washington wrote to Congress repeating his request for the right to inflict five hundred lashes in preference to too frequent examples of capital punishment for military offences.

Nevertheless at the beginning of 1781 Washington had become recognizably for the first time the real Commander-in-Chief of the whole continental army. He sent his best general, Nathanael Greene, to the south to replace Horatio Gates; he vetoed another Canadian expedition; and he told Virginia that it was more important to the national cause for Greene to be reinforced than for their local forces to be tied to their own state by the menaces of the traitor Arnold. Some of Washington's own slaves were seized from Mount Vernon, but he wrote an angry letter to his overseer reproving him for trying to placate the British marauders with refreshments. Throughout the early summer he watched narrowly the antics of Congress and of his French allies. On May 11th he wrote to a friend: 'The resolution of Congress to appoint Ministers of War, Foreign Affairs and Finance, gave, so far as I was able to learn the sentiments of men in and out of the Army, universal satisfaction. Postponing of the first, delaying the second, and disagreeing about the third had a direct contrary effect.'

Greene carried out a valuable defensive campaign in the south and Clinton withdrew Cornwallis north to join Arnold in Virginia. Washington planned to hit the British where they were strongest by assaulting New York. This he could do because he was told that a powerful French fleet under Admiral De Grasse was coming north from the West Indies, after Rodney had left for home. But De Grasse announced that he would not come further north than Chesapeake Bay and could only remain until the autumn. Without a sign on that serene face to disclose his feelings Washington at once altered his programme to an offensive against Cornwallis, encamped at Yorktown, Virginia, near the northern end of the Chesapeake, and directed his energies to persuading the French admiral in Rhode Island to link up with De Grasse.

On September 5th Washington recorded in his diary, which he had reopened that year for the first time since 1778, the glad news that De Grasse had arrived on August 30th. Four thousand French regulars and two thousand Americans marched from New York State to the northern end of Chesapeake Bay where they were picked up in transports and carried down the bay to a point west of Yorktown where Lafayette with a light American division was to meet them. Admiral De Grasse drove off a strong British fleet that attempted to interfere and Washington was able to write to the French admiral that the 'enterprise against York . . . [is] as certain as any military operation can be rendered by a decisive superiority of strength and means'.

On October 6th, 1781, the siege began according to the recognized canons of the eighteenth century. The Franco-American forces numbered some 20,000 men (excluding navy) and Cornwallis had about eight thousand — the equivalent of half a modern division. Under cover of well-directed artillery the first trench or 'parallel' was opened. On October 14th two of the enemy's outer works were taken at the point of the bayonet, Colonel Alexander Hamilton distinguishing himself with Lafayette's light division. The following mercifully small casualties were reported during this siege: the French: 50 killed and 127 wounded, the Americans: 27 killed and 73 wounded, the British: 156 killed, 326 wounded and 70 missing. But as Cornwallis had been completely surrounded and ran out of ammunition he had to surrender with over seven thousand men who marched out with their band playing 'The World Turned Upside Down'. On October 19th, Dr. Thacher saw the French and Americans draw up in line, the French in smart uniforms with a band 'of which the timbrel formed a part, a delightful novelty . . . the Americans, though not in uniform nor their dress so neat, yet exhibited an erect soldierly air'. Cornwallis, a brave and able general, was treated with punctilious politeness. 'My lord', said Washington, 'you had better be covered from the cold.' 'It matters not, sir,'

TOWARDS VICTORY

responded Cornwallis gloomily, 'what becomes of this head now.' Cornwallis, however, survived to win great battles in India. And though Clinton, who could not or would not relieve him, lingered on in New York, for the British the war was over that day. George Washington hastened to Mount Vernon and to Martha who had been down with jaundice and on his way saw her only son, Jacky Custis, die.

No military struggle disturbed 1782. Washington sat outside New York watching the British garrison, now under Sir Guy Carleton. In due course the British evacuated their stronghold of Charleston in South Carolina. The American soldiers grew 'soured' as they kicked their heels and longed for their firesides when winter came. Washington was troubled by a thousand public and private cares. His mother complained that she was poverty-stricken; his brother Samuel was overwhelmed with debt; he had the memory of a painful quarrel with Alexander Hamilton; and he angrily rebuked his overseer, Lund Washington, for not sending him annual accounts of his crops. But, above all, he sorrowfully contemplated the 'predicament he was in as a citizen and a soldier' when his men began to clamour louder and more insistently for their just rights. Unlike Cromwell, he did not imagine an inscrutable Providence had plucked him out to be a military dictator or a king. Inflexibly he did his duty by Congress. On March 15th he addressed a meeting of discontented officers, presided over by Major-General Gates, who, with the 'stigma' of Camden now obliterated, had rejoined the victorious army. Standing at a 'desk or pulpit' in a temple at Newburgh the Commander-in-Chief fumbled in one pocket for his manuscript and in another for his spectacles. 'Gentlemen,' he began, 'you will permit me to put on my spectacles, for I have not only grown grey, but almost blind in the service of my country.' Under the impact of reasonableness the threatened storm dispersed. Four days later he wrote to the President of Congress that the articles of the treaty between America and Britain were 'as full and satisfactory as we have reason to expect', though he thought the 'general pacification was inconclusive', or, in other words, that the French had done less well out of it. But when De Grasse had sailed back from Chesapeake Bay to the West Indies, Admiral

Rodney had returned and attacked him with an inferior fleet, captured or destroyed eight of his ships and taken the French admiral himself prisoner. So far as the sea was concerned, De Grasse had won the war for America and lost it for France.

In 1783 several letters from Washington to Hamilton, to whom he was reconciled, showed the trend of his thoughts. He stressed the need for a United States Constitution 'competent to the general purposes of government' and said he felt it his duty to point out the defects in the existing confederation. He demanded of Congress speedy demobilization of his army and fair treatment for his men. At last in November 1783 after Sir Guy Carleton had marched his troops from New York to their ships, Washington prepared to go to Congress to surrender his commission. At a New York tavern he drank with his comrades, shook each by the hand in silence, and walked with them to the barge which was to carry him on the first stage of his journey home to Mount Vernon, where he could repose a mind 'always at a stretch' and resume 'those domestic and rural enjoyments which far surpassed the highest pageantry of this world'.

4. PRESIDENT AND ELDER STATESMAN (1783-1799)

General Washington was now 'a private citizen on the banks of the Potomac ... under the shadow of my own vine and my own fig tree, free from the hustle of a camp ... envious of none'. 'I am determined to be pleased with all', he told Lafayette; 'and this, my dear friend, being the order for my march, I will move gently down the stream of life, until I sleep with my fathers.' He had returned to Mount Vernon in time to distribute Christmas presents to the four lovely fatherless children of Jacky Custis. Soon he gazed out over the snowbound fields and began to plan the reconstruction of his estate and of his fortunes shattered by the war and by the depreciation of the currency. 'I made no money from my estate' he told a relative, 'during the nine years I was away from it and brought none home with me.'

Slowly his old round was resumed. In February he would 'employ all day in marking the ground for the reception of my

PRESIDENT AND ELDER STATESMAN

shrubs'. Spring brought back the grafting of the cherry trees. Throughout the summer he rode out daily to inspect his different farms and to supervise the crops. Foxhunting and fishing enlivened his autumn and winter. A novel occupation was the breeding of the first American jackasses. A 'jack' had been presented to him by the King of Spain and dogs by French admirers. The weekdays were always fully absorbed, and on Sundays churchgoing was even rarer than of old. Often his diary recorded for Sunday: 'at home all day alone' or 'at home all day writing'.

Yet an air of sadness disturbed these years of retirement from the public service. Martha was often ill. The much loved neighbours, the Fairfaxes, had long ago left Belvoir for England. One winter day Washington went across to view the ruins of their house which had been destroyed by fire. He begged his old friends, George and Sally, to come back to Mount Vernon and rebuild their home. But one day came the news that George William Fairfax was dead. Other friends and relatives died: General Nathanael Greene, whose son, his namesake, Washington offered to adopt; Samuel, his extravagant and prolific brother, in 1783; and in 1787 his favourite brother, John Augustine, the 'intimate of his youth and the friend of his ripened age'; and Colonel Tilghman, one of his former aides.

In the autumn of 1784, accompanied by his closest personal friend, Dr. James Craik, Washington set out along the once familiar trail to visit his properties beyond the mountains; they travelled as far as Pittsburgh only to find his 'bounty lands' there in possession of squatters who defied him to oust them, as they claimed ownership by right of first settlement. However, to Washington, the chief interest of the trip was that it confirmed his belief that the navigations of the rivers Potomac and Ohio could be linked and a direct route cut between Virginia and Detroit. He pressed this development policy on the Virginian Assembly. The obstacle to his plan was that the Potomac River ran along the boundary between Virginia and Maryland. Therefore to enhance its commercial prospects these two states, so long rivals, had to come together in defiance of the Articles of Confederation which forbade inter-state treaties without the consent of Congress. Nevertheless in the spring of 1785 a meeting to promote the project was held at Mount Vernon and in due course two companies were formed to improve the waterways of the Potomac and James Rivers. Washington became the president of the former company and was granted fifty shares in each, which he at first refused and then took on trust for charitable ends. But out of the Mount Vernon agreement arose something more important than a mere commercial arrangement; from it grew the idea of a closer union of all the American states.

Another presidency accepted by Washington was that of the Society of the Cincinnati, a somewhat aristocratic edition of a veterans' association or ex-servicemen's league. Membership, which was hereditary, was confined to American and foreign officers who had served for three years or had been incapacitated in the army. Washington was soon upset by an outcry begun against the society by the leading civilian politicians who had always feared the influence of a standing army. He wrote to Thomas Jefferson, the former Governor of Virginia, and to his friend, Alexander Hamilton, for their advice and after considering it proposed various drastic alterations in the constitution of the society and even tried to abolish it. It never recovered from this uneasy birth and was to become an historical relic and not a lobby.

At the close of 1784 Lafayette came to Mount Vernon to say goodbye, promising he would return there every spring. But Washington in a letter of curious foreboding wrote to him that he feared they would never meet again. 'I called to mind the days of my youth and found they had long since fled to return no more; that I was descending the hill I had been fifty-two years climbing, and that, though I was blest with a good constitution, I was of a short-lived family, and might soon expect to be entombed in the mansion of my fathers. These thoughts darkened the shades and gave gloom to the picture, and consequently to my prospect of seeing you again. But I will not repine; I have had my day.' The two friends were indeed not to meet again. But Washington was to be twice President of the United States before he died; and Lafayette was to be engulfed in the French Revolution and to survive as a retired actor in two events that shook the world.

In those years Washington had his portrait painted several times and his bust modelled by the celebrated sculptor, Jean Antoine Houdon: 'In for a penny in for a pound is an old adage', he wrote. 'I am so hackneyed to the touches of the painter's pencil, I am altogether at their beck, and sit like patience on a monument, whilst they are delineating the lines of my face. It is a proof among many others of what habit and custom can effect. At first I was as impatient at the request and as restive under the operation as a colt is of the saddle. The next time I submitted very reluctantly but with less flouncing. Now no dray moves more readily to the thill than I do to the painter's chair.'

The peaceable occupations of farming, riverland development and artist's model did not completely fill a life of retirement from the world. The former Commander-in-Chief had an ample and often embarrassing correspondence. His urban friends kept him in the political picture and his mind was far from disinterested in the problems of the new nation; he could not forget what he had learned when he was in the army. 'We are a young nation and have a character to establish', he told his brother. There was truly a need to establish it.

The main weakness of the Articles of Confederation of 1781 had been that they provided for no effective national executive government, but conferred all powers upon Congress which with its delegates from thirteen states was too unwieldy for its tasks — even though its power did not include the right to coerce or to levy taxes. With the end of the war the confederate states had fallen asunder. Attendance at Congress was slack. All the states indulged in an internecine war of tariffs and depreciated currencies. With Hamilton and an able young Virginian named James Madison, George Washington considered the question how to invigorate Congress. Clearly though he realized the deep dislike of the individual states for the idea of a strong central government which would abridge their own separate sovereignties, he was convinced that victory and independence would be of slight value unless they conquered such prejudices: 'To be fearful of investing Congress . . . with ample authorities for national purposes appears to me the very climax of popular absurdity and madness.' Holding these opinions he felt that he could not refuse to represent Virginia in the Convention which was summoned to meet at Philadelphia in May 1787 to frame a new Constitution. The very convention had in fact its original impulse in the Mount Vernon meeting over the improvement of the Potomac waterway. And in Virginia the idea of strengthening inter-state relations had been sponsored by Washington's friend, Madison. Inevitably Washington was elected president of the Convention and keenly approved the work of giving Congress the powers 'indisputably necessary to perform the functions of government'.

The Philadelphia Convention decided after profound deliberations that the executive power should be invested in a single person who was to be chosen by electors nominated by the legislatures of individual states. The President thus chosen was given apart from these undefined 'executive powers', certain prerogative powers — such as the right to veto bills — administrative powers and appointive powers — such as the right to choose ambassadors and other high executive offices, with the consent of the Senate. It seems clear that what most delegates to the Convention imagined that they had created was a modified monarchy with powers carefully circumscribed. The pattern they had in mind to avoid was George III. It was assumed that the House of Representatives (elected in numerical accordance with state populations) and the Senate (two members from each state) would act as an effective check on the President. Moreover the House was given the right to impeach the President before the Senate. Thus everything that ingenuity could devise was put on paper to control the presidential authority, although it was agreed that the practical needs of government required that the executive should be a single individual. There was, however, nothing in the theory of the Constitution to prevent the powers of the President from withering away if he did not choose to exercise them. Thus the new institution from the first depended upon the character of the man who was elected to the office.

From this time forward Washington was genuinely exercised in his mind whether he ought to undertake the Presidency of the United States if it were offered to him. His old natural diffidence returned, and he told Hamilton that he hesitated to abandon his hopes of 'an unclouded evening after the stormy day of life' to the call of public duty. It was plain to him that the first President, whatever use he made of his powers, would become the target of much criticism — had he not said years before that censure was the inevitable lot of the public man? — and the lessons of the Cincinnati affair had shown him how icy the climate of democracy could be. But when Congress called him unanimously to the post on April 6th, 1789, he knew he could not refuse. It was a sacrifice. Few men have become rulers of their country with less satisfaction. And so four and a half years after he had left New York to give up one trust, he went back there reluctantly to assume another.

George Washington left Mount Vernon in no very cheerful mood. He regarded his new office as a public responsibility that he would have preferred to avoid and emphasized to his friends his lack of experience in the work of civil administration. 'Integrity and firmness' were, he said, all he could promise; and he added that his mistakes should be 'of the head, not of the heart'.

The awaiting Congress saw their President appear in a black velvet suit with gold buckles on the knees and shoes, yellow gloves and carrying a cocked hat with an ostrich plume. His thin hair was powdered and 'clubbed behind in the fashion of the day' and he had a sword hanging at his side. When he made his inaugural address it was noted that his face had a grave, almost sad look. He deliberately refrained from either proposing specific subjects for legislation or from suggesting amendments to the Constitution. On the contrary, he called upon Congress to devise and adopt them. Indeed at the beginning he regarded his position as equivalent to that of a constitutional monarch to whom the Senate would act as an advisory council.

Because of this conception of his office Washington took immense care over his public and private conduct and over what has been called the 'dignified element' in his new office. His practice was to refuse all social invitations and to make no calls, but to give a formal reception every Tuesday. It was decided that he should be known simply as Mr. President and not as his Highness. He shook hands with no one and acknowledged salutations by a formal bow. The President's lady also played her part with precision. To supplement the Tuesday levees, she also held receptions on Fridays which her husband attended. Dinner parties were a regular and terrifying function at which the President wore a settled look of melancholy. If a visitor showed signs of staying too long, Martha would say: 'The General always retires at nine, and I usually precede him.' Such precautions were merited. For adverse comments on his behaviour were soon to be heard and even his method of bowing was critically scrutinized.

To familiarize himself with national problems Washington undertook a number of tours both of the eastern and southern states. When he was in Massachusetts he insisted that John Hancock, the Governor, should pay his respects to him first, thus asserting the supremacy of the Federal Government over the states. For he was fully determined that as a whole the new government should be a strong government with real power — and influence, he said, was not power.

It was not surprising that Washington should regard himself virtually in the light of a monarch. For the Constitution had made no provision for ministers or executive officers responsible to Congress. As Lord Bryce observed, almost the only reference in the Constitution to the President's ministers is that contained in the power given to him to 'require the opinion in writing of the principal officer in each of the executive departments upon any subject relating to the duties of their respective offices'. These executive officers were responsible not to Congress (whom they could not even address) but to the President, and the President was responsible directly to the electorate (even though he could be impeached). This separation of powers between the President, Congress and the federal judiciary was of the essence of the American Constitution and was regarded by all, including Washington himself, as a bulwark against tyranny. Washington, who was anxious to avoid any suspicion of nepotism or favouritism, was nevertheless determined to find the best men for his ministers. Alexander Hamilton, his gifted former aide, became Secretary of the Treasury; General Henry Knox, his former artillery expert, was made Secretary of War; and two Virginians, Thomas Jefferson and Edmund Randolph, became respectively Secretary of State and Attorney-General. John Jay, a New Englander, selected the position of Lord Chief Justice. Jefferson and Randolph were keen believers in states' rights, whereas the others were federalists. The consequence was that Washington's original 'Cabinet' was from the outset divided against itself and this division among his counsellors added substantially to his own perplexities. It must be realized, however, that this group of Secretaries did not constitute a Cabinet in the English sense of the phrase, although it was frequently summoned to meet as a body

PRESIDENT AND ELDER STATESMAN

after 1793. Washington was not the first among equals. He listened to what his chosen counsellors had to say, but he was not obliged to accept the opinion of the majority or even restrained from seeking for advice outside their number. In the summer of 1789 Washington was severely ill with anthrax and while he recovered slowly he told his friend, Dr. Craik, that 'want of regular exercise with the cares of office, will, I have no doubt hasten my departure for that country whence no traveller returns'. Some of his friends thought indeed that after this disease he never recovered his old vigour.

Throughout his Presidency Washington felt his way with profound cautiousness and deliberation. His ill-health, the pronounced differences of outlook among his intimate advisers, and his own desire to be 'above party' all helped to give an impression that a weak man had taken command. But these were not the only reasons. From the earliest days of his public life it had been Washington's habit to act modestly in the exercise of personal power and to show deference to Congress. If he had chosen from the start to make energetic use of all the rights conferred upon him by the Constitution the political history of the United States might have developed very differently, but then Washington would not have been Washington. His refusal from 'motives of delicacy' to influence the decisions of either House and his determination not to indicate any preference when elections to Congress were taking place set a peculiarly difficult example for his successors to follow. Yet perhaps because of his very delicacy and restraint such views as he did feel called upon to express were heard with respect by his contemporaries and helped to strengthen the institution of the Presidency.

On domestic matters Washington was inclined to follow the advice of the brilliant young Hamilton, not because he had no mind of his own but because from the outbreak of the War of Independence the older and the younger man had been accustomed to think along much the same lines; both of them were convinced of the need to create a strong nation with a central government truly able to govern. For this reason Washington supported Hamilton's efforts to put the national finances on a firm footing, even though this meant that some of the states were called upon to contribute more than others to the liquidation of the national debts and even though, as in every debt settlement, some injustices were done to individuals. Washington accepted too Hamilton's doctrine that the Constitution must not be interpreted with narrow literalness and that there were in it 'implied powers' that the Federal Government might invoke. Such a doctrine was no departure for him. Since he had always believed that the federal administration must be effective if the United States were to be a power among nations, it was only logical that he who willed the end should also will the means.

In 1790 a somewhat curious bargain had been made between the followers of Hamilton and Thomas Jefferson whereby the former agreed that the new federal capital should be sited on the Potomac River, while the latter accepted the assumption of payment of the state debts by the Federal Government. It was the first of many examples of the Congressional 'deal'. Washington thoroughly approved this bargain as he held that 'the cause in which the expenses of the war was incurred was a common cause', while he was delighted that the new capital was to be so near Mount Vernon. The plans for the new capital were entrusted to a French architect, Major Pierre Charles L'Enfant, by commissioners appointed by Congress. Washington studied L'Enfant's plans with close attention and also Dr. Thornton's designs for the Capitol. Unhappily L'Enfant insisted in dealing directly with the President instead of the commissioners and succeeded in offending Thomas Jefferson who was an amateur architect with ideas of his own. In the end Washington had to acquiesce in the dismissal of L'Enfant but the city of Washington is laid out largely after L'Enfant's model. And in it the first President has a finer and more enduring memorial than any statues or inscriptions.

The treaties that concluded the War of Independence left several questions unsettled. Although the United States had been confirmed in her sovereignty over the continental territory as far north as Canada and as far west as the Mississippi, nothing had been clearly settled about the rights of navigation on the Mississippi or about the use of the port of New Orleans at its mouth, which was Spanish. Moreover, the future trading relations between Great Britain and America had not been decided, although the Americans had promised to pay outstanding debts and not to

PRESIDENT AND ELDER STATESMAN

discriminate against the loyalists. Washington, who interested himself closely in foreign affairs (he acted as his own Secretary of State until Jefferson returned from France) was convinced that the position of the United States in the world depended upon her degree of political unity. Other nations would respect her and enter into treaty relations with her if they believed that the Federal Government was capable of fulfilling its pledges. Hence in his mind foreign relations and domestic affairs were intimately linked.

In the autumn of 1789 the news of the French Revolution reached America. Enthusiasm was natural, for it was felt that the allies of the United States were hastening to follow in their footsteps. Washington, though he greeted the event with the ambiguous word 'wonderful', remarked with his customary caution that this might be the 'first paroxysm only'. And he grasped the significance of the Revolution from the point of view of America. France was her ally and if in consequence of the Revolution an armed conflict began between Britain and France, the United States Government might be committed to a fresh war with the peace settlement still incomplete. He therefore explored the ground carefully, sending new envoys to England and France, giving instructions that the British Government was to be sounded to see if it would now agree to surrender the forts it still held in the west and also be prepared to negotiate a treaty of commerce. The British, for their part, were irritated because the obligations to the American loyalists undertaken by the treaty of 1783 were not being fulfilled and outstanding debts were not being paid. In 1793 the thing that Washington dreaded occurred — England and France went to war. He hastened back from Mount Vernon to Philadelphia and summoned his Secretaries for advice. The presidential Cabinet was violently divided. Eventually a compromise was reached. It was decided to publish a proclamation not (in so many words) of American neutrality but of 'friendly and impartial conduct'. A French Republican Minister (the French having beheaded their king) was to be received but licences were not to be granted for the fitting out of French privateers in American ports. At the same time a British Minister was also received and in 1794 John Jay was induced to leave the bench of the Supreme Court to go on a special mission to England to negotiate a treaty of amity and commerce. Differences in foreign policy now accentuated the division between the followers of Jefferson (the Democrat Republicans[1]) and of Hamilton (the Federalists), the former being pro-French, the latter pro-British.

In December 1793 Jefferson resigned the post of Secretary of State. Washington still anxious to rise above party kept the balance even by replacing Jefferson with another Democrat, Edmund Randolph, and by sending in the following year the Francophil James Monroe to Paris. Never in the whole of his life was Washington confronted with a more heart-rending problem than that presented by the French Revolution. The Democrats considered that both sentiment and duty combined to oblige the American Government to do everything short of war to help the struggling French Republic in its war with England. Throughout America they formed societies to propagate this point of view. Washington was determined on neutrality and on a final settlement with Great Britain. In March 1795 the treaty which Jay had concluded in London reached the President. Though the Senate upheld the treaty by the bare majority necessary and with qualifications it was vehemently attacked in the House of Representatives. But the pro-French party was unlucky. Some intercepted letters obtained by the British threw doubt on the patriotism of Edmund Randolph, who was compelled to resign his office. After this, in the words of Professor Corwin, Washington 'proceeded to reconstruct his Cabinet on the basis of loyalty to his own policies, and in so doing created a precedent which, with negligible exceptions, has guided Presidents in the choice of departmental heads ever since'. The House tried to go beyond its prescribed rights in insisting upon the President placing all the papers relative to the London negotiations before it. The President refused on the ground that no such obligation was imposed upon him by the Constitution. And both Monroe in Paris and Gênet, the French Minister in the United States, over-reached themselves by the eccentricities of their behaviour. The Jay Treaty was ratified and this so frightened the Spaniards that in 1796 they concluded a treaty with the United States conceding the opening of the Mississippi to American trade and providing

[1] Both the modern Democrats and Republicans trace their descent from Jefferson. I prefer to call the Jeffersonians Democrats slightly inaccurately because the modern Republican Party really dates from the eve of the Civil War.

for free transit of freight through New Orleans. Thus in the end the foreign policy of George Washington proved a triumphant success. He kept the nation out of war and he obtained satisfactory settlements from both Britain and Spain. And when Napoleon Bonaparte emerged from the French Revolution and the friend of America, the Marquis de Lafayette, found his way into prison, the President's words of caution were shown to have been justified.

In thus directing the conduct of foreign relations Washington had begun the shaping of the presidential office. He had first tried to determine foreign policy in accordance with the apparent intention of the Constitution by going in person to meet the Senate to discuss a treaty; but the Senators were unwilling to consider the treaty in his presence and henceforward the Senate as a whole did not take part in treaty making. They still, however, could exercise their power to reject the appointment of diplomatists employed in treaty making and of course could refuse to ratify the completed treaties.

As we have seen, Washington accomplished all this despite a singular lack of co-operation from his Secretaries. Not only had Jefferson and Randolph resigned but even Hamilton deserted him in February 1795. Washington had the utmost difficulty in filling the vacant Cabinet offices. At one time he offered the Secretaryship of State to four different men each of whom excused himself in turn. The famous jurist, John Marshall, refused to become Attorney-General and Washington's old friend, Major-General Henry Lee, rejected the Secretaryship of War. It is not too much to say that it was largely Washington's personal courage, balanced judgment and imperturbability in the face of every type of criticism that saved the American executive system from falling into immediate decay. But he was not insensitive. In July 1796 he wrote to Jefferson inviting him to bear witness that 'truth and right decisions were the whole objects of my pursuits'. 'Until within the last year or two ago,' he added, 'I had no conception that parties would or even could go to the length I have been witness of.'

It had been with marked reluctance that Washington had agreed to serve as President for a second term, but he had been persuaded and was pleased that the vote of the electoral college was unanimously in his favour. One of his first tasks was to deal with a rebellion. It was not the first occasion when the new Republic had shown signs of disintegrating. In 1787 there had been a rising under Daniel Shays in Massachusetts, which he had then thought should have been more rigorously suppressed. Now when in 1794 a movement, whose leaders first gathered on Braddock's Field, began in western Pennsylvania in protest against the federal excise duties the old Commander-in-Chief took no chances. 'I consider this insurrection', he said, 'as the first *formidable* fruit of the Democratic societies ... instituted by the *artful* and *designing* members ... primarily to sow the seeds of jealousy and mistrust among the people, of the government . . .' 'If these self-created societies cannot be discountenanced', he asserted, 'they will destroy the Government of the country.' Taking personal command in his capacity of Commander-in-Chief imposed *ex officio* on the President of the United States, he rallied a force of fifteen thousand men and compelled a capitulation without conflict. The wisdom of his energetic measures in saving blood was manifest.

In the following year the President made another contribution to internal peace by bringing the Indian wars which had started again in the north-west to an end at least for the time being. His hope for permanent peace 'based on mutual good will' was however delusive. Many of his successors had still to try to cope with the Indian problem.

Thus Washington as President secured peace both at home and abroad for his country. He had surmounted the obstacles of increasingly virulent party strife and had managed without active help from some of the leading political figures of the time. It is easy enough, history teaches us, for a national leader to buy unity at home at the expense of war abroad or to use his domestic difficulties as an excuse for a weak foreign policy. The independent character of the American people flowing logically from the facts of their early history — of colonies with differing traditions, of men and women who could always find freedom in the wilderness — has often been the cause of desperate conflicts at home. That should not deceive anyone about the reality of their fundamental political unity, the most notable political achievement of modern civilization. And that unity owes much to the Presidency

PRESIDENT AND ELDER STATESMAN

of Washington who has survived as a figure above party, a hero acclaimed indeed as a sage by every party. That is as he would have wished it to be.

Thus Washington, while following out his conception of the Presidency as a kind of monarch — like the English monarch of our own times — high above party, had been driven by the realities of politics to enhance the powers of his office. As Commander-in-Chief he had dealt with an internal crisis. As chief executive he had conceived and controlled his own foreign policy, leaving to the Senate the right only to approve or disapprove. Finally he had constructed a homogeneous Cabinet responsible only to himself, leaving the Senate simply as one of the two co-ordinate branches of the legislature and not, as many had intended it and as he himself at first imagined it, as an advisory council to the executive. On the other side Washington had not tried to make Congress carry out his own constitutional or legislative projects. Nor perhaps could he logically have done so, so long as he regarded himself as above party.

Washington resolutely refused to stand for the Presidency a third time. As early as January 1795 he had told an old friend: 'I can religiously own that no man was ever more tired of public life, or more devoutly wished for retirement than I do.' In May 1796 he wrote to Hamilton asking his assistance in completing his farewell address which he wished to publish in all the newspapers. An early draft had been prepared during his first term with the help of the Democrat, Madison. Now Hamilton was invited to curtail it if too verbose and relieve it 'of all tautology' so that the whole should be 'in plain style and be handed to the public in an honest unaffected garb'. In June he asked Hamilton if the moment to announce his retirement was not overdue. Among the last, as among the first acts of his Presidency, was his appeal for an adequate national defence programme and as late as February 1797 he vetoed a bill that did not satisfy his wishes. In his final speech to Congress he urged the need for an American navy.

The farewell address (September 17th, 1796) epitomized Washington's experiences as President. He pleaded for national union before local patriotism, for country before party, for neutrality in foreign affairs. Consistently he had set himself to be above parties. 'I was no party man myself,' he wrote, 'and the first wish of my heart was, if parties did exist to reconcile them.' Similarly he had been an immovable non-interventionist. 'The United States', he had said, 'are too remote from Europe to take any share in the politics of that country [sic]'; again 'I trust we shall never ... become unnecessarily a party in their political disputes'. And again: 'My sincere wish is to have nothing to do with the political intrigues or squabbles of European nations.' And so in the address he warned against 'the baneful effects of the spirit of party, generally', while on foreign policy he observed: 'The great rule of conduct for us in regard to foreign nations is, in extending our commercial relations, to have with them as little *political* connection as possible ... Europe has a set of primary interests which to us have none, or a very remote relation ... Our detached and distant situation invites and enables us to pursue a different course.' Unhappily he could not legislate for eternity or at least for the age of the aeroplane. As for the 'baneful spirit of party' Washington may have noted that the House of Representatives could not even reach a unanimous vote on a farewell motion of thanks to him for his public services. Among the minority that voted against a felicitous form of address was the young representative for the new state of Tennessee, Andrew Jackson. It has been stated, perhaps with some exaggeration, that no President except Andrew Johnson (who was impeached) left office in such an atmosphere of opprobrium as George Washington.

John Adams succeeded Washington as President — the same John Adams who had proposed Washington as Commander-in-Chief in 1775 and later criticized him for setting himself above other men by refusing to accept any pay. Washington got back to Mount Vernon on March 15th, 1797. Two months later he wrote to the then Secretary of the Treasury, Oliver Wolcott, about his future plans: these were 'to make and sell a little flour annually; to repair houses (going fast to ruin), to build one for the security of my papers of a public nature, and to amuse myself in agricultural and rural disputes ...' To a nephew he confessed that he was again short of money and had been obliged to sell off his lands in Pennsylvania and in the Great Dismal Swamp to 'defray the expense of my situation'.

Although he announced that he did not intend to stir more than twenty miles from his own vine and fig tree, he was, in July 1798, at the age of sixty-six called out for the last time on public duty. Owing to the truculence of the French Directory there was a threat of war with France and President Adams invited Washington to become Lieutenant-General and Commander-in-Chief of the Army for the emergency. Washington accepted very hesitantly and insisted in a long and acrimonious correspondence with a number of gentlemen all stiffly standing on their ancient rights that Alexander Hamilton should be his second-in-command. Although his duties did not often compel him to leave home, they kept him fully occupied during the winter of 1798-99. While an undeclared naval war with France did in fact break out, no land fighting developed: Napoleon had other battles to wage. But Washington remained in nominal command of the 'provisional' American army until his death.

Apart from this, the last three and a half years of Washington's life passed peaceably. His habits were regular and abstemious. He had a heavy correspondence and many visitors. Each day he rode out to inspect his estates; each night he recorded with a farmer's meticulousness the vagaries of the weather in his diaries. He seldom had time to read and turned to letter writing regretfully; but he found occasion to welcome the exiled Polish hero and patriot, Thaddeus Kosciusco, to America and to invite him to Mount Vernon. And once his thoughts turned back, as the thoughts of old men will, to the days of his youth: he wrote to Sally Fairfax of Belvoir, now an elderly widow in England, recalling 'those happy moments, the happiest of my life which I have enjoyed in your company'.

George and Martha found pleasure in the company of Nelly Custis, Martha's grandchild and Lawrence Lewis, one of Washington's nephews, who had come to Mount Vernon to act as Washington's host. It was a happy moment for the old people when these two fell in love. They were married on Washington's birthday, February 22nd, 1799, and in November Martha's first great-grandchild was born.

We are fortunate in having a description of Washington in his retirement from a British actor: 'He was a tall, erect, well-made man ... who appeared to have retained all the vigour and elasticity resulting from a life of temperance and exercise. His

GEORGE WASHINGTON

dress was a blue coat buttoned to the chin, and buckskin breeches ... his eyes ... burned with a steady fire ... they were one grand expression of the well-known line: "I am a man, and interested in all that concerns humanity." '

On December 12th, 1799, General Washington noted in his diary: 'A large circle round the moon last night. About 10 o'clock it began to snow, soon after to hail, and then to a settled cold rain.' He rode out as usual to inspect his farms, and sat down to dinner in his wet clothes. Next morning the snow fell three inches deep and the wind blew from the north-east, but Washington went out in the afternoon to mark some trees down by the river for removal. On Saturday the 14th he woke very early in the morning complaining that he felt ill; yet he forbade Martha to get out of bed to call a servant for fear that she would catch cold. Such was his love. When the physicians came they bled him twice severely, thus in all probability killing him. That afternoon his old friend, Dr. James Craik, sat by the bed and Washington murmured to him: 'Doctor, I die hard, but I am not afraid to go.' As night came he told his secretary: 'I am just going. Have me decently buried, and do not let my body be put into the vault in less than three days after I am dead.' Some ten minutes later he passed away 'without a struggle or a sigh'. Martha Washington, who sat at the foot of the bed, asked: 'Is he gone?' and on being informed it was so, she said: ''Tis well. All is now over. I have no more trials to pass through. I shall soon follow him.'

NOTES

1. *Did Washington Love a Married Woman?*

A question which Washington's biographers always have to consider is whether he loved Sally Cary, wife of his friend George William Fairfax. The evidence for this belief consists chiefly of a number of ambiguous sentences in a letter said to have been written by him to the lady on September 12th, 1758, about four months after he became engaged to Martha Custis and four months before he married her. This letter was first published in the *New York Herald* in 1877 and the original has never been seen

NOTES

by historians. There are three schools of thought about this letter among American historians:

(a) The late Professor Nathaniel Wright Stephenson maintained that it was probably a forgery, arguing that, in view of the prolonged public controversy over it, had it been genuine by now it would have have come to light.

(b) Rupert Hughes and Professor L. M. Sears argued that the letter was genuine, that its interpretation was obvious, and that it was supported by other (if equally ambiguous) evidence: 'He loved once at least and that a married woman ... The fire burned so hotly as nearly to consume his honour.' (Sears)

(c) Mr. J. C. Fitzpatrick, the learned editor of the most complete edition of Washington's correspondence, accepts the letter as genuine, but maintains that the ambiguous sentences clearly refer to Martha Custis, his love for whom Washington was relating in confidence to Sally Fairfax.

As both Mr. Fitzpatrick and Professor W. C. Ford, another editor of Washington's correspondence, accept the letter as probably genuine and as it well attunes with the style of Washington's other letters to women, the case for its authenticity is strong. Its interpretation can be argued both ways; but taking account of the date at which it was written — exactly half-way between Washington's engagement and his marriage — the innocent character of the rest of the correspondence between him and Sally Fairfax (she was not the only lady to whom he wrote when on campaign — as a bachelor he also wrote to Sally Fairfax's sister-in-law, another married woman) and the fact that he did not conceal from Sally's husband that he was in correspondence with his wife, Mr. Fitzpatrick's interpretation seems the most natural. Ultimately the solution turns not on exact texts, but on our general view of Washington's character.

2. *Was there a 'Conway Cabal'?*

The evidence for the existence of a deliberate conspiracy both in the Army and in Congress to deprive Washington of his post as Commander-in-Chief and to put Gates in his place in the winter of 1777-78 depends mainly on Washington's own letters and the letters of one or two members of his entourage. The other side of the case has been well put by Rupert Hughes, Bernard Knollenberg and Samuel White Patterson. Knollenberg shows that of the Congressmen only Dr. Benjamin Rush was really committed to preferring Gates to Washington. On the other hand, there was obviously dissatisfaction in Congress over Washington's defeats at Brandywine and Germantown and it was natural that Gates, the victor of Saratoga, should have had ambitions. Unquestionably Mr. Fitzpatrick and some of Washington's earlier biographers have exaggerated the evidence because they have followed too closely Washington's own angry accusations against the so-called 'Junto'. Nothing is easier than for a commander in the field, harassed by crucial duties, to overstress and resent (especially in private letters) the murmurings of distant critics; this is more especially the case when that man has a quick temper and is convinced that he has done his duty. On the whole, it seems fair to say that, in default of better evidence, it cannot be accepted that there was any *organized conspiracy* against Washington, and that in this sense the Conway Cabal was mythical.

SELECT BIBLIOGRAPHY

T. S. ANDERSON: *The Command of the Howe Brothers* (1936).
M. D. CONWAY: *Washington and Mount Vernon* (1889).
J. C. FITZPATRICK: *The Diaries of George Washington* (1925); *George Washington Himself* (1922); *The Writings of George Washington* (1931 seq.).
P. L. FORD: *The True George Washington* (1897).
W. C. FORD: *The Writings of George Washington* (1889); *George Washington* (1900).
LOUIS GOTTSCHALK: *Lafayette Comes to America* (1935); *Lafayette Joins the American Army* (1937); *Lafayette and the Close of the American Revolution* (1942).
RUPERT HUGHES: *George Washington. The Human Being and the Hero 1732-1762* (1926); *George Washington. The Rebel and the Patriot 1762-1777* (1927); *George Washington. The Saviour of the States 1777-1781* (1930).
A. P. JAMES: *Writings of General John Forbes* (1938).
BERNHARD KNOLLENBERG: *Washington and the Revolution. A Re-appraisal* (1940).
S. W. PATTERSON: *Horatio Gates* (1941).
L. M. SEARS: *George Washington* (1931).
N. W. STEPHENSON and W. H. DUNN: *George Washington* (1940).
JAMES THACHER: *A Military Journal* (1827).
W. R. THAYER: *George Washington* (1922).

THOMAS JEFFERSON

JACKSON
ON
JEFFERSON

MR. JEFFERSON has plenty of courage to seize peaceable Americans ... and persecute them for political purposes. But he is too cowardly to resent foreign outrage on the Republic.

LINCOLN
ON
JEFFERSON

THE principles of Jefferson are the definitions and axioms of free society ... All honour to Jefferson — to the man who, in the concrete pressure of a struggle for independence by a single people, had the coolness, forecast, and capacity to introduce into a merely revolutionary document an abstract truth, applicable to all men and all times, and so to embalm it there that today and in all coming days it shall be a rebuke and a stumbling-block to the very harbingers of reappearing tyranny and oppression.

THOMAS JEFFERSON

CHAPTER III

THOMAS JEFFERSON

THOMAS JEFFERSON, like Washington, was a Virginian, and he admired and loved the first President. But these two Presidents represented different phases in American history. Washington personified the transition from the rule of a well-meaning, if inept, English aristocracy to the self-government of a new nation that was slowly recognizing its own unity. Jefferson in his ideas and in his virtues — and perhaps in his faults — typified the United States that was to come and as it was to be down to modern times. Seldom in history has a man who was not a successful soldier nor an outstanding administrator nor even a persuasive man of letters so decisively moulded the future of his country. Though Jefferson held nearly every great office in the Union, from the Governorship of Virginia to the Presidency twice over, it was his political thought, as expressed in the Declaration of Independence and in the teachings of the party that he led, which constitutes his claim to historical fame. For example, the complete freedom that every American possesses to become a millionaire or a bankrupt, a philosopher or a servant of the Yellow Press, an honest politician or a gangster is the realization of a Jeffersonian ideal.

But Jefferson also did much to develop the presidential office into a major factor in American political affairs. Through the part he took in creating a nation-wide party, by his direction of a party Cabinet devoted to his own views, and because of the prestige he obtained from his party leadership, he reduced the gap between the executive and the legislature — whenever Congress was controlled by the same party that chose the President. Moreover by his extraordinary action in authorizing the purchase of the vast territory of Louisiana without consulting Congress he proved that there were unexplored resources of power on which the chief executive could draw in a national crisis. Finally Jefferson by following Washington's example in refusing to stand for a third term in office consecrated a precedent that was not to be broken until our own days.

THOMAS JEFFERSON

Thus in several ways Jefferson enhanced the presidential powers, although perhaps unintentionally. For it is paradoxical that a political thinker who in fact believed whole-heartedly in the freedom of the individual should in practice have tended to weaken the careful balance of power within the Constitution that had been devised for the very purpose of preserving individual freedom. Indeed if attacks on the federal judiciary inspired by him had not been defeated, Jefferson might have come down to posterity as one of the strongest Presidents in American history. Yet whatever the differences between his practices and his preaching, Jefferson believed fervently in the liberty of the individual, in the freedom of the press, in liberty of thought, in a decent education for everyone, and in the need to abolish Negro slavery. Some of his ideals may have been misused and others have been found hard to support in a continent so diversified as that of North America. But his ideas endure and it is to be hoped that they will persist as long as there are English-speaking peoples on the earth. At heart all civilized men are Jeffersonians.

1. AUTHOR OF THE DECLARATION OF INDEPENDENCE: GOVERNOR OF VIRGINIA (1743-1781)

The Jeffersons, who were of Welsh descent, were among the earliest settlers in Virginia. Thomas's father, Peter, had a sane mind in a healthy body. His education, according to his son, was 'quite neglected' but he read lavishly in the Bible and in Shakespeare and in other books from his small but well-chosen library and had 'sound judgment and was eager after information'. A man of unusual strength and commanding stature he became a prosperous farmer, surveyor and public man. The mother was a more shadowy figure. She belonged to an aristocratic family, celebrated in early Virginian history, the Randolphs, and we are told she possessed a 'cheerful and hopeful temper and disposition'. Peter Jefferson failed neither in his public nor his private responsibilities. With Joshua Fry, a versatile Professor of Mathematics, who was at one time Washington's superior officer, he was chosen to continue the boundary line between Virginia and North Carolina, and became a Justice of the Peace and a member of the

House of Burgesses. He had six daughters and two sons and was a guardian to another boy. Thomas was the eldest child, born on April 13th (New Style), 1743.

The estate where Jane Randolph gave birth to Thomas was named Shadwell (Albemarle County) on the road from the Virginian capital, Williamsburg, to the wilderness. To the east lay a peaceful horizon, to the west were long rolling hills stretching towards the Blue Ridge Mountains. Jefferson attended an English school when he was five and a Latin school at nine, and received a correct classical grounding from a Whig clergyman. He learned to ride and swim and became an enthusiastic naturalist. When he was fourteen his father died, leaving his family in very comfortable circumstances. The 'whole care and direction of myself was thrown on myself entirely, without a relation or friend to advise or guide me,' Thomas wrote in his autobiography, ignoring his mother. The habit of command, and from that habit a sense of leadership, may have grown through his being a clever boy surrounded by women. Certainly he took seriously his duties as the eldest son of a widow. It is truer of him than it was of Washington that he was never young. The stilted letter which he wrote at the age of sixteen to ask his guardian for permission to go to William and Mary College at Williamsburg to pursue his studies and save money is at once grave and precocious. From childhood he was an intellectual.

Williamsburg was only a small town, indeed it was scarcely more than a village with some two hundred houses and a thousand inhabitants. Nor was William and Mary a university in the modern sense. Jefferson wrote of the college buildings as 'a rude misshapen pile, which but it had a roof would be taken for a brick kiln'. But Jefferson was fortunate in his teachers. Doctor William Small, a Scottish Professor of Mathematics, took the promising young student under his wing and instructed him in ethics, rhetoric and literature. Through him Jefferson met the then Governor of Virginia, Fauquier, whom he considered 'the ablest man who had ever filled that office' and in company with Small, Fauquier and George Wythe, a friendly and high-minded lawyer, enjoyed one of the best kinds of education, that provided by intelligent conversation. But he also slaved at his books, rising at dawn and working until two the following morning. His only exercise was a brisk run at twilight. To the classics he added a wide knowledge of modern languages and literature: he was to become known to his acquaintances as 'the greatest rubber off of dust' they had ever met. Hard work was his gospel. In later years he likewise expected his eldest daughter to educate herself from daybreak to bedtime. He must have been as formidable a father as he was assiduous a student.

It is true that a letter survives speaking of Jefferson's wild oats at Williamsburg — which he nicknamed Devilsburg — but these appear to have consisted merely of extravagances on his horses and clothes. The temptations of the flesh and the spirit did not noticeably incommode him. Though he fell in love and danced with his idol, 'Belinda' (Rebecca Burtwell), he kept her otherwise at arm's length. When he proposed he made it clear that before marriage he contemplated a two or three years' trip round the world: it was not astonishing that the lady married another. Evidently he fell out of love as quickly as he fell into it. For six months he was 'so abominably indolent' that he did not even bother to see the girl and his only surprise was when her chosen swain invited him to be his 'bridesman'.

If he was indolent over affairs of the heart, he was unwearying in the cultivation of his mind. He studied law at his friend Wythe's office for five years before being called to the Virginia Bar and during that period he read widely and earnestly, taking copious notes on political science as well as on religion and history in his commonplace books. He evolved some curious theories about the Anglo-Saxons and proved to his own satisfaction that Christianity was not a part of the common law. But he was not altogether inhuman: to a friend he confessed that while he was 'always fond of philosophy even in its drier forms — from a ruby lip it comes with charms irresistible'.

From the beginning the young Jefferson showed a close interest in politics, a subject in which Patrick Henry, a brilliant self-made lawyer, may have been his first mentor. Jefferson met Henry first on his way to college. Henry was a wild exciting orator, but lacked Jefferson's tireless industry. Henry's favourite pleasure was to put on his hunting shirt and spend weeks in the woods, camping at nights and cracking jokes by the fireside. But in 1765 his voice rang round America when he moved resolutions in the Virginia

DECLARATION OF INDEPENDENCE

Assembly condemning the British stamp duties. 'I was yet a student of law at Williamsburg', Jefferson recorded. 'I attended the debate however at the door of the building of the House of Burgesses and heard the splendid display of Mr. Henry's talents as a popular orator. They were great indeed; such as I have never heard from any other man. He appeared to me to speak as Homer wrote.' Jefferson himself was no orator; he had a husky unmanageable voice. When his grandson asked a contemporary how Thomas Jefferson became so useful a pleader (he made three thousand dollars a year when he began to practice in 1767) the reply was: 'Well, it is hard to tell because he always took the right side.' In 1769 he was chosen by his own county as member of the House of Burgesses and took part with George Washington and other famous Virginians in the meeting at the Apollo Room of the Raleigh Tavern where it was decided to impose an embargo on British imports as a reply to the Townshend duties. This was the first big Virginian stride up the road to independence.

Like Washington, Jefferson found himself a home of his own before he was married and, again like Washington, he selected as mistress of his estate a young and charming widow, not unblessed with this world's goods. Jefferson's new home was built in a lovely but lonely spot on top of a little mountain, Italianized as Monticello. Jefferson was his own architect and supervised the building. This was to become 'rather elegant, and in the Italian taste... one large square pavilion, the entrance of which is by two porticoes, ornamented with [Doric] pillars. The ground floor consists of a very large lofty salon... decorated entirely in the antique style; above it is a library'. Two small wings were to be joined to the pavilion and over the basement, which contained the kitchen, there was to be a terrace. But in the year of his marriage only one central room or 'pavilion' was ready for habitation. He was lucky to have that, for early in 1770 his old home, Shadwell, had been burnt to the ground and he lost many of his books. As his interest in architecture gave him a home, so his love of music helped to bring him his wife. He was an amateur of the violin, the lady, Martha Wayles Skelton, daughter of another Virginian lawyer, played the harpsichord and spinet. In mid-1771 he wrote to England to purchase a mahogany 'fortepiano' for Martha: was it his wedding present to her? On New

Year's Day, 1772, they married and travelled through the snow to the one-roomed home at Monticello. It was a well-founded alliance. Martha's inheritance from her father of forty thousand acres and one hundred and thirty-five slaves 'doubled the ease' of their circumstances and they were to have six children, of whom, however, only two, both girls, grew to adolescence.

The years of the courtship and the building of Monticello had been fairly peaceable, so peaceable that Jefferson spoke of the people as having 'fallen into a lethargy'. It looked for a moment as if the cracks between Britain and America would be papered over in spite of Patrick Henry and his revolutionary friends in Virginia. It is true that there had been 'incidents' in other colonies. At Boston British soldiers, deeply provoked, had fired on a mob. It was here that John Adams, a testy and slightly vain little lawyer and schoolmaster of Puritan descent and turn of mind, did one of the bravest acts in his life in undertaking the defence of British soldiers for this 'Boston massacre' on payment of a fee of one guinea. In 1772 a body of Rhode Islanders had attacked the crew of a British revenue cutter which had run ashore when trying to enforce the laws against smuggling. But the British Government had repealed the obnoxious Townshend duties except for a threepenny tax on tea and, in general, political passions did not run high. There was nevertheless stirrings and in 1773 Jefferson, with Patrick Henry and other younger members of the Virginian Assembly started a committee of correspondence to keep in touch with committees in other colonies, that were in time to become powerful engines of revolution.

Solidarity between Virginia, the most populous of the thirteen colonies and Massachusetts, the most revolutionary, was promptly exemplified when the British Parliament passed its coercive acts, including the act to close the port of Boston, in revenge for the 'Boston tea party'. Jefferson and his friends decided to arouse the people of Virginia by a public demonstration. They 'cooked up a resolution . . . for appointing the first day of June, on which the [Boston] port bill was to commence, for a day of fasting, humiliation, and prayer, to implore Heaven to avert from us the evils of civil war, to inspire us with firmness in support of our rights, and to turn the hearts of the King and Parliament to moderation and justice'. Is there a touch of irony in the picture of Jefferson who,

DECLARATION OF INDEPENDENCE

if he was anything, was a free-thinker, going around canvassing Puritan preachers to preside over these ceremonies? The Governor of Virginia at once dissolved the Assembly that passed the fasting resolution, but the members met again in the Apollo Room and instructed the committee of correspondence to propose to the committees in the other colonies the summoning of a continental congress, an attack on one colony being considered an attack on all. On August 1st a convention was called at Williamsburg to appoint Virginia's delegates to the first Continental Congress.

On his way to the Williamsburg Convention Jefferson was taken ill but his views on what the colonies should now do to clarify their relations with England were embodied first in the resolution that had been passed in his own county of Albemarle and secondly in the draft instructions which he drew up for the Virginian delegates to Congress. Jefferson's opinion was that the English Parliament had no right of any kind to legislate for the American colonies. He argued that just as when the Danes and Saxons migrated from their native lands to settle in England they established their own societies and own laws in their new homes, so the settlers who arrived in America had been completely free to legislate for themselves. Admittedly their allegiance to the Crown had been retained, but the English Parliament had no more right to pass laws binding upon the colonies than they had (before the Act of Union) to bind the Scots. How could an assembly representing 160,000 people legislate for a nation of 4,000,000? Jefferson's history was rickety, but his conclusions were firm. He protested indignantly against the attempts that had been made by the British Parliament to impose taxation on Americans as 'a deliberate and systematic plan to reduce us to slavery'; and he furthermore denied the right of the Crown to send soldiers to America or to make grants of land which the colonists had conquered by their own unaided efforts. His political philosophy, in spite of its veneer of learning, was empirical, as Professor Chinard has clearly shown, representing 'the harsh, hard-headed, practical and fierce determination of the pioneer who stakes out a piece of land in the wilderness, ready to hold it against all claim jumpers'.

Jefferson's draft instructions concluded with an appeal to the

THOMAS JEFFERSON

King: 'Open your heart, sire, to liberal and expanded thought. Let not the name of George the third be a blot on the page of history... Let no act be passed by any one legislature which may infringe on the rights and liberties of another.' At this stage the other Virginian statesmen were not ready to endorse so drastic an outlook. But they ordered that Jefferson's paper should be printed as a pamphlet called *A Summary View of the Rights of British America*. It was widely read and shook the prevalent opinion that although the English Parliament had no right to tax Americans, it could 'regulate' the 'external commercial relations' of the colonies. In its radical political doctrine and its cavalier attitude to King George III the *Summary View* was the forerunner of the Declaration of Independence, and when at the end of June 1775 Jefferson arrived at the second Continental Congress in Philadelphia (to which he had been chosen as a delegate to replace Peyton Randolph, Speaker of the Virginian Assembly) he had won a name as a wise and daring statesman and a man of culture who could use his pen eloquently and bitingly.

Before Jefferson went to Congress he took part in two significant gatherings in Virginia where resolutions were voted that did much to forward the American Revolution. The first gathering was that of the second Virginian Convention which met on March 20th in a little wooden church at the village of Richmond and carried a motion by the small majority of 65 to 60 votes in favour of raising a force for the protection of the country. The way was blazed by Patrick Henry with incomparable oratory; Jefferson argued 'closely, profoundly and warmly' in his support; and George Washington was also 'prominent' though 'silent'. Six weeks later, or two weeks after the skirmish at Lexington — the 'accident' that, according to Jefferson, 'cut off our last hope of reconciliation' — the Governor of Virginia summoned a meeting of the Assembly to hear some placatory 'propositions' from the English Prime Minister, Lord North. North's proposal was that the colonies should be exempted from all taxes imposed by the English Parliament if they in turn would make voluntary contributions to imperial defence and establish a fixed civil list for the payment of governors and judges. This not unreasonable com-

DECLARATION OF INDEPENDENCE

promise came too late now that the first shots had been exchanged and passions aroused and in any case conflicted with Jefferson's view that the colonies were under no constitutional or moral obligation to England except to recognize the supremacy of the Crown. The proposal, he said, 'only changes the form of oppression without lightening the burden'. The House of Burgesses therefore confined themselves to reaffirming the resolutions passed at Richmond in its capacity as a revolutionary convention and to approving an answer drawn up by Jefferson virtually rejecting North's scheme, though leaving the final decision to Congress. On June 10th Jefferson's answer was adopted and on June 26th he reached Philadelphia.

Jefferson was no orator, a defect which he shared with two other revolutionary leaders, Washington and Franklin. Jefferson himself wrote of their methods of gaining results:

> I served with General Washington in the legislature of Virginia before the revolution, and, during it with Dr. Franklin in Congress. I never heard either of them speak ten minutes at a time nor to any but to the main point which was to decide the question. They laid their shoulders to the great points, knowing that the little ones would follow of themselves.

John Adams, himself an able and witty speaker, and the leading delegate for Massachusetts, gave generous testimony to Jefferson's influence in spite of this shortcoming — indeed he questioned if it were a handicap at all, for he averred that a successful public speaker unavoidably makes enemies. Many years later he wrote of Jefferson that 'although a silent member of Congress, he was so prompt, frank, explicit, and decisive upon committees and in conversation . . . that he soon seized upon my heart'. His 'reputation for literature, science, and a happy talent of composition', Adams added, raised Jefferson's prestige: 'Writings of his were handed about remarkable for their peculiar felicity of expression.'

Jefferson was consequently appointed a member of two momentous committees, one to frame an address on 'the causes of taking up arms', the other to answer (on behalf of all the colonies) Lord North's conciliatory propositions. The result of the deliberations of the first committee was a compromise since the conservative elements, led by the influential John Dickinson, did not want to go to extremes. The other committee wrote its reply

THOMAS JEFFERSON

on the lines of that of Virginia and emphasized that the colonies would not negotiate under armed threats. It was a brief session, Congress rose on August 1st and Jefferson went home not to return to Philadelphia until October. Meanwhile hostilities had begun earnestly and Washington had left for Boston to take command of the confederate armies. The political atmosphere had thus worsened beyond repair. Although the *Address on the Cause of Taking up Arms* had ended (some writers attribute this paragraph to Jefferson) by saying: 'We have not raised armies with ambitious designs of separating Great Britain and establishing independent states,' in November Jefferson wrote to a friend in England: 'We want neither inducement nor power to declare and assert a separation.'

After Christmas Jefferson again left Congress and did not go back until the middle of May 1776. His decision to leave at this crucial time and for so long reflected not only anxiety about his family from whom he had received no letters at all that autumn, but also the fact that at that point of American political history more concern was felt over the conduct of the individual states than over the joint work of Congress. Washington after all had begun the fight with his continental army and must be left to win it as best he could: what he needed was the loyal backing of the states; for the tradition of self-government by the separate colonies was old, the notion of any kind of central administration novel and inchoate. To Jefferson Virginia was still his own country. And he was determined to see that the impulse for independence came from there. His return to Philadelphia was delayed by the death of his mother on March 31st, but he was also anxious to ensure that before he left a declaration in favour of the independence of the colonies from England should be passed by the Virginia Assembly. Soon after he returned to Congress he heard, as he hoped, that he and the other Virginian delegates had been instructed to propose that the united colonies should be declared free and independent states.

Robert Henry Lee was the actual mover of the Virginian resolution in favour of independence on June 7th, but Congress decided that it would postpone final consideration of the question until July 1st. Meanwhile a committee consisting of five members, Jefferson, John Adams, Benjamin Franklin, Roger Sherman and

DECLARATION OF INDEPENDENCE

Robert Livingston, was chosen to draw up a Declaration of Independence, while other committees were formed to prepare a plan for a confederation and to state the American terms for concluding foreign alliances. It was agreed that Jefferson should write the original draft of the Declaration of Independence, which he did, devoting deep care to a pronouncement that was to put the American case before the entire world. His draft was first shown to Adams and Franklin who offered a number of suggestions for its alteration and polishing. It was then approved by the whole sub-committee and laid on the table of the House on June 28th. Jefferson said that in writing the declaration he made no direct use of any book or pamphlet on political philosophy, though he did not 'of course consider it his duty to invent new ideas': his aim was simply 'to place before mankind the common sense of the subject'. Such disavowals did not conceal, however, that the fountainhead of much of his thought was John Locke's *Two Treatises of Government*, which had been written to justify the English Revolution of 1688. Was it improper to recognize that a main source of the Declaration of American Independence was an English political scientist? The argument in short was that men when they enter political society do not surrender to the authority of the government certain natural and inalienable rights: and if those rights are violated by any government, then that government is a tyrant and its subjects are entitled to rebel against it and put another government in its place. The 'natural' rights are not historical realities — no one, neither Locke nor Jefferson could seriously have imagined that they were — but ideal political concepts intended to restrain the power of the State over the individual. Jefferson summarized those ideals in the immortal phrase 'Life, Liberty and the Pursuit of Happiness'. The Declaration in its final form therefore consisted of a preamble and two parts: the preamble explained the reasons for separation; the first part expounds the Lockian democratic political philosophy; and the second lists the Americans' grievances against George III which entitled them to rebel. All references to the English Parliament were meticulously excluded from the Declaration because Jefferson's opinion, as expressed in his *Summary View*, that the English Parliament never at any time had any rights over the colonies, was now generally accepted. In its final form

Congress shortened the Declaration omitting some of the more generous flights of fancy — for instance, the phrase that the King had 'waged cruel war against human nature itself' and left out Jefferson's passage in which he blamed the King for obstructing the abolition of the slave import trade. But the balance and sweep of the prose were almost all Jefferson's. The sentences that follow the preamble, so familiar to every American schoolchild, are a reminder of the art that went into its composition.

> We hold these truths to be self-evident, that all men are created equal, that they are endowed by their Creator with certain inalienable rights, that among these are life, liberty and pursuit of happiness — That to ensure these rights Governments are instituted among men, deriving their just powers from the consent of the governed. That whenever any form of Government becomes destructive of these ends, it is the right of the people to alter it or to abolish it, and to institute new government, laying its foundation on such principles, and organizing its powers in such form, as to them shall seem most likely to effect their safety and happiness.

It is not difficult to write philosophical criticisms of this justly famous document: its whole historical basis is dubious. But its purpose was to make history and not to record it. And in its bold assertion that the true objects of government were to secure the pursuit of happiness and to preserve individual liberty it left the Middle Ages far behind and offered to a pioneer people the control of their own destinies.

The resolution in favour of independence proposed by the Virginians was passed by Congress on July 2nd and on July 4th the amended Declaration was adopted, although it was not engrossed until July 19th nor signed by representatives of all the states until August 2nd, 1776. The student of facsimiles of the Declaration today is always startled by the size of John Hancock's signature on the engrossed copy, for it is at least twice as large as that of any of the other signatories. John Hancock signed first as the then President of Congress. He was a dandy and a former smuggler, who had once had the ambition to be appointed Commander-in-Chief in preference to Washington. He has had to manage instead with this little but noticeable corner of American historical fame.

DECLARATION OF INDEPENDENCE

Early in September Jefferson, having obtained permission from Virginia to resign his seat for 'private reasons on account of my domestic affairs' left that historic Congress and went home.

To Thomas Jefferson independence was not an end in itself but a means to a fuller and freer life. To him freedom of thought and equality of opportunity were intellectual passions. For he felt with his mind, as one of his biographers has said. Steeped in the writings of the English seventeenth-century political philosophers, he imagined a gracious world in which an aristocracy of virtue and not of rank or wealth should rule. Even the best of governments, he believed, must be limited in their scope: the purpose of constitutions should be, he thought, above all, to guarantee the development of all that is finest in men, to ensure that no government, good, bad or indifferent, had the power to impinge upon those 'natural' and 'inalienable' rights which are the hallmark of a free people. His political theory plunged a knife into the body of all state socialist doctrine — and few Americans have yet fancied pulling it out.

Jefferson therefore hurried home to take a seat in the Virginian House of Burgesses (a Senate had also been created by the Constitution of 1776). He had regretted that his duties in Congress had prevented his being present in his own country to shape its new constitution: now he was at least determined to frame its laws.

The first Bill drafted by Jefferson was one to abolish the right of entail, which enabled parcels of landed property to remain in one hand and not be split up. A Bill to abolish primogeniture (the right of the eldest son of the family to inherit in the event of intestacy) had a similar purpose — striking 'at the very root of feudalism in Virginia'. A wide distribution of property and the destruction of the hereditary landed aristocracy were thus promoted. Secondly, Jefferson was appointed to a committee to revise the state laws. Hitherto the criminal code, inherited from the English Common Law, had been a harsh one. The revision was carried through in a conservative manner, the best parts of the old code being retained. Thirdly, there was a group of educational Bills — a Bill 'for the more general diffusion of knowledge', a Bill to transform Jefferson's old college of William and Mary into a genuine university, and a Bill to establish a public library. Jefferson would have divided the country into educational districts with elementary schools, where children could be educated at the public expense, and more advanced schools through which children could advance up the educational ladder. The wealthy classes were, however, unwilling to pay the cost and the Bills were not then placed on the statute book. A fourth and even more progressive group of Bills aimed at obtaining complete religious toleration in Virginia. 'Reason and free inquiry', Jefferson insisted, 'are the only effectual agents against error.' He succeeded by 1779 in securing the disestablishment of the episcopal church and earlier had repealed the laws making punishable the maintenance of unorthodox religious opinions or failure to attend church. But it was not until 1789 that his Bill for religious freedom, guaranteeing complete toleration was enacted. Finally Jefferson tried to obtain the abolition of slavery in Virginia by the deportation of all slaves in the same way that the Spaniards had deported the Moors. This Bill was inevitably defeated in a state where Negro slavery was deemed the economic life blood. But he wrote: 'Nothing is more certainly written in the book of fate than that these people are to be free. Nor', he added, 'is it less certain that the two races equally free cannot live in the same government.' Nevertheless he was satisfied with what he had achieved. The revised code of law was passed in its entirety after six years with the help of a serious and intelligent lawyer named James Madison. And four of the Bills (the repeal of entail, the abolition of primogeniture, the Bill for religious freedom and the Bill for public education) Jefferson regarded in later life as having given Virginia 'a system by which every fibre would be eradicated of ancient or future aristocracy; and a foundation laid for a government truly republican'. As early as 1777 he felt confident that Virginia would be a model republican community — the people laying aside 'the monarchical and taking up the republican government with as much ease as would have attended their throwing off an old, and putting on a new suit of clothes'. Of this young liberal republican state Jefferson, himself aged but thirty-six, was now elected Governor.

Jefferson became Governor of Virginia on June 1st, 1779, at a me when what was least needed was a philosopher king and hat would have been most serviceable would have been a

DECLARATION OF INDEPENDENCE

simple-minded soldier. For after their defeat at Saratoga in 1777 the British had abandoned as hopeless their attempt to conquer the northern states and the stormy waves of war had reached Virginia.

From their base in New York the British were sending out seaborne expeditions to vulnerable points on the American coastline, and no state was more open to attacks from the sea than Virginia with its many easy landing-places in the mouths of the rivers. In May 1779 a British force carried out its first large-scale raid, landing at Portsmouth in the James River and in October 1780 another and larger force established itself at the same place. Four months later Benedict Arnold sailed up the James and raided Richmond, the new Virginian capital, seizing stores and burning property. As Governor, Jefferson was much blamed for the success of these raids. But the critics did not, and perhaps could not, fully appreciate the general strategic situation. History has taught us that where a nation lacks command of the sea it cannot defend a vulnerable coastline at every point. Moreover it was Washington's policy, with his limited resources, to hold the British army in New York and to keep the far southern states of Georgia and South Carolina loyal to the confederation by countering British attacks on them and therefore he could not spare large security detachments to guard the whole of Virginia. As the wealthiest and most populous as well as strategically central state Virginia had necessarily to be employed as a base, an armoury and even a prison camp rather than as a minor battlefield.

Jefferson abided dutifully by Washington's strategy. 'No inclination is wanting either in the legislative or executive powers to aid them [the American forces in the south] or to strengthen you,' he wrote to the Commander-in-Chief on November 20th, 1779, 'but we find it difficult to procure men.' He treated the prisoners sent to Virginia after the Saratoga campaign with humanity, entertaining some of them at Monticello, although he ordered a British commander who had been inciting the Indians to be put into irons. In the spring of 1781 his problems reached their culminating point when Virginia was simultaneously committed to a campaign against the Indians on her north-west frontiers, to supporting General Greene in his operations in the deep south, to preventing Cornwallis's withdrawal northwards, and to resisting the depredations of Arnold. On April 1st Jefferson informed Greene that 'an enemy 3,000 strong, not a regular within our State, nor arms to put into the hands of the militia are circumstances which promise difficulties. Yet I shall think it essential to do everything we can for you to prevent the return of Cornwallis's army'. And Jefferson disclosed his grasp of essentials when he wrote to the French Minister in the same month that 'should a superiority in the continental seas be obtained by your fleet, it will save everything from North to South'.

Yet although Jefferson toiled as best he understood how, he was not cut out to be an organizer of military victory. His deference to liberal constitutional principles was ingrained. As late as 1780 he acquiesced in a scheme for a reduced military establishment and was reluctant to approve any defensive measures, however urgent, without an elaborate consultation with the legislature. Untiring and honest, he lacked driving power and was paralysed by intellectual scruples. Virginia never had enough money or men or even military intelligence to provide the basis for successful local resistance. Jefferson frankly blamed his failures on 'mild laws, a people not used to prompt obedience, a want of provisions of war and means of procuring them'; but even his fondest admirers have recognized that some of these obstacles might have been overcome by a patriotic appeal and a display of administrative energy. In 1781, five days after he himself had been compelled to flee at a few hours notice from his house at Monticello to avoid capture by a British raiding party, a young member of the Virginia House moved for an inquiry into his conduct as Governor. Although at the end of the year the Assembly exonerated him and indeed returned their sincere thanks, Jefferson, conscious of his rectitude, shied at the hint of reproof. His term of office as Governor which finished on June 1st, 1781, too early for him to take official part in the glories of Yorktown, significantly finds scarcely any mention in his autobiography. In letters to friends he announced that he was now taking final leave of public life — 'every fibre' of political ambition he told James Monroe, was 'thoroughly eradicated'. Had he not neglected his private affairs for thirteen years? Had he not been 'suspected and suspended' in the eyes of the world 'arraigned for treason of the heart and not merely for weakness of the head'? 'I have', he declared, 'retired to my farm, my family and books from which I think nothing will ever more separate me.' And except for one brief appearance in the House to defend his conduct as Governor, he kept his word until, two years later, an unforeseen event took place that disrupted his plans and obliged him to start his life again: that was the death of his wife.

2. MINISTER IN PARIS: SECRETARY OF STATE
(1781-1793)

The earlier part of this period of retirement from politics were months of unalloyed happiness for Jefferson, happiness such as is known only to men who have served their country honourably and seek a rest to rebuild their bodies and to refresh their minds in untrammelled freedom. We owe a description of Jefferson to a Frenchman who visited Monticello at this time:

> A man, not yet forty, tall, and with a mild and pleasing countenance, but whose mind and understanding are ample substitutes for every exterior grace. An American, who without ever having quitted his country, is at once a musician, skilled in drawing, a geometrician, an astronomer, a natural philosopher, legislator, and statesman . . . I found his first appearance serious, nay even cold; but before I had been two hours with him we were as intimate as if we had passed our whole lives together; walking, books, but above all, a conversation always varied and interesting.

Thus the Marquis de Chastellux. More intimate friends, ambitious hardworking men like James Madison, were less impressed, feeling that a born statesman was frittering away his talents as a rural philosopher because guilty of a pique. But if Jefferson allowed his social conscience to relax he did not want in application. For it was during this interlude in his life that he wrote his *Notes on Virginia*, a truly remarkable compendium of knowledge. Barbé-Marbois, the Secretary of the French Legation, had been instructed to collect information for his government about the various American states. Jefferson was invited to answer a number of questions about the flora and fauna, the habits and customs of Virginia. He offered a magnificent reply;

in a comprehensive document, later to be printed and to become an American classic, Jefferson ranged over many subjects in a work of literary art as polished in style as it was catholic in knowledge. In his *Notes* he told of the wild animal life of Virginia, the riches of its soil, the majesty of its mountains and the diversity of its waterways which included the Ohio, 'the most beautiful river on earth'. He gave a fascinating account of the domestic behaviour of the Indians, condemned Negro slavery — 'I tremble for my country', he wrote, 'when I reflect that God is just' — criticized the Virginian Constitution, and analysed the state laws and institutions. Here is a celebrated example of his style:

> The passage of the Patowmac [Potomac] through the Blue ridge is perhaps one of the most stupendous scenes in nature. You stand on a very high point of land. On your right comes up the Shenandoah, having ranged along the foot of the mountain an hundred miles to seek a vent. On your left approaches the Patowmac, in quest of a passage also. In the moment of their junction they rush together against the mountain, rend it asunder, and pass off to the sea. The first glance of this scene hurries our senses into the opinion that this earth has been created in time, that the mountains were formed first, that the rivers began to flow afterwards, that in this place particularly they have been dammed up by the Blue ridge of mountains, and have formed an ocean which filled the whole valley; that continuing to rise they have at length broken over at this spot and have torn the mountain down from its summit to its base.

After Mrs. Jefferson had given birth to her sixth child in May 1782 she was taken ill. For four months Thomas, tender and anxious, took turns in the work of nursing and was never out of call, living in a constant state of suspense. When the expected death took place, he fainted and his daughter was to write later 'of the violence of his emotion when, almost by stealth, I entered his room by night to this day I dare not describe to myself'. On his wife's tombstone he had inscribed in Greek these words:

> If in the melancholy shades below,
> The flames of friends and lovers cease to glow
> Yet mine shall sacred last; mine undecay'd
> Burn on through death and animate my shade.

SECRETARY OF STATE

There can be no doubt that love, as true men know it, died for him that day, September 6th, 1782. Like many clever men he was always to find satisfaction and sympathy in the company and letters of the other sex. He wrote to them somewhat in the same playful slightly romantic style that Washington assumed, but it meant nothing. He devoted himself to the care of his three daughters. 'I have placed my happiness', he told the eldest, Martha, 'on seeing you good and accomplished.' And he at once sought forgetfulness in a return to public life. 'Before my wife's death,' he wrote to Chastellux, 'my scheme of life had been determined. I had folded myself in the arms of retirement, and rested all prospects of future happiness on domestic and literary subjects. A single event wiped away all my plans and left me in a blank which I had not the spirits to fill up.' In December Congress nominated him one of the commissioners to negotiate the peace treaty ending the War of Independence, but his ship was held up by ice and, when he was about to leave, it was too late for him to fulfil his mission. Instead he allowed himself to be appointed a Virginian delegate to Congress and reached Annapolis in November 1783. Here he was disappointed in the smallness of the attendance; and now that the war was over many states had lost interest in the confederation and indeed a quorum to ratify the peace treaty was not available until mid-January. Nevertheless Jefferson was an active delegate and absorbed himself in his work, drafting, it is said, some fifty state papers. In particular he was responsible for advocating the use of the Spanish dollar as the unit of American currency and for drawing up the first draft plan (to be embodied in the Ordinance of 1787) whereby the newly colonized lands in the west became federal and not state property and in due course blossomed into new states. Jefferson would have excluded slavery from all such territories, but this was not acceptable to a Congress in which slave-owning states were in the majority.

In May 1784 Congress decided that its representatives in Europe should be instructed to negotiate treaties of commerce for the advancement of American trade. Jefferson took a leading part in framing these instructions, which aimed above all at mitigating the violence of war for neutrals, and when they were approved, he himself was named to go to help John Adams and

THOMAS JEFFERSON

Benjamin Franklin, who were already in Europe, in the negotiations. Jefferson gladly embraced this chance to travel abroad and fetched his daughter Martha from school to accompany him. After a short tour of New England father and daughter sailed across a stormy summer sea to reach the fascinating and, as they soon discovered, expensive French capital.

The task before the three American negotiators was, as Jefferson soon perceived, a hard one. They foregathered in Paris and drafted a 'general form' to be submitted to the governments that were prepared to treat with them. But 'everything in Europe was quiet'. Old ignorances and fresh prejudices had to be overcome: 'there was a want of confidence in us', Jefferson noted and added, a year later, that this was due to the 'non-payment of our debts and the want of energy in our Government'. It was indeed the case that the authority of the Federal Government was not yet accepted and that several war debts were outstanding, while the novel restrictions on belligerents' rights put forward by Jefferson impeded progress in treaty making. Only Frederick the Great, the old King of Prussia, proved willing to sign a commercial agreement on these terms.

Thus Jefferson had a good deal of spare time at his disposal. But he was by no means idle, for he acted not merely as a negotiator, but an ambassador, a consul-general and, as we should say today, a press attaché rolled into one. On March 10th, 1785, Benjamin Franklin was called home and little John Adams, with his puritan wife, Abigail, with whom Jefferson was on the most friendly terms, left for London. Asked by the French if he had replaced Franklin, Jefferson made a practice of replying: 'No one can replace him. I have only succeeded him.' Jefferson shared Franklin's wide interests, although he seems to have been rather less comfortable in the gay and irresponsible atmosphere of Parisian society. He made serious friends of a number of highly cultivated French ladies including the remarkable lady who nearly married Edward Gibbon and who actually married the Swiss banker, Neckar, and a vivacious English lady, Maria Cosway, the wife of a minature painter, to whom he wrote a letter which provided ammunition for romantic biographers. He found Vergennes, the Foreign Minister, 'frank and honourable'. In the Marquis de Lafayette he had a ready-made friend through whom he kept in touch with the

SECRETARY OF STATE

liberal elements in French political society. His eldest daughter, Martha, he placed in a convent to be educated — although he pulled her out of it quickly when she showed signs of becoming a Roman Catholic. His second daughter Maria (or Polly) he sent for to join them. His third daughter, Lucy, had died in America.

To collect intelligence of value to his country Jefferson travelled extensively in Europe. In March 1786 he visited England, a country of which he gained the poorest possible impression. 'That nation hates us, their ministers hate us, and their King more than all other men.' He found a good word to say for British agriculture and a slightly better one for our landscape gardening. It is a pity that his experiences were searing: for in general American travellers, though they have hastened to note our aristocratic manners, have been melted by our modest hospitality. Probably at that time prejudices were too strong, old enmities too near. In the summer of the following year he travelled through the south of France and Italy, going first to take the waters at Aix as a cure for a bad hand. His letters during his tour are full of notes on agriculture and industry, as befitted a commercial representative, but there is no reason to suppose that he did not delight in the beauties of southern Europe. In particular he fell in love with Nîmes and gazed at Rome in proper amazement. Finally after he had joined John Adams in Amsterdam in March 1788 for an urgent financial transaction, he returned to France by way of the Rhine and Strasbourg.

During the years 1787-89 Thomas Jefferson watched with fascinated intensity the dawning of the French Revolution, attending both the meetings of the Assembly of Notables that met in February 1787 and of the States-General that began its extraordinary career in May 1789. Of the coming convulsion he had little inkling; he was enchanted to believe that the influence of America was shaping the political destinies of France, while the more conservative revolutionaries were proud to consult the author of the Declaration of Independence. Earlier he had become conscious of the inequalities of the French social system, quoting with approval Voltaire's saying that every man was either a hammer or an anvil. And he was able to contrast complacently the state of affairs in his native land where 'no distinction between man and man has ever been known, but that of persons in office exercising powers by authority of the laws and private individuals. Among these last the poorest labourer stood on equal ground with the wealthiest millionaire.' He saw precariously balanced at the summit of the ill-balanced European system the decadent institution of monarchy. 'I can say with safety,' he wrote severely to Washington, 'there is not a crowned head in Europe whose talents or merit would enable him to be elected a vestryman by the people of any parish in America.' The French King he regarded as a well-meaning fool too much governed by his queen and irresistibly inclined to overeating. Nevertheless he was not in favour of the rough overthrow of the monarchy — the 'single curse' of France was to him the form of its government rather than its 'good' and 'well-disposed' ruler.

It must have been an almost unbearable temptation to the American political philosopher to obtrude his advice upon the French revolutionaries; he did indeed go so far as to draw up in 1789 a charter of rights which he suggested the French King ought to guarantee. But his persuasions were directed towards moderation, almost towards conservatism, certainly in favour of constitutional monarchy. He lent his house to Lafayette for the holding of a constitutional discussion after the fall of the Bastille and that famous fourth of August when the French aristocracy in a frenzy of overpowering enthusiasm divested themselves of their ancient privileges. Perhaps he overstepped the bounds of diplomatic propriety a little in his concern over the future of France, but no one objected. It was surely a little hard on Jefferson that he should have had to watch the new French Constitution being framed without the right to take part in the deliberations, while in Philadelphia a new American Constitution was being thrashed out and he could do nothing about it but post sage letters from Paris three thousand miles away.

Jefferson's letters home about the new Federal Constitution reaffirmed that Lockian political philosophy which he had embodied in the Declaration of Independence. Speaking of the Shays Rebellion of 1786, when the Massachusetts farmers had risen against the debt collectors, he said 'the tree of liberty must be refreshed from time to time with the blood of patriots and martyrs. It is its natural manure.' Thus he commended the right to rebel. In criticizing the Constitution of 1787 — which, on the whole, he

SECRETARY OF STATE

approved — he insisted on the need to add to it a Bill of Rights, those 'natural' rights, which if violated by a government afforded the true ground for rebellion. Also he deplored the re-eligibility of the President, since his experiences in Europe made him fear anything that savoured of monarchy.

With his two daughters Jefferson left France a little regretfully in September 1789; in his old age he looked back on this 'great and good country' with its 'benevolent people' as his second home. But the chief thing his five years in Europe had taught him was that home was best. To see Europe, he told James Monroe:

> will make you adore your own country, its soil, its climate, its equality, laws, people and manners. My God! how little do my countrymen know what precious blessings they are in possession of, and which no other people on earth enjoy.

Thus spoke, thus felt this one hundred per cent American long before he set off back to Monticello.

A week after Jefferson returned to America he received a letter from Washington inviting him to become Secretary of State in the new government, a position 'involving many of the most interesting objects of the executive authority' both in home and foreign affairs, as the President temptingly put it. Jefferson hesitated to accept: 'My wish', he explained in later years, 'had been to return to Paris, where I had left my household establishment, and to see the end of the Revolution, which I then thought would be certainly and happily closed in less than a year.' But pressed, he allowed himself to be persuaded, and after attending the marriage of his daughter Martha at Monticello to her second cousin, Thomas Mann Randolph, he left for New York in March 1790 and began vainly to look for a house on Broadway.

To Senator Maclay of Pennsylvania we owe an excellent description of Jefferson at this date: 'Jefferson', Maclay wrote, 'is a slender man, has rather the air of stiffness in his manner. His clothes seem too small for him. He sits in a lounging manner, on one hip commonly, and with one of his shoulders elevated above the other. His face has a sunny aspect. His whole figure has a loose, shackling air. He has a rambling, vacant look, and nothing of that firm collected deportment which I expected would dignify the presence of a secretary or minister. I looked for gravity, but a laxity of manner seemed shed about him. He spoke almost without ceasing; but even his discourse partook of his personal demeanour. It was loose and rambling; and yet he scattered information wherever he went, and some even brilliant sentiments sparkled from him.'

It is said that he was less happy in New York than in Paris. In his *Anas*, the autobiographical notes that he prepared in his retirement, he records how shocked he was at the political outlook of the leading New Yorkers. Dinner table conversations, he said, were all in favour of a 'kingly' government — by which Jefferson apparently meant a strong central executive authority and not the constitutional monarchy that Washington tended to approve. 'I found myself', he asserted, 'for the most part the only advocate on the republican side of the question.' Certainly none of the other members of Washington's 'Cabinet' had the same perfervid, almost religious faith in republicanism — the faith of an American Algernon Sidney — which the Secretary of State held. General Henry Knox, the blunt and burly Secretary of War, swore that he would not give a copper for the present government: 'It is the President's character and not the written constitution', he averred, 'that keeps it together.' The Attorney-General, though another Randolph from Virginia, vacillated upon most questions — 'the poorest chameleon I ever saw', Jefferson called him. The Vice-President, who was only consulted in the absence of the President, was Jefferson's former friend and colleague, John Adams, but, according to one of his namesakes, he too 'dallied in his writings with monarchy in such a way as to lay him open to the charge of believing in it'. But Jefferson's worthiest opponent was the Secretary of the Treasury, Alexander Hamilton.

Hamilton was a youthful genius of only thirty-two. In almost every respect he differed from Jefferson. He was small and stocky, Jefferson tall and slender. His private morals were not above censure, as Jefferson's were. 'I'm no philosopher,' Hamilton boasted in one of his earliest surviving letters, 'my ambition is prevalent so that I contemn the grovelling condition of a clerk or the like . . .' and his unrelenting application and inspiring personality made him at an early age one of the leading men in the new nation. Hamilton was self-made, whereas Jefferson was born to govern, if he wished — though he did not always wish. Hamilton

SECRETARY OF STATE

was an earnest believer in Christianity; Jefferson was probably an agnostic. Hamilton was a soldier, Jefferson a man of peace. Hamilton was a splendid orator; Jefferson spoke in public as little as need be. Hamilton did not mind making enemies; Jefferson was tactful, accommodating and sensitive. And from a difference in outlook on life arose fierce political differences. Hamilton thought the British Government was 'the best in the world' and would, it appears, have preferred the American President to have been elected for life as head of a strong central government, functioning as a kind of elective constitutional monarch. Jefferson wanted the President to be elected only for a term of seven years and sought for guarantees of individual liberty to be included in the Constitution. Hamilton foresaw a commercial America dependent upon a sound financial structure. Jefferson thought that the ideal political society was an agricultural one. From the disputations between these two great men sprang a violent spirit of party which has been the enduring heritage and burden of the American people. In consequence few American historians can discuss the differences between Hamilton and Jefferson in completely scientific impartiality, and, since Hamilton was on the surface, pro-British and Jefferson pro-French it is hard for an Englishman or Frenchman to do so. It is no coincidence that among Hamilton's most enthusiastic literary admirers was an Englishman or that one of Jefferson's most thoughtful biographers is of French descent. One thing, however, may be safely said: that there was an almost pathological enmity between the two men that distorted the merit of the services of each. Thus when Jefferson wrote that Hamilton favoured 'a monarchy bottomed in corruption' he was using words in a way that was unphilosophical. Both men, according to their lights, were patriots and fathers of their country. In his series of pamphlets called *The Federalist* Hamilton wrote an enduring defence of the republican constitution, just as in his Declaration of Independence Jefferson immortalized the cause of American freedom. Both of them advocated an independent foreign policy freed from European intrigue. Neither was guilty of ambition in any ignoble sense — they fought each other for no mean or selfish ends.

The first contest between Jefferson and Hamilton was settled amicably at a dinner party. Jefferson was opposed to the assumption by the Federal Government of the debts contracted by the individual states during the war on the ground that this would benefit speculators. Hamilton as a New Yorker was against the permanent seat of the Federal Government being established in the south. On June 20th, 1790 Jefferson wrote to his son-in-law: 'Congress are much embarrassed by the questions of assumption and residence . . . mutual sacrifice of opinion and interest [is] . . . the duty of everyone'; and he told him that although he would prefer the states to raise money to pay their debts in their own way, he decided that he must yield 'for the sake of union, and to save us from the greatest of all calamities, the total extinction of our credit in Europe'.

Next year, however, Jefferson expressed his opinion that Hamilton's plan for a national bank violated the Constitution but he was overruled by Washington. At the end of the same year he criticized adversely Hamilton's report on national manufactures which recommended the provision of bounties to aid the development of American trade for the same reason, namely that the Federal Government had no right to exercise far-reaching powers not specifically provided for in the Constitution. Washington vainly tried to reconcile the two giants among his advisers. But Jefferson made it plain that his disapproval of Hamilton's plans for strengthening the economic powers of the Federal Government was no mere 'speculative difference'. Hamilton's 'system', he said, flowed from principles adverse to liberty 'and was calculated to undermine and demolish the republic by creating an influence of his department [the Treasury] over the members of the legislature'. In long and moving conversations with the President (of which Jefferson rewrote his accounts years after Washington and Hamilton were in their graves) Jefferson emphasized his desire to retire from office, while he begged Washington to retain the Presidency for another four years. When Washington told him that this difference of opinion over the National Bank ought to be tolerated, Jefferson retorted that the Bank, product of an unnecessary national debt, and the system of bounties were bound to give rise to a stock-jobbing interest that would be immoral in a pure republic. When Washington said he did not believe that there were ten important men in the country who wanted a monarchical system, Jefferson answered flatly that Hamilton did.

SECRETARY OF STATE

Broadly Washington followed Hamilton's advice on matters relating to the Treasury and took Jefferson's counsel on foreign matters, the peculiar concern of the Department of State. There were at that time three main problems, American relations with Spain, with Great Britain and with France.

By the treaty that ended the War of Independence the British Government had conceded to the Americans all the territory from the east coast as far as the Mississippi River but the country west of the Mississippi and New Orleans near the mouth of the river still belonged to Spain. Jefferson was a southerner and the author of a book on Virginia, in which the Mississippi was counted as one of its rivers, and as Secretary of State he pressed the claims of the United States Government to the rights of common navigation on the river and to the possession of a port at its mouth. When it seemed likely that the Spanish Government would be involved in a European war he instructed the American representative in Spain to advocate the American claims 'warmly'. Nature, he insisted, had determined and justice demanded that the Spaniards should concede the American requirements, however distasteful the surrender of territory might be to them. Jefferson saw with prophetic vision the importance of the Mississippi in the future history of the United States. Though he was willing to take advantage of Spanish weakness by rigid diplomatic pressure, he never contemplated war and in the end — though not at this date — he was to secure not just rights of navigation on the river but the whole of the Mississippi valley for his country.

In his relations with Great Britain Jefferson also took a strong diplomatic line. He rebutted the assertions of the British Minister in the United States that the American Government had failed to carry out the terms of the peace treaty and in reply to such arguments compiled a State paper as remarkable for its categorical nature as for its legalistic ingenuity. He explained that American debts, the settlement of which had been promised, could not be paid if Great Britain refused to accept American exports carried in their own ships; he inquired how 'hard money' could be found by a government which had been obliged to fight a prolonged war with paper credit; he distinguished between the principal owed and the interest that had accrued — 'there is no instrument or title to debt', he averred, 'so formal and sacred as to give a right to interest on it under all possible circumstances'; and finally he maintained that Britain herself had broken the treaty by failing to evacuate the western forts and by not restoring Negroes who had been carried away during the war.

But it was in American relations with France that Jefferson found his most perplexing problems. Although the French Revolution had developed more violently than he had expected, he was confident that the French cause was the cause of freedom throughout the world and could not be repudiated by the American people. As early as 1791 he wrote that 'a check there would retard the revival of liberty in all countries' and he was frankly interested in the reactions of events in France on domestic politics, fearing that the overthrow of republicanism in Europe would excite the followers of Hamilton to transform the Presidency into a monarchical institution. But there were other than theoretical questions to be decided. By the Franco-American treaty of 1778 the United States had agreed to give advantages to French privateers and to guarantee the security of the French West Indies. There was even an argument that this treaty would oblige the Americans to go to war on the French side, when the new republic was attacked. In March 1793 it had become known in America that the French had guillotined their King and a little later that Britain and France were at war. Washington, as we have seen, accepted Jefferson's view that the treaty was not voided by the establishment of the French Republican Government and that the new French Minister, Citizen Gênet, must be received. At the same time Jefferson acquiesced in American neutrality. Gênet arrived at Charleston in May 1793 on a ship bearing the cap of liberty on its prow and proceeded to capture British ships and fit out privateers. His main duty was to induce the American Republic to enter the war on the French side. Though Jefferson was sympathetic to the French cause, the behaviour of Gênet, whom he described as 'hot headed, all imagination, no judgment, passionate, disrespectful and even indecent towards the President' gave him much embarrassment especially as he did not want war. In the end he was compelled to demand Gênet's recall by the French Government — 'he will sink the republican interest if they do not abandon him', he told Madison — but 'instead of returning to a French prison Gênet fell in love with Cornelia, daughter of George

SECRETARY OF STATE

Clinton, the republican governor of New York, and lived happily ever afterwards, a worthy citizen devoted to agriculture and science'. (Hirst.)

Jefferson's tenure of office as Secretary of State did much to fix American principles of foreign policy for at least one hundred years. 'We wish not', he laid it down on March 23rd, 1793, 'to meddle with the internal affairs of any country, nor with the general affairs of Europe.' At the same time he stressed American claims to expand in the western hemisphere and would have considered taking over the Spanish or French West Indies, if they should have fallen as ripe fruits to be gathered. Unlike Woodrow Wilson, but like Franklin Roosevelt, he did not expect the American people to be neutral in their minds; he frankly rejoiced that the bulk of the American people were pro-French. But he himself was at heart neither pro-French nor pro-British. Writing a little later, in 1796, a French representative said that: 'Jefferson ... is an American and hence he cannot be sincerely our friend. An American is the born enemy of all Europeans.' And later still, when he became Vice-President Jefferson observed: 'The first object of my heart is my own country: in that is embarked my family, my fortune, my own existence. I have not one farthing of interest nor preference of any one nation to another but in proportion as they are more or less friendly to us.' Jefferson's policy — like that of all patriotic Americans of his day — was 'America First'.

It is impossible to say how far Jefferson's sensitive mind, assaulted by the press attacks of the Hamilton party, was induced to long for retirement and how far his desire to resign was due to a simple weariness of public affairs after over ten years in harness. Plainly he was not the ambitious intriguer pictured by some of his critics. Yet his clear formulation of political principles during his term of office as Secretary of State had done much to form the Democrat Republican party, of which two later American parties were to claim to be the heirs. As the recognized leader of this party it was inevitable that sooner or later he should return to office. Meanwhile his restless spirit sought a respite. Satisfied that the government of the United States was in safe hands so long as George Washington, that 'wise, good and great man', was President, he insisted in giving up his office. With characteristic

THOMAS JEFFERSON

courtesy Washington sped him homewards with a testimony to his 'integrity and talents and earnest prayers for his happiness'. It was on the last day of the exhausting year of 1793 that his resignation took effect and on January 16th, 1794, he was back in Monticello.

3. VICE-PRESIDENT, OPPOSITION LEADER AND PRESIDENT (1793-1805)

'The principles on which I calculate the value of life', wrote Jefferson to Vice-President John Adams in April 1794, 'are entirely in favour of my present course', and to President Washington he said: 'I return to farming with an ardor which I scarcely knew in my youth ... Instead of writing ten or twelve letters a day which I have been in the habit of doing as a thing of course, I put off answering my letters now, farmerlike, till a rainy day.' For company he had his married daughter, Martha, and her husband and his handsome young daughter, Maria. A French noble who visited Monticello in 1796 found his host 'in the midst of the harvest from which the scorching heat of the sun does not prevent his attendance'. 'His Negroes', he said, 'are clothed and treated as well as white servants should be.' The work of the Negroes made the estate almost self-sufficing and their children were employed in a nail factory. The master invented a novel plough and practised a six-course rotation of crops on his four farms. The house was renovated with balustrades over its one storey and was ranked 'with the most pleasant mansions in France and in Europe'. From the house on the little mountain the view was truly magnificent and the conditions might well have contented a pure philosopher. But Thomas Jefferson, though at the age of fifty he already regarded himself as 'an antediluvian patriarch', was at heart no dweller in an ivory tower. He enjoyed his rest, but his mind soon turned to politics again. President Washington had been left with some hard problems to solve. At home there was the 'whisky rebellion' which Jefferson thought was repressed too firmly, and overseas or on the seas there was a rising danger of war with England. During the opening stage of its fresh war against France the British Government adopted rigorous measures to

VICE-PRESIDENT—PRESIDENT

blockade its enemy with adverse consequences for American commerce. British cruisers were ordered to bring into port every neutral ship carrying flour or corn to a French port or taking provisions to the French colonies. The French retaliated with measures against neutral vessels, but shrewdly threw open their hitherto closed ports in the West Indies to American trade. Jefferson gave out that he favoured a trade embargo to punish the British: 'This, you will say,' he told a correspondent, 'may bring on war. If it does, we shall march like men; but it may not bring on war, and then the experiment will have been a happy one.' He was disgusted when the Senate rejected a Non-Importation Bill and asserted that the Upper House had never been intended to thwart the people's will. Meanwhile some sections of the American public were eager for war, and the President, becoming alarmed, denounced the activities of the pro-French 'democratic societies'. Jefferson thought it 'wonderful' that Washington should have permitted himself to be the organ of such an attack 'on the freedom of discussion, the freedom of meeting, printing and publishing'. This was, however, the only harsh expression he used against his former chief: most of his political criticisms in his retirement were directed against Hamilton and his associates, whom he called 'Anglomen', 'Monocrats' and a number of other odd names, and accused of trying to establish an autocracy.

Hamilton himself was already ruined. In the summer of 1791 he had drifted into an intrigue with a married woman and had been blackmailed by her husband for his pains. The unsavoury story came to be known to Monroe and other Congressmen and ultimately in 1797 Hamilton was obliged to publish the whole sordid story to the world to defend himself against the charge of corruption. His political ambitions were damned for ever and although he continued to direct the Federalist party, he never sought political office again. In the autumn of 1794 Washington decided to settle the American differences with Britain peaceably if possible and sent Chief Justice Jay — and not Hamilton, who would have liked to go — to London with this mission. Jay had a good case and concluded a treaty by which the British at last surrendered the frontier forts, met damages inflicted by some of their navy's interferences with neutral trade, and opened the British West Indies to American ships. The treaty, which did not meet every grievance, was so unpopular in America that Jay was hanged in effigy in the streets. The Senate confirmed the treaty, but from this occasion may be dated the bitter divisions in American party politics.

Jefferson was determined that the Democratic party, of which he was the acknowledged leader, should destroy Hamilton and the 'pro-British' 'monarchical' Federalists. The extreme nature of his views was shown in a letter to an old friend, Philip Mazzei: 'In place of that noble love of liberty and republican government which carried us triumphantly through the war, an Anglican, monarchical party has sprung up, whose avowed object is to draw over us the substance, as they have already done the forms, of the British Government... It would give you a fever were I to name to you the apostates who have gone over to these heresies, men who were Samsons in the field and Solomons in the council, but who have had their heads shorn by the harlot England.' Although he wanted his friend Madison to be the party candidate for the Presidency on Washington's retirement, he was obliged to stand himself as the leader of the Democratic party and was defeated by only three electoral votes by his former colleague, the puritan John Adams. When Jefferson knew of the result he expressed his pleasure to Adams: 'I leave to others the sublime delights of riding in the storm, better pleased with sound sleep and a warm berth below' and he told Madison that Adams was perhaps 'the only sure barrier against Hamilton's getting in'. Under the voting system of those days Jefferson became Vice-President and one suspects that he protested his pleasure over his warm berth too vigorously. At least from then on he expended all his energies in strengthening his party and preparing for the next contest. In January 1797 he said of Washington that he was 'fortunate to get off just as the bubble is bursting, leaving others to hold the bag'. With sure political instinct Jefferson saw how heavy was the bag that Adams had been left holding.

Adams aimed at following in Washington's path as a President above party (as Jefferson said, he did not care for Hamilton and his ways) and, like his predecessor, found his chief cares in questions of foreign policy. At first he approached his Vice-President to suggest that he might care to go back to France as a special envoy, for the French Government, now largely directed by

VICE-PRESIDENT—PRESIDENT

the rising Napoleon Bonaparte, was the European danger spot. Jefferson was not without hopes that Bonaparte would behave like a Washington rather than a Cromwell. And just as he had wanted earlier to avert a war with Britain, he was even more anxious that war should not have to be waged against the old ally of the United States. The situation was grave. Three hundred American ships were seized by the French and in March 1798 three American envoys were told on their arrival in France to negotiate by three Frenchmen known as X, Y and Z that to facilitate an agreement they must bribe the members of the new French Government or Directory. The cry went up 'Millions for defence but not a cent for tribute' and for a time feeling in the United States became as rabid against the French as four years earlier it had been against the British. In June Jefferson shared in this unpopularity when he was believed to have dispatched a certain Dr. Logan on a private peace mission. But President Adams and his Hamiltonian Cabinet overplayed their hands in meeting the crisis; they gave the impression that they were exploiting it for party ends when they brought in an Alien Act, intended to secure the deportation of French propagandists, and a Sedition Act, aimed at the suppression of the opposition newspapers. These acts were in fact little used, but they proved a political error and Jefferson was so shocked that he said they were sufficiently grave violations of the Constitution to justify the secession of individual states. Although he was Vice-President Jefferson secretly drafted a protest known as the Kentucky Resolutions which was an able exposition of the Democratic case against the Adams administration. Appealing, as this resolution did, to the deep-rooted American love of individual freedom, it was a powerful instrument in turning public opinion against the government. And although in the end President Adams, a patriotic man and a statesman above party pettiness, succeeded in averting war with France, he had because of the outcry aroused by his earlier measures forfeited his chance of re-election.

Jefferson burrowed on, determined that in 1800 he should be chosen President. In 1797 he had opened a correspondence with Colonel Aaron Burr, a New York lawyer, as remarkable in his own way as his colleague Alexander Hamilton. Burr, left a wealthy orphan when a boy, had received an excellent education and had distinguished himself in the army where he rose to the rank of lieutenant-colonel, but retired with broken health and a squandered fortune. He was married to a New Jersey widow with five children by her first husband who was ten years his senior. Burr's talent for intrigue was noted by Washington. After winning a reputation at the New York Bar Burr interested himself in politics and succeeded in overthrowing the hitherto invincible Federalists in his state. Founder of Tammany Hall as a New York electoral machine he now became Jefferson's running mate in the election.

Jefferson felt that a warm wind was blowing pleasantly behind him. In January 1799 he told Madison that there was strong reason to believe that the 'X Y Z delusion' was wearing off and that French willingness to agree to a liberal treaty had put an end to the national panic. In 1798 the elections to the House of Representatives and the Senate had gone in favour of the well-organized Democratic party and thus at this early stage in American history a President held office with a hostile Congress by his side. Jefferson noted in the summer of 1800 that the Federalists had been unable to carry a single big measure in the lower House during the whole session and three months later he announced from Philadelphia that 'the arrogance of the proud hath ceased and the patient and meek look up'. The presidential election of 1800 was fought on party lines, the electors not being impartial, as the authors of the Constitution had intended, but pledged either to the Democratic or Federalist official candidates. Since, however, the Constitution had prescribed that the candidate with a clear majority over other candidates was to be elected President and the candidate with the second largest number of votes was to be elected Vice-President, this purely party vote resulted in a deadlock, for the two Democratic candidates, Jefferson and Aaron Burr, who headed the poll, had an equal number of votes. The election therefore reverted to the House of Representatives where the election was by states.

After a series of hopeless manœuvres to use the deadlock to keep the Federal Government in the hands of his party, Hamilton threw the vote in the House of Representatives to Jefferson. (This electoral anomaly was put right by a subsequent amendment to the Constitution.) One curious episode completed this remark-

VICE-PRESIDENT—PRESIDENT

able election. John Adams, who took his defeat badly — although he told Jefferson that he would be his loyal 'subject', a phrase that cannot have pleased the new President, spent his last day in office in creating new judges. At midnight on March 4th, 1801, Jefferson sent his Attorney-General armed with a watch into the office of the Secretary of State to take possession and stop any further appointments of judges or others from being signed. These appointments were nicknamed, therefore, the Midnight Judges and this odd incident ushered in Jefferson's administration after one of the most virulent election campaigns of the many that are known to American history.

When at the age of fifty-eight Thomas Jefferson, his red hair now tinged with grey, looking like 'a tall large-boned farmer', took up his office of President, the residence of the Federal Government was modern Washington. The move from Philadelphia had taken place during the previous summer; but the town was not a quarter built. The discontented Congressmen 'clustered together in eight or ten boarding-houses as near as possible to the Capitol, and there lived, like a convent of monks, with no other amusement or occupation than that of going from their lodgings to the Chambers and back again'. The new capital was a bleak village set in the midst of a swamp: 'We want nothing', wrote Gouverneur Morris, 'but houses, cellars, kitchens, well informed men, amiable women, and other trifles of this kind, to make our city perfect.' It was from a boarding-house that Jefferson walked across to deliver his inaugural address.

Jefferson saw to it that simplicity was the keynote in Washington, for he at once abandoned the lingering relics of monarchical ceremony maintained by his two predecessors. The clothes that he wore he reckoned were of a republican cut — a red plush waistcoat, green corduroy trousers and down-at-heel shoes. Washington's weekly levees and formal state dinners were abolished. Thomas Jefferson was 'Mr.' President with a vengeance. Yet the Executive Mansion became the centre of life and society and an invitation was much sought after. When necessary, buxom Dolly Madison, the jolly wife of Jefferson's Secretary of State, acted as his hostess, but the dinner parties were most famous for their scintillating conversation and excellent champagne. Besides Madison the other members of Jefferson's

Cabinet were Albert Gallatin, a Swiss-born financier who was Secretary of the Treasury, General Dearborn, of New Hampshire, Secretary of War, Levi Lincoln, another New Englander, the Attorney-General, and Robert Smith, a rich Baltimore lawyer, a *pis-aller* as Secretary of the Navy. His was a party Cabinet, as he was a party leader; yet it was still not a Cabinet in the English sense — there was no collective responsibility. Jefferson insisted that all departmental papers should have his personal approval and if the Cabinet was an exceptionally harmonious body, in, notable contrast with those of Washington and John Adams, it was because of its partisan character and Jefferson's recognized pre-eminence in his party.

Nevertheless, Jefferson's first inaugural address was not only the pronouncement of a lifelong liberal faith, but also in part the offer of an olive branch to his political enemies. 'Every difference of opinion', he reminded his audience, 'was not a difference of principle': 'We are all republicans: we are all federalists.' He went on to deny that a republican government, broad-based on the rule of law, could not be strong, even though it left men free 'to regulate their own pursuits of industry and improvement'. He described as his ideal 'a wise and frugal government' and he summed up his foreign policy in the sentence: 'Peace, commerce, and honest friendship with all nations, entangling alliances with none.' Jefferson's first inaugural — more than Washington's farewell — address enshrines the historical political outlook of the American people.

In his private letters Jefferson showed that he honestly believed that though he had been elected after a virulent party struggle, he represented the vast majority of true Americans, who had been merely led astray from their basic republican convictions by the unfortunate 'X Y Z affair' in France. On March 6th, 1801, he wrote: 'We shall put her (the ship of State) on the republican tack and she will now show by the beauty of her motion the skill of her builders.' On March 18th he told Tom Paine: 'The return of our citizens from the frenzy into which they have been wrought, partly by ill-conduct in France, partly by artifices practised upon them, is almost extinct.' And on March 27th he informed General Henry Knox: 'I was always satisfied that the great body of those called Federalists were real republicans as well as Federalists.'

VICE-PRESIDENT—PRESIDENT

It followed logically from this outlook that Jefferson refused to sweep away ruthlessly all the office-holders of the previous regime on the ground that to the victors belonged the spoils. 'Malconduct', he announced, 'is a just ground of removal: mere difference of political opinion is not.' Nevertheless by the end of his first term of office a substantial number of the men appointed to posts by Adams were in fact removed, including Adams's own son, John Quincy, who had been a customs officer in Massachusetts. Many justices of the peace made by Adams were dismissed and where judges could not be got rid of, sound republican marshals and district attorneys were established as counterweights. In dealing with the federal judges themselves Jefferson had a stiff row to hoe. Yet Jefferson was sure that they must be dealt with; for, he asked: 'Had not the Federalists retired into the judiciary as a stronghold?'

Entrenched in the stronghold was one of Jefferson's principal opponents, John Marshall, who had been Adams's Secretary of State and was now Chief Justice of the Federal Court. Marshall was a humourless Federalist and a man of outstanding ability and intellectual daring. The question in dispute between the President and the Chief Justice was which branch of the government had the power to decide upon the constitutionality of legal enactments. In the original draft of his inaugural address Jefferson had claimed that he could declare an act (the one he had in mind was the Sedition Act) to be 'in palpable and unqualified contradiction to the constitution' and therefore a 'nullity'. But he did not press this claim and passed the decision over to Congress. In February 1803, however, Marshall ruled in the case of Marbury versus Madison that it was essentially the function of the Supreme Court to determine whether a given enactment was constitutional. In reaching this decision he seems to have followed the intention of the makers of the Constitution and such judicial precedents as existed — notably in the state courts. Jefferson denied that this was the case, maintaining that it was the right of the executive so to decide. The final source of authority, he urged, was in the people, and if the people considered that any branch of the government had behaved in an unconstitutional manner they could pronounce their views at the next election. Thus Jefferson stressed the power that the President derived from his being — in fact, if not in theory — popularly elected. Jefferson's ideas were logical from the democratic point of view: politically it seemed wrong for one of the three co-ordinate branches of the government to have the right to pronounce, even by the process of the judicial review, on the constitutionality of the acts of the other two branches. Jefferson took up the challenge that the judiciary — a judiciary filled largely with his political opponents — could override acts of the executive or of the legislature if they conflicted with the Constitution by the most obvious means open to him, namely by trying to establish Congress's power over the judges through inducing the House of Representatives to impeach one of them, Mr. Justice Chase, before the Senate; for impeachment was the only constitutional method by which a judge could be removed from office. The case against Chase appeared to be good, for he had attacked the principles of democracy from the bench, dubbing them 'mobocracy', and the matter was profoundly argued. In the end a number of Republican Senators deserted their own leaders and Chase was acquitted. 'The assault against the judiciary', as it has been called, was one of the most dramatic and fascinating episodes in Jefferson's life — for Jefferson honestly believed that the claim of the judges to lay down the law of the Constitution endangered the nicely balanced system of American democracy. It was one of the few occasions on which Jefferson suffered a permanent political defeat.

Jefferson's political programme may be summed up in a slogan dear to Victorian England: 'Peace, Retrenchment and Reform'; indeed in October 1801 he wrote to an American diplomatist, 'peace is the most important interest and recovery from debt'. In retrenchment his administration at first showed excellent progress. Gallatin introduced a sinking fund and the national debt was much reduced and as at the same time taxes were scaled down — the notorious whisky excise was abolished — this could be achieved only by reductions in public expenditure. The small army was cut down further and Jefferson planned to withdraw all the American diplomatic agents gradually from Europe, leaving only consuls. Surprisingly Jefferson found that some citizens were opposed to the suppression of taxes. However the whole structure of the Jeffersonian policy was threatened by the factor

VICE-PRESIDENT—PRESIDENT

that no government can control independently — that of foreign affairs.

In the first place within six months of Jefferson's becoming President, the United States was at war. Admittedly the enemy was not formidable — it was only Yusuf Caramelli, Pasha of Tripoli, who in an old-fashioned way had sent his corsairs to prey on American commerce in the Mediterranean. Nevertheless American frigates had to be released from the inexpensive quiet of the Washington navy yard and their subsequent successful exertions interfered with the President's plans to save money by reducing expenditure on the Services. A far more dangerous crisis arose in May 1801 when it became known that the Spanish Government had signed a secret treaty with Napoleon yielding to him the whole of the territory named Louisiana after King Louis XIV which lay between the Mississippi and the Rockies, West and East Florida, and the town of New Orleans. Louisiana was an area of about a million square miles comprising the modern states of Arkansas, Colorado, the Dakotas, Iowa, Kansas, Louisiana, Minnesota, Missouri, Montana, Nebraska, Oklahoma and Wyoming, into which the growing American population would inevitably need to expand, while the Mississippi Valley was an essential channel of commerce. To Jefferson this decision by Spain to sell American hinterland to a virile European Power was the most dangerous crisis that the United States had had to meet since they became independent.

When the crisis became known the French had not yet taken possession of Louisiana, but the Spanish authorities at New Orleans had suspended the right of American merchants to deposit their goods there free of duty while waiting trans-shipment as secured by treaty. This caused uncontrollable indignation in the whole of the west and Jefferson feared that he might be driven by pressure of public opinion to immediate war on France. On April 18th, 1802, he wrote a remarkable letter to Robert Livingston, the American Minister in France: 'There is', he said, 'on the globe one single spot the possessor of which is our natural and habitual enemy. It is New Orleans, through which the produce of three-eights of our territory must pass to the market ... Spain might have retained it quietly for years ... The day that France takes possession of New Orleans fixes the sentence which is to restrain her for ever within her low water mark. It seals the union of two nations who in conjunction can maintain exclusive possession of the ocean. From that moment we must marry ourselves to the British Fleet and British nation.' This from the erstwhile Anglophobe! For a moment Jefferson did not know where to turn. He said that the navy, which he had previously hoped to leave permanently moored in the Washington navy yard, must at once be strengthened and suggested that France should be firmly asked to cede New Orleans and the Floridas. But a strong navy could not be created overnight and to ask Napoleon to yield up territory was like asking a bulldog for its bone.

Fortunately for Jefferson it did not come to such extremities. Napoleon had other and apparently more manageable schemes of conquest. The more sensible and practicable solution of offering to buy New Orleans and the Floridas from France was put forward by Jefferson and approved by Congress and in January 1803 James Monroe was sent post-haste to Europe as special envoy to assist Livingston in the negotiations. On Easter Sunday Napoleon, while in his bath, sent for two of his ministers and informed them that he was ready to sell the entire territory of Louisiana and the island of New Orleans and the offer was at once transmitted to Livingston. Jefferson had obtained an appropriation of only two million dollars from the House of Representatives for the purpose of the negotiations, but he had privately notified his envoys that they might go as high as fifty million livres (or about five and a half million dollars). The Americans' original and, as they stressed, modest aim had been to purchase only West Florida and the island of New Orleans, but in the end somewhat to their own surprise they obtained the whole of Louisiana plus New Orleans for a mere sixty million livres. But the negotiators were not a little annoyed to find (as Henry Adams wrote) that having been sent to buy the east bank of the Mississippi they had bought the west bank instead. The agreement was signed on May 8th, 1803. Jefferson, that stickler for constitutional etiquette, had trailed his coat invitingly. Not only had he consented to a purchase price much higher than that approved by the House of Representatives for a different purpose, but he had clearly acted in an unconstitutional manner in acquiring foreign territory purely on his own responsibility. His conduct is one of those historical instances where true statesmanship is not baffled by traditional procedure. Congress was in no mood to question his wisdom and in October the purchase was enthusiastically approved. The President was authorized to take possession of the territory and to organize its government as he thought best.

The Louisiana Purchase was the beginning of a Greater America, but Jefferson himself glimpsed the ultimate unity of this huge territory only through a glass darkly. In a letter to Dr. Joseph Priestley of January 29th, 1804, he wrote: 'The dénouement has been happy; and I confess I look to this duplication of area for the extending of a government so free and economical as ours, as a great achievement to the mass of happiness which is to ensue. Whether we remain one confederacy or form into Atlantic and Mississippi confederacies, I believe not very important to the happiness of either.' In fact Old Man River proved to be a uniting and not a separating force. The distinguished American historian, F. J. Turner, called the Mississippi the 'bond of union'. The peaceful acquisition of Louisiana was to free the United States for some years from those foreign entanglements which Washington and Jefferson had both dreaded so much. And from the new America was to arise a more vigorous and ruthless form of democracy than the intellectual Jefferson ever dreamed of — the democracy of President Andrew Jackson.

Jefferson, who had thus stepped into the shoes of the King of Spain (as Professor Channing wrote), was convinced that the French and Spanish inhabitants of the new territory were not yet ripe for the benefits of American democracy. They were therefore not incorporated into the Union at once; instead Louisiana was divided into five districts each with a commanding officer. Jefferson was willing to suspend the full benefits of freedom until the 'immense swarm' of Americans flocking to these districts should instruct the foreign elements in the virtues of self-government.

Jefferson's dispatch of an expedition to explore the Missouri River and reach the Pacific if possible, which he organized at the same time as he was sending Monroe to France, was another instance of his clear vision of a Greater America. This mission headed by Jefferson's former secretary and would-be beau of Dolly Madison, Captain Merriwether Lewis, and Lieutenant

THOMAS JEFFERSON

William Clark set out in May 1804 and having surmounted many astonishing adventures reached the Pacific, returning in November 1806, after a march of eight thousand miles, bringing with them bears that were let loose in the gardens of the presidential house. In purchasing the Mississippi territory and setting on foot the exploration of the Missouri and the arduous march to the Pacific and back, Thomas Jefferson staked a powerful claim to be the imperial father of the United States, as we know them today.

In spite of these triumphs of statesmanship Jefferson's conduct of his first administration did not leave him free from criticism and anxieties. In particular Jefferson's alleged atheism was seized upon and his patronage of men like Tom Paine and Joseph Priestley was brought forward in evidence. In fact, as he explained to his friend Dr. Rush in April 1803 he conceived himself to be 'a Christian in the only sense He (Christ) wished anyone to be; sincerely attached to his doctrine in preference to all others; ascribing to himself every *human* excellence and believing he never claimed any other'. He was attacked for not proclaiming days of thanksgiving and of fasting and for otherwise failing to identify Church and State. In general he complained to Mazzei: 'Every word of mine which they can get hold of, however innocent, however orthodox, is twisted, tormented, perverted, and like the words of holy writ, are made to mean everything but what they were intended to mean.' Like most men in responsible office, he forgot the days when he was out in the street throwing stones himself.

On top of this, private difficulties crowded in upon him. In the spring of 1804 his younger daughter, Polly, who had married her cousin John Wayles Eppes in October 1797, died at the age of twenty-six leaving him with only one child: 'My evening prospects', he confessed 'now hang on the slender thread of a single life.' Most of his older friends and colleagues in the struggle for independence were also passing away. In 1804 the Vice-President Aaron Burr and Alexander Hamilton, long violent and skilful political rivals in New York, met in a duel in which Burr was the challenger. The encounter took place on July 11th on a grassy platform overlooking the Hudson. Hamilton's was indeed a career to cause the most thick-skinned historian to pause and meditate. Magnificent orator, ingenious financier and scintillating statesman, he was ruined by a low intrigue and died in a meaningless duel, for no one could have censured him had he refused the challenge, and indeed his intention was, it is said, to fire in the air. Though Jefferson was then over sixty and already contemplating his end, he was to survive for another twenty-two years. He was never to meet another Hamilton.

John Adams was one of the few survivors of the older generation of American statesmen. He and Jefferson were no longer on speaking terms, but in June 1804 Mrs. Adams wrote the President a letter of condolence on the death of his daughter, which might have proved the immediate means of burying the hatchet. Far from burying the hatchet this correspondence put it on view. For Jefferson in his reply reminded the lady of her husband's 'personal unkindness' in making the 'midnight appointments', while Abigail Adams, a woman of spirit, retorted in kind, giving her view on the removal of judges and in particular the dismissal of her son. Another unfortunate incident was that James Callender, a Scottish hack writer, who had been given fifty dollars by Jefferson in 1800 and had been released by him from prison early in his administration had recently reprinted a highly scurrilous pamphlet about the former President. Callender in fact was an impartial libeller; for not only did he blackguard Hamilton as well as Adams, but later he turned on a new tack and assaulted the morals and conduct of Jefferson himself. In the end, however, the airing of mutual grievances between Mrs. Adams and Jefferson in this correspondence did lead to a reconciliation between two great Americans.

As early as March 1804 the attacks of the opposition party had provoked Jefferson — who was no moral coward, as some of his critics implied — to stand for office again. 'I sincerely regret', he then wrote, 'that the unbounded calumnies of the Federal party have obliged me to throw myself on the verdict of my country for a trial, my great desire having been to retire at the end of the present term to a life of tranquillity.' He won the election by the decisive majority of fifteen out of seventeen states (Vermont, Kentucky, Tennessee and Ohio had been added to the original thirteen states in the Union). The reduction of taxation, the Louisiana Purchase, and the President's success in keeping the United States out of a major war were all sound election planks.

He at once let it be known that he would not seek a third term. It was his opinion that eight years as President, with public confidence renewed in the holder of the office at the half-way mark, was the right length for a term (in earlier days he had come out for a seven-year term, the President not to be eligible again). 'General Washington', he said in January 1805, 'set the example of voluntary retirement after eight years. I shall follow him.'

4. SECOND TERM AND RETIREMENT
(1805-1826)

Jefferson was sixty-two when, accompanied by an admiring crowd, he went up Pennsylvania Avenue, Washington to deliver his second inaugural address. In it he was able to look back with some complacency upon the record of his first term. 'The suppression of unnecessary offices, of useless establishments and expenses', he reminded his audience, 'enabled us to discontinue our internal taxes.' Consequently 'it may be the pleasure and pride of an American to ask, What farmer, what mechanic, what labourer ever sees a tax-gatherer of the United States?' — for the revenue was paid 'chiefly by those who can afford to add foreign luxuries to domestic comforts'. He turned to speak of the Louisiana Purchase in a more optimistic vein than he had used in his private correspondence: 'Who, after all,' he asked, 'can limit the extent to which our federative principle may operate effectively?' 'The larger our association', he asserted, 'the less it will be shaken by local passions; and in any view, is it not better that the opposite bank of the Mississippi should be settled by our own brethren and children, than by strangers of another family?' Of the Indians, the extent of whose hunting grounds had been further reduced by the Louisiana Purchase, he said: 'Humanity enjoins us to teach them agriculture and the domestic arts.' Of the press, about whose freedom he was less enthusiastic than he had been when he was a critic of the government, the most that he could say was that it was an 'interesting experiment' to see how far a virtuous government could survive, though 'written down' by 'falsehood and defamation'. His address ended with an appeal for national unity and for the blessing of that Supreme Being in

SECOND TERM AND RETIREMENT

whose hands they were and who had led them, as Israel of old, into the Promised Land.

It was plain enough that Jefferson would need all the extraneous help he could extract to master the problems that were now awaiting him. In the first place, in spite of the Louisiana Purchase, he found his government still unavoidably entangled with European nations. Three weeks after Napoleon had signed the agreement selling this vast American territory to the United States Government, he had plunged again into war and by 1806 both France and Spain were fighting England. Out of that war arose a fresh American lust for expansion and fear of involvement.

Jefferson's hope was that he would now be able to acquire the Floridas from Spain and so round off the south-eastern corner of the national map. Appetite had grown with eating, and the southern pioneers and adventurers were clamouring for their share of the Spanish west. There were several ways of approaching the matter. Jefferson at first affected to believe that the terms of the Louisiana Purchase had included West Florida, but he could not induce Count Talleyrand, the French Foreign Minister, to acknowledge it. Indeed the President was conscious of a little awkwardness about the whole situation, for had not Congress originally voted him money to buy the Floridas and had he not failed to buy them? His opponents, the beaten Federalists, made the most of it. What, they asked, was the use of Louisiana? This huge acquisition, they alleged was full only of roving buffalo and saltmines and they jested in verse:

> Jefferson lately of Bonaparte bought
> To pickle his fame, a mountain of salt.

In the House of Representatives the former Democratic leader, the eccentric John Randolph of Roanoake, criticized the Spanish policy of the President on another ground, namely, that he had not fulfilled his promises of admitting the inhabitants of Louisana into the Union. This Randolph was a youngster of dazzling brilliance, a compelling orator, a wealthy Virginian of an independent turn of mind who fought alone and feared no man — a kind of Byron of politics. He was to prove an obstacle to Jefferson's plan to obtain the Floridas.

Jefferson's policy towards Spain was so realistic that his critics said it verged on blackmail. His idea was to threaten the Spanish Government with war and thereby induce it to compromise with a sale of land for cash. 'If as soon as she [Spain] is at war we push them strongly with one hand, holding out a prize with the other we shall certainly obtain the Floridas, and all in good time.' So Jefferson wrote to a confidant in August 1803. To mature the armed threat to Spain, Jefferson even contemplated an alliance with his old enemy, England, suggesting that as soon as England was at war with Spain, the United States should proffer her an alliance on condition that she should 'stipulate not to make peace unless Spain acknowledged the rightful boundaries of Louisiana' — by which he meant the inclusion of West Florida. This plan was stillborn because at that date the alliance of the United States would have been of small value to Britain and the terms proposed were scarcely practicable. In October therefore Jefferson changed his tactics and proposed that a deal should be made with the Spaniards through their powerful friend Napoleon. 'Is not Paris the place?' he asked Gallatin, 'France the agent? The purchase of Florida the means?' In November the Cabinet approved the plan of mixing bids with menaces (December 8th, 1805). Publicly Jefferson sent a fierce message to Congress, outlining the alleged Spanish 'spoliations' on the Louisiana frontier and apparently paving the way to war. Congress and the press were aroused to fever pitch but three days later received a cold douche when a confidential message from the President explained that negotiations with Spain were to continue, 'but the course to be pursued will require the command of means which it belongs to Congress exclusively to yield or to deny'. John Randolph of Roanoake, whose duty it would normally have been to sponsor the appropriation to buy the Floridas, withheld his co-operation, believing or pretending to believe that the plan was to bribe Napoleon into forcing Spain to give way. 'I consider it a base prostitution of the national character to excite one nation with money to bully another out of its property.' In the end the perversity of Randolph's vituperation detracted from the magnetism of his oratory. But the chance to persuade Spain to sell had passed, and the United States had to wait another sixteen years to obtain this lovely state in the Gulf of Mexico.

The America of Jefferson's day was a land of extraordinary

SECOND TERM AND RETIREMENT

men and unique opportunities. (The opportunities were less marked for women. 'The appointment of a woman to office', wrote Jefferson to Gallatin in January 1807, 'is an innovation for which the public is not prepared, nor am I'.) The purchase of Louisiana aroused in particular the adventurous spirit of Colonel Aaron Burr, the former Vice-President of the United States, who had been compelled to retire into the background since the day when he had killed Alexander Hamilton. The Democrats had refused to put him forward again in 1804 for the Vice-Presidency preferring his old New York rival, George Clinton. Burr's restless nature sought some outlet. He went to see Jefferson in search of a diplomatic post, but Jefferson, who had no reason to love him, refused it. Now that Burr's wife was dead and his daughter on whom he doted was married, he fancied that some enterprise in the west would be more profitable and amusing than a barrister's career. The first thing needed was money and he went to both the British and Spanish Ministers in Washington with the story (true or false no one knows to this day) that he would support a separatist movement. Nothing came of this, but later he found a curious backer, an Irish man of letters named Harman Blennerhassett, who lived with his wife on a beautiful island in the river Ohio; they were all agog to engage on these fantastic and far-reaching plans which promised them the chance to mix with the great or the near-great. Burr also sounded two distinguished southern gentlemen, General Andrew Jackson of Tennessee, a former Senator, and General James Wilkinson, the Governor of New Orleans, who had played an odd part in Washington's life in connection with the so-called Conway Cabal. The plan which Burr appears to have put forward was that he should collect and train a force to invade Mexico in the event, which then seemed likely, of war breaking out with Spain. As a cover plan and also as an investment he purchased four hundred thousand acres of land (known as the Bastrop estate on the Washita River in Upper Louisiana) where a voluntary American 'garrison' could cultivate the soil until an opportunity presented itself for a march into Mexico. In October 1806, just when foreign affairs were in a particularly delicate condition, General Wilkinson (who himself had been intriguing with the Spaniards) wrote to Jefferson to inform him that Colonel Burr was planning an immediate attack upon the Spanish possessions in America in order to carve for himself an independent empire in the west.

Jefferson acted at once, for he felt that such a disruptive threat to the Union (if genuine) must be stopped at all cost. On November 27th the President issued a proclamation against 'sundry persons conspiring and confederating together' and eight weeks later sent a special message accusing Burr by name to Congress. On February 18th, 1807, Burr was arrested after a number of boats and stores that had been got ready for him had been intercepted. How far Burr was guilty or not guilty of treasonable conspiracy has never been conclusively ascertained. General Jackson believed implicitly in Burr's innocence. Burr himself in his old age is reported to have said: 'I never got within ten thousand leagues of a wish to break up the United States by a separatist or secessionist movement, though I did hope to establish an empire in Mexico and to become its emperor.' Threats of secession were not infrequent during the early years of the confederation — Jefferson, as we have seen, was at one time ready to acquiesce in secession — and so too were frontier 'enterprises': had not George Washington attacked the French on the frontier in time of peace? The only thing that can be said with certainty is that at the time that Jefferson published his proclamation Burr was not equipped for desperate moves; for the so-called 'flotilla' of boats and barrels of provisions that were seized *en route* from Blennerhassett's island to New Orleans were better suited to found a colony than to nourish a military campaign.

After he had been indicted by a Grand Jury for high treason and misdemeanour Aaron Burr was put on trial before Chief Justice Marshall in whose circuit he had been arrested. Jefferson threw himself anxiously into the fray, doing all that was in his power to secure a conviction and writing private letters in which the defendant was prejudged. It seems that Jefferson thought that by making an example of Burr he would 'save the Union', while, if Marshall should allow Burr to be acquitted, the judiciary would be disgraced and the pretentions of the Supreme Court to overrule the executive be for ever discredited. Because of the strong views that he held of the relations between the executive and the judiciary Jefferson refused to appear under subpoena as a witness at the trial. Marshall was not dismayed. Burr, he

SECOND TERM AND RETIREMENT

maintained, had committed no 'overt act' of treason and the defendant was acquitted, though in ambiguous terms, by the jury. Professor Gilbert Chinard, a warm admirer of Jefferson, has written severely of his conduct in this case. It was, he says, a struggle between the executive and the judiciary, in which Marshall came out as a staunch champion of legality, while Jefferson vainly tried to twist the law or, if it could not be twisted, to invoke political arguments for its destruction. 'Self-preservation', Jefferson announced, 'is paramount to all law.' No doubt it was true that in a time of national crisis exceptional acts overriding the established law might have become necessary. So at least our European democracies have always believed. The philosopher king had learned more than one lesson from experience since he became President of the United States.

The truth would appear to be that both sides were right. It was Jefferson's conviction that the American Constitution was founded on an equal balance between three powers, the executive, the legislature and the judiciary. To that extent he was right as President to refuse to appear as witness in a judicial court where his testimony was not fundamental to the verdict. He was right too in thinking that Burr's plot, as described to him by General Wilkinson, was a menace to the Union. And had the documents that were unearthed by Henry Adams many years after the trial then been available it would have been very difficult for the jury not to convict. But Marshall surely was equally right in maintaining that it was the duty of the judiciary to safeguard the freedom of the individual, in the light of the principles laid down in the Constitution, even from the executive — or as many would say, especially from the executive. And although it was plain that what Burr had been doing or thinking of doing was embarrassing to the Federal Government, it would have been stretching the definition of treason far to have denounced him as guilty on the existing evidence alone.

The attempt to buy Florida and Burr's plot were less important consequences to the United States of the war in Europe than the disputes with Great Britain and France over the freedom of the seas which finally led to the Anglo-American war of 1812. The Napoleonic wars had proved highly profitable to the neutral Americans: for once the power of the British navy had swept all their enemies' shipping from the seas, almost the entire carrying trade of Europe fell into American hands. American ships carried Spanish goods to Spain for her colonies and Dutch goods to Holland from hers. It was a roaring business which could only be stopped if the British succeeded in blockading almost every port in the world. The British Government did its best to impose such a blockade, for it was its most potent weapon of war; on it the British people pinned their hopes, as they did again in 1914 and 1940, until such a time as a European tyrant should overreach himself. In January 1804 a blockade was declared of the French and Dutch West Indian ports. The American carrying trade evaded this restriction by fetching the cargoes just the same but landed them in American ports, paid the duties on them and reshipped them before taking them to Europe. The British Court of Admiralty had acquiesced in this procedure since legally the voyage had been 'broken'. In 1805, however, a fresh case of this kind (the Essex Case) came before the British Admiralty courts which, virtually reversing their previous judgment, decided that since the goods were intended for sale in Europe and not in the United States, their shipment was, in fact, 'direct'.

The anger of the American mercantile community over the decision in the Essex Case was intense and Jefferson had to take political action. His choice lay between a diplomatic move, retaliation of some kind and a declaration of war. He tried diplomatic action first: the Jay Treaty of 1794 was about to expire and Jefferson hoped that his special envoy in London, James Monroe, might be able to effect a compromise. Meanwhile, exercising his full rights of presidential leadership, he proposed to Congress that a Non-Importation Bill should be passed so that if national satisfaction was not exacted the import of all goods from Britain and British possessions would be forbidden. This was the same policy that had been applied against England with some success during the days before the War of Independence.

Jefferson suspended the operation of the Non-Importation Bill which Congress passed at his behest while the negotiations continued in London (and in doing so he enlarged his presidential powers). In June 1805 he was optimistic: 'Every communication from Mr. Monroe', he wrote, 'strengthens our expectations that the new pretence of the British to control our commerce with

SECOND TERM AND RETIREMENT

belligerent countries will be properly restricted.' Monroe and his colleague, William Pinckney, did all they could, but the situation grew worse. In May 1806 a British Order in Council declared a blockade of the whole coast of Europe from the mouth of the Elbe to the port of Brest, and on January 7th, 1807, in reply to Napoleon's 'Berlin Decrees' (also restricting the American carrying trade) another Order in Council forbade neutrals to trade between any two ports in the possession of France or her allies. A further long-standing American grievance came to a head at this time. British-born sailors had been in the habit of deserting to serve in American ships where pay was higher. After a number of incidents between the two nations arising out of these technical desertions (the matter was complicated because the laws of naturalization differed) a British warship, the *Leopard,* stopped an American frigate, the *Chesapeake,* by firing at her, killing some of her crew, and forcibly searching her for deserters. The action took place not far from the American coast and was the first occasion on which the British had dared to board a vessel belonging to the American navy. Popular indignation was aroused and if Jefferson had had more than gunboats at his disposal war might have followed. Thus, as often, Retrenchment was the mother of Peace. Jefferson knew the limitations of his gunboats and was pacific at heart. All he did was to publish a proclamation ordering British armed vessels out of American waters and to remark that 'reason and the usage of civilized nations require that we should give them [the British] an opportunity of disavowal and reparation'.

The possibilities of diplomatic action were now exhausted. Jefferson recalled Monroe from London, refusing to submit to the Senate the 'hard treaty' that he and Pinckney had extracted. In December the President put into force the Non-Importation Act and also sent a special message to Congress recommending that no American ships should be allowed to leave American ports for Europe. This self-denying ordinance was at once passed by Congress and for over two years all American overseas trade came almost to a standstill. Farm prices declined, many merchants went bankrupt, and the embargo was ignored by law-defying spirits. No wonder Jefferson wrote to Gallatin: 'This embargo law is certainly the most embarrassing one we have ever had to execute. I did not expect a crop of so sullen and rank a growth of frank and open opposition by force could have grown up in the United States.' Again the philosopher in office was learning the ways of men. Disobedience spread through the New England states and, what was more disconcerting to the Administration, the embargo proved more damaging to America than it did to Britain. Yet Jefferson by his policy had postponed the outbreak of war and given time for a militia force to be raised and an American fleet to be built. Moreover having tried the method of protecting neutral rights by economic sanctions as well as by normal diplomatic approaches, if war came, his conscience could be clear.

It was always to be Jefferson's belief that if the embargo had been kept on a little longer than it was the British Government would have capitulated and war would have been averted. In that case, as he told Congress in his eighth annual message, his 'candid and liberal experiment' of gaining his ends without fighting would have succeeded. But, as we were to learn in our own time, economic sanctions are unlikely to be effective unless the nations which impose them are willing and ready in the last resort to go to war. Jefferson in any case did not want war nor did the New England states. In February 1809 a 'sudden and unaccountable revolution of opinion in Congress' insisted on the removal of the embargo. Jefferson signed an Act ending the embargo on March 1st and substituting for it a non-intercourse act forbidding all trade between the United States and Britain or France until they revoked their discriminatory measures.

Thus Jefferson's eight years in office ended in political confusion and economic depression. But taking all in all, he was able to look back with pride on his achievements. He had abolished all internal taxes. He had substantially reduced the national debt. He had acquired for the United States the immense potentially rich area of Louisiana and the valuable town of New Orleans. Moreover — and perhaps in terms of humanity this was his noblest work — he had persuaded Congress to pass a Bill prohibiting the importation of any more African slaves into the United States after the year 1807. 'These', said the address presented to him by the Virginia Legislature, 'are points in your

SECOND TERM AND RETIREMENT

administration which the historian will not fail to seize, to expand, and to teach posterity to dwell upon with delight. Nor will he forget our peace with the civilized world, preserved through a season of uncommon difficulty and trial; the good will cultivated with the unfortunate aborigines of our country, the civilization humanely extended among them; the lesson taught the inhabitants of the coast of Barbary, that we have the means of chastising their piratical encroachments, and swing them into justice; and that theme, which, above all others, the historic genius will hang upon with rapture, the liberty of speech and the press preserved inviolate without which genius and science are given to man in vain.' This was a just enough encomium. Though his years in office had sloughed off some of the more innocent fancies of the political theorist and convicted him of some of those inconsistencies that are the natural product of his profession, they had forged a statesman who had served his country well.

Jefferson handed over the executive house without regret to his former Secretary of State, the dry but wise Madison and his attractive wife. The Democratic nomination for the Presidency had rested in effect between Madison and another loyal Virginian follower of Jefferson, James Monroe. Monroe had complained to Jefferson that his difficult negotiations in London had cast a reflection on his abilities and prejudiced his chances. Jefferson soothed him, but had no doubt that Madison had the first claim to the succession. Madison served for eight years and Monroe then became President for the next eight. Thus for nearly a generation Jefferson's political ideas steered the United States on their course. In many ways Jefferson's political principles guide his country yet.

So far as the Presidency was concerned, Jefferson had shaped the institution primarily through being the founder and leader of a party that was to dominate American politics until the time of Abraham Lincoln. In due course it was to become a recognized custom of the Constitution that the President was the chosen representative of a political party, and thus to the power and privileges that went with the office were added all the influence of party leadership. When his party predominated in the two Houses of the Legislature, Senators and Congressmen had a certain political and moral obligation to follow his directions or take the consequences of 'bolting' the party. It was in fact only by the association of party leadership and the tenure of the presidential office that the chief American executive was enabled to influence legislation and thus break down the separation of powers enshrined in the Constitution.

Jefferson was nearly sixty-six when he returned thankfully to Virginia; for the remaining seventeen years of his life he seldom moved from Monticello except for an annual visit to his other estate of Poplar Forest seventy-five miles away. Yet if he stayed away from the world, the world did not stay away from him. The domed white house on the hill, with its doric pillars, balustrades, and octagonal passages, was always full of visitors, and, as the years rolled by, pilgrims — men, women and children from every state of the Union and even from overseas — came there to gaze curiously on the venerable author of the Declaration of Independence. Whether they were old friends or merely energetic sightseers — all partook expensively of the unstinting Virginian hospitality. Their host was a national heirloom — but unsupported out of the national funds.

The President of the United States receives no pension. Farms that had worked long for absentee landlords and employed slave labour proved unprofitable undertakings to Jefferson as they had to Washington. A life in retirement from the great world, though pleasurable, was a long and unsuccessful struggle against debt. Whatever he may have advocated as a public man, Jefferson was rigorously punctilious about the payment of his British creditors, and this was not easy for a planter whose resources were rarely liquid and whose investments fell in value.

In a letter written soon after his return Jefferson described his daily round: 'My mornings are devoted to correspondence. From breakfast to dinner I am in my shops, my gardens, or on horseback among my farms: from dinner to dark I give to society and recreation with my neighbours and friends [it should be remembered that both Madison and Monroe lived near]; and from candlelight to early bedtime I read. My health is perfect . . . I talk of ploughs and harrows . . . A part of my occupation . . . is the direction of the studies of such young men as ask it . . . I endeavour to keep their attention fixed on the main subjects of all science, the freedom and happiness of man.' Each day he rose at dawn, lit his own fire, walked his gardens and rode through his plantations. 'He was always a miser of his time', wrote one of his grandsons. 'He said, in his last illness, that the sun had not caught him in bed for fifty years.' Though he had one or two illnesses, notably in 1819, on the whole his health was excellent for his age. Even after he found walking a trial, he never missed his two or three hours on horseback or failed, as a preventitive of catarrh, to dip his feet daily in cold water.

One of his most burdensome physical trials was his large correspondence, which he frequently spoke of as being 'afflictingly laborious', and in his later seventies he wrote feelingly: 'Is this life? At best it is but the life of a mill-horse who sees no end to his circle but in death.' Yet he was, on the whole, a conscientious and entertaining correspondent; a letter from the ex-President was worth having for he could lift any topic out of the commonplace and illuminate it with his eager interest.

For a long time Jefferson followed politics closely and was applied to for advice. He was instrumental in reconciling Monroe, at first disgruntled about the 1808 presidential nomination, with President Madison, whose Secretary of State he became. Jefferson sadly watched the dawning of another war which he had done so much to postpone and had hoped to avert. Still convinced in his mind that it was England, not France (though Bonaparte, he recognized, had betrayed the republican cause) who was the enemy of international freedom, he judged harshly: to him England was 'the nation who never admitted a chapter of morality into her political code' and her government the 'most unprincipled' one of the day. When at length grievances over the impressment of seamen and over the British interpretation of the rights of belligerents at sea led to the unfortunate war of 1812 Jefferson supported it with patriotic fervour. 'She may burn New York', he declared, 'in which case we must burn the city of London by hired incendiaries, of which her starving manufacturers will furnish abundance ... We have nothing to fear from their armies', he wrote, 'and shall put nothing in prize to their fleets. Upon the whole I have known no war entered into under more favourable auspices.' In fact the war did not prove as simple to win as Jefferson imagined. Owing to what he termed blockheaded (and certainly elderly) generals, American attempts to invade Canada failed and in revenge for the destruction of public buildings at York (now Toronto) British troops set the presidential house and the Capitol on fire. Jefferson gloomily observed the course of the war worsening and was convinced that the 'violation of women' was the habitual British practice in war. In October 1814 he wrote to President Madison that as the entire objects of the war had now, in his opinion, been changed by England, they must prepare to fight interminably. Happily things were less bad than they seemed and in June 1815 he was able to rejoice in a 'single-handed victory' for American arms. At the same time he could reflect on the 'sample of bathos' provided by Napoleon Bonaparte's exile to St. Helena — Jefferson would have preferred that 'he should have perished on the swords of his enemies under the walls of Paris'. There was, however, one political reflection that seems to have eluded him: that was that the war of 1812 had strengthened the powers of the American President — a presage of a greater strengthening in wider wars.

With the unprincipled English and the hammer of the French Republicans both defeated, the United States could revert to the policy which Jefferson had always advocated of freedom from European entanglements except for one or two outstanding questions that had to be settled with Spain — namely the future of Florida and perhaps of Cuba. Spain presented another complication in that during the Napoleonic wars the Spanish colonies in Central and South America under the inspiring leadership of the Creole, Bolivar, had broken off their allegiance to the Crown and formed themselves into independent republics. Jefferson advised Monroe to act in concert with England to prevent European intervention. There is some controversy among American historians about how far Jefferson helped to influence the famous declaration in which President Monroe announced that the American continents were not henceforward to be considered as subjects for future colonization by any European Powers and that any European interposition for the purpose of oppressing the Latin-American states would be treated as evidence of unfriendliness towards the United States. There is in any case no doubt that Jefferson thoroughly approved the 'Monroe Doctrine' so ex-

SECOND TERM AND RETIREMENT

pounded; equally there is no question that he realized at that time the United States were not powerful enough to enforce the doctrine unless it had behind it (as it had) the sanction of the British navy.

When in September 1814 Jefferson learned that the library of Congress had been largely destroyed in the firing of the Capitol by the British, he determined upon a magnificent personal sacrifice by offering his own library to replace the loss. It was a generous offer, less generously accepted. In the end Jefferson's nine or ten thousand carefully chosen volumes were purchased for the purpose and there they remained until another fire consumed about two-thirds of them in 1851.

Reading — the Greek tragedies were among his favourite books — was one of the chief consolations of Jefferson's old age, but it was not the only one. He could rejoice in the company of his descendants, his daughter Martha, who survived him, her husband who became Governor of Virginia, their eleven children and half a dozen of their grandchildren. The memories of Thomas Jefferson's understanding of and generosity to the younger members of his family have been lovingly preserved from that day to this.

But to the historian the most fascinating consolation of Jefferson's old age was the correspondence which he entered into with John Adams, second President of the United States, to whom he was reconciled in 1812. We have seen how towards the end of Jefferson's second term a letter from Mrs. Adams had opened the way to the renewal of an old friendship, but the path had been barred by painful political recollections. Now that the two former Presidents had both retired a mutual friend arranged that good relations should be restored. As soon as the sage of Monticello heard that Adams had said 'I always loved Jefferson and still love him' the green light went up. After a preliminary exchange of samples of homespun cloth and of cordialities Adams wrote: 'You and I ought not to die before we have explained ourselves to each other.' When the correspondence began (at the time of writing it has still not been published in its entirety) Jefferson was sixty-eight and Adams was seventy-six. Adams appears to have written more letters but Jefferson contributed longer ones.

THOMAS JEFFERSON

They did not confine themselves to happy memories of the days when they were fellow labourers in fighting for independence and in fashioning the Republic: their minds ranged over a wide field, the habits of Indians, history and politics, religion and philosophy. Their frankness was moving and their intimacy complete. An enterprising publisher wanted to get hold of the letters in the lifetime of the writers, but this offer was indignantly refused, for they were not writing for the public or for posterity but only for their own pleasure. Jefferson recalled how in his boyhood 'the great Outassete, the warrior and orator of the Cherokees', had often been the guest of his father; he dilated upon the 'Wabash prophet' who claimed to have been in constant communication with the Great Spirit; Adams wrote two essays on the nature of grief; and both of them exchanged bold and realistic thoughts on the subject of old age and death. Adams's fear was that his 'machine would not surcease motion soon enough'; he 'dreaded nothing so much as "dying at top" ' and expiring, like Dean Swift, "a driveller and a show". Jefferson confessed he too had ever dreaded 'a doting old age ... I dread it still'.

In these and other letters Jefferson disclosed his extraordinary optimism about the future and his faith in the destiny of his country. 'I do believe', he said, 'we shall continue to grow, to multiply and prosper until we exhibit our association, powerful, wise and happy beyond what has yet been seen by men. As for France and England with all their preeminence in science, the one is a den of robbers, and the other of pirates.' In another letter to Adams he avowed: 'I think with you that it is a good world, on the whole; that it has been framed on a principle of benevolence and more pleasure than pain dealt out to us. My temperament is sanguine. I steer my bark with hope in the head, leaving fear astern.' This was the same man who at the age of nineteen had asked: 'Is there such a thing as happiness in this world?' and had answered 'No'. Adams commented on the letter: 'I admire your navigation.'

There has been much speculation on Jefferson's religion, but it is a subject on which quotations from his many writings can be used in various ways; not even Adams, who was fascinated by theology, succeeded in drawing him out. Once Jefferson wrote: 'I am a materialist — I am an Epicurean', but surely no one was

SECOND TERM AND RETIREMENT

less of a materialist than Jefferson. In his letter to Adams, condoling with him on the death of his wife, there is a passage which can be construed to show that he believed in immortality. Assuredly he believed in a benevolent God — as an optimist must — and there are some indications that he accepted the moral teachings of Christ. On the whole, it may be hazarded that 'he cleaved ever to the sunnier side of doubt'. But it is given to few to read the hearts even of those dearest to them and maybe Jefferson's biographers are well advised to follow his own direction: 'Say nothing of my religion: it is known to my God and myself alone: its evidence before the world is to be sought in my life; if that has been honest and dutiful to society, the religion which has regulated it cannot be a bad one.'

Two events in particular brightened Jefferson's last years. General Lafayette, who had been loved as an ardent youngster by George Washington, now paid a visit to Monticello. As the old hero, 'permanently lamed and broken in health by his long imprisonment in the dungeon of Olmutz', embraced his host, there was not a dry eye among those present. Secondly Jefferson found an absorbing interest in the foundation of the University of Virginia of which he became the first rector. His plans for giving his native state a complete and integrated system of education stretched back many years and were of the logic of his democracy. Progress had never been as fast as he wished, but he was always determined that Virginia should have at least an institute for higher education 'more comprehensive, more healthy and central' than William and Mary College where he had been a student. He canvassed for the university, begged for it, planned its architecture and framed its law. The site chosen for the buildings on Jefferson's counsel was within view of Monticello and so for five years from 1819 to 1824 he was able personally to supervise its construction. His argument for the salubriousness of the spot he wanted was that a larger number of people over eighty lived in the neighbourhood. The old Anglophobe had to send to England for the best professors. In compensation, 'for the first time in the history of the country, higher education was made independent of the Church and to a large extent the foundation of the University of Virginia marks the beginning of the secularization of scientific research in America'. (Chinard.)

THOMAS JEFFERSON

A visitor who saw Jefferson in his last years found him 'stooping and lean with old age, thus exhibiting the fortunate mode of decay which strips the frame of its most cumbersome parts leaving it still some strength of muscle and activity of limb'. All his teeth remained intact to the end. He himself complained, probably with exaggeration, of loss of memory; and he dreaded the approach of each winter, expressing the half-joking wish that he could sleep through it like a dormouse. But his moral courage and immovable faith in the future fortified him to the end: in his last letter to Adams (March 25th, 1826) he wrote apropos the rising generation: 'Theirs are the halcyon calms succeeding the storms which our Argosy has so stoutly weathered.' In the spring of that year his health declined and on June 24th he had to write to General Roger Weightman refusing an invitation to visit Washington to take part in the fiftieth anniversary celebration of Independence Day. 'All eyes are opened or opening to the rights of man,' he declared, 'the general spread of the light of science has already laid open to every view the palpable truth that the mass of mankind has not been born with saddles on their backs nor a favoured few booted and spurred ready to ride them legitimately by the grace of God.' He faced what was to come philosophically 'as an event rather unpleasant than terrible . . . like a traveller expressing his apprehension of being caught in a rain'. As Independence Day dawned both John Adams and Thomas Jefferson lay dying. The day before, Jefferson had asked: 'Is it the Fourth?' 'It soon will be', was the reply. Those are his last recorded words. At about one o'clock on July 4th, 1826 he passed away.

Jefferson died in such financial straits that the terms of his will could not be carried out. Even in his lifetime he had been obliged to ask permission from the Legislature of Virginia, which he had served so honourably, to sell his farms by lottery so as to meet his obligations. When this fact became known a collection had been raised on his behalf which he accepted with gratitude, characteristically rejoicing that the gift did not come out of taxation. But soon after his death Monticello was sold to pay his debts. One of his final requests was, however, honoured. An obelisk of coarse stone was placed upon his grave bearing these words:

SECOND TERM AND RETIREMENT

> Here was buried
> Thomas Jefferson,
> Author of the Declaration of American Independence,
> Of the Statute of Virginia for Religious Freedom,
> And Father of the University of Virginia —

for those were the testimonials of his life and work by which he wished most to be remembered.

SELECT BIBLIOGRAPHY

HENRY ADAMS: *History of the United States* (1891).
JAMES TRUSLOW ADAMS: *The Living Jefferson* (1936).
CARL BECKER: *The Declaration of Independence* (1922).
CLAUDE G. BOWERS: *Jefferson and Hamilton* (1925); *Jefferson in Power* (1936).
E. CHANNING: *The Jeffersonian System 1801-1811* (1906).
GILBERT CHINARD: *The Commonplace Book of Thomas Jefferson* (1926); *Thomas Jffrson* (1929).
H. J. ECKENRODE: *The Revolution in Virginia* (1916).
P. L. FORD: *The Writings of Thomas Jefferson* (1893).
F. W. HIRST: *Life and Letters of Thomas Jefferson* (1925).
MARIE KIMBALL: *Jefferson, The Road to Glory 1743-1776* (1943).
A. A. LIPSCOMB and A. E. BERGH: *Writings of Thomas Jefferson* (1905).
F. S. OLIVER: *Alexander Hamilton* (1909).
S. K. PADOVER: *Jefferson* (1942).
S. N. RANDOLPH: *The Domestic Life of Jefferson* (1939).
S. H. WANDELL and M. MINNIGERODE: *Aaron Burr* (1925).
P. WILSTOCK: *Correspondence of John Adams and Thomas Jefferson 1812-1826* (1925).

ANDREW JACKSON

THEODORE ROOSEVELT
ON
JACKSON

WITH the exception of Washington and Lincoln no man has left a deeper mark on American history... a true American, who served his country valiantly in the field of battle against a foreign foe, and who upheld with the most staunch devotion the cause of the great Federal Union.

A VERY charming English historian of our day has compared Wellington with Washington; it would have been far juster to have compared him with Andrew Jackson. Both were men of strong, narrow minds and bitter prejudices, with few statesman-like qualities, who, for brilliant military services, were raised to the highest civil positions in the gift of the State.

ANDREW JACKSON

CHAPTER IV

ANDREW JACKSON

ANDREW JACKSON has been called the first President of the Plain People. The choice of the retired Tennessean soldier to lead the nation was made by a popular vote in most of the states and it was the vote of a substantial and growing electorate in which the industrial and commercial classes of the north, the southern planters and the western pioneers were all represented; Jackson's deliberate appeal was to the masses, for he had an almost religious faith in democracy, which did not betray him.

It was in the success of his appeal to the people throughout the whole nation that lay Jackson's peculiar contribution to the evolution of the Presidency. Jackson had been chosen as candidate and topped the electoral poll in 1824 against the opposition of virtually all the established politicians in his party. Moreover, after he became president in 1829, it was against the inclination of many influential members of his party and of the majority of the Senate that Jackson forced through his own policies. For the first time in American history the chief executive was both the choice and the voice of the plain people.

Not only did Jackson thus directly represent the plain people, for whom he embodied the increasingly articulate nationalism of his age, but in a sense he was a plain person himself. For he was a self-made man with little formal education and his earliest interests were earthy: he loved race horses more than political philosophy. Fundamentally he was a less complicated figure than any of his predecessors. In contrast with Washington and Jefferson, Jackson became a practising Christian. From a youth of gaiety and gambling he came to an old age fondling his dead wife's Bible and attending the Presbyterian Church.

It is one of the paradoxes of Jackson's character that though he was a full man, he had several womanly traits. In his tantrums and his susceptibility to flattery, in his devotion to sometimes worthless friends, in his concern over personalities rather than principles there was much that was feminine. And some historians have attributed his political and military success to his feminine gift of intuition. Once his instincts selected an object he went bald-headed to achieve it. The risks that he took in his New Orleans campaign would have appalled the well-trained professional officer, whilst his defiance of Congress in his campaign against the United States National Bank dismayed many an experienced statesman. Yet his intuitions rarely led him astray. Though the arguments by which he justified his actions could not, and will not, withstand the analysis of a logician, the actions themselves invariably accorded with the spirit of his times. He knew what he wanted and what he wanted the mass of American people wanted too. He saw and met the demand for rugged leadership free from the customary balancings and heart-burnings of the professional politicians.

Nevertheless there was continuity in Jackson's policies. In many ways and in a changing world he was the true heir of Thomas Jefferson. Jackson did not offer — he did not pretend to offer — positive ideas for a Brave New World. All he sought to do was to give the opportunist his opportunity. Like Jefferson he feared a monopolist bank and the menace of the 'Money Power'. Except (and it is a big exception) when large claims by South Carolina endangered the Union, Jackson was as good a states' rights man as his predecessor. And Jackson was as little friendly to the claim of the Federal Supreme Court to make constitutional decisions as Jefferson had been.

Though Jackson wore the Jeffersonian mantle, he himself played a distinctive role in American history. In his use of the veto, in his treatment of the members of his Cabinets as officials subject to his own orders, in his employment of his special group of advisers — the 'Kitchen Cabinet', he asserted the power of the chief executive in a manner that no man had done before. 'We are in the midst of a revolution', declared Jackson's political rival, Henry Clay in 1833, 'hitherto bloodless but rapidly tending towards a change of the pure Republican character of the Government, and to the concentration of all power in the hands of one man.' Yet his opponents wrongly nicknamed him 'King Andrew', for Jacksonian democracy was in reality the complete antithesis of one-man rule. The final meaning of Andrew Jackson's life is to be found in his association with the man in the street for whom he spoke. 'You know I never despair,' he once said, 'for I have confidence in the virtue and good sense of the people.' The unique place which the Presidency holds in the political system of the United States as an effective instrument of democratic government owes as much to Andrew Jackson as to any one man.

1. ATTORNEY-GENERAL, CONGRESSMAN, SENATOR, JUDGE (1767-1813)

It was due to luck or 'manifest destiny' or whatever other name we choose to give to the enterprise of his parents that Andrew Jackson, 'the first Irish President of the United States', was not born in Ireland. His father was an Irish tenant farmer, his mother, born Elizabeth Hutchinson, was the daughter of an Irish linen weaver. The Hutchinsons were a prolific clan; and it was in order to join a group of sisters and friends who had settled in the New World that Elizabeth, her husband and two small boys, Robert and Hugh, embarked at Carrickfergus in the spring of 1765 to cross the sea and win their fortunes. They must have found it a wearisome journey before they reached the frontier town of Salisbury in North Carolina and thrust forward in company with the wagons of other belated pioneers to their destination, 'the Garden of the Waxhaws'. And when they arrived they might well have been almost as disappointed as Martin Chuzzlewit.

The Waxhaw is a tributary of the river Catawba which emerges from the Blue Ridge Mountains about 250 miles from the sea. For some years land companies had been persuading Irishmen and others to settle upon the red soil of its valley; but by this date the most promising lands had already gone, and in any case Andrew Jackson senior could not afford to buy the best. Still he staked his claim to two hundred acres near the headwaters of Twelve Tree Creek, a few miles from the farms of two of his brothers-in-law, and started to clear the forest, break the soil, and sow his crops. Within two years, worn out perhaps with his exertions, Andrew Jackson senior was dead. He died on March 1st, 1767. Elizabeth Jackson, big with child, followed the coffin across the ice to the graveside; then she retired to a sister's home to give birth to her third son whom she named after his father.

The birth took place in a house somewhere on the borders of North and South Carolina — nobody knows exactly where, but it seems then to have been technically in South Carolina — on March 15th, 1767. Elizabeth, a red-haired, blue-eyed little woman was born to be a pioneer; she vigorously overcame the problems of raising three small boys without a husband to support her: no doubt friends and relatives and the comradeship of the frontier aided her: she settled with a brother-in-law, James Crawford, whose wife was an invalid, took charge of the combined households, and brought up her sons. Andrew with red hair and deep blue eyes like his mother's distinguished himself at school where he 'learned figures', wrote a 'neat legible hand' and found a favourite subject in geography. The community had only one newspaper and the bright boys of the neighbourhood took it in turns to act as public readers. It was Andrew's turn to read when in the summer of 1776 the local newspaper printed Thomas Jefferson's masterpiece, the Declaration of American Independence.

After a year or two the horrors of war penetrated south. At sixteen Hugh, Andrew's eldest brother, volunteered to fight for the American cause and died after a skirmish in 1779. In May 1780 Charleston, capital of South Carolina, fell to the British and in August of the same year Major-General Horatio Gates suffered his humiliating defeat at the battle of Camden. By this date Andrew had become at the age of thirteen a 'mounted orderly'. In the spring of the following year a body of British dragoons, part of General Cornwallis's army, raided the Waxhaws and Andrew (who had already once before had to flee his home) and his brother Robert were taken prisoners. 'I was in one skirmish,' related Andrew in later life, 'that of Sands House — and there they caught me along with my brother Robert and my cousin, Tom Crawford. A lieutenant of Tarleton's Light Dragoons tried to make me clean his boots and cut my arm with his sabre when I refused. After this they kept me in jail in Camden about two months, starved me nearly to death and gave me the small pox. Finally my mother persuaded them to release Robert and me on account of our extreme youth and illness. Then

Robert died of small pox and I barely escaped.' After this the American cause improved. Major-General Greene's able defensive campaign forced Cornwallis out of the Carolinas to meet disaster at Yorktown. 'Take it altogether, I saw and heard a good deal of war in those days', Jackson confessed, 'but did nothing toward it myself worth mention.' He was the only one of his family to survive the war. His mother contracted yellow fever while visiting American prisoners on board an English prison ship at Charleston and died of it in November 1781. It was no wonder that Andrew Jackson always hated the English.

The courage and commonsense of his mother made a lasting impression on the boy who had never known a father. He treasured her words of advice, which were these: 'You can make friends by being honest, and you can keep them by being steadfast ... To forget an obligation or be ungrateful for a kindness is a base crime ... Never bring a suit at law for assault and battery or for defamation. The law affords no remedy for such outrages that can satisfy the feelings of a true man ... If angry at first, wait till your wrath cools.' 'The memory of my mother and her teachings', he said afterwards, 'were, after all, the only capital I had to start in life with.'

This was not strictly accurate, for soon after his mother's death Andrew received a small inheritance of three or four hundred pounds, from a relative in Ireland. But he went to Charleston when the war was over and promptly dissipated it, probably in gambling; he would allow nothing to infringe his birthright to be a self-made man. From Charleston he returned for only a brief spell to the Waxhaws and then moved to Salisbury where, ignoring his mother's wish that he should be a clergyman, he began to read the law. There he was remembered as 'the most roaring, rollicking, game-cocking, horse-racing, card-playing mischievous fellow that ever lived ... the head of the rowdies hereabouts'. But what was more to the point the reckless orphan acquired and employed an infectious charm: he was the natural leader of the young men and his 'ways and manners with young ladies' were long recalled as 'most captivating'. He profited by his friendships. First he completed his legal education in the well-stocked library of Colonel John Stokes, a former light of the North Carolina bar who had a silver knob instead of a hand. Then he persuaded John

McNairy, a fellow law student, who had been nominated a judge in the Western District of North Carolina, to appoint him attorney-general or public prosecutor in that district. In the autumn of 1788 with 180 dollars in hard money, half a dozen law books, a pair of pistols and a brand-new rifle Jackson set out in an emigrant train along a trail beset by Indians, which could only be crossed in safety with an armed escort, to Nashville in what was to become middle Tennessee. In Nashville he was to find a wife and win a reputation.

In 1788 when Andrew Jackson's caravan reached its journey's end at Nashville the outlying districts of North Carolina beyond the mountains were still primitive but were beginning to prosper. Gradually they had been wrested from the Indians and had been annexed by North Carolina in 1766. But the inhabitants of this area did not pay much regard to the government of North Carolina, which could do little to protect them from the surrounding Indians, and took care of themselves as best they could. They did not often dare move far from the blockhouse or the beaten track; frontier justice was rough, land was cheap, cash was scarce and opportunities infinite. The eastern half of the area beyond the mountains had for a time successfully broken away from the mother state under the guidance of a remarkable figure named Nolichucky Jack Sevier, a man of Huguenot descent and a mighty fighter of Indians, who had once brought his warriors across the mountains to inflict a crushing defeat on a British force at the Battle of King's Mountain and became in 1784 the 'president' of the independent state of 'Franklin'. Between 'Franklin', which ended at the town of Knoxville, and the middle and western territories in the rich Cumberland River valley, where McNairy and Jackson came to institute justice, lay the hazardous 180-mile wilderness trail by which they came. The three Cumberland counties (Davidson, Sumner and Tennessee) were but newly colonized and sparsely peopled. The twin founders of this Cumberland domain were Captain James Robertson and Colonel John Donelson. The latter was an old pioneer from Maryland who, after marrying a Virginian girl by whom he had eleven children and losing his money, was persuaded to bring his horde of relatives nearly a thousand miles by water into this new and

ATTORNEY-GENERAL—JUDGE

promising land. Though suffering severe losses at the hands of the Indians Donelson triumphantly kept his rendezvous with Captain Robertson in the spring of 1780. Five years later the veteran pioneer was himself murdered in the woods probably by his old enemies, the Indians, but his widow and family lived on in a blockhouse ten miles from Nashville. Among the daughters dwelling there was the attractive dark-haired Rachel who had married a man from Kentucky, Lewis Robards by name. Rachel had left her husband to go back to her mother at his own request, but later, jealousy yielding to desire, he had sought a reconciliation and joined his wife and mother-in-law in the blockhouse on the Cumberland. It was in a cabin belonging to this blockhouse that Andrew Jackson lodged with another young lawyer, John Overton, when he first came to Nashville.

Nashville itself was then a town of some two hundred houses and there were about five thousand persons in the whole settlement. The nearest town (Knoxville) was 180 miles away to the east, whilst the nearest place of any importance on the Mississippi, Natchez, was a thousand-mile journey by water. The five thousand settlers were surrounded by about sixty thousand Indians belonging to four different tribes, the Cherokees, the Creeks, the Choctaws and the Chickasaws. To the uneasy settlers the Charleston legislature that had dispatched McNairy and Jackson on their errand of justice must have appeared a long way off, and it was significant that they had named their country 'Mero' as a compliment to the Spanish Governor of Louisiana who was a good deal nearer and much more friendly. This anomalous position ended when (later) the settlement came under the direct jurisdiction of the Federal Government. Meanwhile the task of imposing justice must have been formidable. It was to the credit of McNairy and Jackson that they made the law run, cleaned the dirt out of the logwood courthouse, and superseded the lynch law that had hitherto prevailed.

In so primitive a community a lively man had ample chances to build his fortunes. Jackson was not obliged to confine himself to his official duties and his services were in constant demand in the courts where he proved himself a fluent, forceful and convincing speaker. One of his old friends described how 'when excited or angry he would pour forth a torrent of rugged sentences more remarkable for their intent to beat down the opposition than for their strict attention to the rules of rhetoric — or even syntax'. For his services he was usually paid in kind. In Nashville even the taxes were customarily settled in corn, buffalo meat or the like. Land too was cheap, plentiful and simple to transfer. Jackson once said that in the first eight years of his Nashville practice he 'took fees in land enough to make a county' and he received sufficient cattle and horses by way of pay to stock his first farm.

For outdoor excitement there were always the Indians to fight and Jackson was prominent in many a frontier affray. He did not, however, join in the biggest of all expeditions against the Indians, that organized by John Sevier in 1794 against the northern Cherokees, for it was not a campaign authorized by Congress to which the territory had then become subject — and Jackson had become a federal officer. The expedition was none the less successful and established peace on the frontier for a spell.

It was natural enough that in the frontier town the recognized means of settling questions of honour between gentlemen should be the duel. And not on the frontier only. For when in July 1806 Aaron Burr, the Vice-President of the United States, shot and killed Alexander Hamilton, the former Secretary of the Treasury, and escaped punishment, it sealed the propriety of seeking redress for personal grievances on the field of honour. Some fifty years later up in Illinois the peaceable Abraham Lincoln was obliged to accept a challenge, though his selection of 'cavalry broadswords of the largest size' as his weapons may be said to have reduced the affair to its proper proportions. Jackson's sense of proportion was never marked. The first story we have about his seeking to defend his honour by a challenge was actually in a law court where he thought he had been insulted by the opposing counsel during the hearing of a case while he was on his way to Nashville. The second instance concerned his landlady's daughter, the fascinating Rachel Robards. Her husband had grown jealous of the lodger's 'engaging and sprightly manners' — no doubt with reason — and his jealousy had reached such a pitch that the attorney-general was compelled to leave his lodgings. According to his friend and fellow lodger, John Overton, just before he left Jackson met Robards accidentally and a conversation beginning with mild remonstrances from the husband ended in fierce words and a challenge from Jackson. The challenge was refused and the irate husband carried his wife away from temptation back to his Kentucky home. But the pair found no bliss. And Jackson crossed over into Kentucky to help the lady flee back again from her husband to her mother. The husband soon came after his wife and when a fresh reconciliation was refused, announced that he would sue for divorce on the ground that she had 'lived in adultery with another man' since her 'desertion'.

Divorce was no simple matter in those days, and the first step that had to be taken was for the outraged husband to obtain permission of the Virginia legislature (since Kentucky was at that time part of Virginia) to bring his case to court. For some reason that had never been satisfactorily explained Andrew and Rachel assumed that the permission to sue that was granted in the form of a bill was in fact a bill of divorce; and so in August 1791 they became man and wife. They settled on an estate named Poplar Grove in a hairpin bend of the river Cumberland and for a time they were happy. In September 1793, however, after an inexplicable delay, Lewis Robards brought his divorce suit and it was disclosed to the citizens of Nashville that all unwittingly Andrew and Rachel had committed bigamy. On January 7th, 1794, another marriage ceremony was required to put matters legally right.

This curious and unfortunate beginning formed a cloud over the married life of Andrew Jackson that was never to be completely dissipated. Rachel, who for all her adventures was a shy and religious woman, would have liked after her wretched first marriage and the scandal of the divorce proceedings to fashion a life of quiet peace with the fearless hot-tempered Irishman who adored her; but, unluckily for her, Andrew Jackson was not that kind of man. By nature he was restless and ambitious and though he was often to protest that he did not want public office, it was soon to be thrust upon him. And as he rose higher and higher in the political scale the whole miserable story came out again and again to regale thousands of newspaper readers and to be repeated by mealy mouthed enemies who cried stinking fish. Finally Rachel did not obtain the consolation of children. Once she exclaimed in tears: 'Oh, husband! How I wish we had a child!' Andrew answered: 'Darling, God knows what to give and what to withhold.' They found some compensation in an adoption and in the frequent company of Rachel's numerous nephews and nieces. Andrew was a gallant husband and until the day of her death his anger would rise and he would neither forgive nor forget anyone who dared impugn the honour of his wife.

North Carolina was one of the last of the original thirteen states to enter the Union (November 1789) and in doing so she had gladly ceded to the jurisdiction of the Federal Government the two semi-independent outlying communities of 'Franklin' and 'Mero' which thus became a United States Territory under the Governorship of William Blount. The territory soon expanded to cover 60,000 inhabitants, enough to form a new state and in 1796 delegates from the east and the west forgathered in a constitutional convention to discuss how it should be named so that admission to the Union might be sought from Congress. Some favoured the name of Franklin, others that of Washington. Finally it was determined, with the approval of Jackson, to call it by the Indian name of the 'Great Crooked River', Tennessee, a word which, he said 'had as sweet a flavour on the tongue as hot corncakes and honey'. On June 1st, 1796, with the powerful support of Aaron Burr — a support that Tennesseans never forgot — Congress approved the admission of the new state into the Union. The hero of eastern Tennessee, Nollichucky Jack Sevier, became the first Governor, William Blount became a Senator, and Andrew Jackson, now a leading citizen of Nashville, was elected first Congressman. In the winter of 1796 he rode on horseback the whole eight hundred miles to Philadelphia to take up his new duties, arriving there on December 8th, in time to record his vote against too warm a tribute being accorded to President Washington, then on the eve of his retirement. In retrospect Jackson explained that he considered such an address to a President was a servile imitation of an English monarchical custom, by no means to be tolerated in a virgin republic. Jackson's antagonism to Washington had already been exemplified before he came to Philadelphia in a letter which he wrote attacking the President's 'unconstitutional conduct' over the Jay Treaty with England and demanding whether civil war might not follow the acceptance of the treaty. For although he had his reservations about Thomas Jefferson —

he fancied that the sage of Monticello lacked courage — he was a one hundred per cent anti-British and pro-French democrat.

The first impression of Andrew Jackson received by the House of Representatives was not very favourable. He was said to be 'tall, lanky, uncouth-looking' with 'the queue down his back tied with an eelskin' and the manners 'of a rough backwoodsman'. But those who looked more closely would have noticed the square chin and the intense blue eyes, indication of a firmness of character not lightly to be forgotten.

Representative Jackson carried out the first duty of a good politician by obtaining the sum of over 22,000 dollars for his state, as compensation for the expense incurred in the expedition against the Cherokees in 1794; in this transaction he had the valuable backing of James Madison and was also befriended by Albert Gallatin, who was to become Jefferson's Secretary of the Treasury. Apart from acquiring such useful friends, he was fully occupied during his short spell as Congressman and indeed he complained that because he was the sole representative of his state he was overwhelmed with committee work. On his way home after Washington's term ended he wrote to assure his wife that he meant to retire from public life and spend his days 'with you, the Dear Companion of my life, never to be separated from you again'. No doubt he sincerely meant this as he wrote — but Rachel was to be disappointed. For that very November 1797 he returned to Philadelphia, this time elevated to the role of Senator of Tennessee, replacing his friend, Blount. To his wife's brother-in-law, Colonel Robert Hays, he wrote on his way: 'I must now beg of you to try to amuse Mrs. Jackson and prevent her from fretting. The situation in which I left her (bathed in tears) fills me with woe.'

Of Jackson's early career as Senator little is known apart from one letter in which he said: 'It is true that the American mind should be awakened from its lethargy' and complained of 'the execrable system of Executive patronage'. Could he have looked up the passage of years to his own Presidency, however, his indignation might have been less pronounced. Another letter disclosed his interest in foreign affairs: he was hoping that Napoleon would successfully invade the British isles: 'Should Bonaparte make a landing on the English shore, tyranny will be humbled, a throne crushed, and a republic spring from the wreck.' But then suppose Napoleon made peace with England and turned his attention elsewhere? 'Should that happen, perhaps France may give America a sweep of her tail.'

Andrew Jackson's political outlook as a *pukka* Jeffersonian is preserved for us not in his speeches in Congress but in a letter which he composed three years later to examine the credentials of a candidate for the position of Tennessee Congressman. He asked him: 'Have you always been an admirer of the true Whig principles of '76? Have you always been an admirer of the State authorities? ... an admirer of the Constitution? ... opposed to standing armies in time of peace? ... inimical to a standing naval armament? ... opposed to foreign political connexions? ... to an extension of Executive patronage? ... an advocate for freedom of religion and the freedom of the press? ... friendly to economy in the public disbursements? ... a real Republican in principle and practice?'

In April 1798 Jackson obtained leave from Congress to attend to his complicated and neglected private affairs and when he reached home he resigned his seat. He threw himself into re-establishing his fortunes, deciding to combine the business of planter at his estate of Hunter's Hill (to which he had moved from Poplar's Grove) with that of merchant. To this end he sold land to acquire liquid capital, which took the form of some dubious notes from a Pennsylvanian Quaker. Taking in due course as his partner the husband of one of his wife's nieces, John Hutchings, the retired Senator opened his store with a flourish, offering home-distilled whisky as an attractive sales line. But in six months the new storekeeper and farmer executed another lightning transformation and became a judge of the Supreme Court of Tennessee.

For five years Andrew Jackson acted the part of a frontier judge, sometimes sitting with his fellows as an appeal court, sometimes going out on circuit; he was not required to make written decisions but earned the reputation of doing rough and ready justice. In his capacity as judge, as formerly in that of public prosecutor he imposed a healthy respect for the law upon his fellow western pioneers.

Whether attorney, farmer, senator or judge, Jackson retained the position he had won for himself as the political boss of middle

ATTORNEY-GENERAL—JUDGE

and western Tennessee, as Sevier was of eastern Tennessee. Between these two powerful men no love was lost; as early as May 1797 Jackson had written to Sevier to complain that the latter had called him 'a poor pitiful pettifogging lawyer'. In 1802 he exacted his revenge. Sevier (who at that time was not Governor) stood for the elective post of Major-General of the Tennessee militia. Jackson, having satisfied himself that there was nothing to prevent a Supreme Court judge from competing for the office and fancying himself in the novel part of soldier, put up against Sevier and defeated him by a single vote. Sevier was understandably incensed, for could he not boast of 'twenty-eight campaigns and twenty-eight victories', whereas his successful rival had never held any military rank higher than that of judge advocate? 'What,' he inquired, 'has this red-headed upstart ever done that entitled him to be military commander-in-chief of Tennessee?' In October 1803 (soon after Sevier had again been elected Governor) the two men met in Knoxville and angry words were exchanged — both volubly commending their own services to the state. Sevier is reported to have said to Jackson's face that he had never heard of anything Jackson had done to deserve such celebrity except for taking a trip to Natchez after another man's wife. 'Good God!' exclaimed Jackson, 'Do you mention *her* sacred name?' It was all their friends could do to prevent the two bosses of Tennessee from attempting to kill each other on the spot. Eventually the Judge returned to the sentencing of murderers and the Governor to his administrative duties.

In 1803 the Louisiana Purchase excited the hopes and desires of the men of the south-west, and Andrew Jackson bethought himself of fresh employment, more far-reaching than that of a frontier judge: he sought, and was strongly backed, for the post of Governor of the new Territory. In the spring of 1804 Jackson went so far as to pay a special visit to the new capital of Washington to stake his claim, but found the executive mansion was empty. Nevertheless he was optimistic, writing to his wife to tell her that he thought he would obtain the appointment and that they would be able to 'retire to some peaceful grove to spend their days in solitude and domestic quiet'. Andrew's notion of a peaceful grove was not exactly the same as that of his Rachel. In any case the President did not appoint him, and for the next seven years Jackson's lot was cast mainly in his own local theatre. Momentarily the eager voice of the new west was stilled, if not entirely quietened.

In July 1804 Jackson resigned his judgeship and became a planter once more, breeding famous horses, raising cotton, and exchanging the products of the west for the imports of New Orleans. He had his ups and downs. That same year he was obliged to sell his lands at Hunter's Hill to meet his debts and moved somewhat nearer to Nashville to a more compact property of over six thousand acres called the Hermitage. The house was a two-storeyed blockhouse with a loghouse nearby for guests, and around it lay the cotton and wheat fields, the Negro cabins and the precious stables that comprised the estate and earned its income.

Through all his financial vicissitudes and swift changes of role Jackson remained the Democratic boss of western Tennessee. In November 1803 the Tennessee legislature had decided to divide the state into two militia districts and Jackson had thus become the Major-General only of the western division. But his sphere of influence was widening. Jack Sevier, the flayer of the Indians, was now growing old and in 1809 a friend of Jackson, Willie Blount, began a spell as Governor which lasted for six years. Jackson carried out his duties as Major-General with unbridled dash: as early as 1803 (before the Louisiana Purchase) he had warned his volunteers to stand by in view of the menacing attitude of Spain; later he warned them that 'war with England must come soon . . . and that upon the strong right arms and the unerring rifles of the sons of Tennessee must fall the patriotic and glorious duty of defending the nation's integrity and their own firesides'.

There was one potential challenger of Jackson's supremacy. This was a handsome young man from Maryland named Charles Dickinson, who had been the pupil of Chief Justice Marshall and bore a reputation for polished manners and quick shooting. Dickinson soon picked up the dangerously malignant current gossip about Jackson, and asserted that the only military exploit that the Major-General had ever performed had been to capture another man's wife. Jackson warned Dickinson's father-in-law, Captain Erwin, of the painful consequences of such ill-considered observations. In 1805 a quarrel arose over the terms of the settlement following a horse race between Jackson's crack stallion

ATTORNEY-GENERAL—JUDGE

Truxton and Erwin's Ploughboy when Truxton had a walkover because Ploughboy went lame. A friend of Dickinson, Thomas Swann, started the round of insults that ended in tragedy. Jackson caned Swann, though unfortunately he tripped over in the process to diminish the dignity of the event, and virtually challenged Dickinson as the 'base poltroon and cowardly talebearer' acting in the background behind Swann. The final provocation was published in the local newspaper by Dickinson. On May 30th, 1806, the duellists met at a point just across the Kentucky border. Jackson rode there with the fixed intention of killing or being killed. He determined to let the younger man fire first — at a distance of only twenty-four paces — and to risk the consequences. Dickinson hit Jackson on the chest; Jackson then took careful aim and mortally wounded his opponent, who died that night. Returning home Jackson confessed that he had 'pinked me worse than I thought at first' and needed a month to recover. A namesake, writing to him that June perhaps spoke for posterity when he said: 'I must regret the loss of your antagonist, could have wished his wound had not been fatal.' Jackson never boasted and never regretted the deed.

The other outstanding adventure in the years following Jackson's resignation as judge arose out of Jackson's relations with Aaron Burr. We have already outlined Burr's bid to become 'emperor of Mexico' in the story of Thomas Jefferson. Jackson welcomed Burr to Tennessee as the 'always true and trusty friend' of the state. In 1805 Burr stayed with the Jacksons at the Hermitage although what version he gave of his plans is unknown. In any case, like most prominent westerners, Jackson gladly endorsed a scheme to acquire for the American Republic those portions of Spanish territory which lay outside the Louisiana Purchase. But he did not commit himself too far and when he learned through a visit from a certain Captain Fort that there appeared to be a plan on foot to divide the Union and to seize New Orleans he hastened to assert his innocence and loyalty. His suspicions, however, centred not on Burr, but on the Military Governor of New Orleans, General James Wilkinson who (as we know now) was in the pay of Spain. On November 12th, 1806, Jackson used his pen energetically: to the Governor of Louisiana he wrote that he feared that 'treachery had become the order of the day . . . Beware of the month of December'. To Senator Daniel Smith of Tennessee he said: 'I have no doubt but there is a plan on foot to take possession of New Orleans.' To President Jefferson he offered his services and those of his men. On January 15th, 1807, he wrote to a fellow Freemason: 'One thing is generally believed, that if Burr is guilty, Wilkinson has participated in the treason.' Burr, he added, had always maintained that if there was a war with Spain: 'He would obtain an appointment ... and revolutionize Mexico.' But he was persuaded that Burr was no more guilty of treason than he was himself. So he informed Jefferson's Secretary of War in a letter that fairly rattled with anger.

In the early summer of 1807 a subpoena was served on Jackson to appear before the court at Richmond, Virginia, as a witness in the case against Aaron Burr over which Chief Justice Marshall presided and where Wilkinson was the principal witness. This was at the time when war between the United States and Great Britain hung in the balance. Jackson's hatred of England spilled over and he announced that he would deliver a speech outside the courthouse: he did not hold his punches. 'Mr. Jefferson,' he said, 'has plenty of courage to seize peaceable Americans by military force and persecute them for political purposes. But he is too cowardly to resent foreign outrage upon the Republic ... Mr. Jefferson can torture Aaron Burr while England tortures our sailors ... A year or more ago I gave at a dinner to Aaron Burr in Nashville the toast — "Millions for defence; not a cent for tribute." They change that tune on this side of the mountains. Here it seems to be — "Millions to persecute an American; not a cent to resist England!" Shame on such a leader! Contempt for a public opinion rotten enough to follow him!' This stupendous speech — the authentic voice of western indignation — resounded throughout America. It was scarcely surprising that the prosecution dared not put Jackson on the witness stand. 'He can talk as well as shoot,' said one of his audience. 'Yes,' was the reply 'and he talks as if he was ready to shoot now.'

In 1808 Jackson's anger with Jefferson expressed itself in his support of Monroe against Jefferson's candidate for President, Madison. But having thus shot his arrow into national politics, Jackson for a time concentrated chiefly on the rapid repair of his private fortunes. Soon affluence smiled on the Hermitage. In

ATTORNEY-GENERAL—JUDGE

1810 Rachel adopted the orphaned offspring of one of her sisters and named him Andrew Jackson. Their family life unfolded itself joyfully. Mrs. Jackson (who, now a plump and pleasing forty, like Mrs. Washington senior, enjoyed a quiet pipe by the fire) proved a charming dispenser of southern hospitality at the Hermitage and Andrew found his excitements in drilling his militiamen, racing his horses, fighting his cocks and finally in 1811 in making ready to come to the aid of General William Henry Harrison in his campaign against the Indian chief, Tecumseh.

In 1812 the chance at last came for Jackson to demonstrate his military ardour. War with England was what the commander of the militia district of western Tennessee had always wanted. Two months before war was declared he penned at the Hermitage a stirring appeal to arms: 'Shall we, who have clamoured for war, now skulk into a corner? . . . Are we the titled Slaves of George the Third? the military conscripts of Napoleon? or the frozen peasants of the Russian Czar? No — we are the freeborn sons of . . . the only republic now existing in the world . . .' Alas! when five months later after the official declaration of war, on June 12th, 1812, the orders for the freeborn sons of Tennessee arrived, they were to take them hundreds of miles by water to New Orleans and place themselves at the disposal of — General James Wilkinson. Jackson loyally obeyed his orders and in the remarkable time of thirty-nine days brought his picked force of over 2000 men to Natchez, 150 miles north-west of New Orleans. Wilkinson did not welcome the eager militiamen who had really been sent there with a view to invading Florida and when the decision was taken not to pursue this plan the Secretary of War in Washington sent blunt orders to Major-General Jackson to dismiss his men from the public service. Jackson refused to disperse his division, which included some two hundred wounded, and leave it stranded so far from home. Paying for their supplies largely out of his own pocket he took them back again to Nashville. 'He's tough,' said his men, 'tough as hickory.' And from that time Jackson's nickname was to be 'Old Hickory.'

A rather shocking incident was to be the epilogue to the expedition to Natchez. Jackson's Chief of Staff was a man of first-class ability and marked oratorical power, Thomas Benton. Jackson wisely dispatched Benton to Washington to explain there why he had disobeyed his orders and to exact his expenses. But while Benton was away Jackson became unwillingly involved as a second in an affair of honour between a young friend of his and Benton's younger brother. Benton, hearing on his return an exaggerated account of Jackson's championship of his brother's enemy roundly condemned him for sponsoring a duel between 'young men who had no harm against each other'. Jackson threatened to horsewhip Thomas Benton, as he had caned Thomas Swann four years earlier. But Benton, who was now a lieutenant-colonel in the regular army, was of sterner stuff than Swann and a shooting affray ensued in September 1813, in which Jackson was severely wounded by the elder Benton. At one time it seemed as if Jackson would lose an arm in consequence. But at forty-five his constitution was of iron and his will unbreakable. And when he heard on his sickbed that the Creek Indians had risen and massacred two hundred and fifty persons at Fort Mims (Alabama) he at once determined to lead the men of Tennessee to avenge the crime. Like Oliver Cromwell, Andrew Jackson in his middle age was to win a soldier's reputation and through it ultimately to become the leader of his country.

2. MAJOR-GENERAL AND GOVERNOR OF FLORIDA (1813-1821)

The Indians who had carried out the massacre at Fort Mims belong to the Creek tribe and dwelt in the area to the south of Tennessee, which today lies in the state of Alabama. The massacre itself was a flare-up in the war between the white American pioneers and the Indian aborigines that had been continual since the dawn of American history. Some historians have blamed the Creek rising specifically on British agents; others have claimed that the Spaniards were concerned in it. One biographer of Jackson states that it was an example of that 'flagitious perfidy and dishonour that uniformly characterized the policy of England in her use of the Indians against us in our two wars with her'. It seems clear, however, that the celebrated Indian leader, Tecumseh who dreamed of a union of all red men against the persistent encroachments of the white, was the man who struck the spark. His dream of unity found an echo in the heart of a half-breed Creek leader named Bill Weatherford or 'Red Eagle' and the men who followed him were called Red Sticks after the crimson war clubs they carried.

Major-General Jackson struggled up from his bed of pain to lead his militiamen into the Creek country. 'The distressed citizens of that frontier who have escaped the tomahawk implored the brave Tennesseans for aid. They must not ask in vain.' Speed, he felt, was essential if the outbreak was to be checked. On October 7th, 1813, he took command at Camp Blount (so named in honour of Governor Willie Blount of Tennessee) and sent forward Colonel John Coffee, husband of one of Rachel's nieces, with his mounted infantry to establish contact with the enemy. The campaign is a notable exposition both of Jackson's military methods and his character. The problem how to beat the enemy, once contact had been established, was not a very difficult one. The Creeks were primitive in their tactics, had little ammunition, and were compelled to depend mainly on the bow and arrow. In every contest they were outnumbered. But the logistics of Jackson's advance were enough to cause a professional soldier to shudder. For to reach the Creek country the men of Tennessee had to go by boat as far as Huntsville, thence by portage across the 'American Alps' to the Upper Coosa River and thence again across trackless country to the Creek encampments, 300 miles from Tennessee. In Washington a plan for a three-forked advance had been concocted, but winter would have come — in fact it did come — before any such elaborate plan, which required difficult timing without adequate means of communication, could be put into effect.

Jackson therefore decided to strike on his own, trusting that the problems of supply would somehow be solved. He moved off to a flying start. On November 3rd Coffee destroyed the northernmost Creek village of Tallushatchee, killing about as many of the Red Sticks as they had killed white men at Fort Mims. Six days later receiving news through his well-organized spy system that friendly Indians were about to be attacked by the Red Sticks near the village of Talladega, Jackson ordered a forced march to the rescue and induced his primitive enemies to rush into a trap where they were overwhelmed by rifle fire; three hundred at least were killed out of perhaps a thousand, whilst Jackson lost only fifteen killed. At Talladega Jackson was but eighty miles from the heart of the Creek country, where there was a sacred hickory grove in which no white man had ever trod. But Jackson had outrun his communications and was obliged to withdraw to his advanced base of Fort Strother. There his real troubles began. His supply contractors had failed him and his troops mutinied. Jackson's men who originally numbered some twenty-five hundred divided into three brigades (each equivalent to a small modern battalion) consisted partly of volunteers enlisted for a year and partly of militiamen called out for three months. On one occasion he threatened to shoot the first man who moved; on another he said he would fire his solitary six-pounder gun on the mutineers. Jackson wrote to Governor Blount: 'The war is over, if a strong front can be presented' and to General Pinckney, his nominal superior commander: 'Had I been able to follow up immediately the victory at Talladega, the enemy would never have been able to recover from their defeat.' But the news of the mutinies spread gloom in the back areas and the Governor wrote to Jackson advising him to come home until the winter was over. He did not know his man. Jackson was set on his 'strong front' and retreat was not in his reckonings: instead of obeying the Governor's counsel, he told Blount exactly what he thought of his 'milk and water observations': 'Arise from your lethargy — despise the fawning smiles or the smarting frowns of such miscreants — with energy exercise your functions — the campaign must rapidly progress, or you are forever doomed, and the country ruined.' Blount accepted this rousing response in good part, and although for a time Jackson had to cling to his forward base with only two or three hundred men — the remainder having, in spite of all his exhortations, gone home — in the end reinforcements reached him in time for him to maintain his pressure on the Creeks. In January Jackson moved south and inflicted two fresh blows on the Creeks before retiring to replenish his supplies and further recruit his forces. By March he had at his disposal a force of some five thousand men, including a regiment of regulars, that very regiment in which Thomas Benton was lieutenant-colonel. Mrs. Jackson was appalled. 'I cried aloud', she wrote, 'and praised my God for your safety. How long, Lord, will I remain so unhappy? No rest, no ease. I cannot sleep. All can come home but you.' But it was the Creeks who had reason for fear. Neither a fractured hand nor recurrent dysentery nor lack of men and supplies could compel the ruthless amateur general to loosen his grip. On March 14th General Jackson ordered the shooting of a seventeen-year-old militiaman, Private John Wood, who, he thought, had tried to revive the dead embers of mutiny. On March 24th after he had located the main defensive position of the Red Sticks he gave his orders: 'Let every shot tell.' The Creeks had fortified an area of some 100 acres within a horseshoe bend in the river Tallapoosa and there Jackson prepared to annihilate them. He sent Coffee with his mounted infantrymen to the rear and friendly Indians to impound their canoes. His six-pounder was mounted on a strategic hillock and his regulars were held ready to storm the wooden barricades when the opportunity was ripe. Of eight hundred Red Indian fighting men who faced the assault that day at Horseshoe Bend (or Tohopeka) not one wounded brave survived to tell the tale: all were killed or taken prisoner. 'The carnage was dreadful,' Andrew told his Rachel. A few days later Bill Weatherford, Red Stick himself, rode into Jackson's camp to surrender. On April 28th Jackson was back at the Hermitage and a month later the Federal Government, shaken to the core by so speedy and so complete a victory, appointed him a major-general in the regular army. A new career had thus begun for this tough and relentless man. As his first task he imposed the peace terms, taking from the Creeks one half of their entire territory as a condign punishment and in order to secure the frontiers of western advance (Treaty of Fort Jackson, August 9th, 1814). By this means too he cleared a new route between Tennessee and the Gulf of Mexico.

In the Red Stick campaign we see many of the characteristics that were to make Jackson so compelling a figure on the national stage. His tenacious harrying of his enemy, his stubbornness, his refusal to be dissuaded from his plan of campaign because of the obstacles envisaged by his advisers, were ingredients in a recipe that were to fashion one of the strongest Presidents in the history of the United States. As in his duel with Charles Dickinson, so in his war with the Creeks, and so later in his mighty struggle with the United States Bank, Andrew Jackson gave no quarter and expected none.

ANDREW JACKSON

The Red Stick campaign had been one of the few positive successes on the American side in the first two years of the war of 1812 against Britain. This war, which began in June 1812, had come about largely because of the breakdown of international diplomacy and it was ironical that the British Orders in Council, imposing severe restrictions on American maritime trade and therefore acting as one of the most powerful causes of the war, were abandoned by the British Government five days after the outbreak of hostilities. The Federal Government had been ill prepared for war and had a very small army and navy, while the British, being engaged in a life-and-death struggle with Napoleon in Europe, could only spare limited resources for a campaign on the American mainland. The contest had therefore been chiefly confined to the sea, British depredations off the American coast being more than balanced by the daring attacks of United States frigates on English commerce ranging as far east as the Irish Channel. On land the Americans had captured Toronto in the spring of 1813, but an expedition against Montreal had failed. In 1814 the defeat of Napoleon had enabled the British to send reinforcements which eventually compelled the Americans to withdraw from upper Canada. Meanwhile command of the sea permitted small British expeditionary forces to occupy Maine and to sack Washington. It was three days before this latter event that Andrew Jackson arrived at Mobile, about 150 miles east of New Orleans in the Gulf of Mexico, to take up his new command. By that date the war was coming south.

The British plan appears to have been to take advantage of the discontent that they expected to find among the French, Spaniards and Indians in the Louisiana area to arouse antipathy to the war just as they had already created an anti-war movement in New England. Spanish Florida, though nominally neutral, offered them a possible advanced base, a fleet and expeditionary force assembling in the West Indies were to be the means. Their intentions were to be thwarted by two things, the skill of the American artilleryman and the restless energy of Andrew Jackson.

Jackson made up for what he lacked in orthodox military training by the speed of his moves and the strength of his personality when the time for action came. As one of his biographers says, he was, 'a man who could blunder against his opponent and then defeat him by sheer fighting'. His first decision was to destroy the hostile nest in Florida and in July he opened an acrimonious correspondence with the Spanish Governor, Don Matteo Gonzalez Manrique. The Spaniard retorted with counter-accusations, whilst expressing the hope that God would preserve Jackson for many years (as indeed He did). Jackson at once wrote to the Secretary of War, about to flee from Washington, asking permission to seize Pensacola, the Spanish town where the British were drilling Indians and near which, at Fort Barrancas, they had a naval base. 'How long', he demanded, 'will the government of the United States tamely submit to disgrace and open insult from Spain?' while he warned the government that the consequences of his 'hostile evasive spirit' would be 'an eye for eye, tooth for tooth, and scalp for scalp'. After notifying the Secretary of War of his 'lively emotions of satisfaction' at the successful repulse of a British amphibious attack on the fort guarding Mobile, he waited no longer but took matters into his own hands and marched his men to Pensacola.

On November 7th, 1814, after the Spaniards had fired on the messenger who brought Jackson's ultimatum, the American troops stormed Pensacola. Seven days later General Jackson was able to report to James Monroe (who had become Secretary of State in President Madison's Cabinet): 'The undaunted bravery of our columns displayed on entering the city with a heavy battery on the fort upon our right, the British flotilla on our left, strong block-houses and batteries in our front had drawn a tribute of respect from our enemies.' Jackson had feinted to the west of the town and then sent the bulk of his troops round to the east, thus surprising both Spaniards and the British naval force which was obliged to blow up Fort Barrancas and withdraw. 'I have broken up the hot-bed of the Indian war,' boasted Jackson. He then went to New Orleans, where his presence was urgently demanded and which he knew would be the objective of the coming British offensive.

Jackson has sometimes been criticized for going to Pensacola at all instead of moving at once to New Orleans; his object, he explained afterwards, was 'to clear his left flank of the enemy'. In any case his prompt action, taken without the authority of the government, impressed both friends and foes with his capacity and daring, eliminated a potential enemy base and stifled local defeatism in Louisiana. As soon as he reached New Orleans on December 1st he reorganized its defences: the city was put under martial law; and after a trip down the Mississippi he declared that 'with a few auxiliary batteries it can be made impregnable against any invading foe'. But besides the long approach up the river there were no less than five other water routes by which the enemy could advance on the city and Jackson had left himself little time to collect the men and guns that were necessary for its defence. Two days after Christmas the British under the command of Sir Edward Pakenham (brother-in-law of the Duke of Wellington) landed. It is yet another quirk of history that, unknown to the men who were to fight and die in the battles of New Orleans, on the following day at Ghent in Belgium a treaty of peace was signed which, when confirmed by the British Government and by the American President and Senate, was to bring this purposeless war to an end.

The presence of General Jackson had done something to cheer the panic-stricken city of New Orleans; he even impressed his lovely French hostesses and it was noted that he had 'two sets of manners, one for headquarters, the other for the drawing room'. But he had little time for the drawing-room, for every exertion was needed to meet the coming attack. Jackson felt confident that the enemy would first assault Mobile and then make a long detour to outflank New Orleans from the north. This fixed idea did not, however, materially influence his dispositions since with his limited resources he could not possibly defend every line of approach. Instead he took the wise military course of placing obstacles wherever he could and of keeping in reserve a reliable mobile force which he could send to any point of attack. This reserve included eight hundred mounted riflemen under his trusted relative by marriage and friend, now Brigadier-General Coffee, a Tennessee division, two regiments of regulars, dragoons from the Mississippi territory and the Orleans Carabiniers. As soon as he obtained authentic intelligence that five American gunboats which were responsible for the defence of Lake Borgne, 12 miles east of the city, where the British fleet anchored, had been overwhelmed and that the British had found an unobstructed route by which to advance inland, Jackson determined to go out to meet them and to attack them that very night. If he himself had been surprised by the British landing, he would counter promptly with another surprise. At eight o'clock on the foggy evening of December 23rd, with a force only about half the strength of his enemy's he inflicted a check on the invaders with the valuable support of an armed schooner whose guns fired on the British bivouacs from the Mississippi. He did not succeed, as he had hoped, in driving the British advance guard back into the lake and before daybreak he prudently drew off his men to a fortified line.

The position which Jackson's army now took up lay behind a disused canal, twenty-five feet wide and four feet deep. Two thousand Negroes had been put to work on strengthening this natural defensive obstacle and on building two further ramparts behind it. Taken aback by the fierceness of Jackson's riposte and by the need for reinforcing his own troops it was not until four days later that the English general carried out his next move. He then brought naval gunners from the British fleet in an attempt to silence the American artillery which had been firing from the river on his left and he ordered a reconnaissance in force to test the value of the main American defences. Two American armed schooners were successfully attacked, but the guns from one of them were saved and mounted on the west bank of the river. Next day there was a short skirmish to the right of the American line where, an English captain related: 'In the thick cypress forest and under the long Spanish moss not an Indian could be seen, and the sole evidence our troops had of their presence was the flashes of their rifles and the deadly effect of their aim. That was enough.'

The skirmishes and cannonades of December 23rd and 28th are sometimes described as battles, but the casualties were small and the events were mere preliminaries to the decisive struggle of January 8th when the British, now some seven thousand strong, launched a full-scale attack on the prepared American positions. Jackson had manned his defences skilfully, although he had only a motley army of about four thousand and insufficient arms or entrenching tools. (He had accepted the services of some local pirates as useful additions to his resources.) His line was less than a mile wide with its flanks resting on the river and on a swamp.

On the west bank of the river he placed a small force of militiamen under General Morgan of Louisiana to protect the naval guns there and to prevent any British outflanking move. In front of the canal he had eight batteries and the left centre of his line was protected to some extent by the cypress wood. The British commander finally chose somewhat reluctantly to launch a frontal assault on this excellent defensive lay-out. For he felt that owing to the nature of the ground in front of the canal he could not undertake a siege operation by constructing 'regular approaches'; that he needed to get to New Orleans quickly so as to obtain supplies; and he was confirmed in his judgment by intelligence that the American army was smaller than his and included a large proportion of militia. Surely, he consoled himself, whatever the obvious military dangers of a frontal attack might be, the veterans of Wellington's Peninsula campaign were capable of overcoming them.

From the beginning everything went wrong for the intrepid British. A detachment that was sent across the river to cope with General Morgan and silence the American cannon that had been annoying the British left was unduly delayed, the early morning fog which should have concealed the main assault lifted too soon, and the timing of two columns under orders to attack on the right and left simultaneously went wrong. As the first British column came forward bravely to the left of the cypress trees it was met by the fire of two batteries — an old Spanish eighteen-pounder and two six-pounders, and then by sustained rifle fire from the men of Kentucky and Tennessee. 'They couldn't stand it', observed an American regular, Major Butler, who was there. 'In five minutes the whole front of their formation was shaken as if by an earthquake... in less than ten minutes the first line of the enemy's column had disappeared, exposing the second, which was about a hundred yards in its rear.' The level plain of Chalmette yielded no cover to the British battalions as they advanced bunched together four ranks deep. 'Almost incredible as it may seem, this whole column numbering... 2500 or 2600 men was literally melted down by our rifle fire... No such execution by small arms was ever done before', concluded Major Butler, 'and I don't believe it will ever be done again.' General Pakenham and his second-in-command were killed whilst trying to rally their men.

GOVERNOR OF FLORIDA

Major-General Keane, who commanded on the left, was severely wounded in trying to save the day. From the American point of view there was only one blemish on the victory: the contest on the west side of the Mississippi went against them, Morgan's militiamen retiring before the attack of the British regulars. Jackson's mortification at what he called an 'inglorious flight' knew no bounds; but the American success on the main front soon relieved the situation. Eleven days after the battle the remainder of the British army decamped and began to re-embark in their ships and a month after that the citizens of New Orleans learned that the war was over. Perhaps the most satisfying experience in the whole of Andrew Jackson's life came when Major-General Keane of the British army humbly begged him for the return of his sword lost on the field of Chalmette. The orphan had exacted his revenge for the mother and two brothers who had died during the War of Independence.

It was indeed, as Jackson informed Monroe, an overwhelming victory in which the enemy had been cut to pieces. Against the British losses of nearly three thousand the Americans had only a handful of casualties. It was no wonder that Jackson thanked that Providence who always intervenes on one side or the other — but never on both — in the celebrated battles of history. But Jackson did not forget his men. On March 21st in a farewell address he expressed his 'joy, gratitude, and exaltation — these', he said, 'are the saviours of their country — the patriot soldiers who triumphed over the Invincibles of Wellington and conquered the Conquerors of Europe!' They had not all been patriots, however; for a month earlier he had upheld the sentence of a court martial condemning six militiamen from west Tennessee to be shot for mutiny.

Rachel Jackson reached New Orleans in time to share her husband's triumph. Before he left that city of grateful merchants and lovely women, he submitted decorously (if with suppressed anger) to a fine for contempt of court for defying a federal judge during the period of martial law. Then, as the summer of 1815 began, he returned with his wife and adopted son to Tennessee where he was greeted as 'the idol of the State and the hero of the nation'.

In November 1815 General Jackson went from Tennessee to

Washington to attend a conference on the reorganization of the American army now that the war was over. On his way he stopped at Lynchburgh in Virginia to partake of a banquet in company with the venerable Thomas Jefferson. No two men differed more in character and outlook than the high-tempered border captain and the intellectual idealist, though both in their own ways worked unselfishly to create a Greater United States. They never cared much for each other, for Jackson regarded Jefferson as a moral coward, while Jefferson appears to have questioned Jackson's fitness for the highest offices. But on this occasion they were reconciled, formally at least, both of them promising their support to James Monroe as the presidential candidate of 1816. Thus the old and the new Democratic leaders met, bowed and parted. In Washington Jackson agreed most reluctantly to the army being reduced in size and exuberantly defended to the embarrassed officials his high-handed procedures in New Orleans. When he got back home he learned that one of his aides-de-camp, John Reid, a young man of charm and promise, who had started to write the story of Jackson's campaigns, had suddenly died. Jackson selected a wealthy Tennessee lawyer, John Henry Eaton (of whom more later), to complete Reid's work on condition that the proceeds (a dollar a copy) should go to Reid's widow and children. Thus Jackson's first biography was published nearly thirty years before he died.

Jackson spent the next two years in improving the military resources at his command in expectation of a renewal of war in the south that he felt was certain to come. A few quarrels enlivened this phase as well as a fresh negotiation with the Indians. It was discovered that in the Treaty of Fort Jackson the General had blithely annexed four million acres of land that were the recognized hunting grounds of friendly Indians and did not belong to the beaten Creek. Jackson induced the Indians concerned to sell their lands, a transaction which earned the hearty approval of the Federal Government. Jackson himself is reported to have said of the outcome: 'Yes, yes; it is good — as far as it goes. But none of these treaties can last more than a score of years. The white race will by that time demand access to every acre east of the river (Mississippi) and they will have it too. Nothing can stop them. I feel sorry for the Indians. If the English would let them

GOVERNOR OF FLORIDA

alone they wouldn't make much trouble. They can lay all their misfortunes at the door of England.'

When Monroe was duly elected President, Jackson was indirectly approached with the offer of the Secretaryship of War. But he preferred to remain active in the field and to engage in a long-distance struggle with that department. He laid it down that all War Department orders to his subordinates should be directed through him, on the face of it an entirely reasonable stipulation, although the President would not admit it, since he maintained that it infringed the rights of the executive. Nevertheless Monroe begged Jackson to stay in command, and Jackson consented, for he foresaw trouble coming, trouble with which he knew how to deal. At Christmas 1817 the trouble came. The War Department ordered Jackson to take personal command of the frontier between Georgia and Spanish Florida where incidents conducive to war had taken place and the Seminole Indians and a group of escaped Negroes had insulted the star-spangled banner. Jackson had not the slightest doubt about what ought to be done, 'the whole of East Florida should be seized', he said — although without implicating the government. 'Let it be signified to me through any channel', wrote Jackson to President Monroe on January 6th, 1818, 'that the possession of the Floridas would be desirable to the United States and in sixty days it will be accomplished.' He knew that Monroe would not object to forcing the hand of the Spanish Government and a letter that Jackson had at this time from a friend in Washington easily satisfied him that he had the unofficial backing of the President for violating Spanish neutrality. In April therefore he crossed into Spanish Florida and at once arrested and executed (after courts martial) two British subjects for stirring up the Indians against the United States. 'Every principal villain', he informed Rachel, 'has been either killed or taken.' On May 28th he occupied Pensacola, capital of Florida, for the second time — though he denied that he intended to extend the territorial limits of the United States — and left Monroe's Cabinet to work out how to justify the accomplished fact and the unauthorized deeds. The majority of the Cabinet was perplexed about how to handle the baby thus placed squarely on its doorstep. The Secretary of War, Calhoun, even advised that Jackson should be put under arrest. For although of course the

United States Government wanted East Florida (who would not?) it was none too easy to explain away diplomatically the invasion of neutral territory and the summary shooting of British subjects living in a Spanish domain. Fortunately for Jackson he had a friend at court in the bold and intelligent son of John Adams, John Quincy Adams, who was now Secretary of State. In a number of State papers Adams managed to prove, at any rate to his own satisfaction, that Spain and Britain and not Andrew Jackson were in the wrong. And although the United States Government had temporarily to give up Jackson's conquests as pledges of good behaviour, this made little difference, for in February 1819 the Spaniards finally elected to sell Florida which they could neither defend nor keep in order. Jackson never doubted the absolute discretion of his conduct — later he was to convince himself that the President had actually ordered him to invade Florida — and just before the treaty of sale was signed he appeared in Washington to help brief his defenders in the House of Representatives. Though the attack on him was led by another southerner of genius, Henry Clay of Kentucky, motions of censure on his conduct were handsomely defeated. 'I fortunately arrived here', he wrote to his ward, Andrew J. Donelson, at West Point, 'in time to explode one of the basest combinations ever formed.' The Major-General, his blood cooled and his honour satisfied, then rode home after attending popular demonstrations in his honour in New York, Philadelphia and Baltimore. The southern planter personified the nationalist impulse of the American people.

It now seemed momentarily to the pious Mrs. Jackson that her husband would really carry out his often repeated threat to retire into private life; for in the spring of 1819 he devoted himself to building a new 'Hermitage' for her in a secluded meadow and supervised the laying out of a garden after the English style. His military pay afforded him protection against the customary financial worries of his class and he had his race horses to play with and a flock of guests to entertain. But he did not allow his interested gaze to be distracted from the problems of the frontier. And when it looked for a moment as if the Spaniards would fail to honour the Florida Treaty, he was at once ready with another daring proposal for Washington. Taking Florida, after all, was child's play — he had done that twice already — why not seize Cuba too?

The next time General Jackson entered Pensacola, however, it was in a new capacity; he was persuaded in March 1821 against his better judgment to become the first United States Governor of Florida. To the restless soldier the post was a sinecure, but he did not give it up until he had once more stirred this quiet Spanish town out of its sleep. As one of his biographers soberly observes: 'Jackson's administrative achievements were less striking than his quarrels.' On an appeal from a handsome mulatto woman named Mercedes Vidal — he always had a weakness for a pretty woman — Jackson proceeded to throw the former Spanish Governor into his own jail on the ground that he had secreted papers that proved the dusky beauty was an heiress. The Spaniards reacted to this with more vocal indignation than violence. Rachel Jackson who, despite her dislike of the climate, had accompanied her husband to Pensacola, soon realized with pleasure that she would not be required to stay there long. 'The office does not suit my husband,' she wrote to her brother, 'there never was a man more disappointed than he has been. He has not the power to appoint one of his friends, which I thought was in part the reason for his coming. But it has almost taken his life ... I was afraid there would be a rebellion, but the Spanish troops were all gone to Havana; only some officers remaining here yet. Rebellion would have been terrible. You know how he deals with rebellions. Let us thank the Lord there was none ... The glory of his office is nothing. I shall never forget how quickly the leaves withered of the laurel crown they put upon the General at New Orleans. There is but one Crown that never fades or withers. O, let us seek it while yet we may.' Alas, poor woman, how she hated the Sabbath-breaking Spaniards of Pensacola, almost more than she disliked the gay French of New Orleans. All she wanted in life was to have her hot-tempered husband safely anchored by the fireside at the Hermitage. But the victor of Tohopeka and Chalmette, the hero of New Orleans and the terror of the Indians, though he now resigned his commission and retired into private life, was one of the most famous and popular men in his country. As soon as the Virginia dynasty and the Adams family had exhausted their welcome from the

ANDREW JACKSON

American people, a representative of the new America, of the empire carved out in Tennessee, Kentucky, Louisiana and the Floridas, would be sought. And the American Moses was by no means hidden among the bullrushes.

3. PRESIDENTIAL CANDIDATE AND THE FIRST TERM (1822-1832)

Tremendous changes had been taking place in the United States since the day when Thomas Jefferson's second term ended and during the period when Andrew Jackson had moved from the Tennessee bar to the Florida battlefields. Irresistibly the frontier had advanced and as it advanced the nation had become divided into three distinct sections. In the north the 'Money Power', which had been Alexander Hamilton's god, had achieved new conquests: merchants and industrialists had prospered exceedingly; and millions of dollars had been made out of the fur trade and the mercantile marine. New York State, the most populous in the Union, was to be further benefited by the building of the Erie Canal, linking the Great Lakes and the Atlantic by way of the Hudson River, which was completed in 1825. In the south King Cotton reigned — Jackson's two plantations, the Hermitage and Melton's Bluff, which he owned in Alabama, both earned him his principal incomes from the cotton fields tended by Negro slaves. But most significant of all had been the development of the west, the virgin lands reclaimed from the forests beyond the mountains. Here the population had risen from a million in 1800 to two and a half million out of the total population of over 9,600,000 in 1820. Land was still cheap and even becoming cheaper, but there was a chronic scarcity of cash; the east provided the capital for the west, but the west could seldom meet its obligations and defaults both by individuals and banks were commonplace. A hungry and single-minded search for quick wealth drove the pioneers forward and little attention was paid to those arts and comforts that are the produce of a settled community, although Fenimore Cooper was soon to appear to record the romance of the Wild West.

Between 1812 and 1818 five new states (Louisiana, Indiana,

FIRST TERM

Mississippi, Illinois and Alabama) had been cut out and fitted into the Union, one slave state and one free state in turn, but in the latter year the question of admitting Missouri, which lay north of the line that hitherto divided free from slave states, threatened a political crisis. A compromise was reached, however, whereby both Maine, a free state, and Missouri, a slave state, entered the Union (bringing the total number of states to twenty-four) and it was agreed that henceforward slavery should be excluded from the territory acquired by the Louisiana Purchase north of the parallel 36' 30". Old Jefferson and others nevertheless foresaw that here was a problem that would have to be resolved or end in tragedy.

The author of the Missouri Compromise was Henry Clay, the Kentucky Congressman, who had led the attack on Andrew Jackson's methods of suppressing Indians in Florida. Clay, who was ten years younger than Jackson, had been born in Virginia and, like Jackson, was a self-made man. 'I know my deficiencies,' he once boasted (not altogether accurately), 'I was born to no proud patrimonial estate. From my father I inherited only infancy, ignorance and indigence.' He had studied the law under that same George Wythe, who had been Jefferson's friend and tutor. In 1797 Clay had migrated to Kentucky and ten years later won a place in national politics. By the eighteen-twenties Federalism was dead (if indeed it had not died on the Burr-Hamilton duelling field). But the Republican or Democratic party was divided between the conservative successors of Jefferson, like Madison and Monroe, who still wished to constrict the activities of the Federal Government and to practise peace, retrenchment and reform, and men like Clay, who sought a protective tariff and a system of 'internal improvements' (that is, the building of roads and canals at the national expense) for the benefit of the new America. It has indeed been said that the war of 1812 and Clay's carefully balanced protective tariff of 1824 were two political events which bound the United States together and offset the fissiparous tendencies of north, south and west. Clay, though no soldier, had been a 'war hawk' in 1811. Under these historical circumstances it was clear that the era when Virginia or Massachusetts always found the President of the United States would soon be over; that new parties must arise reflecting the economic changes of the times; and that a chief executive who appealed both to the south and west as well as to the 'underprivileged' of the north would one day rule America. There were several candidates. One was Henry Clay; Andrew Jackson was to be another.

As early as October 1815 Major-General William Carroll had written to ask Jackson if he were a candidate for President. At that time Jackson was perfectly content with Monroe with whom he was on the friendliest terms. But by 1825 Monroe would have finished his two terms, and who was to replace him? Most of the members of Monroe's Cabinet were keen candidates. John Quincy Adams, Monroe's Secretary of State, had claim of precedent to succeed. William Harris Crawford, the Secretary of the Treasury, who came from Georgia, was the candidate of the old unpopular Republican caucus, and was backed by Jefferson, Madison and Monroe. John Caldwell Calhoun, another southerner, the Secretary of War, also had high hopes. And outside the Cabinet there was always Henry Clay, the 'Kentucky gamester of politics'. Jackson knew for whom he would not vote — Henry Clay, his critic, and Crawford, with whom he had quarrelled when he was Secretary of War, to whom, Jackson announced, he would have preferred the Devil. Adams and Calhoun, both of whom he thought had backed him on the Florida question (for he did not then know of Calhoun's proposal for his arrest) he considered were at least respectable. But Jackson's friends had other ideas. If a southerner's turn to be President had come, why not the military chieftain himself, who was popular throughout the whole country? For this end they worked in their devious and devoted ways. Sixteen days after the Governor of Tennessee had presented the retired warrior with a ceremonial sword, the General Assembly in Tennessee dropped a bombshell into the political world by voting (July 20th, 1822) that Jackson should be nominated for the Presidency. Jackson was now fifty-five and suffered from the dysentery that he had picked up in his early fighting against the Indians. Rachel sighed: 'I do hope they will leave Mr. Jackson alone. He is not a well man ... he has done his share ... the Lord's will be done.' Still when Andrew turned his mind from his cotton crops and the dozen or so youngsters whom he was helping to educate, ambition stirred and the

FIRST TERM

old warhorse scented battle far off. In response to the Tennessee resolution he declared: 'The people have the right to elect whom they think proper, and every individual composing the republic when the people require his service, is bound to render it regardless of his own opinion of his unfitness for the office he is called to fill.' The quartet of candidates were perturbed at the news and a scheme was even hatched to divert Jackson on a mission to Mexico, which had become independent of Spain in 1819 and had acquired an emperor. Jackson refused the appointment on the unassailable ground that he did not wish to present credentials to a tyrant. In May 1823 in letters published in the press written in response to a gift to Rachel of a home-manufactured grass hat or bonnet from Philadelphia he disclosed that he was a protectionist. By the autumn of that year his own hat was in the ring. When his chief opponent in Tennessee Colonel John Williams — that 'subtle fiend', Jackson once called him — stood for re-election to the Senate at that time Jackson's friends induced him to let his own name go forward in opposition as the only method of defeating him. Jackson was elected without difficulty while very few of those in the Tennesee legislature who voted against him were subsequently re-elected. Having thus asserted his supremacy in his own state, Senator Jackson, somewhat to his own astonishment, found himself setting out to join the other presidential candidates in Washington.

In the capital Jackson impressed the pundits. He was at once appointed chairman of the Senate Committee on Military Affairs; he buried a number of hatchets; he voted for most of the protectionist duties, except for that on frying pans, and said that he would support the tariff 'so far as I believe it will tend to foster the means of national defence'. His vote was given too for federal expenditure on new roads which he considered could also be justified on the ground of military necessity. Nor did he prove the terror of the drawing rooms that some expected him to be. 'Great pains', he wrote, 'had been taken to represent me as [of] a savage disposition; who always carried a scalping knife in one hand, a tomahawk in the other ... instead of this they ... found a man of even temper, firm in his opinions advanced and always allowing others to enjoy theirs ...' He met his rivals amicably at dinner parties, even shaking hands with Henry Clay and, as he wrote to

Rachel, 'kept entirely aloof from the intriguers and caucus mongers, with a determination that if I am brought into that office (of president) it shall be by the free unsolicited voice of the people' (December 21st, 1823).

The free unsolicited voice of the people was by no means against Jackson for President. In the election of 1824 he obtained ninety-nine votes in the Electoral College against Adams's eighty-four, Crawford's forty-one and Clay's thirty-seven; Calhoun had dropped out of the fight to become vice-presidential candidate. It cannot be stated certainly whether Jackson had the majority of the popular vote, although this was probably the case. As no candidate had won a clear majority, the decision now went to the House of Representatives voting by states. The final vote depended on the way that three of the states which had voted for Clay now cast their ballots. From an early stage Clay had determined that he would use all his influence on behalf of Adams although he did not hurry to let his resolve be known; and Adams was elected. But before this happened a busybody friend of Clay had approached Jackson to sound him in a roundabout way whether if he were chosen President, he would appoint Clay his Secretary of State. Jackson replied: 'Go tell Mr. Clay, tell Mr. Adams that if I go to that chair, I go with clean hands.' Thus when Adams was elected with the help of the votes of the Clay states and Adams chose Clay as his Secretary of State, Jackson thought that the 'inference was irresistible': Clay had exerted his influence on behalf of Adams in return for a promise of office: the 'Judas of the West' had received his 'thirty pieces of silver'. American historians have not recorded an agreed verdict on whether or not there was a corrupt bargain. All the outsider can do is to note that a man of Henry Clay's talents was outstandingly qualified to be Secretary of State (was the post then such a prize?) and to observe that one of Jackson's deepest admirers could not bring himself to believe that a man of so upright a character as Adams could have been party to a dirty deal. Jackson himself believed it to his dying day. He resigned from the Senate and returned to Tennessee intending to smash Adams and Clay and to cleave his way to unchallengeable victory in the election of 1828.

Generalship consists largely in knowing how to make the best

FIRST TERM

use of one's staff. Ought one to be aware exactly how one's staff operates or to be content, if it achieves results? In organizing and directing the 1828 electoral campaign Jackson's staff was careful to conceal the seamy side from him. The backwoodsman was no fool; he had seen enough of life to grasp a great deal about it; and the manner in which he could baffle his enemies by keeping his temper at the right time and also by losing it at the right time was perfectly clear to him. Yet there was an air of innocence, which was assuredly not assumed — for it appears in his most intimate correspondence — about the way in which he believed that virtue lay all on his side and wickedness all on the other. Perhaps it was not so strange. For black and white are the primary colours of party politics, and party politics, so distasteful to the first American President, were now an essential of the American way of life. But certainly Jackson had reason to agree with one of his advisers that 'no man in this country, living or dead, has been abused to the extent that you have'. All the ghosts of his past were conjured up and paraded before his electorate. First, there was his birth: it proved necessary to obtain affidavits about the character of his mother, the site of whose very grave had been forgotten. Then there was his marriage: the story of bigamy and adultery was retold in all its inaccurate details: then came Jackson's duel with Dickinson, his relations with Aaron Burr, his execution of Private Wood, of the two Britishers in Florida, of the six Tennessee militiamen who had threatened mutiny:

>   All six militiamen were shot
>   And O! it seems to me
>   A dreadful deed — a bloody act
>   Of needless cruelty.

So versified the doggerel writers on the other side. Even the victories of New Orleans were attributed, much to Jackson's wrath, to James Monroe, while his Florida campaign was described as a deliberate and unjustifiable breach of orders.

In October 1825 Jackson resigned his seat in the Senate, an action which accorded with the wishes of his staff as well as his own. He paid a special visit to the Tennessee legislature for the purpose of explaining to them that since they had been good enough to nominate him again as presidential candidate in the next campaign, he was better out of Washington. He went on to urge that no member of Congress ought constitutionally to be allowed to accept office during his first term or two years after that. It was said that this was the longest political speech Andrew Jackson ever gave.

For Jackson the years of John Quincy Adams's administration were prosperous as well as exciting. One season he received the excellent price of thirty cents a pound for his cotton. He was pleased with a visit of the venerable General Lafayette to the Hermitage. His stables worried him a little. 'From the scarcity of money and the high prices at which fine horses stand', he wrote to a friend in 1828, 'I have almost determined to abandon breeding horses and turn my attention to mules.' His staff were all in favour of his keeping his thoughts on his farm — 'say nothing and plant cotton' was their tactical advice. While they were attacking President Adams for some incautious remarks about the federal role in his inaugural address and Henry Clay for proposing to send a delegation to a Pan-American conference, they did not want their leader to commit himself about policy — it was so easy to offend the south or the west or the north with a single unrehearsed sentence about the tariff or internal improvements. In the west Jackson was represented as a supporter of the American system of high tariffs and national improvements, but in the east as their enemy. The Jacksonians were content to fight the battle on their hero's record and even his slanderers, they reckoned, at least helped to keep his name vividly before the electorate.

Thus it came about that in this mud-slinging campaign there were few real principles involved. You were either a Jackson man or you were not. Neither of the contestants for the Presidency themselves appeared in the arena. Jackson took part in one celebration at New Orleans and that was all; otherwise he was confined to writing a few letters, for example, to assure an inquirer that he had 'presided for several years as Royal Arch Mason in the Grand Lodge of Tennessee'. President Adams was even more restrained, for he considered it beneath his dignity to fight. It was left to Henry Clay to rebut the charges of Adams's adversaries, to question the wisdom of appointing a 'mere military chieftain' to high office and, in general, according to the Jacksonians, 'to

FIRST TERM

manage Mr. Adams's campaign not like a statesman of the Cabinet, but like a shyster pettifogging for the defendant in a bastardy case before a country squire'.

On December 17th, 1828, the final results of the presidential campaign were known at the Hermitage: Jackson had beaten Adams by 178 electoral votes to 83, carrying every state south of the Potomac and west of the Appalachians, as well as Pennsylvania and New York. 'No man has ever had such a triumph before', Old Hickory was informed by his delighted lieutenants. John C. Calhoun was elected Vice-President.

On the same day that the wonderful news arrived, Mrs. Jackson was taken seriously ill. She had been ailing for a long time. Suffering from melancholia, her only pleasure had been to sit in an upper room by the fire, reading her Bible and smoking her pipe. Some said that the renewed slanders about her marriage had deeply upset her, but she was making ready to accompany Jackson to Washington on December 22nd when her heart gave out. Jackson could not believe that she was dead and kept vigil by her body all that night. No political questions could be raised with him until on Christmas Eve the funeral ceremonies were completed. By her graveside the widower said: 'In the presence of this dear saint I can and do forgive all my enemies. But those vile wretches who have slandered her must look to God for mercy.' According to one of the Negro domestic slaves at the Hermitage, thenceforward every night 'the General would kneel before the picture of Miss Rachel and tell his God that he thanked Him to spare his life one more night to look on the face of his love'.

Thus it was with a broken heart, as he confided to his old friend, John Coffee, that President Jackson travelled to take up his duties at Washington and he refused to pay the customary courtesy call on the retiring President on the ground that Adams had been responsible for the continued attacks on his wife's name. Yet the arrival of Jacksonian Democracy in the federal capital afforded a unique spectacle. Thousands of backwoodsmen invaded the city and the surrounding towns to proclaim their hero. 'I never saw anything like it before', said Senator Daniel Webster, who belonged to the other side. 'They really seem to think the country is rescued from some dreadful peril.' Jackson's Cabinet did not impress. Martin Van Buren, the secretive and intelligent boss of

ANDREW JACKSON

New York, 'the little magician' who had got aboard the bandwagon in excellent time, was appointed Secretary of State. Senator John Eaton, chief of Jackson's personal staff, was given the War Department — not an onerous duty. The little known Samuel D. Ingham of Pennsylvania went to the Treasury; a clever Georgian lawyer named Berrien became Attorney-General; and John Branch, a former Governor of North Carolina, attended to the Navy. All Jackson considered to be 'able amiable men'. Of the eleven thousand minor offices in the President's gift some nine hundred were cleared of their incumbents to make room for the seekers after loaves and fishes, thereby finally establishing the spoils system in national politics. Jackson called this process 'cleansing the Augean stables'. After the first inaugural address (carefully worded to offend none) a mob followed their leader into the White House, overwhelming the social *élite*. 'It would have done Mr. Wilberforce's heart good to have seen a stout wench eating in this free country a jelly with a gold spoon at the President's House', so Van Buren was informed. Jackson quietly withdrew while the populace helped themselves from tubs of punch on the presidential lawn. Thus was ushered in a new and significant era in American history.

There are times in the political history of most countries when a group of astute men eager to run the government but lacking a popular leader in their own ranks will search for a figurehead behind whom they can creep into office, gaining the realities of power while he has only the shadow. It is a dangerous game; for the leader they have picked may be exposed as a man of straw or — worse still from the point of view of the promoters — prove to possess unexpectedly stubborn ideas of his own. In modern Europe we have experienced two such figures of straw — Hindenburg and Pétain, both military heroes: and in Hitler we have seen the dog that bit the hand that fed him. Unquestionably there were some politicians behind General Andrew Jackson who expected to exploit a heart-broken and ageing military hero for their own profit. But also grouped around the new President were a number of able radical-minded reformers eager for a new political deal. These men were called by Jackson's opponents his Kitchen Cabinet. They did not expose themselves in public more than they could avoid; but they were said to form 'the power behind the throne greater than the throne itself'. The truth would appear to be different. In spite of his loyalties, his pig-headedness, his vanity, his romanticism and his simple faiths, Andrew Jackson was no man's fool. He used the clever journalists and other members of his Kitchen Cabinet just as much as he needed them to carry through his own policies. In the words of Professor Schlesinger, they gave the 'driving energy' to Jacksonian democracy.

In Jackson's official Cabinet — as distinct from his Kitchen Cabinet — there were, apart from the Secretary of State, Martin Van Buren, a collection of mediocrities. John Henry Eaton, the Secretary of War, 'my best friend', as Jackson once called him, was the link between the Kitchen Cabinet and the actual Cabinet. Eaton had a vulnerable point — and that was his second wife. Margaret Eaton was the attractive daughter of a Washington boarding-house proprietor, in whose establishment Jackson had stayed when he came to the capital as a Senator in 1823. After various youthful amatory adventures she had been swept off her feet by a handsome young sailor named Timberlake with fair hair and a propensity for getting his accounts muddled. She had made a favourable impression on Jackson: 'Mrs. Timberlake', he reported home in December 1823, 'plays on the piano delightfully and every Sunday evening entertains her pious mother with sacred music.' Her looks rather than her music exerted an even more exciting impression upon Senator Eaton who was a widower and shared the same boarding-house. He showed his interest by helping her husband to straighten out his accounts and stick to the sea. After Timberlake died in 1828 Eaton married the widow apparently under some pressure from his friend, Jackson. Margaret Eaton was an ambitious young woman and when her husband joined Jackson's Cabinet it might have seemed that she had all she wanted.

Unfortunately Washington society decided to cold-shoulder Mrs. Eaton. The men did not much mind if she had been Eaton's mistress before he married her, but they drew the line at her becoming his wife. The ladies maintained that she was not chaste; they considered that she was vulgar; and they recognized that she was beautiful. Nothing was better calculated to arouse the ire of

Andrew Jackson than this organized boycott of his best friend's wife. Had he not spent over thirty years in fighting aspersions on the honour of his own wife, whom calumny had driven to the grave? Eaton had stood by him and he would stand by the Eatons. Moreover he regarded the attack on the Eatons as a move directed against himself not only by his political enemy, Henry Clay, but also by 'treacherous friends'. 'These are the men who cry out principles, but who are on the scent of Treasury pap. And if I had a tit for every one of these pigs to suck at, they would still be my friends. They view the appointment of Eaton as a bar to them from office . . . I was elected by the free voice of the people . . Major Eaton was necessary to me . . . Mrs. Eaton is as chaste as those who attempt to slander her.' But the rot spread into his own Cabinet and even into his own family. Clay, at first blamed for the conspiracy, was succeeded in Jackson's mind by his own Vice-President, John C. Calhoun. On January 29th, 1830, the President addressed a serious State paper to his Cabinet on the subject: 'I will not part with Major Eaton from my Cabinet, and those of my Cabinet who cannot harmonize with him had better withdraw, for harmony I must and will have.' The Secretaries hastened to explain that they had no control over their wives' prejudices.

Meanwhile Jackson had discovered something else distasteful about Vice-President Calhoun; he found that he had won his friendship on false pretences, for he had really been against him over his invasion of Florida in 1818, although he had conveyed the impression that he had been Jackson's supporter. Clay and Calhoun then were tarred with the same brush. Moreover Calhoun — 'mean, vindictive and cowardly' — had tampered with his Cabinet. The 'able amiable men' of 1829 became by 1831 'puppets' and 'Judases'. There was nothing left to do but break it up. Van Buren and Eaton resigned and the other Secretaries were sent for by Jackson and told that they were dismissed. 'Calhoun and his puppets,' he then explained, 'male and female, have been secretly at work to destroy me and they have been too successful to blind my connections and part of my family, and would have effected it . . . I have always viewed those who secretly pirate upon female character worse than the pirates on the high seas . . .' Eaton and his provocative lady retired to Tennessee. Van

FIRST TERM

Buren went to England. A brand-new Cabinet took their place. And Jackson, relieved from the preoccupation of defending Mrs. Eaton's morals, was able to concentrate upon affairs of State.

Four big political questions dominated Jackson's first term, the reduction of the national debt, internal improvements, the future of the United States Bank, and the tariff. Many of the wire-pullers behind the new President expected him to favour internal improvements and had hoped to dip their hands into the pork barrel. But just as Jackson proved less amenable about patronage than they had hoped, he was also unexpectedly obstinate about internal improvements. It is true that in the previous Congress he had voted as Senator for building roads of military value, but as President he was primarily anxious to reduce the national debt and, secondly, doubted the constitutional rightness of spending federal funds in benefiting the individual states. That Jackson should be opposed to internal improvements was contrary to the desires and expectations both of Eaton and Jackson's western supporters and of many highly respected Senators and Congressmen. An enjoyable era of log rolling had been foreseen — 'you back my canal and I will back your road'. This prospect suddenly vanished when the President vetoed the Maysville Road (Kentucky) Bill and the Washington Turnpike Bill. 'The veto', wrote Jackson to Van Buren, who had counselled it, in July 1830, 'has become what my enemies neither wished, or expected, very popular. I have no doubt but it will be sustained by a large majority of the people.' And it was.

In his efforts to abolish the debt and to resist the expenditure of federal funds on state projects Jackson trod in the footsteps of Jefferson. He did so too in his campaign against the National Bank. It will be remembered that Jefferson had strongly objected to the idea of a national bank when it was first put forward by Alexander Hamilton, but had been overruled by Washington. This bank had been allowed to die, but in 1816 a second bank had been incorporated with the sole right to keep (and use) government deposits and to lend money to the government. One-fifth of the capital had been subscribed by the government and one-fifth of the directors were government nominees, but the moving spirit behind the Bank was its president, the able and cultivated Nicholas Biddle, who directed its operations in a dictatorial fashion from a Greek temple in Chestnut Street, Philadelphia. The Bank represented everything that the western pioneers most disliked: to them it was a soulless creditor stifling the enterprise of hard-working debtors. To the eastern working-class leaders too it was a bloodsucking monopoly, and many regarded it as a standing danger both to the rights of individuals and of states. The west would have preferred state banks under local control, but Jackson himself was opposed to this idea also, and inclined to think that no banks should have the power to issue notes, that there should be no currency but coin. Although the Bank's charter was not due to expire until 1836, after his first term ended, Jackson told Congress in his first annual message in 1829: 'Both the constitutionality and expediency of the law creating this Bank are well questioned by a large proportion of our fellow citizens; and it must be admitted by all that it had failed in the great end of establishing a uniform and sound currency . . .' and he went on to suggest the foundation of another bank not open to these objections. Such a bank, he confided to his intimates, would be limited to the ten-mile square which enclosed the federal capital (the District of Columbia) and would be allowed branches elsewhere only with the permission of the states. In fact the absence of a uniform and sound currency was scarcely the fault of the existing Bank as it did not have the exclusive right to issue notes and indeed tried to discourage the state banks from the miscellaneous issue of notes. To the impartial historian it would appear that the Bank had performed a useful service in assisting the expansion of American trade and commerce and financing the work of the Treasury. Jackson's attack on the Bank was directed and sustained against the advice of the majority of both his Cabinets and, in particular, of his first two Secretaries of the Treasury. But although Jackson as a 'hard money' man was inspired by economic objections to the Bank, his main public criticisms of it were on political and constitutional grounds and, in choosing these grounds his instincts did not fail him, whilst Henry Clay, who constituted himself the champion of the Bank, and hoped to win the next presidential election on this question, backed the wrong horse. With a few exceptions all the most influential orators of the day were ranged on the side of the Bank. But it was to be proved that Jackson

FIRST TERM

knew how to appeal over the heads of the politicians to the majority of the electorate.

On the tariff Jackson's views were more fluid and less pervasive. In his first inaugural address he had argued that import duties should be equitably distributed so as to affect agriculture, commerce and industry equally 'perhaps the only exception' being 'products essential to our national independence'. He had inherited a very high tariff from the former administration. The tariff of 1828 had imposed heavy duties both on manufactured goods and raw materials and was designed for electioneering purposes rather than to be a genuine instrument of fiscal reform. It had been passed somewhat to the dismay of its promoters and at once aroused an outcry in the southern states where it hit business severely. The centre of the criticism was South Carolina, Jackson's native state, and the leader of the resistance movement was Vice-President Calhoun. A document secretly written by Calhoun (the 'South Carolina Exposition') asserted that the tariff was not only inequitable but unconstitutional (for the Constitution did not in so many words empower the Federal Government to impose protective duties) and maintained that individual states had the right to call conventions which could veto or 'nullify' so obnoxious an act. It was this doctrine of 'nullification' rather than his attitude to Mrs. Eaton or to Jackson personally that made Calhoun so dangerous an opponent of the administration. Jackson was not concerned with the profound historical and constitutional theories that lay behind the question: he laid hold of the essential point that 'nullification' was a threat to the Union. On April 13th, 1830, the President explained his position in offering a toast at a banquet in memory of Jefferson. 'Our Federal Union,' he proposed, 'it must and shall be preserved.' Calhoun answered with another toast: 'The Union — next to our liberty the most dear.' It was recognized that the South Carolina Nullifiers, however drastic their methods, had substantial justice on their side, and in 1832 Congress scaled down the tariff of 1828 while preserving its protective structure; and a year later Henry Clay started to press through the Senate an even more moderate tariff bill. Although the ground was thus being cut from under their feet the South Carolina extremists, having tasted blood, on November 24th, 'nullified' both the tariff acts of 1828 and 1832.

It was now that Jackson moved. On December 10th, 1832, he published a skilful proclamation condemning the Nullifiers and asking Congress (by implication) for power to levy the duties by force if necessary. He let it be known that if this power were refused he would upon his own responsibility raise a military force to compel South Carolina to obey. 'Tell them,' he is reported to have said, 'if one South Carolina finger be raised in defiance of this Government ... I shall come down there and once I am there, I will hang the first man I can lay my hands on to the first tree I can reach.' Privately he told his Secretary of War on December 17th: 'If I can judge from the signs of the times, Nullifications and Secessions, or the language of truth, *disunion* is gaining strength; we must be prepared to act with promptness and crush the monster in its cradle before it matures to manhood.' How far Jackson's precautionary measures and threats of force and how far Henry Clay's much more moderate tariff bill (passed by both Houses on March 1st, 1833) were responsible for the capitulation of South Carolina is hard to estimate. But in January the South Carolina Convention suspended and on March 15th repealed the ordinance of nullification, and all sides were able to claim a victory. It had always been an inviting speculation what would have happened if Jackson had been in office when the American Civil War — logical successor to the nullification movement — broke out. It seems likely that he would have quickly moved south at the head of an army and struck a military blow in relief of Fort Sumner. He would certainly have gone to Charleston with crushing strength in 1833 if South Carolina had not yielded.

Anger with Calhoun, the father of nullification, and determination to prevent the recharter of the United States Bank decided Jackson to stand again for the Presidency in 1832. As soon as his resolution was known, Henry Clay advised the Bank to apply for recharter and a bill for that purpose was passed by both Houses. The President at once vetoed it and the future of the Bank became the main subject of controversy during the election. But the election was also fought on Jackson's record. Mrs. Eaton's chastity and the spoils system were among the other topics engagingly discussed by the opposition press. The majority of the people relied on 'Old Hickory'. They appreciated his firm stand against the Nullifiers, against the 'monster bank', and against the log-rollers. And it was the electorate who spoke. For the first time in the history of the United States all the presidential candidates were nominated by national conventions chosen by the people and not by a Congressional caucus or by the state legislatures. Henry Clay was the candidate of a new party, the National Republican party. Martin Van Buren, whose appointment as American Minister to Great Britain had been rejected by the Senate, much to Jackson's disgust, was his running mate as Vice-President as well as his openly avowed choice for succession to the presidency in 1837. A third candidate stood on the odd platform of opposition to Freemasonry (Jackson of course was a Mason). Jackson swept back into office with a four-fifths majority (219 electoral votes to Clay's 49) although the popular majority was less marked. With his authority thus confirmed he was able to return to the work of dealing with the Nullifiers. But that he was not the man of blood and iron sometimes pictured by his enemies was shown when he decided on the eve of his second term to sign Henry Clay's tariff bill — even although it had been opposed by Jackson's own supporters in the Senate — and this act by removing the southerner's immediate grievances helped to preserve the Union for a generation.

4. JACKSON'S SECOND TERM AND RETIREMENT (1833-1845)

Although his wife was dead and he had no children, Andrew Jackson was never really lonely. Not only did he find a constant and absorbing interest in public affairs, which, because of his temperament, took on the form of an ever recurring struggle with the devil, but he was surrounded both by cronies of his own generation, chiefly retired officers of his campaigning days, and by representatives of the next two generations after him. Three young men, all his namesakes and wards, with their families, provided sources of companionship, pleasure and sometimes perplexity. The most promising of the three was Andrew Jackson Donelson, a nephew who had been on his staff when he was Governor of Florida and afterwards acted as his secretary. Donelson had married Emily, a niece of Rachel Jackson, and she proved to be a girl of high spirit and independent mind. Because Rachel had intended to take Emily Donelson with her to the White House to assist her in the duties of hostess, Jackson had brought the Donelsons to live with him there. But Emily refused to be friendly with the redoubtable Margaret Eaton; her husband supported her, and for a time the young couple were exiled in Tennessee. During Jackson's second term they returned with their three young children to the White House where they both proved valuable aides. Emily's death of tuberculosis at the age of twenty-eight cast a dark shadow over the closing months of Jackson's Presidency.

Another of Jackson's wards was the son of John Hutchings, who had been his partner in the Nashville store. Andrew Jackson Hutchings had failed to distinguish himself at college, but after he came into the estates carefully preserved for him by his guardian he became an excellent farmer. He was the recipient of a remarkable letter from the President in April 1833 on the subject of marriage:

> One word to you as to matrimony — seek a wife, one who will aid you in your exertions in making a competency and will take care of it when made, for you will find it easier to spend two thousand dollars than to make five hundred. Look at the economy of the mother and if you find it in her you will find it in the daughter. Recollect the industry of your dear aunt, and with what economy she watched over what I made and how we waded through the vast expense of the mass of company we had. Nothing but her care and industry, with good economy could have saved me from ruin — For economy and prudence I would bring to your view General Coffee and Polly.

One fancies it was not the 'economy' of his future mother-in-law which had induced the young Nashville attorney-general over forty years before to travel hundreds of miles to help his Rachel run away from her first husband. But Hutchings took the advice —for he married Polly Coffee.

The third nephew who bore Jackson company was his adopted son, Andrew Jackson II, who was nineteen when Andrew Jackson senior became President. Andrew junior had always been petted and spoilt and must have been a disappointment to his father who

SECOND TERM AND RETIREMENT

had designed him for the Presidency. Perhaps he had asked too much of him, but at any rate he rejoiced in his son's wife, Sarah, a charming Philadelphia Quakeress, and especially in their daughter Rachel, who was, he said, 'as sprightly as a little fairy and lively as a little partridge'. He put them in charge of the Hermitage while he was still in Washington. The young man showed a singular inability to manage so large an estate, for he ran into debt, did not make the best of the crops, and allowed himself to be outsmarted when he repurchased the old Jackson estate of Hunter's Hill. A stream of letters flowed from the White House to the Hermitage: 'Why will you not, my dear Andrew, attend to my admonition about your money matters — never incur debts when you have the money to discharge your contracts?' 'You are entering into life, unacquainted with the world, and the duplicity of mankind.' 'My son, why will you not learn to transact your affairs like a man of business?' The young man's extravagance and carelessness were to some extent mitigated by the husbandry of a good overseer. The President's main concern with the Hermitage overseers was, however, that they should treat his Negroes compassionately and the first thing he asked his friends who went there to report on was the health of his slaves. In October 1834 the Hermitage was burnt down and became a total loss. With reluctance Jackson consented to its being rebuilt after a different pattern from that which his wife had known, with a handsome white pillared front that still survives. The President's admirers wished to meet the cost of the rebuilding, but he proudly refused. Nevertheless, — like Washington and Jefferson — Jackson had to spend most of his retirement in re-establishing his estate and fortune.

The White House also underwent some structural changes at this time which made it a much more comfortable place to live in. The many guests who were entertained there were impressed by the elegance of the upholstery and lavishness of the meals. The President himself, it was noticed, was limited to the simplest fare, for he suffered from chronic indigestion as well as intermittent headaches. But the vigour both of his body and his mind enabled him to throw off even the most serious illnesses and to scatter medical advice among his family and friends. Nothing is more touching than the picture of the ageing statesman handing out

ANDREW JACKSON

doses of medicine to the children whose presence lighted the last days of his residence in Pennsylvania Avenue.

If in his private life affairs went on the whole more smoothly during his second term than his first, Jackson still had considerable troubles with his official family — the Cabinet. After he had dismissed his first Cabinet because his Secretaries' wives had refused to invite Margaret Eaton to dinner, he collected a somewhat abler team. But the way in which he treated the members of his Cabinet was scarcely calculated to encourage the best men to serve him. He regarded them as junior officers whose job it was to furnish periodic reports on their own special duties and receive their orders from him rather than that of counsellors of State. If he sought advice that he was prepared to weigh impartially he usually turned to his Kitchen Cabinet rather than to his Secretaries. Because of differences over the Bank question he had to change two Secretaries of the Treasury, while the direction of foreign policy he kept largely to himself. He found one congenial spirit in Roger Taney of Maryland, who came into the Cabinet as Attorney-General and was nominated Secretary of the Treasury in the latest stages of the battle over the Bank. Taney both shared the President's views and offered wise suggestions; Jackson found him a 'sterling man' and was very angry when the Senate rejected his nomination to the Treasury. With factiousness the Senate also refused to confirm Taney's appointment as a judge, but when the elections of 1834 produced a more friendly Senate Jackson named him Chief Justice of the Supreme Court, a choice that was approved and thus he succeeded Chief Justice Marshall. Only one member of the Kitchen Cabinet was promoted to the official Cabinet after the departure of John Eaton: this was Amos Kendall, a former Kentucky journalist, who became Postmaster-General in 1835. In Taney, Kendall and Benjamin F. Butler, who took Taney's place as Attorney-General, President Jackson at length had a first-class staff with which to engage in his fight to destroy the United States Bank, a fight that occupied most of his energy during his second term.

It is necessary to understand clearly the reasons why Jackson was so vehemently opposed to the renewal of the charter of the United States Bank. A somewhat childlike belief in the virtues of 'hard money' lay at their base; but the public grounds of his criticisms were mainly constitutional, political and moral, for hard money cut no ice in the west. The Bank had been incorporated by an act of Congress and in two important test cases the Supreme Court had decided that because it was a federal creation the individual states had no power over the branches of the Bank set up within their borders. Since the Bank used its influence and resources to restrict the note issues of the state banks by compelling them to keep adequate reserves of gold and silver it was unpopular in many states, particularly in the south and west where illimitable credit was the fulcrum of economic life. Politically there was no question that several of the directors and officials were anti-Jackson men, although the Bank as such did not actively combat Jackson's election in 1828. Lastly stood the moral argument that the Bank, as a monopoly, soullessly exploited the temptations to which all flesh is heir so as to swell its own profits and to corrupt the hard-working though innocent pioneers and toilers for the comfort of the idle middlemen of the eastern cities. 'Those who borrow', it was said, 'are encouraged in their extravagant modes of dressing and living which are far greater than their means will justify. Many are building little palaces in very expensive style, and the children of many are dressed as though they were the sons and daughters of princes . . . what may remain of the wrecks produced by these splendid follies will after a few years be seized by this Mammoth Bank.' Amos Kendall summed up the Jacksonian position by asserting that the Bank 'impaired the morals of our people, corrupted our statesmen and was dangerous to liberty'.

These arguments were set out by Jackson in the message he sent to Congress when he vetoed the bill to renew the charter of the Bank before the election of 1832. The constitutional case against the Bank was cleverly expounded and if this involved a direct attack on the Supreme Court, that after all was in tune with the Jeffersonian tradition: 'The opinion of the judges', the veto message had observed, 'has no more authority over Congress than the opinion of Congress has over the judges, and on that point the President is independent of both. The authority of the Supreme Court must not therefore be permitted to control the Congress or the Executive when acting in their legislative capacities, but to have only such influence as the force of their reasoning deserves.'

As soon as the election, in which the future of the Bank had loomed so large, had been won, the President submitted a memorandum to his Cabinet (March 19th, 1833) explaining his plans. The 'results of his reflections,' he stated, 'were that the Bank charter should not be renewed', that the 'ground gained by the veto' should be maintained, that a new national bank should be established in the District of Columbia with the right to open branches elsewhere though only with the permission of the states — but that such an institution should be recommended only after a period of trial without any national bank at all — and, finally, that the public funds should not be kept in any one favoured institution but in selected banks in different states. It was logical and sensible that if the charter of the Bank was not to be renewed in 1836 steps should at once be taken to place the government funds elsewhere. A clause of the original Bank charter laid it down with comparative clearness that the Secretary of the Treasury had the right to order the withdrawal of the public deposits provided that he explained his reasons for doing so to Congress.

Nicholas Biddle, the President of the Bank, who had a Napoleonic love of power, counter-attacked with all the weapons he had to prevent the institution which he had done so much to build from being destroyed. He granted loans to individuals for purely political reasons, hired some of the most persuasive lawyers in the country to defend his cause in the Senate and the House, and distributed generous credit in the hope of enlisting supporters throughout the country interested in the victory of the Bank. It was his belief that he had not only the majority of Congress on his side but also the majority of Jackson's own Cabinet. A merciless struggle ensued between him and the obstinate demagogue at the White House.

The next move by Jackson after his memorandum of March 19th was to rid himself of his Secretary of the Treasury, John McLane, who disapproved of the withdrawal of the deposits, by kicking him upstairs into the office of Secretary of State, and substituting a weaker man, William Duane. On June 26th he ordered Duane, out of consideration for the 'purity of our government and the liberty of our people', to select a number of state banks willing to accept the public funds and then to replace the National Bank by them as the depositaries. Duane refused and the sterling Roger Taney was invited to grasp the nettle. In the height of the sum-

SECOND TERM AND RETIREMENT

mer of 1833 while he was holidaying in Virginia as a respite from the heat of the capital Jackson wrote to Vice-President Van Buren (who discreetly kept out of these controversies): 'I am busy all my working hours, reviewing the Bank question.' In Taney he had a lieutenant who, if possible was more royalist than the King. On August 5th Taney wrote to Jackson: 'I should feel deeply mortified if after so many splendid victories, civil and military, you should in the last term of your public life meet with defeat.' On September 18th a statement was composed giving the Cabinet the President's reasons for removing the deposits after October 1st and explaining that the Bank was a 'sure lodgment for a dangerous influence in this country' and five days later Taney was nominated Secretary of the Treasury to do the deed.

Jackson's opponents struck back. Henry Clay led a series of attacks on the President in the Senate, while everywhere the Bank contracted its credits. The withdrawal of the deposits naturally affected the Bank's own financial situation but clearly the deflationary movement was ordered by Biddle in an attempt to thwart the policy of the government. 'Nothing', Biddle wrote, 'but the evidence of suffering abroad will produce any effect on Congress . . . A steady course of firm restriction will ultimately lead . . . to the recharter of the Bank.' The Jacksonians at first retorted by denying that there was any real economic distress in the country following the withdrawal of the deposits, but they later took the more politic course of blaming the distress on Biddle.

The struggle between Jackson and the Bank reached its climax during the autumn and winter of 1833. The Senate refused to confirm Taney's appointment and rejected Jackson's nominees as bank directors. These were mere pinpricks. The elections went in Jackson's favour and in February 1834 the Governor of Pennsylvania came out with a forceful denunciation of the Bank's conduct in deliberately creating a depression. Although in March Henry Clay persuaded the Senate to censure the President (the motion was carried by twenty-six votes to twenty) a week afterwards the House of Representatives, inspired by a friend and a disciple of Jackson named James K. Polk, approved the administration's policy towards the Bank in four comprehensive resolutions. Biddle saw that influential public opinion had turned against him and accepted his defeat; once more the credit of the

Bank was expanded and he prepared for the loss of the charter by obtaining permission to reconstitute the Bank in Pennsylvania. He himself withdrew to devote himself to a study of the classics in his country house but ultimately he died in poverty. One final triumph remained for Jackson. A number of changes in 1836 had transformed the Senate into a much more friendly body. Senator Thomas Benton (whom he had threatened to horsewhip a quarter of a century before and was now his friend and admirer) induced the Senate to expunge from its own journals the resolution of censure and to send the pen with which it was expunged as a gift to the President.

Speaking of his foreign policy one of Andrew Jackson's contemporary admirers wrote: 'No part of his administration, successful, beneficial and honourable as it was at home, was more successful, beneficial and honourable than that of his foreign diplomacy. He obtained indemnities for all outrages committed during his time. He made good commercial treaties . . . and left the whole world at peace with his country.' This praise, though deserved, gives an exaggerated impression because Jackson never had any severe problems of foreign policy to handle in the sense that they were known to Washington and Jefferson or were to confront Theodore Roosevelt and Woodrow Wilson in later times. Spain and France had no foothold left on the American continent and the more pressing disputes with Great Britain had been settled by Jackson's predecessors. Jackson's gifts as a diplomatist were not truly tested, although the secondary affairs he had to settle were managed in such a way as to suggest that Jackson as President would not have behaved with the same imperviousness to the susceptibilities of European Powers as Jackson the General had done.

One achievement that reflected credit on Jackson and his first Secretary of State, Martin Van Buren, was the reopening of the trade of the British West Indies to American enterprise. Before their time the American method of attaining this object had been to try to force the hand of the British Government by a war of tariffs and embargoes. Jackson's representatives soothed instead of provoking and a compromise fair to both sides was reached.

In seeking a settlement with France over what were known as the 'spoliation claims' Jackson was slower to appreciate the need

SECOND TERM AND RETIREMENT

to pacify European *amour-propre*. The claims arose mainly out of injuries done to American property seized on merchant ships during the Napoleonic wars. The 1830 Revolution in France had interrupted the negotiation of these claims, but the friendly attitude towards King Louis Phillippe shown both in an address by Jackson and in the conduct of a wise minister in Paris had paved the way to a treaty which was ratified in February 1832. The French Chamber, however, was reluctant to carry out the agreement and Jackson then decided on strong measures, threatening to sequester French property to meet the claims. A sentence in one of his messages to Congress on the subject deeply offended the French and a comedy of conflicting prestige ensued. The French demanded an apology: the Americans said that they would neither apologize nor explain and added, by way of good measure, that the President's messages to Congress were purely domestic matters. Finally, in December 1835, Jackson denied that he had intended to menace or insult the French and reluctantly agreed to British mediation. 'Why England as mediator?' he asked: 'She will manage to cheat either us or France or both at some stage of the business.' But the matter was amicably arranged and the United States Treasury received its money.

The most delicate question of foreign policy related to Texas. When Mexico became independent of Spain in 1823 Texas went along with it, but the ambition of the United States Government was to purchase Texas as it had purchased Louisiana. Jackson authorized the price to be raised from one million to five million dollars, but he was unlucky or perhaps unwise in the choice of the representative whom he sent to do the bargaining. Jackson consistently refused his consent to any scheme that would savour of corruption although he did not object to some indirect means of achieving the end. Ultimately another Tennesseean detached Texas from Mexico and afterwards helped to acquire it for the United States. Sam Houston was a remarkable young man who, like Jackson, began his career as a Nashville lawyer and had served with Jackson in his Creek campaign and later became Congressman and Governor of Tennessee. But twelve weeks after his marriage, at the age of thirty-five, he left his wife and resigned his Governorship and went off to live with the Indians on the Texan border under the adopted name of the Raven. In due course Houston entered

ANDREW JACKSON

Texas and became the leader of the American settlers there who, in 1835, began a war of secession from Mexico. Houston's plan was not dissimilar from that of Aaron Burr which had so shocked Jefferson and Jackson had repudiated. But unlike Burr, Houston was successful: he defeated the Mexican army and took its general prisoner. Jackson handled the whole business with kid gloves. When it looked as if Houston was going to be beaten, he wrote in answer to an appeal from a Texan: 'The writer does not reflect that we have a treaty with Mexico, and our national faith is pledged to support it. The Texans before they took the step to declare themselves independent which has aroused and united all Mexico against them ought to have pondered well. It was a rash and premature act. Our neutrality must be faithfully maintained.' Even after Houston's victory he told his friend Kendall: 'I have determined to maintain strict neutrality over Mexico.' Houston was nevertheless informed that the United States were willing to mediate if both sides asked. They did not ask and Jackson was reluctant to do anything that might divide the Union or result in war. On his very last day in office, however, he nominated a chargé d'affaires to the Texan Republic and thereby recognized its independence. And from his retirement he employed all his personal influence with Houston to bring the independent republic into the Union.

Two other events in Jackson's second term remain to be noted. The first was his management of the Indian problem. In his first annual message Jackson had stated that the Indians were to be given the choice of remaining where they were and submitting to the laws of the state in which they dwelt or of emigrating westwards. The Indians — particularly the Cherokees — were reluctant to leave their old hunting grounds, but the discovery of gold in north-east Georgia stimulated the desire of the white men to expel them and Jackson did not interfere when the government of Georgia in defiance of the existing treaties tried to force them out. Jackson laboured consistently to induce the Indians to cross the Mississippi and approved numerous treaties directed to this purpose. The other event was Jackson's promulgation of what was called the 'Specie Circular' which stipulated that all persons buying land from the Federal Government must pay for it in coin or bullion. The aim of the circular was partly to prevent

SECOND TERM AND RETIREMENT

inflation and partly to discourage speculation. Both the economic wisdom and the constitutional right of the circular were called into question and it was decently buried by a joint resolution of Congress after Jackson had ceased to be President.

As early as December 31st, 1829, Jackson had written a letter to a friend to be published if he died recommending that Martin Van Buren should succeed him as President. Van Buren had distinguished himself as Secretary of State during Jackson's first term and as Vice-President had carefully avoided all political controversy. Jackson admired qualities in him which he did not pretend to possess himself — his urbanity, his fine intelligence, his diplomacy and his breeding. Yet, it has justly been said, without Jackson, Van Buren might never have reached the heights of his political desires; for Jackson put forth his still burning energies to ensure that Van Buren was elected, expressing his disgust with his own state of Tennessee when it refused to be represented at the Democratic national convention and chose an independent candidate of its own. Van Buren beat General Harrison, the National Republican or Whig candidate, by 170 electoral votes to seventy-three.

In imitation of Washington Jackson published a farewell address setting out at some length the achievements of his two administrations. He had sought the assistance of Chief Justice Taney in writing his address, instructing him that the themes should be the maintenance of our 'glorious union' against sectional jealousies and the successful fight against corrupting monopolies' and 'a thousand ways of robbing honest labour to make knaves rich'. The finished article contained an earnest admonition against the dangers of disunion. 'Has the warning voice of Washington been forgotten?' Jackson asked, 'or have designs already been formed to sever the union?'

On the day of Van Buren's inauguration, March 4th, 1837, Jackson was far from well but he drove with his successor to the Capitol and acknowledged the cheers of the crowds delighting in the warmth of an early spring. Looking down on the scene from a side window Senator Benton 'felt an emotion which had never passed through him before'. It was, he thought, no pageant that he witnessed but 'a real scene — a man and the people'. 'For once', he observed, 'the rising was eclipsed by the setting sun.'

What were the qualities that won for Jackson so large a place in the affections of the American people? It was not so much that they felt he was one of themselves but rather that they were convinced that he was their true protector. They believed rightly that he fought for them without giving quarter against any who would exploit them. Indeed Van Buren said of him: 'The conciliation of individuals formed the smallest, perhaps too small a part of his policy. His strength lay with the masses, and he knew it.' Once he had made up his mind, not so much through conviction of his intelligence as by an intuitive decision, he seldom hesitated and never compromised: 'Every step', said Benton, 'was a contest, every contest a victory.' After Jackson became President he was the ruler and not the servant of his passions; he did not lose his temper, but kept it and expended it as the occasion warranted. Benton summed up by saying that 'abhorrence of debt, public and private, dislike of banks, and love of hard money — love of justice and love of country' were the ruling passions with Jackson. Jackson himself in a letter to Van Buren written a fortnight after he left the White House, expressed his satisfaction that he had fought the good fight: 'When I review the arduous administration through which I have passed, the formidable opposition I have met to its very close, by the combined talents, wealth and power of the whole aristocracy of the Union, aided, as they were, by the money monopoly, U.S. Bank with its power of corruption, with which we had to contend, the result must be not only pleasing to me but to every patriot.' A more complicated person might have had his doubts, but Jackson knew he had been fated to be the Hammer of the Bank and the People's Friend.

Jackson returned to the new Hermitage to repair his private fortunes. 'The burning of my house and furniture', he confessed, 'has left me poor . . . I returned with barely ninety dollars in my pocket.' Indeed he was not too proud to accept the repayment of a loan of fourteen dollars by an old soldier. Much of his time was to be occupied in struggling to straighten out his affairs which had been reduced to chaos by the incompetence and extravagance of his adopted son. In 1838 he officially joined the Presbyterian Church: he had long delayed doing this for political reasons, although he had not hidden from his intimates that he had been

SECOND TERM AND RETIREMENT

brought up 'a rigid Presbyterian, to which I have always adhered'. Those who knew him well said that there was in him 'a deep-seated vein of piety' and that 'if he had been born in the time of Cromwell he would have been a puritan'. Certainly his faith was of a rigid Calvinist type, as a letter written to Andrew Jackson Hutchings on the death of his child shows: 'It is probable', he wrote (January 25th, 1835), 'that you doted upon him too much, to the neglect of Him who gave the boon, so He has taken him from you, to bring to your view that to Him your first love is due, and by this chastisement to bring you back to your duty to God.'

The ending of Jackson's second term had coincided with an American economic crisis — the crisis that Jackson had vainly tried to arrest by his hard money policy. The Jacksonian era had been one of tremendous expansion and unlimited optimism. The number of banks had much more than doubled and an orgy of 'wild cat' buying occurred. The placing of the government's funds in the state banks and the decision which was taken by Congress to distribute a Treasury surplus among the states had contributed to a dangerous expansion of credit, which the Specie Circular had helped too summarily to check. The banks suspended payments in coin, confidence was shaken, and finally prices fell. Jackson persisted that all his measures had been wise (American economic historians do not think so), although he pressed President Van Buren to establish an independent Treasury to retain the government revenue and issue notes instead of relying on the 'pet banks'.

The financial confusion affected Jackson personally. His son, who, against his advice, had gullibly backed the notes of others, was found to have involved himself in debts which Andrew Jackson could only pay by borrowing on his own credit or by selling his lands. His crops failed to realize what he hoped and he was driven to appeal to friends to rescue him from his difficulties. Speaking of his son he confessed to one old friend, Major Lewis: 'When I discovered his embarrassments, found how he had been swindled and imposed upon, that he had been adopted and raised by my dear wife and myself, was my only representative to perpetuate my name, and when I viewed the goodness and amiability of his dear wife and little children, I could not withstand from stepping forward to extricate him.'

Jackson was not, however, so steeped in his private cares as to forget politics and followed the changing scenes with undimmed interest. At the age of seventy-three he 'took the stump' in Tennessee and Kentucky on behalf of President Van Buren who stood for re-election against the Whig candidate, General Harrison, a simple but appealing hero of the Indian wars. Van Buren was well beaten, but Harrison died soon after his term began and was succeeded by the Vice-President John Tyler with whom Jackson was on not unfriendly terms. It was during Tyler's administration that Congress voted for the repayment with interest of the fine that had been imposed upon Jackson after his victory at New Orleans. Tyler at once approved the bill, which alleviated, though it did not solve, Jackson's financial troubles. The main political question at this time was the annexation of Texas. Houston's 'independent republic' was now anxious to enter the Union, but the proposal was resisted by many politicians in the north who did not want so large an area where slavery was permitted to be added to the south-west. Moreover the measure was disliked on moral grounds for it was felt to be the culmination of an unsavoury plot. Jackson, for his part, argued that the original terms of the Louisiana Purchase, correctly interpreted, gave the United States the right to Texas and always referred to the question not as one of 'annexation' but of 'reannexation'. 'The future safety of our country', he averred, 'and its best interest demand it . . . We must regain Texas, peaceably if we can, forcibly if not.' But Houston, whose influence was still paramount in Texas, was unwilling to give up the advantages of his bargaining position, especially as the United States Government had three times rejected his requests for annexation, and Jackson was again begged to employ his influence with his old subaltern: Senator Robert J. Walker went so far as to tell him: 'I think the annexation of Texas depends on you.' Jackson wrote Houston 'patriotic' letters to keep him 'out of the snares of England and France' and was pleased with a reply which said: 'Texas is presented to the United States as a bride adorned for her espousals.' But he was sadly disappointed when he heard that Martin Van Buren rejected the eager lady. It was obvious that

SECOND TERM AND RETIREMENT

the west wanted Texas and that therefore Van Buren could not again in 1844 be the Democratic candidate for the Presidency. Instead Jackson approved the choice of the comparatively unknown James K. Polk, sometime Governor of Tennessee, as the party nominee. To Polk he wrote: 'We must and will have Texas with and in our glorious Union. The Federal Union must be preserved.' Polk won the election, but even before he took office a joint resolution of the two Houses of Congress approved annexation and Jackson could rejoice. His eyes then turned to the north-west corner of the Union and in May 1845 he wrote to tell the new President to ignore British claims to the Oregon Territory which had during the early eighteen-forties been populated by an ever-swelling stream of immigrants crossing the breadth of the continent in their dauntless caravans. 'Dash from your lips the counsel of the timid', wrote the indomitable old imperialist. 'No temporizing with Britain.'

Jackson's last days were thus by no means unhappy, although he confessed to his nephew Donelson that his health was 'feeble and his afflictions great' and that 'poverty stared him in the face'. Once again his old friends came to the rescue and he learned of their kindness with tears in his eyes. All his friends were loyal from Sam Houston in Texas to the scattered members of his Kitchen Cabinet. Two of the latter, Amos Kendall and F. P. Blair, hitherto the editor of the official Democratic organ, quarrelled with each other and Blair and Lewis were dismissed from their posts by President Polk, though he was named 'Young Hickory'. But all of them were faithful to Jackson. Even Major Eaton, who had deserted the Democrats for the Whigs and was deemed by Jackson 'a lost man', hastened to the Hermitage when he heard his old friend was sinking.

In March Commodore Elliott of the United States Navy returned from Palestine bringing with him a 'splendid sarcophagus' which was offered to Jackson as a suitable resting place for his bones and those of his wife. The sarcophagus was wrongly supposed to have been made for a Roman Emperor. Jackson answered: 'I cannot consent that my mortal body shall be laid in a repository for an Emperor or a King.' Dropsy had developed in the spring of 1845, but Jackson, half-blind, unable to write and scarcely to eat, went on dictating his letters of political wisdom almost to the end. His last letter was written to President Polk on June 6th congratulating him on his united and harmonious Cabinet. It was two days later, on Sunday, June 8th, 1845, that his adopted son, many friends and relatives and his Negro slaves gathered to watch the old chieftain die. He met death with his customary courage. Five years earlier he had quoted the words of a hymn:

> Why do we mourn departed friends or shake at death's alarms?
> 'Tis but the voice that Jesus sends to call them to his arms.

He asked for his 'specs', wiped them and took one last look at his family and friends; then turning to the Negroes he said: 'I want all to prepare to meet me in Heaven; I have a right to the Tree of Life. My conversation is for you all. Christ has no respect to colour. I am in God and God's in me. He dwelleth in me and I in him.' Then his shoulders slumped and he passed away without a struggle. And the Negroes wailed: 'The Old Massa's dead.'

SELECT BIBLIOGRAPHY

J. S. BASSETT: *The Life of Andrew Jackson* (1913); *Correspondence of Andrew Jackson* (1926).
THOMAS H. BENTON: *Thirty Years View* (1854).
A. C. BUELL: *History of Andrew Jackson* (1904).
J. H. EATON: *The Life of Andrew Jackson* (1824).
MARQUIS JAMES: *Andrew Jackson. The Border Captain* (1933); *Andrew Jackson. Portrait of a President* (1937); *The Raven, a Biography of Sam Houston* (1929).
JAMES PARTON: *A Life of Andrew Jackson* (1859).
JAMES PHELAN: *History of Tennessee* (1888).
A. M. SCHLESINGER: *The Age of Jackson* (1946).
MARTIN VAN BUREN: *Autobiography* (ed. Fitzpatrick) (1920).

ABRAHAM LINCOLN

THEODORE ROOSEVELT
ON
LINCOLN

ABRAHAM LINCOLN, the rail-splitter, the Western country lawyer, was one of the shrewdest and most enlightened men of the world, and he had all the practical qualities which enable such a man to guide his countrymen: and yet he was also a genius of the heroic type, a leader who rose level to the greatest crisis through which this nation or any other nation had to pass in the nineteenth century.

WOODROW WILSON
ON
LINCOLN

THE passion for letters had been strong upon him since a boy, and his self-training had with unerring instinct followed a fine plan of mastery. By reasoning upon the principles of the law, as they came to him out of a few text-books, by poring upon books of mathematics, by reading up and down through such books of history or adventure as fell in his way in search of the experience of other men, by constant intimacy of talk and play of argument with men of every kind to whom he had access, he had made himself a master of brief and careful statement, of persuasion, and of oral debate: thoughtful, observant, steering in what he said by an unfluctuating compass of logical precision, and above all lucid, full of homely wit and anecdote such as was fit to illuminate practical subjects, and uttering phrases which struck his opponent like a blow, but fair, unmalicious, intellectual, not passionate.

ABRAHAM LINCOLN

CHAPTER V

ABRAHAM LINCOLN

It is important at this dividing point in American history to lift our minds above the rough-and-tumble of ancient political controversy and to recall what had gone before. On the one hand, the United States of America had been constantly expanding and absorbing eager immigrants — especially Scots-Irish and Germans — into its melting pot. On the frontiers the consciousness of unity had grown. On the other hand, with the development of new federal territories, each with differing climates and resources and sometimes with its own cultural traditions, arose a form of 'sectionalism' at least as clearly defined as any which the original thirteen states had known. To the Creole in New Orleans or the peon in California the federal system can have had but little meaning. The history of the United States to 1861 is largely a story of conflict between the growth of sectionalism and the growth of national unity (indeed some would say it is so still) and it culminated inexorably in the Civil War.

The American Civil War was the testing ground for the written constitution of the United States and for the institutions which it embodied, including the Presidency. Was it indeed possible for a democratic system of government to function over so vast a geographical area — a system which Aristotle had claimed was suited only to a small city state? Could one popularly chosen chief executive really speak for so varied a citizenry, ranging from the town dwellers of the eastern seaboard to the farmers of the western prairies and the cotton aristocracy of the south? In days when telephones and wireless did not exist and railways and telegraphs were in their infancy was it a practical thing for one man to administer affairs that concerned German and Irish immigrants, Frenchmen and Indians and the many other nationalities that were scattered throughout the Federal Union?

Admittedly the Constitution had provided for a decentralized form of government which only placed limited spheres of authority under the control of the administration at Washington. Yet even

ABRAHAM LINCOLN

in the early days of the Union, when the thirteen states formed a more compact community, doubts were expressed about the possibility of the permanent coherence of so many widely dispersed political groups. President Jefferson (as we have seen) suggested that states had the right to secede if the Federal Government exceeded its constitutional power, as he claimed it had done when Congress passed and John Adams signed the Alien and Sedition Acts. Likewise Jefferson had regarded with equanimity the possibility of America being divided into more than one confederation, if the United States proved unable to absorb all the territory acquired by the Louisiana Purchase. During the war of 1812 and earlier New Englanders had advanced to the edge of secession from the Union because they maintained that the foreign policy of the Federal Government was ruining them. In 1833 South Carolina had almost seceded when its Convention 'nullified' the federal tariff.

In fact the right to secede was resisted and the Federal Union preserved by war under the Presidency of Abraham Lincoln. In the study of the life of this great statesman which follows it will not be possible to elaborate the arguments for secession against preserving the Union — a complicated exercise in political philosophy. It is sufficient to say that Lincoln accepted the ultimate view of all his predecessors on the need to preserve the Union — though in terms of mere precedent he was a revolutionary — just as he was a revolutionary when he made his famous speech on slavery in which he said that 'a house divided against itself cannot stand'. (In most other respects Lincoln was a conservative who loathed extremes and was ready to confirm any compromise that did not involve the rupture of the Union or the extension of slavery.)

Thus, with the victory of the north enforcing the preservation of the Union, the institution of the Presidency was strengthened; it might have been further strengthened if Lincoln himself, with his tolerant ideas on reconstruction had survived the victory and been able to put into effect the ideas of an unquestionably national statesman devoid of all feelings of rancour or revenge. But this was not to be. Nevertheless the Presidency came through the process triumphantly. (It is perhaps notable that the southern Confederation also acquiesced in the value of the institution by electing a President as its war leader.) Moreover Abraham Lincoln found that the Constitution had provided a source of authority, hitherto virtually unexplored, which he could employ in time of crisis — namely the powers available to the President in his *ex-officio* position as Commander-in-Chief. Many major decisions were taken by him in this capacity without his consulting Congress which was manœuvred into situations where it could do nothing else but acquiesce in them. He resisted, as far as he could, the demands of Congress to intervene in the running of the war. Later Presidents, especially Woodrow Wilson and Franklin D. Roosevelt, were able to draw generously on the precedents thus created by Abraham Lincoln, when they had to master problems arising not out of civil, but out of international war.

Finally, laying aside questions of political power, Lincoln by his leadership in the war did much to fashion the course of American history. It is the task of the philosopher or the priest and not of the historian to determine whether the American Civil War, which cost hundreds of thousands of lives, divided families, and spread misery that endured for generations, was justifiable. All that the historian may venture is that if President Lincoln had not gone to war to preserve the Union, then he would have been removed from office and another would have fought the war in his place. As things were, Lincoln's humanity, his desire to find compromises, especially with the border states, his decision to postpone the emancipation of the slaves until he was sure that the time was propitious, and his anxiety to achieve reconstruction without greed or malice, added much vigour to the northern cause. Whether he was a great War Minister will always be a matter of controversy; as the spokesman and head of the Federal Government he was magnificent. The Presidency emerged from its fiercest test not merely fortified but ennobled.

1. THE SELF-MADE CONGRESSMAN (1809-1849)

The paternal grandfather of Abraham Lincoln, after whom he was named, had been a close friend of the mighty American hunter and explorer, Daniel Boone, and it was no doubt because of this friendship that he, his wife Bethsheba and their three sons, Mordecai, Josiah and Thomas, had in 1782 left the old Dominion of Virginia to seek wealth and adventure in Kentucky which Daniel Boone had done so much to develop. The Lincolns found more adventure than wealth. Four years after their arrival, as Abraham was starting to clear a plantation in the forest, he was shot dead by an Indian lurking in the brushwood. While the two elder boys ran for assistance Thomas, a child of six, was left to the mercy of the Indians; just as one of them was about to seize the child his brother Mordecai took accurate aim with his rifle and killed the intruder, and soon the rest fled. Thomas was to become the father of the future President.

The Lincoln fortunes declined in Kentucky where Thomas eked out a very modest livelihood as a carpenter. Thomas was a shiftless meditative man, a 'piddler', to whom the spirit of the pioneers had not been given in a generous measure and who preferred gossip to hard work. In June 1806 he married Nancy Hanks, of a family that had come to Kentucky from Virginia about the same time as his own. Nancy was no great catch — she was illiterate as well as illegitimate, though her son was to declare that her father had belonged to the Virginian aristocracy and that she was a genius. Loving research has only made her into a contradictory figure. All we really know is that she laboured and scrubbed and washed like the wives of a thousand other pioneers and that there was a settled melancholy about her out of which she was shaken only when a circuit preacher came to the neighbourhood to raise the hewers of the forest to the ecstasy of Christian worship. Though there was much beauty in primitive Kentucky, life was hard and often short and nasty. It was in a one-door one-window log cabin by a weedy piece of farmland three miles from Hodgensville that Nancy gave birth to a son on February 12th, 1809.

Three years after he was born Abraham's parents moved to another farm named Sinking Spring near Knob Creek which ran out of a tributary of the river Ohio, where the child, 'as solemn as a papoose', learned to fish and master his ABC. When he was eight the family (he had an elder sister named Sarah) moved again, out of the slave state of Kentucky into the free state of Indiana, where the rich black soil was expected to offer better

THE SELF-MADE CONGRESSMAN

prospects to the impecunious cultivator than the red clay of Kentucky. Thomas Lincoln traded his Kentucky farm for four barrels of whisky and floated a flatboat across the Ohio River to begin life again in a three-walled cabin or 'half-faced camp' with the fourth open side filled by a logwood fire. Pigeon Creek Farm, South Indiana, proved at first as stern a disappointment to the Lincolns as Sinking Spring Farm, Kentucky had been. Smallpox attacked the farm animals and in October 1818 it carried off Abraham's mother at the age of thirty-six. Her husband fashioned a coffin out of a log left over from building the cabin and it was said that some months afterwards the boy Abraham persuaded a wandering preacher to deliver a sermon over her grave.

In this self-sufficing frontier community a family could scarcely manage without a woman, and a year after his mother's death Abraham acquired as a stepmother an old flame of his father from Kentucky. The stepmother was a woman of considerable energy and a little property and from the age of twelve Abraham experienced no longer that abject poverty he had known as a child. From being 'a mere spindle' of a boy he shot upwards to become a useful contributor to the family income. 'He can sink an axe deeper into wood than any man I know', one of his employers said. He became the best wrestler in the county, a skilled butcher, and a muscular farmhand. But other ambitions stirred his heart, whether derived from some forgotten schoolmaster at one of the three schools he attended in Indiana we do not know: he sought keenly after knowledge, inscribing arithmetical sums on a wooden shovel and reading every book he could obtain, from the Bible to *Robinson Crusoe*. 'The things I want to know', he told his friends, 'are in books; my best friend is the man who'll git me a book.' When he was eighteen he gained his first glimpse of a wider world. He was hired in 1828 to make a flatboat voyage down the Mississippi over a thousand miles to New Orleans to sell there a local farmer's produce in exchange for cotton, tobacco and sugar. On this journey he must have heard of the powerful political movement that was later that year to sweep Andrew Jackson into the White House. But it was during a second trip three years later that we have a clear record of his impressions. Then he was profoundly struck by the sight of a Mulatto girl being sold by auction in the streets of New Orleans and of Negro slaves 'chained, maltreated, whipped and scourged'.

By this time the Lincoln family, still poor and optimistic, had moved on again in an ox-drawn caravan from Indiana to Illinois, which had been admitted into the Union in 1818. Abraham now left his father and stepmother (his sister had died in giving birth to a child) and entered the employ of Denton Offutt, the merchant who had sent him the second time down the Mississippi. Offutt owned a store at the village of New Salem on the river Sangamon, an obscure locality that later disappeared from the map. The store did not prosper, as Offutt drank the profits and his clerk was more concerned to make the store a social centre than to drum up business. In New Salem the gaunt six-foot-four store clerk soon became a public figure. He had an irresistible gift for telling funny stories and acquired a reputation for kindness and bravery. When the local bullies tried to bait him he thrashed their leader in a wrestling match and the two became fast friends.

Meanwhile the task of self-education continued. The storekeeper was always to be found reading anything and everything he could lay his hands on. One day (after Offutt's store had failed and he had for a spell a store of his own) he had a stroke of good luck. This is the story as he afterwards told it: 'One day a man who was migrating to the West drove up in front of my store with a wagon which contained his family and household plunder. He asked me if I would buy an old barrel for which he had no room in his wagon, and which he said contained nothing of special value. I did not want it, but to oblige him I bought it and paid him, I think, half a dollar for it. Without further examination I put it away in the store and forgot all about it. Some time after, in overhauling things, I came upon the barrel, and emptying it upon the floor to see what it contained, I found at the bottom of the rubbish a complete edition of Blackstone's *Commentaries*. I began to read those famous works... The more I read, the more intensely absorbed I became... I read until I devoured them.'

Then Lincoln tried to write verse, stories and constitutional essays for his own amusement. In the quiet of the forest he practised public speaking and in March 1832 he bravely offered himself as a candidate for the State Legislature in the Whig

THE SELF-MADE CONGRESSMAN

interest. Lincoln's 'beau ideal of a statesman' was Andrew Jackson's opponent, Henry Clay of Kentucky. In his election address Lincoln advocated such 'internal improvements' as a local railroad and better water communications and also pronounced his firm faith in education. Between the address and the election he volunteered to go and fight the Indians who were threatening to invade their former hunting grounds in Illinois under the veteran chief of the Sac tribe, Black Hawk. Evidence of Abraham's popularity was given when he was elected captain of a mounted company without any mounts. His immense strength ensured respect for his rudimentary discipline, but his men saw only one Indian, a drunk who blundered into their camp by mistake and whose life Captain Lincoln saved. Returning to New Salem Abraham addressed the public: 'Fellow citizens, I presume you all know who I am. I am humble Abraham Lincoln. I have been solicited by many friends to become a candidate for the legislature. My politics are short and sweet, like the old woman's dance. I am in favour of a national bank. I am in favour of the internal improvement system and a high protective tariff. If elected, I shall be thankful; if not, it will be all the same.' The county did not choose him this time, but he carried almost all the votes of New Salem. Meanwhile Offutt's store and two other stores with which he had been associated had failed. He did not worry; he kept on reading — Blackstone, Shakespeare, Keats, Gibbon, Tom Paine. He earned a living by splitting fence rails or helping with the harvest. One day a local farmer found him sitting barefoot on a woodpile reading. 'What are you reading?' asked the farmer. 'I'm not reading,' he answered, 'I'm studying.' 'Studying what?' 'Law, sir', said he 'proud as Cicero'. 'Great God Almighty!' exclaimed the farmer as he passed on.

Everybody loved this humorous, ardent and abstemious young man. To his father's indifference about worldly things and his mother's shadowy melancholia was added his own consuming urge to make good at politics and the law. 'His ambition', said one of his intimate friends, 'was a little engine that knew no rest.' He had a superstitious belief that he was destined for great things. Poor but proud, strong and independent, thirsting for knowledge and with a unique power of perseverance, seldom had a man so obscurely circumstanced, with so few material advantages moved so quickly towards his goal. Perhaps his finest asset was his gift for friendship. Good friends lifted him from his haphazard existence and had him appointed an assistant surveyor and postmaster of New Salem. He liked being postmaster, for he could read all the newspapers coming that way and the duty of delivering the letters, which he carried in the lining of his hat, was not onerous. So popular was he that in the summer of 1834 he was elected to the State Legislature with the support not only of the Henry Clay Whigs but also of many of the local Jacksonian Democrats. In December at the age of twenty-five he reached Vandalia, the capital of Illinois, to take his seat.

'The election of Mr. Lincoln to the Legislature', wrote his famous biographers, Nicolay and Hay, 'may be said to have closed the pioneer portion of his life.' Gone was the wild carelessness of his boyhood in the woods, the petty chaffering of grocery stores, odd jobbing to repel frontier poverty. He was still poor — indeed he had to borrow two hundred dollars to pay for his outfit — but he was respectable. His famous stovepipe hat about a foot tall (in the lining of which he now kept his own correspondence) became the badge of his new profession; he wore a white shirt and white collar, and a bow tie that was nearly always askew and his trousers tended to bag and his hair to rumple. His lanky shambling figure and his air of clownishness did not deceive his acquaintances, though they sometimes surprised strangers. As a rule his looks were melancholy, though his sense of humour never left him and he never ceased to tell funny stories and this was the least troubled period of his whole life.

Lincoln, it has been said, at first proved himself a curiously routine politician. But every man had to learn his profession, and it was natural that while feeling his way and learning his job he should follow along the recognized party line. If he had proclaimed himself a disciple of Henry Clay — a believer in a high tariff and in the value of internal improvements — it was clearly his duty to do his best to promote by these means the expanding economic life of Illinois. Serving on the Committee on Finance Lincoln laboured to obtain a canal linking the Illinois River with Lake Michigan, to make provision for railroads, and obtain the removal of the capital from Vandalia to Springfield, the most

THE SELF-MADE CONGRESSMAN

flourishing town in his own county of Sangamon. In this last project he was the leader and was successful.

Illinois was being borne along on the crest of a wave of prosperity which coincided with Jackson's term of office as President. The population of Illinois had doubled in ten years. The rich soil, the temperate climate and the timbered part of the state invited settlers though as yet they avoided the prairies. The defeat of Black Hawk promised security and the development of railroads and canals a promising market. To the north of the state speculation in real estate was already beginning in what was to be the mighty industrial town of Chicago. Springfield, the new capital, which Lincoln had helped to sponsor, though it had a mere fifteen thousand inhabitants, was a lively market town that set the tone for the neighbouring farmers who came there to sell their goods and spend their money. Smartly dressed men and women drove through its streets in their carriages. Its atmosphere might have corrupted a poor young politician.

Nevertheless Lincoln more than kept his end up and moral ardour kept breaking through. He was chosen again by his county in 1836 after he had promised 'if elected, I shall consider the whole people of Sangamon my constituents, as well those that oppose me as those that support me'. Altogether there were nine representatives of Sangamon County in the Illinois Legislature (two Senators and seven members of the Assembly) and all of them were over six feet tall; consequently they were known as the 'Long Nine' and among the 'Long Nine' Lincoln was not the least prominent. In 1836 he took another plunge and decided to set up as a lawyer in Springfield, Though Blackstone's *Commentaries*, found in the barrel, had first attracted him to the law, it seems that he received substantial encouragement from Major John T. Stuart who had been with him in the Black Hawk campaign. Stuart lent him law books and after Lincoln had successfully applied for a licence to practise in March 1837 Stuart became his first partner. It must be remembered that the litigation in those times was primitive and a show of wit in the loghouse courtrooms was at least as rewarding as learning. Major Stuart soon became a Congressman in Washington by defeating another rising lawyer named Stephen Douglas, a Democrat, and thus much of the firm's business was to fall on Lincoln. When Lincoln first came to settle in Springfield, he called on a young merchant, named Joshua Speed. 'He had ridden into town on a borrowed horse,' Speed afterwards related, 'and engaged from the only cabinetmaker in the village a single bedstead. He came into my store, set his saddle-bag on the counter, and enquired what the furniture for a single bedstead would cost. I took slate and pencil, made a calculation, and found the sum for furniture complete would amount to seventeen dollars in all. Said he: "It is probably cheap enough; but I want to say that, cheap as it is, I have not the money to pay. But if you will credit me until Christmas, and my experiment here as a lawyer is a success, I will pay you then. If I fail in that I will probably never pay you at all." The tone of his voice was so melancholy that I felt for him. I looked up at him and I thought then, as I think now, that I never saw so gloomy and melancholy a face in my life. I said to him: "So small a debt seems to affect you so deeply, I think I can suggest a plan by which you will be able to attain your end without incurring any debt. I have a very large room and a very large double bed in it, which you are perfectly welcome to share with me if you choose." "Where is your room?" he asked. "Upstairs", said I, pointing to the stairs leading from the store to my room. Without saying a word he took his saddle-bags on his arm, went upstairs, set them down on the floor, came down again, and with a face beaming with pleasure and smiles, exclaimed: "Well, Speed, I'm moved."' Thus began a lifelong friendship. The story is an instance of Lincoln's extraordinary charm, in spite of all his oddities, for normally one thinks twice before inviting a stranger to share one's room.

Lincoln soon became as well known a figure in Springfield as he had been in New Salem. He was re-elected to the legislature in 1838 and 1840, and, though he disliked the studious side of a lawyer's work, getting up the briefs, he was astute in the courts, particularly since, like Jefferson, he tried always to take the right side. Amid the routine work of politician and lawyer one event stands out in these years. Slavery was now becoming more and more a national question. As the United States, under the energetic leadership of Jackson and his protégé, Martin Van Buren, expanded south-westwards slavery, which depended chiefly on the growing realm of King Cotton, threatened to cover wider terri-

THE SELF-MADE CONGRESSMAN

tories and even to sweep northward, despite the Missouri Compromise. In the north earnest men and women, convinced that slavery was incompatible not merely with the Declaration of Independence but with Christianity organized a society to work for its abolition. These New England Abolitionists were considered by many to be fanatics endangering the Union. 'Born in Kentucky, and surrounded as he was by slaveholding influence', wrote William Herndon, a young clerk of Speed's, Lincoln failed 'to estimate properly the righteous indignation and unrestrained zeal of a Yankee Abolitionist'. But when the Illinois Legislature passed a resolution protesting against the formation of Abolition societies, 'as attempting to undermine the sacred right of property' Lincoln was constrained to a moderate protest. He and one other member declared that 'the institution of slavery' was 'founded on both injustice and bad policy' and though they thought that the abolition doctrines would tend to increase its evils rather than to abate them and that Congress had no power to interfere with slavery, they asserted that Congress did at least have the right to abolish slavery in the District of Columbia if invited to do so by the people of the District. It was a relatively small concession to the Abolitionists but it showed the way Lincoln's mind was turning. An address which he gave at that time to the Young Men's Lyceum at Springfield disclosed too that he was worried over the spread of mob violence throughout the nation — of Negroes being hanged without trial in defiance of the law. Though his utterances were cautious there were thus already glimmerings to show that hidden perplexities puzzled the mind of this 'routine politician', a mind that never ceased to absorb and was always willing to learn. Otherwise Lincoln behaved as any other keen Whig politician. In the 1840 election he was an active campaigner for the ineffable General Harrison who was to be swept into office by a torrent that was carrying away the Jacksonians who had seen prosperity fade round the corner and a depression take its place. In a long and witty speech about this time (December 1839) Lincoln also attacked Van Buren's pet sub-Treasury scheme, arguing that a national bank could be better entrusted to handle the nation's finances than politicians who had too often proved themselves corrupt. Lincoln did not conceal that behind all this eagerness for the party cause lay a compelling hope: he wanted to move forward from being a mere local politician to become, like his partner, Stuart, a United States Congressman.

The poor but rising lawyer sought love, though what kind of love he scarcely knew. His mother died young and he did not much care for his father whom he described slightingly as a 'wandering labouring-boy' who 'never did more in the way of writing than bunglingly to write his own name'. Looking back with resentment on the 'stinted living' of his early years in a Kentucky cabin, he hankered after colour and warmth in life as much as after knowledge. Knowledge after all was coming through his own little aided efforts. For knowledge he had always groped and he was to recall how as a child he used to get irritated when anybody talked to him in a way which he could not understand but intended to find out. Ever since then, in daytime with his back sunk in a chair and his long legs cocked up as high as his head, or at night by candlelight in his double bed he read voraciously and unremittingly. Colour he tried to manufacture by the writing of poetry and warmth by seeking a mate.

Lincoln's attitude to women was ambivalent — he both longed for their company and was afraid of it. Deeply sensitive, he strove to rationalize his emotions. William Herndon, who knew him well, wrote that: 'Nothing with him was intuitive. To have profound judgment and just discrimination he required time to think: and if facts or events were forced upon him in too rapid succession the machinery of his judgment failed to work.' His first perhaps legendary love was a young girl named Anne Rutledge with auburn hair and blue eyes, charming and gentle, the belle of New Salem. She was but nineteen when they met and was betrothed to another man. But the other man went home to New York and did not return and if her brother's recollections may be trusted, Anne and Abraham were engaged while he was still a law student. In the summer of 1835 Anne was struck down with typhoid fever and Lincoln came to sit by the bedside of the dying girl. She was buried in Concord graveyard, seven miles north-west of the town of Petersburg, and her death is said to have wrought a noticeable change in Lincoln's moods, even threatening his reason. To one of his friends he is said to have murmured in agony: 'I can never be reconciled to have the snow, rains and storms beat upon her grave.'

THE SELF-MADE CONGRESSMAN

About a year later another girl, Mary Owens, came on a visit to Illinois from Kentucky. She was over twenty-eight, a big brunette with a wealthy father and some willingness to marry. Again it seems that Lincoln committed himself to an engagement, but no sooner had he done so than he began to back out. Here his ambivalence was most marked. He confided to a friend that Mary reminded him of his mother and swore to her that she cheered his loneliness. On the other hand, he said that she repelled him: 'I knew she was over-size,' he wrote after the affair was over, 'but now she appeared a fair match for Falstaff... I knew she was an old maid... too eager... from her want of teeth, weather-beaten appearance in general, and from a kind of notion that ran in my head that nothing could have commenced at the size of infancy and reached her present bulk in less than thirty-five or forty years: and in short I was not at all pleased with her.' The letter from which these excerpts was taken is surely one of the most extraordinary that Lincoln ever wrote. Of course he meant to be funny and succeeded only in being vulgar; but equally certainly the letter covered some real hurt to his pride. Though he did his utmost to persuade Mary Owens not to marry him by warning her of his lack of means — 'You would have to be poor,' he told her, 'without the means of hiding your poverty' — and by telling her not that he loved her but that 'in all cases he wanted to do right', he was evidently surprised when she finally refused him. In her old age she explained that she did so because he 'was deficient in those little links which make up the chain of a woman's happiness'. Others might have said that it was because his sensitiveness presented itself to her in the form of downright rudeness; for women also have their pride.

Third time lucky — or unlucky. In 1839 Mary Todd came to Springfield on a visit to her married sister. She was from Lexington, Kentucky, and was the popular daughter of two first cousins. Gay and lively, not badly educated — she knew some French — her attraction was spoilt by a caustic wit and a forbidding manner. Nevertheless her brother-in-law asserted that: 'Mary could make a bishop forget his prayers.' Abraham, now a rising young politician of thirty, had reason to be moved by light brown hair with a glint of bronze, long lashes, and a lovely complexion and also, maybe, by a social position a cut above his own. It is said that they were first engaged in December 1840 and that by January 1841 it was broken off. Who broke the engagement is not clear, but there was some quarrel leading to separation on what Lincoln called the 'fatal first of January'. 'Poor Lincoln!' wrote a contemporary, 'how are the mighty fallen! He was confined [to bed] about a week but though he now appears again he is reduced and emaciated in appearance . . .' That same month Lincoln himself wrote to his law partner: 'I have within the last few days been making a most discreditable exhibition of myself in the way of hypochondriasm' and, again: 'I am now the most miserable man living . . . Whether I shall ever be better I cannot tell . . . I must die or be better, it appears to me.' Curiously his close friend, Speed, was almost as sensitive as he and was at that time also trembling upon the precipice of matrimony. In a series of consoling and deeply introspective letters to Speed are mirrored the changing quality of Lincoln's own moods. When a year had passed since the breach with Mary Todd, he was himself again. 'I have been quite clear of "hypo" since you left', he wrote to Speed on February 3rd, 1842, and on February 25th: 'I tell you, Speed, our forebodings (for which you and I are peculiar) are all the worst sort of nonsense . . . when your nerves once get steady now, the whole trouble will be over for ever.' By the autumn Abraham and Mary Todd had been reconciled. She seems to have waited for him and wanted him, perceiving perhaps in the gaunt neurotic lawyer, as Sarah Marlborough had once perceived in her John, the essentials of greatness. On November 11th, 1842, he wrote to another friend: 'Nothing new here, except my marrying, which to me, is a matter of profound wonder.'

Mary Todd was an ambitious young woman, who loved 'glitter and show, power and pomp'. When she lived in Kentucky she once met Henry Clay and told him she would like to be mistress of the White House. According to Herndon, who disliked her, she was the whiplash who spurred Lincoln on his way upwards. After she married she told an acquaintance: 'Mr. Lincoln is to be President of the United States some day; if I had not thought so, I would not have married him, for you can see he is not pretty.' There is much testimony that their marriage was not entirely happy. Lincoln with his untidy habits, his melancholia and brooding was probably a trial as a husband; Mary with her

THE SELF-MADE CONGRESSMAN

ungovernable temper and violent headaches, her wilfulness, her pride, her jealousy, her meanness and personal extravagance was assuredly a termagant of a wife (however devoted and intelligent). No doubt, as some witness, there were sunny intervals between the storms. Lincoln at any rate made the best of it and would not allow his sense of humour to desert him. She being under five feet tall he referred to them as 'the long and the short of it'. He was patient — as was John, Duke of Marlborough with his Sarah — 'I think the Lincolns agreed moderately well,' said one who knew them both, 'as a rule Mr. Lincoln yielded to his wife.' She bore him four sons, of whom only one lived a normal span of years. Not long after Lincoln's assassination she was confined for a year (at the age of fifty-six) as a certified lunatic. When after years of wandering she returned to Springfield to die they found her wedding ring on which was inscribed: 'A. L. to Mary. Nov. 4 1842. Love is Eternal.'

Lincoln's partnership with Stuart had been dissolved in 1841 and he had found a new partner in Stephen Logan who was one of the ablest and most successful lawyers in the State of Illinois. Lincoln benefited from his association with such a man and Logan was pleased with Lincoln's assiduity. 'He would study out his case and make about as much of it as anybody,' Logan is reported to have said in later years, 'his ambition as a lawyer increased; he grew constantly. By close study of each case, he got to be quite a formidable lawyer.' For the first time in his life he began to earn a modest income. Yet in the early months of his marriage he lived in a boarding-house and it was here that his eldest son, Robert Todd, was born on August 1st, 1843. That same year he changed from the position of a junior to a senior partner, inviting his young friend, William Herndon, to come in with him. Herndon, an alert and conscientious youngster, was delighted at the idea and became devoted to Lincoln. Unlike his senior partner, however, Herndon was an ardent supporter of the slavery abolitionists and his idealistic outlook on politics may well have had its influence on Lincoln, though he modestly disclaimed that it did so. Lincoln's political ambitions remained vehement. 'If you should hear anyone say that Lincoln don't want to go to Congress,' he wrote to a friend, 'I wish you, as a personal friend of mine, would tell him you have reason to believe he is mistaken. The truth is I should like to go very much.' Both in 1843 and 1844 he was disappointed of the nomination as Whig candidate as Congressman in his own county, although on the second occasion he was made a presidential elector to cast his vote against Polk. It seems that a local understanding was reached, however, whereby Lincoln was to have the nomination in 1846.

President Polk, supported by the dying Andrew Jackson, had approved the annexation of the republic of Texas. This had been the main question on which the presidential election of 1844 had been fought and Henry Clay's opposition had driven the last nail into the coffin of his presidential hopes. On that subject Lincoln's own position was equivocal. 'I perhaps ought to say', he observed in October 1845, 'that individually I never was much interested in the Texas question. I never could see much good come of annexation inasmuch as they were already a free republican people on our own model. On the other hand, I never could very clearly see how the annexation would augment the evil of slavery ... I hold it to be a paramount duty of us in the free States ... to let the slavery of other States alone; while, on the other hand, I hold it equally clear that we should never knowingly lend ourselves, directly or indirectly, to prevent that slavery from dying a natural death ...' Lincoln was nevertheless violently moved by the Mexican war which arose out of the annexation of Texas. The United States Government, having annexed that republic, which had been spasmodically at war with Mexico since Sam Houston raised the standard of revolt in 1835, claimed that its boundary extended to the Rio Grande. Mexico denied the claim and war followed. General Zachary Taylor of Louisiana, though he disapproved of the war, obeyed the orders given him to invade Mexico and won several rapid victories over numerically superior forces. Lincoln's view was that the war was immoral and he had a chance to expound it in Washington since soon after the war began he was elected to Congress.

In the election he had won a notable victory — the only Whig victory in Illinois — over a Jacksonian Methodist preacher named Peter Cartwright. Cartwright was a remarkably vigorous man of over sixty who in his life preached some fifteen thousand sermons. The campaign was waged on personalities, Lincoln being attacked

THE SELF-MADE CONGRESSMAN

as a infidel. One day Cartwright asked him: 'If you are not going to repent and go to Heaven, Mr. Lincoln, where are you going?' 'I'm going to Congress, Brother Cartwright', Lincoln retorted.

Lincoln took a little time to find his feet in Washington and practised speaking on questions of small intrinsic interest in the House of Representatives. He soon won popularity in the same way that he had done in New Salem and Springfield as an inimitable raconteur and mimic. In the House his most notable achievement was his criticism of the Mexican war. On December 27th, 1847, he introduced what were known as the 'Spot Resolutions' which asked President Polk to state whether the spot on which the war had begun really was or ever had been Texas (and thus American) territory. He followed up his resolutions in a brave speech accusing the 'bewildered confounded and miserably perplexed' President of 'unnecessarily and unconstitutionally' declaring war. Still he voted for military supplies for the war and found some difficulty in explaining the consistency of his conduct to his partner Herndon. After the war had been won a Pennsylvanian Democrat named David Wilmot introduced a proviso to an appropriation bill declaring that slavery should for ever be prohibited in any territory which might be acquired from Mexico. By this means the claim that the south had sponsored the Mexican war in order to widen the area of slavery could be rebutted. Lincoln said that he voted forty times in favour of the Wilmot proviso. He also introduced a bill to permit the abolition of slavery in the District of Columbia, the proposal which he had put forward earlier in the Illinois Legislature. The House of Representatives indifferently shelved the proposal.

In the year 1848 Lincoln campaigned actively for General Zachary Taylor, 'Old Rough and Ready', the Whig candidate for the Presidency, who had distinguished himself in the Mexican war — Lincoln had reluctantly decided that his old hero, Henry Clay, stood no chance — and not only delivered a speech in the House attacking General Cass, the Democratic candidate (formerly Jackson's Secretary of War) but ventured into New England to stump for the party cause. The American people, who dearly love a war hero, duly elected General Taylor. On his way back from Congress Lincoln paid a visit to Niagara and told Herndon 'the thing that struck me most forcibly when I saw the Falls was where in the world did all that water come from?'

Lincoln's attitude to the Mexican war had diminished his popularity in his constituency and blasted his hopes of re-election; he was replaced as candidate by his former law partner, Logan, who was beaten. Now for the first and last time in his career he resorted to wire-pulling to obtain an office; but his application for the post of Commissioner for the General Land Office at Washington failed and though he was considered for the Governorship of the new territory of Oregon, he was offered only the minor post of Secretary. It was said that Mary Lincoln refused to go to Oregon and Abraham contemptuously rejected the offer. So he returned a disappointed man to Springfield and for the next five years assiduously resumed the practice of the law. To his contemporaries it might have seemed — indeed it seemed to himself — that his political career was at an end for ever. But within four years the slavery question, which had for so long menaced the peace of the Union, was to arouse him from his lethargy and carry him to the peak of his fortunes and to his death.

2. THE CONTEST WITH STEPHEN DOUGLAS
(1849-1861)

Although he did not completely give up political activity, Lincoln, disappointed with what he regarded as his failure in Congress, threw himself once again into the round of a circuit lawyer. 'His habits were very simple', recorded his partner, William Herndon. 'He was not fastidious as to food or dress. His hat (that famous hat which was his "desk and memorandum book") was brown, faded, and the nap was usually worn or rubbed off. He wore a short cloak and sometimes a shawl. His coat and vest hung loosely on his gaunt frame, and his trousers were invariably too short. On the circuit he carried in one hand a faded green umbrella, with "A Lincoln" in large white cotton or muslin letters sewed on the outside. The knob was gone from the handle, and when closed a piece of cord was usually tied around it in the middle to keep it from flying open. In the other hand he carried a literal carpet-bag, in which were stored the few papers to be used

CONTEST WITH STEPHEN DOUGLAS

in court, and underclothing enough to last till his return to Springfield. He slept in a long, coarse, yellow flannel shirt, which reached half-way between his knees and ankles. It probably was not made to fit his bony figure ... and a young lawyer ... on seeing him thus arrayed for the first time, observed afterwards that "He was the ungodliest figure I ever saw."'

Unlike the other circuit lawyers, Lincoln seldom went home at the week-end, but spent his Sunday with the loungers in the country tavern rather than return to his nagging wife. Here 'his melancholy, taking to itself wings, seemed to fly away'. He was totally indifferent to worldly comforts. When his fellow lawyers talked over the money they made by speculating in real estate or grumbled about the food and drink provided at the inns, he showed no interest. Even in charging fees he was exceptionally modest and, if a case moved him, he would give his services for nothing. His reputation grew in the courts, and especially in the higher courts. After his return from Congress he began to study the law in earnest. To quote Herndon again: 'Once fixing his mind on any subject, nothing could interfere with or disturb him. We, usually, in the little country inns occupied the same bed ... Placing a candle on a chair at the head of the bed, he would read and study for hours ... I have known him to study in this position till two o'clock in the morning. Meanwhile I and others who chanced to occupy the same room would be safely and soundly asleep.' What did he read? Though he advised young students to master the essential legal text-books, Herndon says that he never read one right through himself. Nor was his knowledge of literature wide, though he dipped into Shakespeare, Byron and Burns. Philosophy did not appeal to him. He knew his Bible well and drew upon it to illuminate many of his speeches. He also taught himself Euclid and logic and continued to write poetry. And once he had his teeth into a subject that attracted him, he would never let go.

His method of winning success at the bar was to take plenty of time to prepare his cases and then present them with a moral fervour that was induced by his confidence in their justice. He believed in thorough, lucid and elementary exposition, and carried this principle into his political speeches. 'Billy, don't shoot too high', he told his partner. 'Aim lower and the common people will understand you. They are the ones you want to reach — at least they are the ones you ought to reach.' It was this combination of simplicity and moral fervour that was one of the chief secrets of his public success. Yet if he had died when he was forty his name would now be almost forgotten. For politics, despite their rebuffs for the sensitive man, were his one overpowering love in life. Had he been as the other men of his day — and there were many clever lawyers on that Illinios circuit — with a happy home, an enjoyment of little luxuries and comforts, a pleasure in making money, he might never have become a national figure. As it was, when the question of slavery gave him opportunity to return to the political theatre, he laid aside a profession that was always a bit irksome, and embraced his chance in his long arms.

Since the Missouri Compromise had been passed in 1820 under the impulse of Henry Clay, slavery had more than once threatened to divide the Union. The Foundling Fathers (as Lincoln himself always averred) had expected the institution of slavery to wither away. Neither Washington nor Jefferson had expected it to endure much beyond their lifetime. But economic considerations had renewed its vigour. The invention of the cotton gin by Eli Whitney, a young student from Massachusetts, which enabled a Negro turning a crank to clean fifty pounds of cotton a day, had given a fillip to cotton output with slave labour. Slavery had proved to be only of economic worth where the processes of production were simple routine. Thus it was in the areas where cotton and tobacco growing were the chief industries that slavery flourished. And the price of slaves varied in almost precise ratio with the price of cotton.

The balance of slave states and free states continued exact. While Texas entered the Union in 1845 as a slave state the balance was redressed by the absorption of Wisconsin as a free state in 1848. Though the northern states had altogether a bigger population than the southern slave states this did not matter politically because the Constitution provided that each state should have only two representatives in the Senate. Thus though the House of Representatives might become friendly to anti-slavery movements, the Senate could be counted upon to kill them. In 1850 the balance of states was again endangered because of the victory over Mexico. For the United States had acquired three fresh territories, New Mexico, Utah and California, none of which were covered by the terms of the Missouri Compromise. Henry Clay came forward with a fresh compromise. California was to be admitted as a free state and New Mexico and Utah were to be organized without legislation for or against slavery and were ultimately to settle their own future in this respect. The slave trade was to be abolished — as Lincoln had always wished — in the District of Columbia. Finally a Fugitive Slave Law was introduced whereby slaves escaping from their masters into free states were to be sent back. Clay was supported in his fight for this compromise by the veteran Whig statesman, Daniel Webster, and by the rising young Senator from Illinois, Stephen Douglas, who had married the daughter of a kindly slave-owner. Indeed much of the plan came from Douglas whose pet scheme was to allow states to settle their own future. The Bills were signed by President Fillmore who had succeeded General Zachary Taylor on his death in 1850.

The Compromise of 1850 only postponed the clash over the future of slavery, as many statesmen realized. In the north the movement against slavery gathered momentum and received stimulus both from many of the pulpits and from the publication of the best-selling novel, *Uncle Tom's Cabin*. Many northerners objected to the harsh features of the Fugitive Slave Law and connived at its evasion, while in the south a resentful feeling was arising among the slave-holders that the Federal Government was being badgered into the abolition of a form of property that was reckoned to be worth at least £1,000,000,000. It was openly asserted by many southerners — among others by Lincoln's friend, Speed — that they would rather see the Union dissolved than consent to the abolition of slavery 'especially at the bidding of those who are not themselves interested'. Abraham Lincoln had long expected this threat. For the hope of Jefferson's political heirs that the institution would gradually die had obviously ceased to have any foundation; and if it did not die, it must be killed; and if it were to be killed, it would mean fighting. One day, as Lincoln was walking away from court with John Stuart, his friend said to him: 'Lincoln, the time is coming when we shall all have to be either Abolitionists or Democrats.' Lincoln thought a moment and then answered ruefully: 'When that time comes my mind is made up, for I believe the slavery question can never be successfully compromised.'

In 1854 the slavery question was again brought forward in Congress in connection with the rapid development of the fertile territories beyond the Missouri River which now form the states of Kansas and Nebraska. This time the architect of the compromise was Stephen Douglas. This energetic and resourceful orator and lawyer had won his reputation, like Lincoln, in Illinois, though he was born in Vermont: indeed he is said to have once been a rival for the hand of Mary Todd. Douglas was only five feet high with a large round face, a massive neck and a small nose and was nicknamed 'the Little Giant'. Though four years younger than Lincoln he had always been ahead of him in his career. He had been appointed a judge when he was twenty-seven and at thirty was a Congressman before Lincoln and later a Senator. Douglas was commonly spoken of as the next Democratic candidate for the Presidency. This tough keen politician was not stirred by the moral evils of slavery but was anxious to avoid a rupture between north and south. He therefore offered as a compromise (following the precedent of New Mexico and Utah) that the inhabitants of Kansas and Nebraska should be allowed to decide for themselves when they attained sufficient population to become states whether they wanted to be slave or free. Thus the decision would be taken out of the hands of the Federal Government and settled on recognizable democratic principles. His plan met with stalwart opposition in the north for several reasons. In the first place it meant the repeal of the Missouri Compromise which had excluded slavery from all territory acquired by the Louisiana Purchase (as Kansas and Nebraska were) north of the parallel 36' 30" and thus opened the possibility of slavery coming to parts of the United States where it had hitherto been prohibited. Secondly it in effect invited the slave-owners to settle in these new prairie lands in such numbers as to promise an ultimate decision in their favour and thereby fomented corruption, violence and perhaps civil war. The whole country was roused by the Kansas-Nebraska Bill as it had seldom been moved before. There were virulent newspaper campaigns and fierce debates in Congress. When the Democratic President, Franklin Pierce, signed the bills the storm did not abate, but heightened. The compromise plan acted as a cataclysm on American politics. Both the old parties were split largely into the very geographical sections that Douglas had hoped to reconcile, and, as Herndon wrote, 'it drove together strange, discordant elements in readiness to fight a common enemy', and 'brought to the forefront a leader in the person of Lincoln'.

When Stephen Douglas returned from the Senate to Illinois in the autumn of 1854 he embarked on a speech-making tour in defence of the Kansas-Nebraska Compromise. He met with an abusive reception in Chicago, where he lived, but as he moved south to Springfield he was heard with more sympathy. Abraham Lincoln, who disliked the repeal of the Missouri Compromise and was the acknowledged spokesman of Douglas's opponents in Central Illinois, determined to answer him before the vast crowds which gathered in October to attend the state agricultural fair. Twelve days later in a homeric contest of oratory at Peoria Lincoln again answered Douglas in a four-hour speech packed with argument and charged with emotion: this speech was left on record and formed one of the first foundations of his national fame. Douglas had argued his case for the Nebraska Bill in a spirit of sweet reasonableness, affirming that it was not the duty of the Federal Government either to force slavery into a territory or to exclude slavery from it but to leave it to the people who lived there to decide in accordance with the recognized principles of popular sovereignty. Lincoln, who was said to have been seen 'mousing about the libraries of the State House' to collect his facts, replied with a broad and deep survey of the whole subject ranging the history of the United States and culminating in an appeal to his audience not to allow the clock to be set back. In a voice quivering with excitement he declared his hatred of the 'monstrous injustice of slavery itself' and pronounced its inconsistency with the 'very fundamental principles of civil liberty'. But he was careful to show that he was no Abolitionist himself: 'I have no prejudice', he said, 'against the southern people. They are just what we would be in their situation. If slavery did not now exist among them, they would not introduce it. If it did now exist among us, we should not instantly give it up.' Indeed, he continued: 'If all earthly power were given to me, I should not know what to do as to the existing institution.' But Lincoln squarely faced Douglas's central argument about the new territories. Though he would not compel existing slave states to abandon their human properties, he would on no account consent to the extension of slavery to fresh areas of the United States:

> Whether slavery shall go into Nebraska, or other new Territories, is not a matter of exclusive concern to the people who may go there. The whole nation is interested that the best use shall be made of those Territories. We want them for homes of free white people ... Slave States are places for poor white people to remove from, not to remove to. Now Free States are the places for poor people to go to, and better their condition. For this use the nation needs these Territories.

This paragraph was the heart of Lincoln's argument and the projection of his own character. He himself came of a family of poor pioneers. He himself had been a poor white labourer, the honest aspiring man who demanded his chance to improve his lot. Beyond this he sympathized with the black man whom he had not seen in the paternal care of a good slave-owner such as Douglas's father-in-law, but in the stocks at New Orleans. As he wrote to his friend, Speed, in reference to the Fugitive Slave Law, 'he hated to see the poor creatures hunted down and caught', even though 'he bit his lips and kept quiet'. Lincoln resolutely denied that the doctrine of self-government could be applied to the question, for slavery, he said, was itself the negation of self-government. He therefore pleaded for the nation to turn back to the principles of the Foundling Fathers, to the Declaration of Independence, and to the Missouri Compromise. 'Let north and south,' he concluded, 'let all Americans — let all lovers of liberty everywhere — join in the great and good work. If we do this, we shall not only have saved the Union, but we shall have so saved it, as to make it and keep it forever worth saving. We shall have so saved it that the succeeding millions of free, happy people, the world over, shall rise up and call us blessed to the latest generation.'

Illinois, itself a geographical link between north and south, was torn between the two points of view. Yet enough members of Douglas's own party in the state, the Democrats, turned against him to ensure the defeat of the candidate favouring the Kansas-Nebraska Compromise in the Senatorial election which took place in the legislature in the following year. Lincoln, whose local fame had been enhanced by his Peoria speech, was the Whig candidate. But the anti-Douglas Democrats refused to vote for a Whig and so, to secure victory over the 'Nebraska men', as Douglas's followers were called, Lincoln was obliged to swing his own forty-seven votes in the Illinois Legislature to the anti-Nebraska candidate who had but five. 'I regret my defeat moderately', he observed to a friend, but we may suspect that it was a severe shock to his ambition. For it was an ambition now lit by genuine fires of wrath. After he had twice vainly tried to induce the Governor of Illinois to use his influence to obtain the release of a free Negro who had gone to New Orleans, been imprisoned there and was in danger of being sold into slavery, he exclaimed: 'By God, Governor I'll make the ground of this country too hot for the foot of a slave, whether you have the legal power to secure the release of this boy or not.'

In all parts of the United States passion and fear were coming more and more to determine the politics of slavery. Senator Douglas's plan to prevent a conflict between north and south by leaving it to the inhabitants of the new territories to decide for themselves whether or not they wanted the institution of slavery had at first appeared to the majority in Congress to be both democratic and statesmanlike. But events in Kansas now proved that this solution, though excellent in theory, hardly worked in practice. It had been conceded on all hands that Nebraska would become a free state, but in Kansas extremists on both sides employed every method, legitimate and unscrupulous, to ensure that their own point of view should prevail. The Abolitionists used large sums of money which were distributed through Emigrant Aid Societies to provide that sufficient white settlers should make their homes in Kansas and vote down the legalization of slavery. On the other side parties of 'border ruffians', organized in 'Blue Lodges', in the neighbouring slave state of Missouri worked out plans to break across the frontier and either intimidate the northern settlers or cast illegal votes for slavery. The pro-slavery party won the election to the convention and proceeded to write slavery into the state constitution. The free settlers retorted by setting up a rival government and thus the battle of stratagems degenerated into civil war. President Buchanan endorsed and commended to Congress the pro-slavery constitution even though there were said to have been not more than two hundred slaves in the whole territory.

Douglas did not blind himself to what was going on. On the contrary, he vigorously, though vainly, resisted in the Senate the plan to thrust the pro-slavery constitution down the throats of the people of Kansas. In 1857 he received further discomfort from a decision of the Federal Supreme Court in what was known as the Dred Scott case which laid it down that Congress had no power to extinguish a master's right to his slave in any of the new territories. This decision, Douglas was compelled to argue, did not contradict but, on the contrary buttressed his principle that the territories themselves and not the Federal Government must be the arbiters of the question whether they should admit slavery, since a slave-holder could not exercise his rights unless they were enforced by local legislation. Lincoln repudiated this interpretation of the Constitution, arguing that it was a plain violation of the language of the Declaration of Independence, which had intended that in the United States all men should be free and equal, and that Congress therefore had the right to see that they ultimately became so. The Dred Scott decision was therefore twisted to strengthen Douglas's case, but it could not be doubted that the struggle in Kansas had weakened it — for 'popular sovereignty' had brought not peace but a sword. Both events had served to sharpen the argument of principle that was now the leading topic in American politics: this was whether slavery should be allowed to live and therefore breed or whether it should be discouraged and thus, like the 'short-lived' people in Shaw's *Back to Methusaleh*, be assisted to die.

It is necessary to try to understand plainly Lincoln's point of view. It was perhaps most simply expressed in a speech which he delivered to Kentuckians (Kentucky was a slave state) in September 1859. He then said: 'I think slavery is wrong, morally and politically. I desire that it shall be no further spread in these United States and I should not object if it should gradually terminate in the whole Union.' Speaking to the citizens of a slave

CONTEST WITH STEPHEN DOUGLAS

state he chose mild words. A year earlier he had assured a newspaper man that he had no desire to interfere with slavery in the states where it already existed. Furthermore, as he explained in the course of his many speeches on the subject, when he spoke of the moral iniquity of slavery and of the right of Negroes to be treated as free and equal in terms of the Declaration of Independence he did not mean that they should be regarded as equal in all respects with the white man. 'I am not', he declared, 'nor ever have been in favour of making voters or jurors of negroes, nor of qualifying them to hold office, nor to intermarry with white people.' 'Because I do not want a black woman for a slave,' he explained, 'I must not necessarily want her for a wife.' Because therefore he considered slavery to be morally wrong — 'I have always hated slavery,' he once said — and politically wrong, since he believed that 'the broadening territories of the United States should be homes for free white people', Lincoln was determined to resist the 'tendency . . . to make slavery universal and perpetual in this nation'. And thus, at any rate so far as his public utterances were concerned, his view was that the fight lay between those who wanted to extend slavery and those who wanted to prevent its extension and if, rather than acquiesce in the limitation of slavery, the southern slave-holders were prepared to leave the Union, he was determined to prevent them. 'We do not want to dissolve the Union', he said. 'You shall not.'

But while these were Lincoln's public pronouncements he knew in his heart that the problem was not as simple as that. On more than one occasion he told his friends that compromise over slavery was impossible. He acquiesced in the opinion expressed by Senator Seward of New York that an 'irrepressible conflict' existed. Repeatedly he emphasized his argument that when the United States were created, it was the intention of the founders that slavery should ultimately be abolished. Yet, as he wrote in a revealing letter of August 15th, 1855, 'experience had demonstrated that there is no peaceful extinction of slavery in prospect'. The words of the Declaration of Independence that 'all men are created equal' had, he recognized, become 'a self-evident lie'. A peaceful and voluntary emancipation of the slaves in the United States, he realized, had become impossible: 'The Autocrat of all Russia will resign his crown and proclaim his subjects free republicans sooner than will our American masters voluntarily give up their slaves.' 'The problem', he admitted in this remarkable letter, was 'too weighty' for him — 'may God in his mercy superintend the solution.' Lincoln therefore did not fail to see the logic of his position. If slavery was, as he thought, a vast moral evil, it ought to be eradicated. Yet if there was such bitterness over its possible extension, how much more shattering would be the conflict over its proposed abolition. Hoping for the best, perhaps for some kind of patch-work solution, Lincoln did not allow his innermost anxieties to find their way into his speeches. Yet in one speech — perhaps the most famous of all his speeches — which he delivered in June 1858 when he accepted the nomination to stand against Douglas for the Senate, he did allow his doubts to be disclosed. He had read out the draft of the speech first to his personal friends and advisers who with one exception were unanimously against his using it. What he said was this:

> A house divided against itself cannot stand. I believe this Government cannot endure permanently half slave and half free. I do not expect the Union to be dissolved — I do not expect the house to fall — but I do expect it will cease to be divided.

Douglas with his penetrating mind at once perceived the significance of this utterance and seized upon it. For if, as Lincoln had said, the nation could not survive 'half slave and half free' then it followed that slavery must be abolished everywhere. Yet slavery would not be abolished voluntarily and could not be abolished forcibly without civil war. When Douglas accused Lincoln of fomenting a war of extermination between north and south, he retorted that after all the Federal Government had endured for over eighty years half slave and half free and asserted that although he hoped for the ultimate extinction of slavery, he was opposed to the free states interfering with slavery in the slave states. The argument was specious and Lincoln knew it. Douglas had logic, if not history on his side, when he claimed that as the government of the United States had been founded on a white basis therefore it ought to continue indefinitely half slave and half free. President Jefferson had also had logic on his side when he had argued that the best way of meeting the problem of abolishing Negro slavery was to deport all the Negroes. Lincoln fell between two stools when he argued that the Negroes should be gradually emancipated and retained within the nation as an inferior race. But history is not necessarily dictated by logical principles any more than life is. The second part of what Lincoln foresaw came to pass. And as to the first part, though he certainly hoped for the peaceable extinction of slavery, he knew in his heart that without a miracle it could never be.

In 1856 Lincoln had joined the Republican party, a coalition of the former Whig party and anti-Nebraska Democrats who had secured the defeat of Douglas's candidate for Illinois Senator eighteen months before. Abolitionists also joined the new party as well as a number of the northern members of the 'American' or 'Know-Nothing' party, which particularly disliked foreigners and Roman Catholics. The Illinois branch of the party adopted Colonel Bissell, a crippled hero of the Mexican war, as its candidate for Governor in the coming election and during the meeting of the Republican State Convention Lincoln is said to have delivered the finest speech of his life arguing the slavery question 'with the zeal of a new convert'. Unfortunately the speech has not survived. At the National Convention of the party at Philadelphia Lincoln was nominated as vice-presidential candidate, somewhat to his own surprise, though he failed to carry the day. Nevertheless 110 votes were proofs of his extending fame. The platform of the Republican party was broad, but it asserted that it was the right and duty of Congress to prohibit slavery — and polygamy — in the territories. In spite of Lincoln's vigorous campaigning for the Republicans the Democratic candidate for the Presidency, James Buchanan, the 'old fogey from Pennsylvania', as his critics called him, won. In Illinois, however, the Republicans obtained the election of Bissell as Governor.

In 1858 Lincoln was chosen as the Illinois Republican candidate for Senator. His opponent was the redoubtable Douglas whose term was now up. Douglas, who had quarrelled with President Buchanan, was now playing a lone hand and his chief hope of continuing a political career was to retain his hold on Illinois. It was in this, the third series of debates, between the two famous Illinois politicians, the 'Tall Sucker' and the 'Little Giant', that the slavery question was defined in detail. This time by a common arrangement the two antagonists debated with each other directly in the same place at the same time. In those distant days, before the advent of the cinema and of broadcasting, huge audiences could be persuaded to listen for hour upon hour to speeches on national issues by celebrated men. Douglas's 'forte in debating' was said to be his power of mystifying a point and Lincoln's the cool lucidity that yet gave the impression of hidden fires carrying him forward. The speeches were for the most part long and intricate exercises in constitutional interpretation, spiced by personal allusions, circling round the now familiar central theme whether slavery might be extended or not. Douglas continually accused Lincoln of inciting civil war and Lincoln said he did not want civil war, but feared that it was coming. In one debate (at Freeport in north-west Illinois) Lincoln put to Douglas a question that he knew Douglas would find hard to answer, this was: 'Can the people of a United States Territory in any lawful way against the wish of any citizen of the United States exclude slavery from its limits prior to the formation of a State constitution?' If Douglas answered yes, he would in effect deny the validity of the Dred Scott decision — which had allowed that slavery was legal in any part of the Union where it had not specifically been forbidden — and thereby offend the slave-owners and still further widen his breach with his own party. If he answered no, he would jeopardize his chances of re-election in Illinois and reduce his popularity in the north. Since in order to win the Illinois election he dared not associate himself with the slave-owners in effect he answered yes, by maintaining that in spite of the Dred Scott decision, a territory where the anti-slavery party formed the majority could ban slavery by refusing it police protection. Douglas won the election as Senator, but by disrupting his party he forfeited his chance of becoming President three years later. Lincoln, on the other hand, through his speeches that were widely reported and digested and through the reflected notoriety of his fight against Douglas, focused the national attention. He saw that his time would come. Though dejected by his defeat, he was sure of the final victory of the Republican cause. 'The fight must go on', he said. 'The question is not half settled. New splits and divisions will soon be upon our adversaries, and we shall fuse again.'

CONTEST WITH STEPHEN DOUGLAS

Lincoln had met many disappointments in his political career and for this reason he was extremely modest about his chances of becoming President of the United States. 'Nobody has ever expected me to be President', he said in the course of his debates with Douglas. 'In my poor lean, lank face nobody has ever seen any cabbages sprouting out.' But it was these very debates that gave him his unique opportunity. 'You are like Byron', a Chicago editor had written to him,' who woke up one morning and found himself famous. People wish to know about you. You have sprung at once from the position of a capital fellow and a leading lawyer in Illinois, to a national reputation.' Lincoln took all his chances and used them. In the years 1859 and 1860 others helped him on his way and he nursed himself. He preached the doctrine of preserving party unity by sticking to one central theme whilst otherwise being placatory and non-committal and he refused to squander his gifts or to endanger his supreme opportunity by giving offence through unwise observations on side issues.

Douglas after his re-election to the Senate had tended to trim his sails to suit the slave-owners in the hope of reconciling himself with his old party chiefs and pleasing the south sufficiently to catch their votes. Although he did not depart from his principles of 'popular' or 'squatter' sovereignty as the solvent of the slavery question nor withdraw the statement forced from him at Freeport that the territories could, if they wished, effectively ban slavery, he counter-balanced this by asserting that in territories where 'climate, soil and production make it the interests of the inhabitants to encourage slave property, they will pass a slave code'.

Lincoln, for his part, did not attempt to woo popularity in the slave states. For he saw that if only the free states would vote solidly for one candidate the Republican party would win the next election. In a speech delivered in celebration of the anniversary of Thomas Jefferson's birthday he repeated his view that slavery was incompatible with a free society. 'The principles of Jefferson', he said, 'are the definitions and axioms of free society. And yet they are denied and evaded with no small show of success. One dashingly calls them "self-evident lies." ' ... 'These expressions ... are the vanguard — the miners and sappers of returning despotism. We must repulse them, or they will subjugate us. This is a world of compensation; and he who would be no slave must consent to have no slave. Those who deny freedom to others deserve it not for themselves; and, under a Just God, cannot long retain it.' Lincoln exposed the inconsistency of the Dred Scott decision as interpreted by Douglas — who, as he incisively put it, tried to prove that though the Supreme Court had ruled that slavery was legal in any territory, the people of a territory could drive it out again.

Late in 1859 took place an incident which might have appeared to shake the chances of a Republican victory. An Old Testament figure by name John Brown, father of nineteen children and a fanatical Abolitionist, who had taken part in the civil war in Kansas, with a handful of followers, tried to provoke a Negro rising within the borders of Virginia. Without counting the odds — like the Fifth Monarchy Men of seventeenth-century England — he thrust into Harper's Ferry, a town on the Maryland-Virginia border, seized the armoury and arsenal, rounded up slave-owners and freed slaves. The rising was suppressed with little difficulty by Colonel Robert E. Lee and a detachment of United States Marines. After a fair trial Brown was convicted, sentenced and hanged. He died like a saint or a hero, determined that his soul should go marching on. John Brown's effort, Lincoln carefully explained, was not a slave insurrection. 'It was an attempt by white men to get up a revolt among slaves, in which the slaves refused to participate.' It was, he added, the absurdity of the enthusiast. Lincoln was a brooding enthusiast himself, but now he eschewed all absurdities. When he was invited to New York to make a speech, he took pains to avoid the mannerisms or even the humorous style that had been so successful in the west. He gave his distinguished audience a solemn historical disquisition 'using his rare powers to elucidate and convince'. The New York daily newspapers published the speech in full and it became plain, at any rate in the opinion of his friend, Herndon, that he had 'captured the metropolis'.

The New York speech was Lincoln's last big campaigning speech, delivered on February 27th, 1860. Now followed the party conventions to elect the candidates for the presidential election of that same year. The Democratic Convention at Charleston was divided between those who demanded the protection of Congress for the right of the slave-owner to enter new

CONTEST WITH STEPHEN DOUGLAS

territories and the upholders of Douglas's doctrines. The cotton states seceded from the Convention and when it reassembled at Baltimore were joined in the secession by the delegates of seven other states. At Chicago, where the Republicans met, the dividing question was not measures but men. Amid deafening tumult in a vast building called the Wigwam Lincoln's friends worked for his nomination against that of William H. Seward, the experienced New York statesman. Seward was a man who made enemies, while there was a growing conviction that what was needed as Republican candidate was a man who could sway such central states as Illinois and Indiana. In the end out of all the excited noise and wrangle these two main candidates emerged and in the succeeding stillness the gathered delegates voted more momentously than they knew and chose 'Honest Abe Lincoln — the Rail-Splitter from Illinois'.

Back in Springfield Lincoln waited in a newspaper office to learn the result and having heard it, went off 'to tell the little woman down the street the news'. And in Springfield he remained in meditative dignity throughout the electoral campaign. Besides the Republican choice there were three other candidates: Stephen Douglas, still advocating the doctrine of 'popular sovereignty' as the only practical way of averting civil war; John C. Breckenridge of Kentucky, whose policy was to extend and perpetuate slavery through the power of the Federal Government; and John Bell of Tennessee whose 'Constitutional Union' party professed to ignore the question of slavery altogether. There were now eighteen free states and fifteen slave states in the Union. Except in New Jersey, where he shared the electoral votes with Douglas, Lincoln carried the votes of all the free states, while the votes of the slave states were split between his three opponents with Douglas at their head.

After many years of political defeat and personal disappointment Abraham Lincoln had been elected to the highest office in the United States, but seldom in modern history was a statesman called to lead his nation at more critical a period. Lincoln himself had no illusions about what lay ahead; he knew it was no dream of glory. From the time when his innermost melancholy thoughts had found their outward expression in his 'house divided' speech he had known in his heart that the conflict that was approaching was to determine the future of his country as an entity. Before his election on November 6th, 1860, he was heard to say: 'I see the storm coming.' And before the year was out the political leaders of South Carolina had replied to his victory by again raising the standard of secession from the Union.

3. PRESIDENT—TO THE FIRST BATTLE OF BULL RUN (1861)

The election of Abraham Lincoln as President of the United States had been the signal for civil war. The origins of this terrible conflict in which more men were killed than in any other civil war in the modern world cannot be appreciated without an understanding of the earlier history of the United States. The separate states (in the form of colonies) had existed prior to the Union and several of them had entered the Union with misgivings. Once inside the Union the states retained all their political rights except those that were specifically assigned to the Federal Government in the Constitution that was very difficult to amend. Yet the Constitution had been interpreted particularly by Chief Justice Marshall in a broad sense that conferred on the Federal Government more power than many people considered had originally been intended for it. The exercise of this power often offended sectional interests. And on more than one occasion before 1860 a state or group of states had claimed that if the policy of the Federal Government was injurious to them then they had the right to withdraw from the Union. The New England states had made such a claim when Madison was President and South Carolina had once before been on the edge of secession in Andrew Jackson's time. Nor was slavery a novel cause of dissatisfaction to the southern states. Just as Henry Clay's revision of a tariff to which the southern states objected had been perhaps an even more potent reason than Jackson's military threats for holding South Carolina in the Union in the eighteen-thirties, so the Missouri Compromise and the Compromise of 1850 had been conceived to prevent a breach over slavery between the north and south. Indeed it has been said that: 'Until 1854 every time the south faced Congress with the alternatives of concession to slavery or secession it carried its point.'

But in spite of these threatening controversies over the tariff and the spread of slavery, during the seventy years since Washington's first inauguration the Federal Union had become an established fact. The working of the Ordinance of 1787 — sponsored and approved by Jefferson — which laid down that new territories were to come within the jurisdiction of the Federal and not the nearest State Government contributed materially to the growing importance of the Union. So did the national tariff and the policy of 'internal improvements' forwarded by the Whigs. The very nature of one of those internal improvements, the railways, was such as to bind the states more closely together. And with such objective realities pointing to the cohesion of the Union there had developed a patriotic sentiment in its favour. The acquisition of Louisiana from Spain, the war of 1812 against England, the war against Mexico and the periodic airing of grievances against foreign nations, particularly Great Britain, had engendered a spirit of militant nationalism. The three Presidents, whose lives have been sketched in this book, all ultimately concurred in the doctrine that 'the Union must be preserved'. Yet all three of these Presidents were southerners, and another southerner, Henry Clay, who in his life did so much to hold the Union together had said: 'I owe a paramount allegiance to the whole Union — a subordinate one to my own state.'

At the same time that the United States was thus becoming a nation, north and south had distinctive economic histories. The north had found prosperity in commerce, industry and finance, and slavery had been of no value to it. The south had subsisted on cotton, and to a lesser extent on tobacco and agriculture: New Orleans was its only flourishing city of any size. Though American historians have warned us not to exaggerate the significance of slavery in the south, where there were many families who had never owned a slave, the fact remains that at the outbreak of the Civil War there were between three and a half and four million slaves out of a total population of about nine million in the southern states: they must therefore have been a weighty factor in their economy. As in the north and west the cry for the abolition of slavery became more insistent, the southern leaders came to fear that their communities would be ruined if they remained in a Union where the slave-owning states were in a minority. For it must be remembered that although Lincoln himself was a moderate, the Abolitionists, with all their religious fervour against the peculiar institution of the south, were foundation members of the Republican party and their votes had helped to carry him to power. It is hard, therefore, to avoid the conclusion that the future of slavery was the root cause of the Civil War.

Yet after the war was over the leaders of the southern Confederacy denied that it had been started by them over the question of slavery. They argued, on the contrary, that it had been a struggle between the 'historical' federal system, as conceived by the founders of the Republic, and the consolidation of political power at the centre desired by their enemies: 'African servitude', they asserted, 'was only an incident.' President Woodrow Wilson, himself a southerner, in a chapter which he wrote for the *Cambridge Modern History* on the subject found a happy mean in the statement that the cause of the conflict had been slavery 'upon the surface'. 'Perhaps', he added, 'it need never have come to this, had Douglas kept his hand from the law. The movement against slavery had been weak, occasional, non-partisan until the Missouri Compromise was repealed, ten years before. It was that which brought the Republican party into existence and set the sections by the ears. But now that the breach had come, it did not seem to men in the south merely a contest about slavery; it seemed, rather, so far as the south was concerned, a final question and answer as to the fundamental matter of self-government.' J. F. Rhodes, on the other hand, wrote much more definitely: 'If any one is inclined to doubt that there was other than a single cause for secession and the war that ensued . . . let him read the speeches and newspaper articles of the early days of the secession movement in South Carolina' and he quotes Trenholm, one of the South Carolina leaders, as saying: 'The first issue [of secession] was made upon the question of a tariff in which the sympathies of the world were with the South. Now we are joining the issue with the prejudices of the world against us.'

The truth would seem to be that the south were fighting for an outworn creed. No sensible person today would argue that the evolution of the United States into a Great Power through the strengthening of the Federal Government has contributed less to happiness at home or justice abroad than a loose confederation of states would have done. That is not to deny that the south fought for an ideal, just as the north did. The men of South Carolina regarded their state as a little nation, its citizens a free people who were about to become the victims of aggression. In this they were wrong. Abraham Lincoln had declared a thousand times that he did not propose to interfere with slavery in the states where it was already established. They raised the standard of rebellion out of a fear that had no foundation.

No one can understand the character of Lincoln if they do not appreciate that he was a neurotic. That is to make no adverse criticism of a great man, for many famous men have been neurotics; indeed it is unusual for the well-balanced satisfied man to reach the heights of celebrity. To the melancholy woman who was his mother and the ne'er-do-well happy-go-lucky fellow who was his father a genius had been born. Out of the alliance came the hypochondriac politician whose lack of balance could not be righted by his own uneasy marriage. In his mind fears and brave decisions fought for mastery and fits of exaltation alternated with periods of profound depression. Those were not the days of psychiatrists who can explain a man to himself, even though they do not always explain his fears away. Thus Lincoln became a fatalist and cast the blame for events that were the product either of his own character or of historic causes on some inflexible Providence — certainly not on the Christian's God. 'I was always superstitious', he told his friend, Speed, as early as 1832. And before he left Springfield, it is said, he looked into a mirror and saw a double image of himself, which was interpreted by his wife as meaning that he would serve two terms as President, but would not survive the second. One of his best biographers has remarked that on his journey to the capital Lincoln was a changed man, that he lost his power of speech, and was assailed by self-doubts. If this were so, it was in character. It was rational that the triumph of the election should have been followed by a phase of worry and fear, more especially as he knew, after the decision by South Carolina to secede from the Union, that he was to be faced by one of the hardest tasks that had yet confronted an American President. On the other hand, it was surely natural that until he arrived in Washington and had obtained full access to all the official information, he should hesitate to commit himself in public to a specific line of policy. For until March 4th, the inauguration day, his predecessor, the Democratic President Buchanan was responsible for handling the crisis. It is perhaps an odd commentary on the virulence of the party system that the two men did not at once consult together.

As it was, while passions imperilled the Union, Lincoln was engaged upon routine and personal affairs. He was besieged by office seekers. 'Individuals, deputations and delegations from all quarters pressed in upon him in a manner that might have killed a man of less robust constitution. The hotels of Springfield were filled with gentlemen who came with light baggage and heavy schemes. The party had never been in office. A clean sweep of the "ins" was expected and all the "outs" were patriotically anxious to take the vacant places. It was a party that had never fed; and it was voraciously hungry.' (Herndon.) Lincoln wisely offered the post of Secretary of State to Seward, the rival Republican candidate for presidential nomination, and Seward with equal wisdom, though some optimism as to the sway he might exercise, accepted it. Salmon P. Chase, another former rival, a clever but pessimistic man who had buried three wives, was appointed Secretary of the Treasury; and Lincoln after some hesitation selected Simon Cameron, who was known as 'the Czar of Pennsylvania' as Secretary of War. He sounded his friends, Speed and Herndon, about what they would like to have, but both disclaimed any desire for large loaves or fat fish. He paid a call upon his aged step-mother and visited the site of his father's grave. To Herndon on leaving Springfield he said: 'Give our clients to understand that the election of a President makes no change in the firm of Lincoln and Herndon. If I live I'm coming back some time, and then we'll go right on practising law as if nothing had ever happened.' On February 11th, a rainy day, he left Springfield with an oppressive sadness in his heart, never to return.

In the course of the eleven-day ceremonial journey he made several short speeches and both before and during his trip he

FIRST BATTLE OF BULL RUN

wrote some pertinent letters. He tried to reassure the south about his unprovocative intentions. To a North Carolina Congressman he explained that he had no thought of abolishing slavery in the slave states; to Alexander H. Stephens, who was to become the Vice-President in the southern Confederacy, he had written on December 22nd: 'You think slavery is right and ought to be extended, while I think it is wrong and ought to be restricted. That, I suppose, is the rub. It certainly is the only substantial difference between us.' But to any suggestion of extending slavery in any form or by any means he was utterly opposed. Some of his friends within the Republican party strongly favoured a fresh compromise such as the continuation of the 36' 30" line of the Missouri Compromise right across the country to the Pacific with slavery permitted to the south of it and forbidden to the north of it. Others urged the adoption of Douglas's plan of popular sovereignty, against which Lincoln had so long contended. The advocates of this policy can scarcely have understood the man with whom they were dealing. Lincoln was consistent and clear. 'Let there be no compromise on the question of extending slavery', he wrote to Senator Trumbull of Illinois. 'If there be, all our labour is lost, and ere long must be done again. The dangerous ground — that into which some of our friends have a hankering to run is Popular Sovereignty. Have none of it. Stand firm. The tug has to come, and better now than any time hereafter.' Equally firmly he set his face against secession, although he seems at this time to have suffered from the delusion that the secessionists were not an influential minority. Nevertheless the struggle was one which he had long feared and from which he would not flinch. To General Winfield Scott, the seventy-four year old veteran of the war of 1812, who was still in command of the regular forces, he sent a message to be as well prepared as he could be either to hold or retake the Federal forts in the south 'as the case may require at and after the inauguration'. To Seward who offered him advice he replied that he would not change his mind on the central point nor would he permit the Union to acquire any fresh territory — for example, the island of Cuba for which the south was clamouring — into which slavery could spread. On minor aspects of the slavery question he would accept advice but not on the central question itself.

ABRAHAM LINCOLN

In his public speeches he expressed the view that the crisis was an artificial one. By this he meant that the south was agitated over baseless fears: many thought it was unwise of him to say so, however anxious he might have been to calm public opinion, since he must have known that the crisis was real. Yet broadly he did not deceive the people. He told them that it might be necessary 'to put the foot down firmly'; he said that he saw no rightful principle whereby one state could break up the nation; and he swore that he would rather be assassinated than surrender his principles.

Threats of assassination were already in the air and the renowned private detective, Alan Pinkerton, was sent to guard him during the last stages of his train journey which meant crossing the capital of the slave state of Maryland. He therefore drove through Baltimore in the middle of the night almost in disguise, an incident that gave his enemies much food for fun. It was also noticed that he had grown a beard:

> I'll put my trust in Providence,
> And let my whiskers grow,

they made him say. But as this journey with its tiring ceremonies and comic interludes delayed Lincoln's arrival at the centre of affairs, the sands were running out. One after another, Mississippi, Florida, Alabama, Georgia and Louisiana, joined South Carolina in the fold of secession. On February 18th Lincoln heard that Jefferson Davis, formerly Senator for Mississippi, had been elected President of the southern Confederacy, consisting of the first six seceding states. Buchanan, palsied by well-meaning cautiousness, denied the right to secede, but recoiled from the decision to coerce. His Cabinet broke under him and he would give no definite military orders. If the war arose out of southern misunderstandings, if it became inevitable through the firm refusal of Lincoln to compromise over the extension of slavery, the ultimate ferocity of the conflict must be blamed on the ineptitude of the feeble old man who for all his conscientious rectitude might otherwise have been one of the half-forgotten Presidents of the United States.

Lincoln completed his Cabinet with Gideon Welles of Connecticut as Secretary of the Navy, Edward Bates of Missouri

FIRST BATTLE OF BULL RUN

(technically representative of a slave state — Lincoln had looked vainly for a real southerner) as Attorney-General, Caleb B. Smith of Indiana as Secretary for the Interior, and Montgomery Blair as Postmaster-General. Blair was the son of Francis Blair, who had been so intimate a friend of Andrew Jackson and a member of his Kitchen Cabinet. Francis Blair had been one of the founders of the Republican party — although a former slave-owner — and at the age of seventy he was frequently consulted by the new President. He was thus the living link between Jackson and Lincoln. After his arrival in Washington Lincoln took pains to see a number of representative southerners, including a group of politicians who had met in the capital especially to confer as a 'peace convention'. Lincoln was willing to offer concessions to prevent war — anything short of what he deemed a violation of the Constitution or that would permit an extension of slavery. Nothing positive, however, was achieved, and in his carefully prepared inaugural address Lincoln exerted all his powers of persuasion to avert war. The address was an amalgam of all he had said to his friends or used to warn his correspondents. In it he repeated his promise not to interfere with slavery where it already existed and to uphold the Fugitive Slave Law. On the other side he insisted that no state was entitled of its own accord to withdraw from the Union. Secession, he said, was the essence of anarchy, and constitutional amendment was the only legitimate method of changing the institutions of the United States: 'In your hands,' he concluded in an appeal to the south, 'my dissatisfied fellow-countrymen, and not in mine, is the momentous issue of civil war. The government will not assail you. You can have no conflict without being yourselves the aggressors. You have no oath registered in heaven to destroy the government, while I shall have the most solemn one to preserve, protect and defend it.

'I am loath to close. We are not enemies, but friends. We must not be enemies. Though passion may have strained, it must not break our bonds of affection. The mystic chords of memory, stretching from every battlefield and patriot grave to every living heart and hearth-stone all over this broad land, will yet swell the chorus of the Union when again touched, as surely they will be, by the better angels of our nature.'

It was symbolic of the unity of the north that while Lincoln delivered this address, his old Democratic opponent, Stephen Douglas, held the President's hat.*

No response was given by the southern Confederacy to Lincoln's appeal. Throughout the rest of March both sides manœuvred for position. In the mouth of Charleston Harbour, South Carolina, the Federal Fort Sumter was manned by four hundred troops with inadequate provisions and was surrounded by a much superior Confederate force. It was accepted that an attack on this fort would mean civil war and therefore President Lincoln hesitated for over a month to give any orders for its relief by sea lest this should provoke fighting. There still seemed hopes of a settlement since some of the upper southern states, then known as the Border States, notably Virginia, had not yet thrown in their lot with President Jefferson Davis's Confederacy and without them, if it came to the crunch, the south would be in a markedly weaker situation. Thus the blow poised in the air. The Confederacy still fancied that it might be allowed to leave the Union in peace: and there were several influential voices in the north that were advising Lincoln, as Pharaoh had been advised, to let the ungrateful people go.

Lincoln received conflicting counsel from his Cabinet. His Secretary of State, Seward, argued that Fort Sumter should be evacuated and one danger spot thus erased. Lincoln, while counting on the 'soothing aid of time' to heal the crisis, found the idea of abandoning the fort repugnant — even though his chief military adviser said, as was in fact obvious, that it could not possibly be held. On one point, however, Lincoln and Seward agreed, namely that if war came, it must be fought over the issue of union or disunion; the President rigidly refused to allow the breaking of the Union. As to Fort Sumter, he said that he would consent to its evacuation if in return Virginia, as leader of the border states, undertook not to secede. This was a question of hard bargaining and not of policy, for the causes of war remained. But nothing came of this proposed bargain, and in the first week of April Lincoln at last gave notice to the Governor of South

---

* Professor Randall points out that there is no strictly contemporary evidence for this story. It is, however, given independently by two contemporaries, writing at a slightly later date, and is accepted by Nicolay and Hay.

Carolina that 'an attempt will be made to supply Fort Sumter with provisions only; and that if such an attempt be not resisted, no effort to throw in men, arms or ammunition will be made without further notice, or in case of an attack on the fort'. It was thus still left to the Confederate Government to take the fatal decision. Its headquarters were in Montgomery, Alabama, where the first six seceding states had been joined by Texas towards the end of February. Here it was realized that by attacking Fort Sumter it might gain new allies and on this basis the decision to reduce the fort was taken. On April 12th, 1861, the first shot was fired and two days later the garrison of Fort Sumter capitulated for want of provisions. Lincoln replied with a proclamation calling for the enlistment of 75,000 militiamen and now at last summoned a special session of Congress. Four days later on his own responsibility he proclaimed a blockade of the belligerent southern states in answer to the threat of privateering by Jefferson Davis. The fearful dream that had always haunted Lincoln of the house divided against itself thus became a reality.

In the war that now began twenty-three states upheld the cause of the Union against eleven that favoured secession. Texas, Virginia, North Carolina, Tennessee and Arkansas joined the six states that had originally banded themselves under the presidency of Jefferson Davis; but western Virginia split off from the original state and came under Federal leadership. The eleven states had a population of only about five million whites as compared with some twenty-two million who acknowledged the Presidency of Lincoln. Of the twenty-three states four were slave states, Kentucky, Missouri, Maryland and Delaware, and the majority of their populations remained loyal to the Union, but in the first three, internal political and military struggles took place before they were secure. The loyalty of Maryland, western Virginia, Kentucky and Missouri protected the flanks of the northern free states and an excellent system of communications including a good railway network.

Ultimately the disparity in the size of the populations of the two sides was reflected in the strength of the field armies. Even in the early stages of the Civil War it had been estimated that the north had a five to three superiority. The south had to use its manpower to the utmost to keep large forces in the field and indeed, after a brief experiment with volunteers the Confederate Government turned to conscription. What the south lacked in quantity was compensated in some degree by quality. The regular United States Army was so small and so largely absorbed in frontier duties that its rank-and-file took little part in the struggle; but over one-third of the officers, including some of the most promising, notably Colonel Robert E. Lee (who would have been given a high command had he remained loyal to the Union) were found on the Confederate side. The outdoor traditions of the south, the habits of horsemanship and shooting, provided the southern armies with excellent raw material, while many of the best-equipped forts in the Union were in the Confederate area. And there was little or nothing to choose between the two armies when it came to morale. Each was fighting for its own ideals. The Americans, as has been well said, are a warlike but not a military nation. Nowhere was any lack of enthusiasm or heroic courage to be found.

A study of the resources available to north and south by an impartial observer might have shown that there was no doubt which side would win. Nearly all the heavy industry capable of producing weapons and munitions of war was concentrated in the north in addition to the preponderance of the population, and the bulk of the navy and the money power. Yet there were several imponderables that caused contemporary neutral judges to hesitate over the likely result of the war. One of these was the attitude of foreign nations, which were ultimately linked through foreign trade with the agricultural south, and particularly Great Britain which bought so much southern cotton. Might they not intervene with active or secret aid? Secondly, how could an effective blockade of the coastline be maintained in view of the smallness of the fleet that Lincoln had at his disposal? Thirdly, to win the war all that the south needed to do was to carry out a victorious defensive campaign and weary its opponents. Perhaps the Confederates might succeed — as Washington had succeeded — in holding their enemies and inflicting repulses upon them until something turned up. In war something usually does turn up if one waits long enough. Lincoln himself was soon to grasp the important military fact that the Confederates had the substantial

FIRST BATTLE OF BULL RUN

advantage of operating on interior lines. Finally, as events were to prove, the south initially had the better generals.

The area of operations was divided naturally into two parts — the eastern seaboard and the Mississippi Valley. In the eastern theatre the Federal capital and Richmond which, once Virginia had broken with Lincoln, became the Confederate capital, were only a hundred miles apart and much of the fighting swayed between these two towns.

Lincoln was swiftly confirmed in wide powers which he exercised partly as President and partly as the Commander-in-Chief under the Constitution. After his original call-up of 75,000 men for the pitifully short three-month term of service — an appeal which met with an eager response — he asked for forty thousand men as three-year volunteers as well as for regular soldiers and sailors. In his message to the special session of Congress on June 4th he boldly demanded 400,000 men and 400,000,000 dollars. In noble words he described the coming conflict as 'essentially a people's contest', a test of popular government. Rebutting the right of secession as a 'principle of disintegration' he asserted: 'The people will save their government if the government itself will do its part only indifferently well.'

But brave words are no substitute for alert military leaders and adequate long-term military preparations. Lincoln's first adviser, General Winfield Scott, had been an energetic executive of Andrew Jackson but now spent most of his time in bed and could no longer mount a horse. Neither Lincoln nor his Secretary of War had any real experience of military affairs. Moreover the city of Washington was cut off during the opening stages of the war from proper communication with its hinterland and indeed it was not until a New York regiment arrived there on April 25th and the rebels in neighbouring Baltimore had been overcome that it was realized how strongly the country was behind Congress. The mood then changed from dubiety to excessive optimism. Though a case can be presented in favour of the decision it was undoubtedly under the pressure of an over-exuberant public opinion that Lincoln dispatched his half-trained militiamen to march on the rebel capital. The key point was the railway junction of Manassas where a line from the Shenandoah Valley met the line from Richmond. One rebel force was stationed at

ABRAHAM LINCOLN

Harper's Ferry, forty miles north-west of Washington, where the Shenandoah joins the Potomac, and another at Manassas Junction. Lincoln sent 30,000 men under General McDowell to Manassas while another force under General Patterson was ordered to hold the enemy at Harper's Ferry. But Patterson failed to prevent the Confederates from detaching four brigades, one commanded by Thomas J. Jackson ('Stonewall Jackson') to reinforce the Manassas force of 22,000. A battle was fought by the Bull Run stream on July 21st in which Jackson's brigade prevented the Confederate line from breaking beneath the impact of a not unskilful Federal assault until reinforcements arrived to support a counterstroke. In this battle the north lost 1500 prisoners and twenty-five guns. Some of the members of Congress who had accompanied the army from Washington to watch the war being won at a blow were either taken prisoner or compelled to return with the fugitives. Colonel William T. Sherman, who was there, described it as one of the best planned and worst fought battles in history.

Lincoln, cool in crisis, knew that one lost battle had not decided the war, but he saw that a broader and more mature plan was needed. Two days after the battle he wrote a memorandum advocating among other things an effective blockade, the dismissal of the three-month volunteers, a reorganization of the Virginia front, and a strengthening of the forces in the Shenandoah Valley. A new commander, General George Brinton McClellan, a charming young man, with a success to his credit in Virginia, was put in charge of the army before the capital, known as the Army of the Potomac, and a few months later he replaced Winfield Scott as General-in-Chief, who retired at his own request. The defeat at Bull Run, it has been said, 'had the effect of increasing and deepening the zeal, courage and determination of the Administration, the Congress, the army and the country'. But no positive military success was won before winter came — and McClellan was not to fulfil the hopes so pathetically entrusted to him. Soon Abraham Lincoln was to recognize that in order to exercise control over this widely dispersed war and to marshall all the advantages that the north possessed he must become his own Chief of Staff and teach himself to be a War Minister.

4. WAR MINISTER (1861-1863)

General McClellan, who at the age of thirty-four had been appointed General-in-Chief as well as commander of the Army of the Potomac, was unquestionably an exceptional young man whom his admirers nicknamed 'the little Napoleon'; he had passed out first from the Military Academy (West Point), had been a military observer during the Crimean War, and on his return home had qualified as a railway expert, becoming in 1860 president of the Ohio and Mississippi Railroad. He was a clever organizer and appreciated the fundamental military fact that God is on the side of the big battalions. His handicaps were that he fancied himself overmuch as a politician, that he was conceited and lacking in humour, and above all that he was a Democrat and not a Republican. After the defeat at Bull Run he welded a new army and planned to take Richmond, the Confederate capital, by a flank attack launched from the sea.

During the winter of 1861-62 Abraham Lincoln was pulverized by an understandable impatience. He was harassed by the activities of a Joint War Committee of Congress; he was deeply upset by the death of his second son, Willie; and he had many political cares. But these considerations extenuate and do not justify his treatment of McClellan. First, on January 27th, 1861, he published an order that all the armies of the Union were to move forward on February 22nd — a puerile gesture that was naturally ignored. Secondly, without consulting McClellan, he divided his army into corps and promoted the senior generals to be corps commanders; thirdly, he tried to force his own strategy on McClellan and when the majority of the Board of War upheld McClellan's views, he appears to have resented it. For Lincoln wanted McClellan to undertake another direct attack on the Confederate lines at Manassas, while McClellan stuck to his own plan for a campaign in the Virginian peninsula. Consequently when in March the Confederates voluntarily evacuated the Manassas position, Lincoln was furious and relieved McClellan of his post as General-in-Chief, though he left him in command of the Potomac army. On April 2nd McClellan, who had taken his supersession in good part, landed his army near the mouth of the York River in Virginia to begin his peninsular campaign and for some weeks his army camped so near to Richmond that it could hear the church bells ringing. Even now Lincoln did not cease to interfere. Frightened by warnings from military advisers who disliked McClellan and by the sort of politicians who always consider themselves born soldiers, he decided that McClellan had disobeyed the orders which he had been given to leave Washington adequately defended. Therefore, without consulting McClellan, he retained in Washington one of the corps (McDowell's) that had been earmarked for the peninsular campaign. McClellan never forgave this unexpected blow. 'I have raised an awful row about McDowell's corps', he told his wife. 'The President very coolly telegraphed me yesterday that he thought I ought to break the enemy's lines at once. I was much tempted to reply that he had better come and do it himself.'

As events proved, Lincoln soon had an opportunity to try his skill as an amateur general. At the beginning of May Stonewall Jackson with a mere 16,000 men opened a campaign in the Shenandoah Valley which resulted in frightening the Washington politicians while McClellan's army was away in the peninsula. There were three Federal corps in the valley each of which Jackson attacked in turn. Lincoln and his Secretary of War took charge of the three corps and worked out some wonderful paper manœuvres to trap Jackson; but somehow Jackson got away unhurt in ample time to join General Robert E. Lee in repelling McClellan's attack on Richmond.

Lee was a general who believed wholeheartedly that attack was the best form of defence. Though his army was inferior in numbers to McClellan's (perhaps 80,000 against 100,000) he planned to drive him into the sea and hoped with luck to win a victory that would decide the Civil War in favour of the south. McClellan had been grossly misled as to the strength of Lee's army and imagined that his own was greatly inferior in strength. Hence his extreme caution. Lee saw the weak point in McClellan's dispositions: the river Chickahominy cut off his right from the remainder of his army and on June 26th Lee threw Jackson against it. This was the opening episode in a bloody struggle that lasted for seven days. Lee failed to destroy his enemy or drive him into the sea, and indeed McClellan inflicted bigger casualties than he sustained. Lee had saved Richmond, but McClellan by merely

WAR MINISTER

thwarting Lee's plans had contributed to the certain ultimate victory of the north.

A week after the battle Lincoln visited McClellan, was convinced that the general would not resume the struggle, and therefore ordered him to withdraw from the Peninsula. While the withdrawal was being carried out, Lincoln formed a new army in the Shenandoah Valley and his own efforts as a commander having proved unsuccessful, put General John Pope in charge of a force of over 50,000 men. Lee saw a chance and sent Jackson round Pope's flank to cut his communications with Washington. In the second battle of Bull Run Pope was conclusively defeated, a defeat that Lincoln blamed, not altogether fairly, on McClellan for failing to reinforce Pope. Yet only three days after the battle Lincoln put McClellan in command of the defence of Washington that now appeared to be menaced by Lee's successes. Lee did in fact cross the Potomac with a view to invading Maryland and rallying Confederate supporters in that slave state. McClellan, who had reformed his army with splendid promptitude, met Lee in overwhelming strength at the battle of Antietam Creek in which both sides lost heavily. Lee was compelled to retire across the Potomac and Lincoln sent a message to McClellan ordering him to 'destroy the rebel army if possible', which McClellan failed to do. Seven weeks after the battle of Antietam (September 17th, 1862) Lincoln dismissed McClellan and replaced him by one of his own junior officers, General Burnside, who accepted the command with genuine reluctance.

Abraham Lincoln has of course had his apologists, but it is not easy to defend his conduct of the war during 1861-62 at least so far as the Virginia campaign is concerned. Admittedly questions of general strategy must be decided by the chief executive, for on them depend the allocation of resources between one theatre and another. Admittedly too there are political considerations — such as the moral effect of the fall of Washington — on which the politicians must be presumed to have been better judges than the soldiers. But once a general had been put in command of a particular campaign, he must, as the whole history of warfare shows, be allowed to fight his own battle. Lee could never have taken the audacious decisions he did during this campaign had he not been fully sustained by President Jefferson Davis — and Lee, it may be noted incidentally, was a real admirer of McClellan. In spite of his obvious faults, his cautiousness, his apparent lack of the offensive spirit, his poor intelligence, to the impartial student it appears that McClellan, who never lost a battle, was treated abominably by Lincoln. His immediate successors were much inferior men. Fortunately for the cause of the Union, while the Virginia campaigns were being fought, a first-class northern general was winning a reputation in the Mississippi Valley.

Although the campaign around Washington naturally absorbed Lincoln's chief attention the battle for the control of the Mississippi was also of deep significance. Not only was the great river an essential military highway to the south, but on its eastern borders were two states, Tennessee and Kentucky, which might, had they been left alone by the Union forces, have been won over to the Confederate cause or at least kept neutral. Lincoln did not intend to neglect them. The Federal army had an excellent base in Lincoln's own state of Illinois for an advance down the river, while eastern Tennessee was friendly to the Union cause. Lincoln damaged the initial chances of a successful campaign on the Mississippi, as he had done in Virginia, by permitting the existence of a divided command: Major-General Buell was put in charge of the Army of the Ohio, based on Louisville, Kentucky, while Major-General Halleck with the Army of the Mississippi had his headquarters at St. Louis, Missouri. Buell and Halleck not only ignored each other's existence but apparently gloried in doing so. On January 7th, 1862, Lincoln instructed Buell: 'Please name as early a day as you safely can, or before which you can be ready to move southward in concert with Major-General Halleck. Delay is ruining us and it is indispensable for me to have something definite. I send a like dispatch to Major-General Halleck.' Buell and Halleck, however, continued to engage in their own devices. But Halleck was lucky in having an able subordinate in Brigadier-General Ulysses S. Grant, who in spite of some lack of military theory and a one-time propensity for the bottle, knew how to fight. With tenuous resources he captured Fort Donelson and thus cleared the line between Columbus on the Mississippi and Nashville, once Andrew Jackson's home town, on the Cumberland River. The Confederates in Fort Donelson surrendered with 12,000 men and Halleck received the credit, for in

WAR MINISTER

March he was put over Buell. On April 6th-7th a drawn battle was fought by Grant at Shiloh to the south of Fort Donelson, but the Confederate commander was killed and his force withdrew. In this same month an amphibious operation under Admiral Farragut resulted in the occupation of New Orleans at the mouth of the Mississippi and in June Halleck took the strategic town of Memphis on the same river on the western side of Tennessee. Thus the Federal forces had won wide control of the Mississippi and in general had considerably more to their credit than the armies on the Potomac and it was an understandable decision by Lincoln to recall Halleck from the west to become his chief military adviser in Washington. Before he left his command, however, Halleck — a non-co-operator if ever there was one — refused to assist in an operation that might have brought the war to an end more quickly. Admiral Farragut had boldly sailed up the Mississippi with part of his fleet with the object of assaulting Vicksburg, the strongest fortress on the river still remaining in Confederate hands. If Halleck's army had linked up with Farragut's fleet the whole of the Mississippi river might have come under Federal control. After prolonged hesitations Halleck told Farragut he could not help him. This was three days after Lincoln had appointed him General-in-Chief. It was not the last time in American history that her army and navy failed to co-operate. The remainder of 1862 was spent in inconclusive operations in Kentucky and Tennessee. General Buell was replaced by General Rosecrans — a change which made little difference.

The chief object of Abraham Lincoln's policy during the early months of the Civil War was to keep the border states loyal to the Union or at worst neutral. That was why he at first refused to proclaim the emancipation of the slaves belonging to the secessionists, as he was pressed to do by the Abolitionists and by others on military grounds. As early as August 1860 General Frémont, commanding the department of the west, had of his own volition declared the slaves of the rebels in Missouri to be free men. Lincoln took immediate steps to have this announcement rescinded and explained to a friend that such a proclamation was an instance of dictatorship and a surrender of the powers of the government to a subordinate commander. Moreover, he added, it was politically unwise as it risked the loss of Kentucky, Missouri and Maryland to the Union cause. He reiterated these arguments against emancipation in his first annual message to Congress. He reminded Congress that these three states had forty thousand men in the field fighting for the Union. Nevertheless he warned his enemies that they were reactionaries, fighting to limit the rights of the people and to preserve all property inviolate. He 'raised a warning voice' against 'the return of depotism' and asserted that 'labour is prior to, and independent of capital. Capital is only the fruit of labour, and could never have existed if labour had not first existed'. But Lincoln had not become a disciple of Karl Marx: 'Capital has its rights, which are as worthy of protection as any other rights.'

The reasons why Lincoln resisted the pressure put upon him to proclaim the emancipation of the slaves were therefore those of political expediency. In March 1862 he sent a special message to Congress urging that the United States should grant financial aid to any state that of its own accord adopted a policy of gradual emancipation. By this means he hoped to fasten the border states firmly to the side of the north. But the policy of compensated emancipation (though approved by Congress) yielded no fruits except in the limited area of the District of Columbia — and in July Lincoln was driven to the conclusion that 'it was a military necessity absolutely essential to the salvation of the nation, that we must free the slaves or be ourselves subdued'. When he showed the first draft of his emancipation proclamation to his Cabinet on July 22nd, his Secretary of State, Seward, objected that to publish it at that time when the fortunes of the Union cause were low would be interpreted as a sign of despair. Lincoln therefore agreed to wait until a military victory had been won. The battle of Antietam (September 17th), though scarcely a decisive victory, was accepted for the purpose and five days afterwards the President proclaimed that as from January 1st, 1863: 'All persons held as slaves within any State or designated part of a State the people whereof shall then be in rebellion against the United States, shall be then, thenceforward and for ever free.' The Federal Government pledged itself to recognize and maintain such freedom. The proclamation also renewed the offer of compensated abolition for loyal slave-owners and the voluntary colonization of freed slaves, but compulsion did not apply to the freeing of the slaves of owners who had remained loyal to the Union. Thus the purpose of the proclamation was primarily political and not moral. Lincoln's hope was that it would cause confusion among his enemies and enthusiasm among his friends, and enlist the sympathy of Europe for the northern cause. He had earlier expounded his doctrine of expediency to Horace Greeley, the proprietor of the *New York Tribune*: 'If there be those who would not save the Union unless they could at the same time destroy slavery, I do not agree with them. My paramount object in this struggle is to save the Union, and is not either to save or destroy slavery. If I could save it by freeing all slaves, I would do it; and if I could save it by freeing some and leaving others alone, I would also do that.' The preliminary proclamation was made then essentially for reasons of military necessity ('a measure of war of a very questionable kind', the British Secretary of State for Foreign Affairs called it) and by virtue of the powers conferred upon Lincoln by the Constitution as Commander-in-Chief. The proclamation, which Lincoln confirmed, completed and signed on January 1st, 1863, nevertheless sounded the death knell for Negro slavery throughout the United States. The Republican party rallied behind Lincoln, while the Democrats were furious, even though they had been given a political battle cry, namely that the President had assumed 'powers dangerous to the rights of citizens and to the perpetuity of a free people'. 'A free people!' In the end they were crushed by their own paradox. Once again down the years echoed the words of Lincoln's prophetic speech: 'I believe this government cannot endure permanently half slave and half free.'

Though Lincoln was still to suffer many alternating periods of depression and exaltation after the publication of his preliminary proclamation of emancipation and the repulse of Lee at the battle of Antietam Creek, taught by trials and errors, he was to be a firmer and stronger administrator than he had ever been before. His personal stresses cannot be exaggerated, for he was that creature of paradox, a compassionate peaceable man who found himself cast into the bloodiest war that his country had ever experienced. As a civilian he hesitated to acquiesce in measures of discipline which would scarcely have caused a qualm to a soldier President: for instance, he refused to allow deserters to be treated as George Washington and Andrew Jackson would have treated them. He spent what might have seemed to be an undue proportion of his time in listening to the personal grievances of every type of citizen from an aspirant to be a door-keeper to a contractor with a shady scheme for making a fortune. But his very accessibility and informality told in his favour: the reports of 'Old Abe's' practical democracy spread through the Union and heightened his popularity with the ordinary citizen and soldier. Nor was this informal democracy confined to home consumption. Though he did not conceal his boredom in hearing the details of English royal marriages from the British Minister, he wrote a moving reply to an address from the working men of Manchester who approved the abolition of slavery even if (through the blockade of the export of southern cotton) it cost them their jobs.

In his second annual message Lincoln repeated his deep-seated belief that the Union must be maintained whatever the cost. 'One generation passeth away, and another generation cometh, but the earth abideth forever.' Hence he defended his emancipation proclamation and justified the imposition of martial law which meant the suspension of the right of habeas corpus. The President, however, watched closely to see that the right of arbitrary arrest was not abused and the Habeas Corpus Act of March 1863 limited the powers of the military.

Similarly Lincoln showed a new-found firmness in keeping his Cabinet under control. Here his principle was that he would protect men who did good service in helping to win the war, regardless of their political affiliations or the number of their enemies. At the beginning of 1862 he replaced his Secretary of War, Cameron, by one of the administration's foremost critics, Edwin M. Stanton, who proved himself to be a military organizer of violent energy, exceptional competence and with an extraordinary capacity for intrigue. In early 1863 when Seward, his Secretary of State, become the target of Congress criticism, he defended him by playing off his secret opponent Chase, the Secretary of the Treasury, against him. Finally he coped with his restless critics in Congress by stonewalling tactics and in the end they discovered that the President was not such a fool as they thought.

WAR MINISTER

In his relations with his generals the President was still unhappy. On December 13th Burnside (who had replaced McClellan) was defeated in attempting a headlong assault on a fortified position at Fredericksburg. On January 25th, 1863, Burnside was replaced by 'Fighting Joe' Hooker to whom Lincoln wrote a frank letter warning him against rashness and inordinate ambition, though adding: 'What I now ask of you is military success and I will risk the dictatorship.' On May 2nd Hooker was beaten by Lee with a force half the size of the Federal army at the battle of Chancellorsville, at which the Confederates lost Stonewall Jackson, accidentally shot, it was said, by his own men. On June 28th Hooker was in his turn replaced by General Meade, who accepted the appointment reluctantly, as he was opposed to 'the ridiculous appearance of changing generals after each battle'. Meade was a competent soldier, though Lincoln reasonably resented a proclamation of his in which he referred to 'driving the invader off our soil' — for was not 'the whole country our soil'? Meade ran into Lee's army at Gettysburg on July 1st; this is one of the classic examples in history of an 'encounter battle' (Oudenarde was another) and Meade was actually twelve miles from the scene when the fighting began. The Federal army was soon well entrenched while an outflanking movement attempted by Lee is said to have failed in part because Jackson was no longer alive to carry it out. The casualties on both sides were severe, but the Confederate losses were relatively larger, for they amounted to one-third of their men. Lincoln was much disappointed because Meade failed to follow up his victory and drafted a complaining letter, which he had the wisdom not to send. Gettysburg was in fact the turning point in the Civil War and after it Lee offered his resignation, which President Jefferson Davis unhesitatingly refused.

Meanwhile Lincoln had on the whole acted a noble part in his relations with General Grant. Grant was a ruthless man with many enemies who poured their slanderous tales into the President's ears. When Lincoln was told that Grant drank, he asked what brand of whisky he used so that he might send a barrel to his other generals (but Lincoln was also careful to investigate the charges and found they had no basis). In one respect, however, he behaved badly to Grant. Grant had a first-class subordinate in the sharp-tongued quick-witted William T. Sherman. Yet Lin-

ABRAHAM LINCOLN

coln allowed an old lawyer friend of his from Illinois to be put over Sherman's head without consulting Grant, an action which only the splendid loyalty of Sherman himself prevented from causing mischief. It may be said in extenuation that this lawyer had promised Lincoln as the price of his promotion to raise recruits and in the suumer of 1863, after the defeats at Fredericksburg and Chancellorsville, Lincoln was desperately concerned to raise men by any device so as to give Meade and Grant their chance of winning the war. Throughout the spring and summer Grant struggled against nature to build a firm line of communication for an assault on Vicksburg, the possession of which would not only put the whole of the Mississippi under Federal control, but deprive the southerners of a supply centre rich in hog and hominy. Lee's campaign that ended at Gettysburg had been aimed in part at drawing off troops from Grant. To Lincoln belongs the credit for filling both the main Federal armies. On July 4th, the day after Gettysburg, the Confederate commander at Vicksburg compelled by sickness, starvation and bombardment, surrendered with 30,000 men. Four days later Port Hudson, the only remaining Confederate stronghold on the Mississippi also surrendered. In an immortal phrase Lincoln declared: 'The Father of the Waters again goes unvexed to the sea.'

The year 1863 ended with one other notable success for northern arms. Major-General Rosecrans, who at the end of 1862 had fought a drawn battle at Murfreesborough in eastern Tennessee, after six months inaction, managed to manœuvre his opponents out of the important railway junction of Chatanooga and thereafter fought another drawn battle in the valley of the Chickamauga River on September 19th-20th. Lincoln now wisely decided to put Ulysses Grant in charge of all the operations in the west and Grant's first action was to substitute General George Thomas for Rosecrans. After Grant had sent General Sherman and General Hooker to reinforce Thomas the Federal strength outnumbered that of the Confederate by nearly two to one and on November 24th-25th they completely routed this southern army, which had been a thorn in the side of the north for so long, and drove it out of Tennessee into Georgia. After Gettysburg, Vicksburg and Chatanooga Federal victory in the Civil War became almost certain and it was appropriate that at this time Lincoln should make his celebrated speech of dedication at the National Cemetery on the field of Gettysburg (November 19th, 1863). This speech, which most American school-children learn by heart, was not thought particularly well of at the time; indeed some contemporary newspapers waxed sarcastic: the *Chicago Times* thought it 'in exceedingly bad taste'. This is it:

> Four score and seven years ago our fathers brought forth on this continent a new nation, conceived in liberty and dedicated to the proposition that all men are created equal. Now we are engaged in a great civil war, testing whether that nation, or any nation, so conceived and so dedicated, can long endure. We are met on a great battlefield of that war. We have come to dedicate a portion of that field as a national resting place for those who gave their lives that the nation might live. It is altogether fitting and proper that we should do this. But, in a larger sense, we cannot dedicate — we cannot hallow — this ground. The brave men, living and dead, who struggled here have consecrated it far above our poor power to add or to detract. The world will little note nor long remember what we say here, but it can never forget what they did here. It is for us, the living, rather to be dedicated here to the unfinished work which they who fought here have thus far so nobly advanced. It is rather for us to be here dedicated to the great task remaining before us — that from these honoured dead we take increased devotion to that cause for which they gave the last full measure of devotion; that we here highly resolve that these dead shall not have died in vain; that this nation, under God, shall have a new birth of freedom; and that government of the people, by the people, for the people, shall not perish from the earth.

In the spring of 1864 Lincoln summoned Grant from the west to Washington and put him in command of all the northern armies. An Act of Congress appointed Grant Lieutenant-General and Lincoln gave him a free hand, promising him all the support in his power. Grant replied: 'From my first entrance into volunteer service of the country to the present day I have never had cause of complaint — have never expressed or implied a complaint against the Administration or the Secretary of War, for throwing any embarrassment in the way of my vigorously prosecuting what appeared to me my duty.' He now took Lincoln at his word: 'I did not communicate my plans to the President nor did I to the Secretary of War or General Halleck.' Thus after many mistakes and much soul-destroying disappointment Lincoln had found a commander whom he trusted absolutely, a military adviser upon whom he could lean. Lincoln's previous practice of dismissing generals after they had lost one battle had nothing to commend it; nor was there much wisdom in his habit of sending urgent telegrams to his commanders ordering them to pursue the enemy with vigour — as if they might have forgotten their duty. In the history of war it is curious how often the statesman at home is daring and bloodthirsty, the man in command on the field pusillanimous or humane. There have of course been exceptions. Xerxes drove his men with whips into Greece. Frederick the Great exclaimed: 'Fools! would you live forever?' But wars are usually won not by blood baths, but by concentrating an overwhelming force at a decisive point — and that is harder to do in practice than it is in theory, as Lincoln himself found when he tried to surround Stonewall Jackson in the Shenandoah Valley. Indeed Lincoln now told Grant that he did not profess to be a military man or to know how a campaign was conducted and he confessed that some of his series of military orders had been 'all wrong'. Lincoln's qualities as a war leader did not rest on his handling of his generals (surely he went to the other, equally wrong, extreme in giving Grant so free a hand?) or in his amateur strategy and advice but in his bold use of the power he believed he possessed as Commander-in-Chief under the Constitution to raise recruits, gather supplies and thus keep large armies in the field. On March 3rd, 1863, Lincoln had approved a Conscription Act which empowered officers of the Federal Government to draft conscripts from any district which failed to supply in full its quota of volunteers. Men were no longer allowed to escape the draft (as they had before) by paying for provision of a substitute, and Lincoln defended the draft — however revolutionary it seemed to American notions of freedom — as an essential military measure. The constitutional validity of the law was obviously doubtful, but it produced the men. Similarly the validity of martial law was questioned, but Lincoln was determined on its enforcement lest the Conscription Act should be vitiated by wholesale desertions. Likewise in the interests of discipline Lincoln upheld the action of one of his generals (Burn-

WAR MINISTER

side) in arresting a prominent Ohio politician, Vallindigham, for delivering speeches calculated to seduce men from their allegiance; for Vallindigham sincerely believed that 'the war for the negro' should be abandoned. Lincoln ordered that Vallindigham should be put across the lines and banished into southern territory. Thus Lincoln had gradually learned that the executive itself cannot direct military operations; that its function is to use all its powers — and perhaps to stretch those powers if need be — to supply the means of fighting. This was what Lincoln did in 1863; he filled the armies even if it meant overriding the Constitution or Congress or both. 'I conceive', he told Senator Chandler later in another connection, 'that I may in an emergency do things on military grounds which cannot constitutionally be done by Congress.' His courageous use of his position to strengthen the northern armies, his enlistment of the trust of the common people by such clear and noble sentiments as those he expressed at Gettysburg, and finally his selection of Grant for the supreme command in the final stages of the war comprise the reasons why — despite all his mistakes — Lincoln was a splendid leader of his nation in civil war. His Proclamation of Emancipation and his attitude to 'reconstruction' put the last touches to his greatness.

Lincoln's foreign policy has been summarily described as consisting of the decision not to fight two wars at once. The object of the Federal Government's policy was to prevent interference in the Civil War, just as it was the Confederate aim to obtain European assistance. At first there appeared to be a real danger when Lee won his early victories that England and France would recognize the independence of the confederated southern states. Indeed it is said that the Russian Government (smarting at its defeat by the Western Powers in the Crimean War) and the Swiss Republican Government were the only European governments consistently to back the northern cause. In Great Britain, the Whig Government of Lord Palmerston followed a temporizing line and, while promptly recognizing the southern right of belligerency firmly refused direct aid to the Confederacy; thus it earned the hearty dislike of both sides. With the British Government in this mood, it was plainly not the part of wisdom for Lincoln's administration to provoke it; and when Seward as Secretary of State drafted a violent dispatch to the American Minister in London criticizing the British Government for proclaiming 'neutrality' as between the two sides, Lincoln toned it down and left the handling of the protest to the good sense of the minister. Yet when later in 1861 a Federal warship forcibly stopped the British steamer *Trent* which was carrying two southern envoys from Havana to Europe and took them off it, it appears to have been Seward who advocated the surrender of the men since, according to international law, the American captain was evidently in the wrong. Lincoln was momentarily swayed by the excited anti-British feelings provoked in the north by the incident, but he quickly realized that there was no practical alternative to yielding. 'It was a pretty bitter pill to swallow,' he confessed later, 'but I contented myself with believing that England's triumph in the matter would be short-lived, and that after ending our war successfully, we should be so powerful that we could call her to account for all the embarrassments she had inflicted on us.' In one notable instance the British Government did put itself in the wrong and that was by permitting two commerce destroyers to be built in British yards for the Confederate Government. One of these ships, to find notoriety as the *Alabama*, would not have been allowed to leave the Mersey had it not been for a magnificent muddle one week-end when there was no one in London of high enough rank to take the appropriate action. In the end, long after Lincoln was dead, the British Government had to pay 15,000,000 dollars on arbitration in compensation for the exploits of the *Alabama*.

While the British Government followed the proper course of dignified neutrality and the British people's sympathies ranged between hoping that a small nation struggling to be free would win its freedom and approving Lincoln's emancipation of the slaves, America's ancient ally, France, behaved far more provocatively, by profiting from the Civil War to intervene in the internal affairs of Mexico. The Emperor Napoleon III sent 40,000 soldiers to support the claim of his protégé, Archduke Maximilian of Austria, to the Mexican throne. Although this course contravened the doctrine of President Monroe that interference by any European Power with the former Spanish colonies would be regarded as an 'unfriendly act' towards the United States, Lincoln avoided committing himself even when the House of Representatives unanimously censured the administration for not insisting on the

VICTORY AND RECONSTRUCTION

French withdrawing from Mexico. Here again he was true to the policy of one war at a time. He recognized that the United States could protest with more weight and effect after the Civil War had been won. The value of the cautious foreign policy of the Lincoln Administration was realized when Jefferson Davis publicly admitted that he was disheartened by the failure of his government to win recognition from any foreign quarter. Although an appeal was actually made to Lincoln by Francis Blair that north and south should bury the hatchet by joining forces to expel the French from Mexico, the President would not be diverted from his set path. From the south he required unconditional surrender, that is the laying down of their arms and the acceptance of emancipation and of the Union. To this one aim Lincoln, with the first-rate help of Seward, who had come to recognize and prize his leadership, directed all his energies and he insisted that his foreign policy had to be attuned to that purpose, at whatever cost to the national pride.

5. VICTORY AND RECONSTRUCTION (1863-1865)

Although Lincoln insisted on the unconditional surrender of the armies of the southern states, the last thing he contemplated was a harsh peace. Throughout the war he had never uttered a single bitter word about the southern people and in his 'Proclamation of Amnesty and Reconstruction' which he promulgated on December 8th, 1863, he promised full pardon and the restoration of property rights (except in slaves) to all citizens and soldiers (other than those who had held places of honour and trust under the Federal Government and those guilty of ill-treating coloured troops) who subscribed to an oath of allegiance to the United States. The proclamation also provided that if ten per cent of the qualified voters of any state which had been at war with the United States took the oath of allegiance they would be entitled to re-establish a state government. A majority in Congress under the fierce leadership of Henry Winter Davis of Maryland questioned the constitutional right of the President to publish such a proclamation and after several months produced its own Reconstruction Bill which required a majority of the voters in a seceded state to take the oath before they might set up a new government and also prohibited slavery in the reconstructed states. Lincoln refused to sign the Bill, as he denied the right of Congress to abolish slavery and refused to be committed to any 'single plan of reconstruction'. As Commander-in-Chief he claimed that he should determine the conditions of amnesty and calmly and inflexibly upheld his proclamation.

Action was immediately taken under the terms of this proclamation and personal representatives of the President went to three southern states, parts of which were under the military control of the Federal armies, with oath books to sign up loyalists. Considerable progress was achieved in Louisiana and Arkansas. In the former state General Banks, an ex-Governor of Massachusetts, worked hard to collect the necessary votes (12,000 finally voted) and in February 1864 Michael Hahn of New Orleans was elected Governor. Lincoln delightedly wrote to congratulate Hahn saying: 'Now you are about to have a convention which, among other things, will probably define the elective franchise. I barely suggest, for your private consideration, whether some of the coloured people may not be let in, as, for instance, the very intelligent, and especially those who have fought gallantly in our ranks. This will probably help, in time to come, to keep the jewel of liberty in the family of freedom.' This rump government of Louisiana had a somewhat unhappy career. Lincoln had to intervene to prevent the military from thwarting the working of the new Governor and the Convention which he summoned. Under his watchful care it nevertheless survived, a constitution was adopted, schools were opened equally to white and black and the legislature was empowered to confer the vote on coloured men. Louisiana thus gave an example of what Lincoln regarded as the right methods of peaceable reconstruction.

In Arkansas, north of Louisiana and west of the Mississippi, which had come under the control of the Federal forces in the autumn of 1863, Lincoln also succeeded in organizing and nursing a state government of sorts loyal to the Union. Arkansas proceeded to elect two Senators and three Congressmen, but when these gentlemen arrived in Washington to present their credentials Congress told them to go away, since it did not approve of Lincoln's

VICTORY AND RECONSTRUCTION

policy. But Lincoln firmly told General Steele, the Military Governor of the state, that he wished him to give the new state Government 'the same support and protection that you would if the members had been admitted'.

In the slave states that had remained loyal to the Union throughout the war Lincoln's policy, which he had always consistently advocated, was to obtain the compensation of the slave-holders out of Federal funds. This scheme was unanimously disapproved by his Cabinet and resisted by the Democratic minority in the House of Representatives. In 1864 Maryland passed an amendment to its state constitution abolishing slavery without compensation and later Missouri followed suit.

The method that Lincoln thought should be used to put the final seal on the complete abolition of slavery throughout the Union was that of constitutional amendment. In refusing to sign the Reconstruction Bill he had questioned the right of Congress to abolish slavery and logically he had asked the Republican party to include its abolition by constitutional amendment as part of its programme. Lincoln used all his influence — some say a trifle unscrupulously — to secure the necessary number of votes both in the two Houses and in the states to obtain the Thirteenth Amendment, as it was called, which was adopted after his death. Five years after his death another amendment, the Fifteenth, was passed stating that 'the right of citizens of the United States to vote shall not be denied or abridged by the United States or any State on account of race, colour, or previous condition of servitude'.

Thus Lincoln hoped to create a reunited America by means of the unquestionably constitutional abolition of slavery, the establishment of the right of at least educated Negroes to vote, and the acceptance in the seceded states of the authority of the Federal Government in return for Federal recognition of new state governments. Inevitably the heritage of the Civil War was to be hate, misery and a desire for revenge. Too many lives had been lost, too many families had been ruined. The wounds inflicted by war could not be healed by paper constitutions nor could the conquerors be appeased by moral integrity at the White House. No one man, it may be hazarded, could have altered that trend of events; yet can it be doubted that if Lincoln lived a little longer, his influence, enhanced by victory, would have worked power-

ABRAHAM LINCOLN

fully to mitigate the sufferings of the beaten south and given a nobler meaning to the phrase, reconstruction?

Victory had come painfully to the north in 1864-65. The campaign had opened on May 4th, 1864, when Lieutenant-General Grant had taken personal charge of the operations in Virginia and Major-General Sherman had moved south from Chatanooga in Tennessee with the object of capturing Atlanta in Georgia. The operations in Virginia must in some degree have recalled to Lincoln the events of 1861-62. Grant with an army of over 120,000 men, double the size of Lee's forces which awaited him, aimed, as McClellan had done, at taking the Confederate capital of Richmond. Unlike McClellan, Grant moved his army by land, although he sent a small force under General Butler by sea to make a feint on the peninsula. In the Shenandoah Valley, 'the backdoor to Washington', Lee instructed an able commander, General Early to threaten the Federal capital; he was faced by General Sigel who had orders from Grant to move into the valley. In spite of his inferior strength Lee, taking advantage of the wooded country intersected by streams known as the Wilderness and employing well-constructed field entrenchments to protect his troops, twice severely defeated Grant (at Spotsylvania Court House, May 10th and Cold Harbour, June 3rd). Grant had vainly tried to work round Lee's left flank, but had been driven to a frontal assault in which his losses were tremendous. After his first defeat Grant said: 'I am going to fight it out on this line if it takes all summer.' But after his second defeat he abandoned his attempt to take Richmond from the north-east and decided to assault the city from the south. He had learned his lesson and in the end justified the President's confidence; but what, one wonders, would Lincoln have thought if McClellan had taken the offensive, as he had been told to do, and suffered such terrible losses? Now Lincoln, true to his new found policy of restraint, upheld Grant almost without a murmur. He was momentarily shaken when in July Early crushed the forces opposing him in the Shenandoah Valley and, like a reincarnation of the dead Stonewall Jackson, debouched with seventeen thousand men before the forts north-west of Washington. Lincoln could hold himself in no longer. 'Now what I think is,' he told Grant, 'that you should provide to retain your hold where you are, certainly, and bring the

VICTORY AND RECONSTRUCTION

rest with you personally, and make a vigorous effort to destroy the enemy's forces in this vicinity. I think there is really a fair chance to do this, if the movement is prompt. This is what I think upon your suggestion, and is not an order.' In fact troops sent back by Grant to protect Washington arrived in time to check Early and the Lieutenant-General chose a daring young cavalry officer, Major-General Sheridan, to reorganize the Shenandoah front. On October 19th Sheridan turned the tables on Early and at the battle of Cedar Creek won an overwhelming victory. Lincoln had approved Grant's order to Sheridan 'to put himself south of the enemy and follow him to death' and Grant's decision not to return to the capital lest he should loosen his hold on Lee. 'Hold on with a bull-dog grip', Lincoln commanded, 'and chew and choke as much as possible.' Lincoln had to pay the price for Grant's defeats by finding still more soldiers to fill the gaps in his army. He aimed at calling up another half million men and to do so had to make the decision to abolish the exemption which enabled men to evade enlistment by paying three hundred dollars for the provision of a substitute. His advisers did not care for this decision and there was much difficulty in getting it through Congress, but the President insisted and in the end had his way even though it threatened to diminish his popularity.

During those midsummer months when General Robert E. Lee with the impregnable courage of an early Christian was fighting to save the southern cause, Lincoln's own position was shaken. The election was drawing near and the political experts in the Republican party were frightened that it would be beaten if Lincoln were their candidate again. One of them bluntly told Lincoln in August that his re-election was impossible. Some pressed him to make peace, saying that an offer of generous terms would secure the surrender of the south. He gave way so far as to allow feelers to be put out and let the ineffable Horace Greeley go to Canada to talk with the representatives of the Confederacy. The Democrats decided to nominate McClellan as their candidate with a platform promising peace at once. Some of the Republican party managers seriously suggested that Grant should be withdrawn from the field of battle and put up as presidential candidate in Lincoln's place: if Grant could not save the Union, they argued, at least he could save the Republican party. Another general,

Frémont, also announced that he intended to stand, while Lincoln's own Secretary of the Treasury, Salmon P. Chase, who, as the President observed, had the 'White House fever' and a few indiscreet friends, offered his resignation at the end of June which was now accepted without demur. How far all this political manœuvring was really symptomatic of feeling against Lincoln in the north may be open to question, for political circles in the United States always tend to lose a sense of proportion on the eve of a presidential election. Lincoln himself remained firm to his purposes, refused to modify or postpone the army draft, ignored the accusations of dictatorship from men of his own party and prepared to give his backing to McClellan should the Democrats win the election. Though he reiterated that he would make peace if the south dissolved their armies, accepted the full restoration of the Union and acquiesced in the abolition of slavery, he would not compromise — that, he told his supporters, would be worse than losing the election. He thought the case for his re-election rested on the inadvisability of 'swapping horses while crossing a stream', a phrase that has become a permanent part of the English language.

At the convenient moment for Abraham Lincoln military victory came. On September 3rd General Sherman, after a series of turning movements which forced the enemy back, occupied the city of Atlanta, one of the few valuable industrial towns in Confederate hands. This, followed as it was by Sheridan's victory at Cedar Creek, convinced the electors, if they needed convincing, that Lincoln was leading them to victory and on November 8th he was re-elected by 212 electoral votes against McClellan's twenty-one. All the doubters, would-be pacifists and the like, had united behind him. Lincoln accepted his triumph with that humane detachment that characterized most of his actions in the year 1864: 'I do not impugn the motives of any one opposed to me ... but I give thanks to the Almighty for this evidence of the people's resolution to stand by free government and the rights of humanity.'

Those who knew Lincoln most intimately perceived in him during the last months of the Civil War an elevation of character and a strength of purpose, qualified by a willingness to conciliate, where conciliation was reasonable, that they had never detected before. It was as if his mind and spirit had been tempered in a

VICTORY AND RECONSTRUCTION

furnace. But it was not merely the prospect of victory that had uplifted him. Some men — most men perhaps — are made cautious and taught lessons by the highest responsibilities. But with Lincoln the cares of office had disclosed and established all the finest traits in his character. Before he became President he had been a superb politician with the makings of a literary statesman. Yet no man becomes a statesman until he has to resolve the problems of administration for himself. Lincoln proved to be able not merely to cope with the wide problems of a world at war but to inspire the people he served. Like Pericles and Cicero of old, William Ewart Gladstone and Winston Spencer Churchill in our own time, he knew how to speak and learned how to govern. He offered too, to his colleagues and all with whom he had to work, a richness of humanity that was the very flower of his early life. He never ceased to tell stories, to find homely anecdotes to illustrate his arguments, to confess his own weaknesses and in the long run to forget those of others. Like all good introverts he seldom failed to see both sides of a case.

Although we do not know the whole of the story, it seems that Lincoln's private life was happier in those days than it had ever been. True, three of his four sons had died. Willie's death had been followed by that of 'Tad', a lively lad who used to accompany his father on a pony through the streets of Washington. These personal tragedies must have drawn husband and wife closer to each other. Mrs. Lincoln had been publicly assailed as a southern sympathizer and even a spy and she needed her husband's protection as he needed her comfort. One cannot doubt that after twenty years they found a way of living together. Their one surviving son, Robert, who was educated at Harvard and later became a distinguished lawyer and diplomatist, was a source of pride. In the simple life at the White House and more especially in the Soldiers' Home, just outside Washington in Maryland, where the Lincolns had a country house set in a lovely circle of trees, the tired melancholy man with the dark brown deep-lined face must occasionally have found relaxation and peace.

After the election Lincoln concentrated on the problem of how to bring about reunion. Though he took the election to show that the great majority of the voters, whatever their party, were in favour of maintaining the Union, the difficulty was how to stop the war and induce the insurgents to acknowledge the Federal authority. 'On careful consideration of all the evidence,' he wrote, 'it seems to me that no attempt at negotiation with the insurgent leader could result in any good. He would accept nothing short of severance of the Union — precisely that we will not and cannot give.' Thus there appeared no way out but complete military victory — unconditional surrender. Yet Lincoln was ready to explore every means of attaining peace provided that the Union was upheld and the abolition of slavery ensured. On February 3rd, 1865, on the persuasion of General Grant, Lincoln actually went to meet representatives of the Confederacy at Hampton Roads in Virginia. Here Stephens, the Confederate vice-president, asked him if there was any way of restoring the harmony and happiness of former days. Lincoln answered: 'There is but one way that I know of and that is for those that are resisting the laws of the Union to cease that resistance.' Restoration of the Union, he added, was his *sine qua non*. The conference broke down, but before it did so Stephens paid him one compliment. 'I understand then', Stephens said, 'that you regard us as rebels, who are liable to be hanged for treason?' 'That is so,' said Lincoln. 'Well,' said Stephens, 'we suppose that would have been your view. But, to tell you the truth, we have none of us been much afraid of being hanged with you as President.' He was right; for Lincoln expressed the utmost anxiety that Jefferson Davis, the Confederate president, should not fall into his hands.

A month later Lincoln delivered his second inaugural address. The Chief Justice who administered the oath to him was that Salmon P. Chase who, as Secretary of the Treasury, had given him an uncomfortable time in the Cabinet. Lincoln had borne no resentment and had recommended his appointment to the Senate as successor to Andrew Jackson's nominee, Roger Taney. In his speech Lincoln interpreted the dying war with fatalistic precision, reminding his audience with a frankness that other statesmen in other times might well have emulated that God cannot be on both sides of a struggle and might not be on either. The prayers of neither side, he said, had been fully answered. The Almighty had his own purposes. Perhaps, he thought, American slavery had been one of those offences which brought woe upon the world. Yet 'the judgments of the Lord are true and righteous altogether'.

VICTORY AND RECONSTRUCTION

'With malice towards none;' he concluded, 'with charity for all; with firmness in the right as God gives us to see right, let us strive on to finish the work we are in; to bind up the nation's wounds; to care for him who shall have borne the battle, and for his widow, and his orphan, to do all which may achieve and cherish a just and lasting peace among ourselves, and with all nations.' Lincoln rightly expected this address to wear as well as anything he had ever produced, though, he added, 'men were not flattered by being shown that there had been a difference of purpose between the Almighty and them'.

A month later Lincoln was at Grant's headquarters watching and discussing the last military stages of the war. In the south Sherman, after taking Atlanta, had marched with a small force of 60,000 men that could live on the country three hundred miles across Georgia to the sea, capturing Savannah, the port and railway junction, on December 21st; then he turned northwards 450 miles through the Carolinas, while his subordinate, General Thomas, finally conquered Tennessee. Meanwhile Grant with that methodical thoroughness which had yielded him Vicksburg two years before had almost surrounded Lee's forces and had laid siege to Petersburg, the bastion of Richmond on the southern side. Richmond was occupied by Grant's men on April 3rd and six days later at Appomattox Court House, some 70 miles to the west of Richmond, General Lee with the remnants of his ragged veterans surrendered. Though the war limped on a little longer, this was virtually the end.

On April 11th Lincoln made his last speech in the grounds of the White House to a crowd gathered to celebrate the victory. His entire thoughts were now on reconstruction. He justified the Louisiana experiment, insisting that what was important was not the exact constitutional status of the seceded states but how to bring them back into 'proper practical relations' with the Union. For he recognized the immensity and difficulty of the tasks that lay ahead. 'Unlike in a case of war between independent nations' there was no authorized organ with whom to treat. 'Disorganized and discordant elements' had to be welded together, and this he claimed, could only be done by appealing to what was best in the white man and the black. Though no one can confidently measure the might-have-beens of history, surely had Lincoln lived a year or two longer the finest chapter in his biography could have been written.

A few days before he died Lincoln is said to have dreamed of his end, to have seen himself wandering at night through the brightly lit rooms of the White House, all of them empty, to have watched a military funeral, and to have heard a voice say 'the President has been assassinated'. Be that as it may, he undoubtedly told his Cabinet when it met on the morning of Good Friday, April 14th, 1865, of a dream he had had the previous night in which he saw 'a singular vessel moving with great rapidity towards a dark indefinite shore'. He told the Secretaries and General Grant, who was also present, that he had dreamt a similar dream before the battles of Antietam, Murfreesborough, Gettysburg and Vicksburg and interpreted it as meaning that Sherman would gain another success in the south. Grant dryly observed that Murfreesborough was not a victory. Turning to public matters, Lincoln discussed reconstruction and expressed his strong view that vindictiveness was out of place in winding up the past. 'No one need expect he would take part in hanging and killing these men, even the worst of them ... Enough lives have been sacrificed. We must extinguish resentment if we expect harmony and union.'

That Good Friday should indeed have been a day of joy and hope. Lincoln's son, Robert, had come back from the front with Grant, whose aide he had been. In the afternoon the President went for a drive alone with Mary Lincoln and said to her: 'We have had a hard time since we came to Washington; but the war is over, and with God's blessing, we may hope for four years of peace and happiness, and then we will go back to Illinois and pass the rest of our lives in quiet.' Perhaps if Lincoln had been compelled to choose the day on which to end his life he may have chosen that day, the day of victory and of promise for the future. That night he went with his wife and a Major Rathbone and his fiancée to see an indifferent comedy called 'Our American Cousin' at Ford's Theatre. John Wilkes Booth, a handsome young actor and a fanatical secessionist, had managed to steal into the theatre before the performance and bored a hole through the door in front of which Lincoln was to sit in the stage box. The party arrived late at the performance which ceased to allow the orchestra to play 'Hail to the Chief'. The security arrangements could

NOTE

scarcely have been worse. The policeman on duty was a man with a seedy record who had ultimately to be dismissed the force for sleeping on his beat. During the interval he left his post to have a drink. After the interval just after ten o'clock Booth showed this policeman some card (what was written on it is not known), entered the passage behind the box with a pistol and knife, and shot the President through the head. Then, after struggling with the other occupants of the box, he leapt on to the stage, breaking a leg as he fell, but escaped in the general confusion not to be caught until eleven days later he was killed in a burning barn in Virginia. Lincoln did not die until the next morning, but he never recovered consciousness. Of the other occupants of the box that tragic night 'one was to slay the other and end his life a raving maniac' while Mary Lincoln was to wander over the face of the earth, a lost soul. That same evening another fanatic viciously assaulted Lincoln's Secretary of State, Seward, as he was lying ill in bed, but failed to kill him. They did not dare to bring Seward the news of what had happened at the theatre, but on Easter Sunday as he looked out of the window he said to those who were with him: 'The President is dead or else he would have visited me.'

Lincoln's body was taken back to Springfield to be buried as he had desired. The people paid a just homage to him that was rarely paid in his lifetime. The Vice-President, Andrew Johnson, who succeeded, was quite forgotten as the whole civilized world was stunned by so dramatic a death. For few men have thus passed away at the peak of their greatness or at the exact moment of the military victory of their cause. Lincoln's influence wilted all too soon, but his humanity and his political wisdom, his very faults and his sufferings, have made of him a figure that cannot perish so long as the American nation survives.

NOTE

Did Lincoln fail to Turn Up for his own Wedding?

William Herndon, who was to become Lincoln's law partner in 1845 and after his death devoted most of his life to collecting materials for Lincoln's life to supplement his own memories, has

ABRAHAM LINCOLN

an extremely circumstantial story, which has been accepted by some of Lincoln's biographers that on January 1st, 1841, he failed to turn up for his own wedding. The bridal party and bride, it was said, had actually assembled, but the bridegroom failed to appear, and his friends finally found him wandering in a state verging on hysteria. In their life of Mary Lincoln, Carl Sandburg and P. M. Angle have examined this story and point out that there was no notice of any such wedding on that date in the local newspapers (as might have been expected in view of Lincoln's local prominence) or in any correspondence that has yet come to light. An intimate and detailed letter of Mary Todd, written in December 1840 has no hint of an immediate wedding. In Emanuel Hertz's important book, *The Hidden Lincoln*, where much of Herndon's original material is printed, there is a statement by Mrs. N. W. Edwards, Mary Todd's sister, in which she said: 'Lincoln and Mary were engaged, everything was ready and prepared for the marriage, even to the supper etc. Mr. L. failed to meet his appointment. Cause: insanity.' This surely is the basis of Herndon's statement and would seem to confirm what we know from Lincoln himself that the pair were engaged and an immediate marriage in contemplation when the engagement was suddenly broken off. (Since this note was written I have read Professor Randall's detailed study of the question in *Lincoln the President*, Chapter III, which reaches the same conclusion.)

What is not, however, entirely clear is who broke off the engagement. Some said that he had been jilted. Two letters quoted by Sandburg and Angle can be interpreted in a contradictory way on this point. We may, however, guess from the analogy of his behaviour to Mary Owens that Lincoln asked to be released and a letter of Mary Todd in June 1841 would appear to lend support to this view.

SELECT BIBLIOGRAPHY

C. B. BALLARD: *The Military Genius of Abraham Lincoln* (1926).
LORD CHARNWOOD: *Abraham Lincoln* (1919).
D. S. FREEMAN: *Robert E. Lee* (1935).
W. H. HERNDON and J. W. WEIK: *Herndon's Lincoln* (1890).
E. HERTZ: *The Hidden Lincoln* (1938).
ALLEN JOHNSON: *Stephen A. Douglas* (1905).
W. H. LAMON: *The Life of Abraham Lincoln* (1872).
J. G. NICOLAY and J. HAY: *Abraham Lincoln: A History* (1890); *Complete Works of Abraham Lincoln* (1905).
DAVID POTTER: *Lincoln and His Party in the Secession Crisis* (1942).
J. G. RANDALL: *Lincoln the President* (1946).
J. F. RHODES: *History of the United States from the Compromise of 1850* (1920).
CARL SANDBURG: *Abraham Lincoln. The Prairie Years* (1926); *Abraham Lincoln. The War Years* (1939).
CARL SANDBURG and P. M. ANGLE: *Mary Lincoln. Wife and Widow* (1932).
N. W. STEPHENSON: *Abraham Lincoln* (1924); *An Autobiography of Abraham Lincoln* (1926).

THEODORE ROOSEVELT

WOODROW WILSON
ON
THEODORE ROOSEVELT

YES, he is a great big boy. I was ... charmed by his personality. There is a sweetness about him that is very compelling. You can't resist the man. I can easily understand why his followers are so fond of him.

It was very amusing when Mr. Roosevelt was President, to notice how seasoned politicians shivered when he spoke in public, ... shivered at his terrible indiscretions, his frank revelations, whenever he chose, of what was going on inside political circles, his own nonchalant failure to keep any confidence whatever that he chose to make any public use of ... He may have chosen and chosen very astutely what confidences to keep, which to break, but he was strong and popular in proportion as he broke them and gave the people the impression that he was really telling them all he knew about their business, about the men and the motives which were retarding the proper transaction of their business and the proper correction of the abuses under which they were suffering at the hands of men who enjoyed the confidence and protection of the managing politicians.

THEODORE ROOSEVELT

CHAPTER VI

THEODORE ROOSEVELT

MANY American historians have written rather sadly of the period that elapsed between the death of Abraham Lincoln and the election of Theodore Roosevelt to the Presidency. 'We have now', writes James Truslow Adams of the years that followed the Civil War, 'to enter upon the most shameful decade in our entire national history, and to record a moral collapse without precedent and, let us hope, without successor.' It was the age of big bosses in politics and millionaire trust-builders in the economic life of the country and by 1890 even the western frontier, until then always an escape route for independent adventurers in search of a modest competence, was closed. There was an urgent opening for a tough man who would defy the bosses, the millionaires and their instruments and tackle some at least of the problems of a changing nation.

Theodore Roosevelt was in many respects the antithesis of Abraham Lincoln. Lincoln had been self-made; Roosevelt never needed to work for his living. Lincoln did not boast of his ancestry; Roosevelt was one of the *crême de la crême* of New York society. Yet the two Presidents had much in common. Lincoln had migrated from Kentucky, a slave state, to Illinois, a free state, and had tried, though vainly, to reconcile north and south. Roosevelt, though as much a northerner in his sympathies as the keenest captain in the Federal army, was the son of a southern mother and was eager to do justice to the south. Lincoln was indeed Roosevelt's hero in whose speeches he found authority for his national outlook and his own brand of conservative reform.

Once Roosevelt became President he exerted, in order to promote his own foreign and domestic policies, all the powers inherent in his office which had been discovered and sharpened by his predecessors; for example, he used his *ex-officio* position as Commander-in-Chief to take over and govern the Panama Canal Zone. This facet of his power he derived from Abraham Lincoln. At the same time he followed Andrew Jackson in assuming the role of a popular leader and pressing through the legislation which he favoured by applying all the influence that he derived from that role. But to the resources of power that he extracted from the ceremonial character of his office, from his position as popular and party leader, and from his tenure as Commander-in-Chief, Theodore Roosevelt added an ingenious conception of his own, which Professor Corwin has called the 'stewardship' theory of the Presidency. 'My view', Roosevelt wrote in his autobiography, 'was that every executive officer, and above all every executive officer in high position, was a steward of the people bound actively and affirmatively to do all he could for the people, and not to content himself with the negative merit of keeping his talents undamaged in a napkin. I declined to adopt the view that what was imperatively necessary for the nation could not be done by the President unless he could find some specific authorization to do it . . .' Instances of his use of what he called the 'residual executive powers', which he discovered from his stewardship theory, related particularly to diplomatic matters. Finally Roosevelt not only (like Jackson) took advice outside the party bounds of his official Cabinet, but sent his own unofficial observers to report to him in matters of foreign affairs. And when Congress objected to this latter practice, he defied them on the ground that the President could draw advice wherever he wished.

The powers that were thus accumulated were employed for what Roosevelt regarded as the good of the plain people. For he was driven forward by an almost Cromwellian conviction that he was a chosen instrument of righteousness. In him was all that puritanism, that zest for individualism, that ambition to make good by his own unaided efforts which is the essence of the American character. But added to it was a profound sense of public duty which in men of his sort and his day was uncommon. While he was still a very young man the Devil took him up to the top of the mountain and showed him all the kingdoms of the world that were to be had almost for the asking by a man of his talents, but he rejected them in favour of a life of adventure and of public service. And although in the end that chosen life had its disappointments, he served the American people faithfully and honestly, for which they were not ungrateful. Nor did his influence die with him. For may it not be said that many of the political and social

THE ROUGH RIDER

reforms obtained by the Democratic Presidents, Woodrow Wilson and Franklin D. Roosevelt, owed much to the path blazed for them by Theodore Roosevelt, while the increasing recognition by the United States Government of its responsibilities as a world power received its initial impulse during the years of his Presidency?

1. THE ROUGH RIDER (1858-1898)

Theodore Roosevelt was born in a house in East Twentieth Street, New York City on October 27th, 1858. The house is described in his *Autobiography*: 'The black haircloth furniture in the dining-room scratched the bare legs of the children when they sat on it'; the middle room was a library without windows but with furniture 'of gloomy respectability', while the parlour a 'room of much splendour', contained as its *pièce de résistance* a gas chandelier 'decorated with a great quantity of cut-glass prisms'. This house faded into insignificance beside that of his paternal grandfather at the corner of Fourteenth Street and Broadway with its tessellated black and white marble floor and circular staircase. The Roosevelts, descendants of the original New York Dutch, were in fact a wealthy, respectable and well-to-do family who were able to sample all that life had to offer them. Theodore had only one handicap in childhood, ill health, comprising asthma and defective eyesight, which enabled him to escape school altogether and gave him instead two wonderful trips to Europe and Asia before he was adolescent.

Theodore's father was a banker and philanthropist and his son loved him dearly. 'My father', he wrote, 'was the best man I ever knew. He combined strength and courage with gentleness, tenderness and great unselfishness. He could not tolerate in us children selfishness or cruelty, idleness, cowardice, or untruthfulness. As we grew older he made us understand that the same standard of clean living was demanded for the boys and for the girls; that what was wrong in a woman could not be right in a man.' His mother, Martha Bulloch, came from a Georgia family and had removed there from South Carolina, the starting point of the Civil War. Theodore's childhood coincided with the Civil War in which the loyalties and charitable labours of his father were directed to one side and of his mother to the other. The sympathies of the boy, 'Teedie', as he was called, were with his father and once, when he had been reprimanded by his mother, he sought revenge by 'praying with loud fervour for the success of the Union arms when he came to say his evening prayers'. His father then enjoined upon him what he himself practised in his household, a strict neutrality.

The first trip to Europe in 1869 with his two sisters and younger brother was undertaken partly in the hope that it might do Theodore's health good. The family did the grand tour of Europe pretty thoroughly and Theodore chiefly enjoyed the amusements that appeal to a normal boy. In London he liked the zoo, the waxworks at Madame Tussaud's and the Crystal Palace with its stuffed animals more than he had done a visit to the Oxford colleges or the inspection of the 'old tombs' in Westminster Abbey. Already at the age of ten he showed signs of real promise both of a literary kind in his conscientiously kept diaries — such as 'My Journal in the Papel States' — and of artistic merit in his sketches. His main hobby was natural history. One day he went to a natural history museum all by himself, the true proof of boyish enthusiasm. But his ill health remained. He suffered from headaches and bouts of sickness as well as his asthma: when in Austria he recorded in his diary: 'I was sick of asthma last night. I sat up for 4 successive hours and Papa made me smoke a cigar.' Finally he became a little homesick: 'Mama showed me the portrait of Eidieth [Edith] Carow and her face stirred up in me home-sickness and longings for the past which will come again never, alack never.' Edith Carow was the little girl next door who was to become his second wife.

By the time of his second trip abroad in 1872-73, which included visits to Egypt and Syria, natural history had become a passion. On the ship the youth of thirteen noted that a 'snow bunting (*Plectrophanes nivalis*) flew on board and was captured'. In Liverpool and in Paris he occupied himself in skinning birds. Near Hebron he shot and killed 'two very pretty little finches'. Before the family left the United States he had taken lessons in taxidermy from a contemporary of the famous American ornithologist, Audubon. He had determined that he himself would be a naturalist.

In after life Theodore Roosevelt liked to contrast the 'rather sickly, rather timid little boy, very fond of desultory reading and of natural history and not excelling in any form of sport', with the one hundred per cent he-man with plenty of the 'right stuff' in him that he was to become. The contrast was exaggerated, perhaps heightened even for the dramatic effect, for Roosevelt was nothing if not a romantic. His diaries show clearly that he was a courageous boy, fond of outdoor life, who enjoyed horseplay and pretending to be a soldier. His parents gave him no encouragement to be a molly-coddle and his father inspired him to take up boxing and build a physique to throw off his asthma. The second grand tour did him a great deal of good and not long after his return it was decided to send him to Harvard.

Although he had not been to school his education was on a high level. The young Roosevelt had a superb memory, a flood of general knowledge, and exhaustive interests. He thoroughly enjoyed himself at Harvard, where he worked hard and played hard, and joined all the best clubs. He kept up his boxing, giving 'red-haired Coolidge a tremendous thrashing', though he never became a light-weight champion, as he once inadvertently claimed in later life. Though his devotion to natural history did not wane — it never waned — he decided after all not to choose it as his professional occupation, for he found work on the laboratory bench was stultifying. Instead his interests broadened into history and politics and while he was still at Harvard he started to write a learned treatise on the war of 1812. Politics and not science was to be his 'life's work'.

In the autumn of 1878 he fell in love at sight with a girl who lived near Harvard, Alice Lee. He was barely twenty and she sweet seventeen. They became engaged in January 1880: Alice, who had fair hair and blue eyes, came of a good family and Theodore received his mother's blessing. They were married that October. Theodore's father had died in 1878 at the age of forty-six and left his family well provided for. Theodore probably had about £2000 a year in his own right, 'enough to get bread', as he put it, so that he could afford to select any career he fancied. The future must have seemed very warm and bright to this happily married Harvard graduate.

THEODORE ROOSEVELT

Like many young men down from the university in those spacious times Roosevelt was uncertain exactly what he wanted to do next; and he was not obliged to do what he did not want: 'I had been left enough money by my father not to make it necessary for me to think solely of earning bread for myself and my family', he wrote. 'What I had to do if I wanted bread and jam, was to provide butter and jam, but to count the cost as compared with other things.' He began to read the law, but it did not excite him as a profession and he continued his work on his laborious naval history, which he eventually published in 1882. Like most first books this was a conscientious piece of work, though obscure in parts, and it earned him some reputation. What was more important, he decided to enter local politics and learn the art of government from the bottom.

New York City politics lay paralysed in the grip of Tammany Hall, an effective Democratic party 'machine' that had been largely created by that political adventurer, Aaron Burr. The Republican party was consequently normally 'a hopeless minority in the city' and 'the men in control of its organization used it mainly as a basis for combinations or "deals" with Tammany Hall, receiving in return minor offices . . . and various other favours' (Bishop). Why Roosevelt elected to join this 'homeless minority' is not altogether clear. His friends mocked at him for taking up so low an occupation, which they did not consider suited to a gentleman, and assured him that the men he would meet would be rough, brutal and unpleasant. Roosevelt retorted: 'If this is so, it merely means that the people I know do not belong to the governing class, and other people do — and I intend to be one of the governing class.' In the end his courage and enterprise exacted admiration. A Philadelphia newspaper observed: 'The career of this young man, who has gone boldly and honorably into political life, ought to shame thousands who complain that politics are so dirty that no decent gentleman can engage in them.' Roosevelt was elected a member of the Republican club of the Twenty-first District, which being in the wealthy part of the city, was known as a 'silk stocking district'. After his return from a belated honeymoon in Europe and a stay in his widowed mother's New York home Roosevelt was elected to represent his district in the New York Assembly. Thereupon he and his wife moved to Albany, the state capital. Here his Democratic opponents and the hard-bitten tough group of politicians known as the 'Black Horse Cavalry' thought the new member with his eyeglasses, carroty hair, side whiskers and drawl might prove a figure of fun and dubbed him 'Oscar Wilde'. They were soon undeceived.

Roosevelt discovered that there was little reality about party politics in the Assembly and a good deal of concerted blackmail so that it was not easy to find where right and honesty lay. However, he scored his mark by leading an attack on a judge of the State Supreme Court whom he accused of corrupt relationships with business men. The support of the press enabled him to overcome the opposition to the extent of obtaining impeachment proceedings against the judge, although he was acquitted. Roosevelt's friends felt that he had done more than enough for glory. He had, they told him, made the 'reform play' and now that he had proved his capability they advised him to settle down to earn money as a lawyer or in business, leaving politics and identifying himself with the 'right kind of people'. This revealing counsel was ignored and in November 1883 he was re-elected, while the Republican party secured a victory in both Houses of the State Legislature, a victory that was in part attributed to the fresh vigour that Roosevelt had injected into New York politics.

In 1883 Theodore Roosevelt had a recurrence of his asthma and decided to see what an open-air life in the far west would do for his health. Together with a guide he had picked up in Maine who he thought would make a good cowhand he went out into the 'Bad Lands' in the territory of Dakota. (They were called the Bad Lands because the grassless plains had at first held out little prospect of prosperity.) 'It was', wrote Roosevelt, 'a land of vast silent spaces, of lonely rivers and of plains where the wild game stared at the passing horseman. It was a land of scattered ranches, of herds of long horned cattle, of reckless riders who unmoved looked in the eyes of life or of death.' Without exaggeration it was true cowboy country from which the Indians had only recently been driven and where buffalo still roamed. Roosevelt landed in the village of Medora, named by a Frenchman after his wife, the chief features of which were the station and a ramshackle boarding-house. Roosevelt purchased two ranches,

THEODORE ROOSEVELT

one of which was nicknamed the Maltese Cross from the brands marked on its cattle. Although the cowboys called Roosevelt 'Four Eyes' because he wore glasses, he soon won their respect and did not long remain a greenhorn. He modestly admitted that he was 'never more than a fair hunter' and 'never became a good roper', but his sojourn there rid him of his asthma and gained for him a wider insight into the problems of his still growing country. 'I owe more than I can ever express', he wrote in his *Autobiography*, 'to the West.'

During that same year Roosevelt had worked actively at Albany, not only procuring the passage of some useful city reform Bills, but also obtaining the application of the provisions of the national Civil Service Act of 1883 to the large cities in the state of New York. He was much moved by the conditions of domestic manufacture of cigars in tenement houses where men, women and children toiled in disgustingly overcrowded rooms, and tried to put a stop to the evil by legislation; but the law was declared unconstitutional by the courts. It would be a mistake, however, to picture the rising young politician who, as he himself boasted, had 'shot up like a rocket', as an ardent social reformer at this date. His primary concern was with political reform and elimination of corruption of any kind. His ardour for social reform was kindled later, mainly through the influence of the author of a book called *How the Other Half Lives*, Jacob Riis.

In February 1884 Hubris befell Roosevelt, for the gods had seen him too happy and successful. His wife died in giving birth to a baby daughter and within twenty-four hours his mother had also died. 'There is a curse on this house', the unhappy man affirmed. He relieved his feelings by writing a tribute to the two dead women and declared 'when my heart's dearest died, the light went out of my life forever'. Less than a week after the tragedy, he was back in Albany pushing through one of his reform Bills and that June he attended the Republican National Convention at Chicago where he vainly struggled against the nomination of James Blaine as the party's presidential candidate. It may be, Roosevelt grumbled, when he learned that Blaine had been chosen, that 'the voice of the people is the voice of God in 51 cases out of a 100; but in the remaining 49 it is quite as likely to be the voice of the devil, or, what is still worse, the voice of a fool.' As soon as

THE ROUGH RIDER

the Convention closed, he returned to the Bad Lands to seek forgetfulness in the energetic outdoor life on his ranches, interspersed with the writing of articles about the west and history. Refusing to stand again for election to the New York State Assembly, he told his friends that he had given up politics for ever.

Out in the west Roosevelt preached and practised the gospel of 'strenuosity'. He became, or so his *Autobiography* would have us believe, a kind of Wild West film hero: for he did not drink or smoke; he performed feats of extraordinary endurance in the periodic round-ups: he foiled a bully who tried to browbeat him into standing drinks in the saloon; and, appointed a deputy sheriff, he arrested three boat thieves. Indeed he convinced himself that his experiences in the west had made a man of him and all through his life he kept himself fit by violent forms of exercise. It was not until he became President that he 'thought it better to acknowledge that he had become an elderly man' and therefore gave up boxing: 'I then', he recorded, 'took up jiu-jitsu for a year or two.' But let there be no mistake: he never needed to prove to anyone but himself that he was a man of supreme courage. For he had shown that even when as a small boy he thought he heard a thief in the night and followed him, and again when he left his young wife's deathbed to resume his fight for political reform.

In the winter of 1886 bitter weather killed most of the cattle in Dakota and ruined his farms which had never paid and he abandoned them. But by that date time had healed his wounds. In December 1886 he married his childhood playmate, Edith Carow, at St. George's Church, Hanover Square, London and a few months later he returned to public life.

Roosevelt had not remained long out of politics; but in any case the years immediately after the death of his first wife were not congenial to an eager young Republican. In 1884 Grover Cleveland, a Democrat, had been elected President in preference to the somewhat doubtful Republican figure, James Blaine, 'the man from Maine'. In October of that year Roosevelt had addressed a Republican gathering in Brooklyn and in the following year he was persuaded to stand for the mayoralty of New York City against that dangerous Socialist, Henry George, and a highly respectable and wealthy representative of Democracy. Roosevelt came at the bottom of the poll and it was satirically observed that he was 'not the timber of which Presidents were made'. But after all he was only twenty-eight and it was a compliment to suggest that he was timber at all.

During these two years he was busily writing. His whole time on his Dakota ranches was not spent fourteen to sixteen hours a day in the saddle. Round-ups came rarely, and a publisher's contract was always waiting to be fulfilled. There was even time to read Tolstoy. He did not perturb himself unduly about the art of historical biography and indeed (though half-jokingly) invited his friend, Cabot Lodge to 'hire someone . . . to look up in a biographical dictionary or elsewhere' the facts about the last years of Thomas Benton's life which he was then writing and send them out to the ranch so that he might embellish them and finish it. It was only in his *Naval War of 1812* and in his *Winning of the West* that he embodied first-class work, although he always wrote, as he did everything else, with enormous gusto. The *Benton* is a book which shows that to Roosevelt past history was present politics, for his heart was still in politics and not in writing. When in 1889 General Benjamin Harrison, a hero of the Civil War and grandson of a former President, became the Republican President with James Blaine as his Secretary of State Roosevelt hoped to enter federal politics. His friend, Henry Cabot Lodge, who had been an instructor in history at Harvard and who had now become Congressman for Massachusetts, directed his influence on his behalf. 'I would like above all things to go into politics,' Roosevelt told him; 'but in this part of the State that seems impossible, especially with such a number of very wealthy competitors. So I have made up my mind that I will go in especially for literature, simply taking the part in politics that a decent man should.' Later he was delighted when the President, perhaps to pacify a keen but troublesome supporter, assigned him to the modest office of Civil Service Commissioner. There were three such Commissioners and they were paid 3500 dollars for what was almost reckoned a gentle sinecure. The appointment was under an act of 1883 which had until then been administered by a number of quiet gentlemen of unassuming ways. Civil Service reform was not thought highly of by professional politicians, who relied on the 'spoils system' to feed their hungry followers;

THE ROUGH RIDER

was it not the prescriptive right of every good party man — if his party won — to become a fourth-class postmaster? General Benjamin Harrison had no suspicion when he brought the vigorous young Theodore to Washington what he had let himself in for. For however high his ambitions soared, Roosevelt was a single-minded administrator and if he was to be a Civil Service Commissioner then he would certainly see that 'the merit system was extended at the expense of the spoils system' — no nonsense about that. The President might refuse an active young reformer a 'particle of sympathy' but he was not allowed to do more. 'To-day I caught a glimpse of the President', wrote Roosevelt in August 1889, 'and repeated to him the parable of the backwoodsman and the bear. You remember that the prayer of the backwoodsman was "Oh Lord, help me kill that bar; and if you don't help me, oh Lord, don't help the bar".' Two years later he wrote to his sister, Anna: 'I have been continuing my Civil Service fight, battling with everybody. The little grey man in the White House looking on with cold and hesitating disapproval, but not seeing how he could interfere.' Roosevelt held this office for exactly six years, for even when Grover Cleveland came back as President in 1893 he thought sufficiently well of Roosevelt to confirm his appointment and indeed the ardent Republican Civil Service Commissioner was not a little astonished to find that he received his best support in his reforms from a Democratic President and his two Democratic colleagues on the Commission. Six years were enough. In 1895 he was appointed by the recently elected reformist Mayor of New York City to a far more exciting post, that of Police Commissioner. Here there were four Commissioners, two from each party, and in the past they had interfered little with the Superintendent of Police who often amassed a tidy fortune by discriminatory enforcement of the laws. Roosevelt found the job 'absorbingly interesting', though he told his friends they need not 'have the slightest fear about my losing my interest in National Politics'. Roosevelt realized that there ought to be only one Commissioner, but he did his best in his capacity as president of the Commission, where, having forced out the Chief of Police, he held 'undisputed sway', to make his weight felt in reforming the service and carrying out the laws. At night he could be observed prowling the streets of New York in a big floppy hat and dark cloak, the terror of the patrolman. He took steps to see that the right men joined the force and the wrong men left it and was oblivious to all mockery. As Commissioner he was also a member of the Health Department and with the counsel of his friend, Jacob Riis, did what he could to improve housing conditions. He fought to keep favouritism, politics and corruption out of the police. And in two years he made his mark and many friends.

Both as Civil Service Commissioner and as Police Commissioner Roosevelt always 'hit the headlines'. Indeed his friends reprimanded him for giving too many interviews. His name as a reformer spread. In other ways too he earned a reputation, for he found time to complete his *Winning of the West* — 'of all my axes the best worth grinding' — a first-class historical work completed in 1894 which still retains its place in American historical literature. Moreover he and his second wife and their growing family became leaders in the social life of New York. Among his clever circle of friends were Henry Adams, the dry and cynical diarist and historian, whose tragedy was that he was the grandson and the great-grandson of a President, John Hay, the former secretary and biographer of Abraham Lincoln, Cecil Spring Rice, the British politician, and James Bryce, the British author of *The American Commonwealth*. Both in New York and at their seaside home at Oyster Bay, Long Island, the Roosevelts were excellent hosts whose modest offerings were deeply appreciated. But Theodore's mind was always on politics and when in 1897 the Republicans returned to power under the Presidency of William McKinley of Ohio, for whom Roosevelt campaigned in the middle west, his dearest hopes were realized: he went to Washington to become Assistant Secretary of the Navy.

It had been with some misgivings that the peaceable President McKinley had nominated Roosevelt for this office; for war was in the air and Roosevelt was notorious as a fire-eating imperialist. The danger centre was Cuba where a revolutionary movement had broken out in 1895 against the Spanish rulers of the island. Many southerners in the United States had always cast covetous eyes towards Cuba which at one time Jackson had wanted to seize. A profitable trade with the island was lost on account of the civil war there, while much property belonging to American citizens was destroyed. In private letters written before he went to the Navy Department Roosevelt showed that he hankered after war: 'If it wasn't wrong', he wrote in January 1896, 'I should say that personally I would rather welcome a foreign war.' 'Tell Will', he wrote to his sister, Anna, who had married a naval officer, 'that it is very difficult for me not to wish for a war with Spain, for such a war would result at once in getting us a proper Navy and a good system of coastal defence.' Three weeks later he wrote to her again: 'We ought to drive the Spaniards out of Cuba.'

Roosevelt had always been attracted by the navy: he had acquired much practical knowledge about it when collecting the materials for his first book and he was the friend and admirer of Captain Mahan whose celebrated book, *The Influence of Sea Power on History*, was one of the few historical books that had an immediate political influence. The Secretary of the Navy, John D. Long, a mild old gentleman, was soon overshadowed by the personality of his truculent assistant who constantly badgered his chief to prepare for war and did what he could towards that end whenever Long went on holiday. When the situation grew worse a second-class American battleship, the *Maine*, was sent to Cuba on a courtesy call. In February 1898 the news reached Washington that the *Maine* had been blown up in Havana harbour and 266 members of its crew killed. Roosevelt wanted the President at once to order the whole fleet to Havana, but McKinley struggled against war, while a court of inquiry investigated the causes of the disaster. 'We are certainly drifting toward war,' Roosevelt announced happily, 'but the President will not make war and will keep out of it if he possibly can.' But, Roosevelt added, if the report of the court of inquiry said that the explosion was due to outside work, 'it will be very hard to hold the country'. Roosevelt was right, for ever since the rebellion had started in Cuba there had been a deliberate war movement in the United States, the yellow press of Hearst and Pulitzer ably exploiting all the cruelties and stupidities of the Spaniards to this end. On February 25th Roosevelt, then Acting Secretary of the Navy, ordered his squadron to move to their war stations and instructed Admiral Dewey, once war began, to prevent the Spanish squadron from leaving Asiatic waters and to begin naval operations against the Philippine islands.

THEODORE ROOSEVELT

This moment was one of the turning points in American history. Hitherto the growing population of the United States had expanded only across the mainland. But now the frontier of settlement was no longer open. Hitherto wars had been waged only in the interests of national independence to permit consolidation of the federal authority. Now with a population of 75,000,000 people and commercial concerns stretching across the world, and with an expanding navy, the United States Government undertook a war from imperialist motives against a European power. And since that date, much as many of its citizens have wanted to avoid doing so, the United States has become entangled with Europe. Theodore Roosevelt spoke for a rising generation.

Roosevelt's Jingoism was bound up with his gospel of strenuosity. Just as he believed that it was good for the individual to show his mastery of himself by taking violent physical exercise and to endure hardship and even peril to prove that he had the right stuff in him, so he considered it was good for the nation to go to war — though of course only in a righteous cause. 'Roosevelt', said a contemporary, 'did not care whom we fought as long as there was a scrap.' But logically Roosevelt refused to let others do the fighting for him. 'I had preached with all the fervour and zeal I possessed our duty to intervene in Cuba,' he recorded afterwards in his book *The Rough Riders*, 'and to take the opportunity of driving the Spaniard from the Western world . . . and from the beginning I had determined that, if war came, somehow or other, I was going to the front.' As soon as McKinley was driven to declare war, Roosevelt resigned office to enlist in the army. His friends tried to dissuade him. After all he was forty, he was a married man with a wife and several children and were not his services needed in the capital? Thus the specious plea, to which as good men as he have succumbed, rings down the ages. Roosevelt refused to be moved from his resolve. Others might regard his decision, if they wished, as adolescent exuberance and a few might wisely conclude after the event that it was a shrewd bid on his part to win a national reputation, but his determination flowed naturally from his philosophy of life and had no ulterior motive. Had he died — as many who followed him were to die — in the swamps of Cuba, the knowing ones would have given him the epitaph:' There went a rash fool.'

THE ROUGH RIDER

Roosevelt's opportunity came when Congress voted that three cavalry regiments were to be raised from the wild riders and riflemen of the Rockies and Great Plains. Roosevelt modestly declined the appointment as colonel of one of these regiments and instead served as lieutenant-colonel under a friend, Leonard Wood, who had formerly been a surgeon in the regular army. Recruits came pouring in from New Mexico, Arizona, Oklahoma and of course Dakota. Other glad though less rough volunteers arrived from Harvard, Yale and Princeton universities. The First Volunteer Cavalry Regiment assembled at San Antonia, Texas, to undergo a swift military course before embarking for the scene of the fighting. Though he was not their commander the regiment soon became known as Roosevelt's Rough Riders and they were all agog to go. Roosevelt managed to get them on board a transport (intended apparently for another regiment) and for six days they waited fuming in the semi-tropical heat of Tampa Bay. The regiment arrived in Cuba in excellent time to take part in the fighting, but alas without their horses. Brigaded with two regular regiments the Rough Riders at first had some uncomfortable moments. On June 24th they bumped unexpectedly into the enemy and suffered losses. It was a grim campaign in the heat of the jungle. Roosevelt conducted himself with the greatest bravery: while others took cover, wrote a friend who was there in July 1898: 'Theodore preferred to stand up and walk about snuffling the fragrant air of combat. I really believe firmly now that they could not kill him.' The supreme opportunity had come to the regiment on July 1st when Roosevelt's men charged uphill in what he called the battle of San Juan hills. In spite of terrible losses Colonel Roosevelt led his men forward with immense enthusiasm. 'Are you afraid to stand up when I am on horseback?' he asked troopers who hung back. Though reckless in battle, Roosevelt was splendid in caring for his men when they were out of the line; he overcame the lack of adequate transport facilities and hospitals, wrote home to induce his friends and relatives to send food and other comforts to his men and spent every dollar he could borrow on them. The campaign proved short, sharp and, in retrospect, sweet. For on that same July 1st the Spanish fleet ventured out of Santiago Bay and was destroyed. Roosevelt at once demanded that his regiment should be sent on to another theatre of war, Porto Rico. That was not to be and instead the American army went into camps where it was tortured by yellow fever and malaria. Roosevelt had been promoted first colonel and then brigadier-general, while his friend, Wood, became military Governor of the island. Roosevelt did not hesitate to protest to Washington about the conditions in Cuba and soon the Rough Riders — or what was left of them — were brought home to receive an uproarious welcome in the streets of New York, and Brigadier-General Roosevelt, the star of San Juan, was almost as much of a national hero as Andrew Jackson had been after the battle of New Orleans. Though disappointed because he did not receive the Medal of Honour, which an unappreciative War Department withheld, in November he was elected Republican Governor of New York State. 'I am so glad to be Governor,' he told his sister, 'that is, to be at work doing something that counts that all the bothers and worries are of small consequence.'

2. GOVERNOR OF NEW YORK STATE — VICE-PRESIDENT — FIRST YEARS AS PRESIDENT (1899-1904)

Theodore Roosevelt had not been elected Governor of New York State without a stiff fight. In those days politics were extremely tough with the 'big bosses' running efficient and not wholly soulless organizations that paid useful dividends to those who tended them. The voting public were, however, not imbeciles and if one side or the other was caught out in an obvious piece of graft then the other side might have to be let in. This was the position in 1898. The previous Republican Governor had lost the confidence of the electors because he had permitted extravagant repairs on the Erie Canal, an episode which his opponents bluntly called 'the canal steal'. The Democratic boss, Croker, felt sure that his party's chance had come, while the Republican boss, Tom Platt, a seamy old Senator, knew that only desperate measures could avert the catastrophe of loss of office. For this reason he approached Roosevelt, hoping that his reputation for honesty and even more the glory that hung round him as a war hero might induce the electorate to overlook the awkward affair of the Erie

FIRST YEARS AS PRESIDENT

Canal. 'Senator Platt', wrote Roosevelt in his *Autobiography*, 'was entirely frank in the matter. He made no pretence that he liked me personally; but he deferred to the judgment of those who insisted that I was the only man who could be elected, and that therefore I had to be nominated.'

Roosevelt had not been unduly enthusiastic about the nomination, for he would have preferred to return to federal politics and his attractive friends in Washington, and indeed had hoped that President McKinley would dismiss his Secretary of War and appoint him to the post. However this did not happen and, after all, to be Governor of New York State was a stepping-stone to the highest federal offices. As things were, in spite of all his patriotic endeavour — for Roosevelt treated the contest as of national concern — he was elected by a majority of only just over 17,000 votes. Boss Platt was delighted: 'Roosevelt', he wrote, 'made a dramatic campaign. He fairly pranced about the State ... I have always maintained that no man besides Roosevelt could have accomplished that feat in 1898.'

But for all his showmanship Roosevelt was no man's fool. He well knew the power of the bosses and that it was not easy to create an alternative machine. Therefore he showed deference to Platt, while making it plain that he would not be his tool. Platt was now so feeble that he could scarcely leave his house, but he stuck like a limpet to his absorbing self-imposed task of political manipulation, his only other interest in life being 'an arid theology that bore little relation to ethics'. Roosevelt would take breakfast with him and discuss appointments and legislation; but he saw that he had his own way; his two favourite quotations were, 'It is so much easier to be a harmless dove than a wise serpent', and 'Speak softly and carry a big stick, you will go far'. He refused, for example, to accept Platt's nominee as Superintendent of Public Works since this was the official who would have to look after the canals. When the Senator was told, there was an explosion but Roosevelt 'declined to lose his temper, merely repeating that he must decline to accept any man chosen for him and that he must choose the man himself'. Similarly he insisted on the dismissal of the Superintendent of Insurance and his decision was justified when it turned out that the gentleman in question had borrowed 435,000 dollars from a trust company that controlled one of the insurance companies which came within his jurisdiction.

The legislative accomplishment of which Roosevelt was proudest during his term as Governor was an act for taxing state franchises. A franchise was a right granted to a private company to run tramcars along the public streets. Previously the big corporations had paid nothing for this right, though they contributed heavily and impartially to party funds. Platt protested at the proposed legislation for he maintained that if the Bill were passed no corporation would ever contribute again. 'Senator Platt', wrote Roosevelt, 'did not believe in popular rule and he did believe that the big business men were entitled to have their own way. He felt that anarchy would come if there was any interference with the system by which the people in mass were, under various necessary cloaks, controlled by the leaders in the political and business worlds.' The Bill, it seemed to him, was the thin edge of the wedge. But on April 28th, 1899, Governor Roosevelt sent a special message to the Assembly demanding the immediate passage of the Bill. It was towards the end of the session and the Speaker angrily tore up the message. Roosevelt then dispatched another message by his secretary and the Bill went through against the wishes of the bosses of both parties. Even that did not finish the story. The Bill, as passed, left the assessments to the local authorities, 'which meant that Tammany in New York City would have new power over honest Republican business men' (Pringle). The Governor was willing that a better Bill should be substituted but not an emasculated one. Indeed, he gave warning that if the new Bill did not accord with his wishes, he would sign the old Bill. 'They then all went in', Roosevelt told his friend Lodge, 'in good faith to pass my amendments . . . the net result is that we have on the statute books the most important law passed in recent times by any American State legislature.'

Among other laws sponsored or approved by Roosevelt during his term as Governor was a Bill for Civil Service reform and a tenement house Bill to deal with overcrowding. Housing was a question that had disturbed Roosevelt ever since he had been Police Commissioner in New York City. Even after he became Governor he would still pay surprise visits to sweat-shops picked out at random in company with his mentor, Jacob Riis. Accord-

FIRST YEARS AS PRESIDENT

ing to Roosevelt's friend and biographer, Bishop, the Bill abolished sweat-shops in New York City for all time. Roosevelt claimed with no undue modesty to have been the best Governor of his time and maybe, taking account of the boss-ridden politics that then prevailed, he was right. The technique employed by Roosevelt when he was Governor of New York State to force his own programme on the State Legislature was to be adopted by him later when he was the President of the United States. For it was his conviction that it was the duty of a chief executive to give a lead in matters of social and political reform and not merely to administer the law as it stood. No one but he had the combined powers of political magnate and party chief — and if he could not direct and fulfil political programmes of benefit to the community, then who could?

Theodore Roosevelt was fortunate in that during his term as Governor, in which he had so much enjoyed bending Platt to his will and 'standing the New York Republican machine on its head', his home life was ideally happy. The summers were spent at his seaside home of Sagamore Hill, Oyster Bay, which he had owned since he was a young man and where his six children loved to be. Here the Governor would lead camping expeditions or games on a raft: it was lucky for the children of Oyster Bay that Roosevelt was always a boy at heart. Later Roosevelt's love of children was perpetuated when one of the world's most famous dolls, the Teddy Bear, was named after him — 'Teddy' — because that was his nickname, bear because of his hunting expeditions in search of grizzlies.

The last months of Roosevelt's term as Governor were filled with perplexities as to whether he should stand for election as Vice-President during the presidential campaign of 1900. Roosevelt's ultimate ambition of course was the Republican nomination for the Presidency, to which his record gave him every right. But the duties of a Vice-President, apart from presiding over the Senate, were largely nominal and therefore ill-suited to so ambitious and active a politician. Although John Adams and Martin Van Buren had both become Presidents after holding the Vice-Presidency, they were exceptions rather than the rule. And if Roosevelt was to take another federal office while awaiting his chance for the presidential nomination he would infinitely have preferred to be Secretary of State or even Governor-General of the Philippines. The situation was complicated by the fact that Tom Platt, the boss of New York State, wanted to get rid of Roosevelt as Governor (the term was only two years and expired at the end of 1900) while Senator Mark Hanna, boss of the Republican national machine, wanted Roosevelt to stay in New York State and not burst back into national politics: indeed, he was afraid that Roosevelt's popularity might even win him the presidential nomination. In this he was wrong for Roosevelt was loyal to McKinley, who became the party candidate for a second term. Roosevelt was naturally not anxious to be manœuvred out of New York State, where he believed he was doing good as Governor, for what might prove to be a political backwater, more especially when he became aware that the big insurance companies and street car corporations, which resented the franchise tax, were behind Platt in his efforts to inveigle him into standing for the Vice-Presidency. 'All the high monied interests that make the campaign contributions of large size', he wrote to Senator Lodge on February 3rd, 1900, 'and feel that they should have favours in return, are extremely anxious to get me out of the State.' At one time he went so far as to say that he would rather retire from public life than be Vice-President of the United States.

There was, however, another aspect to the question and that was his duty to the Republican party, for, personal predilections apart, nothing must be done to jeopardize the party's chances at the polls and Roosevelt's name would strengthen the 'ticket'. The Democratic party's candidate was to be that extraordinary figure, William Jennings Bryan. Bryan had been born in Illinois in March 1860 and, like Roosevelt, had 'risen like a rocket'. His mother was a Methodist and his father a Baptist, while he as a young man joined the Presbyterians and puritan fervour lent point to political speeches for which he had a natural genius. Bryan preferred eating to drinking for moral reasons and liked speaking almost as much as he liked eating. He migrated to Nebraska to practise law and there sprang into the limelight by winning a normally Republican Congressional district for the Democratic party at the age of thirty. The House of Representatives was as spellbound by his sentimental oratory as had been the audiences in Nebraska. His views were those of an old-

FIRST YEARS AS PRESIDENT

fashioned radical — he was opposed both to high tariffs and imperialism — and they were fortified by an evangelical belief in the virtues of bimetallism: he thought the problems of the middle-west farmers would be resolved if silver was freely coined in the fixed ratio of 1 to 16 to gold. A speech at the Democratic Convention of 1896 which he ended by saying: 'You shall not press down upon the brow of labour this crown of thorns [i.e. the gold standard], you shall not crucify mankind upon a cross of gold' won him the Democratic presidential nomination and in his fight against McKinley that year he was beaten only by 7,035,638 popular votes to 6,467,946. His oratory was of spell-binding character which, one of his biographers says, lost its effects after the hearers went away. Nevertheless, in those days when public oratory was still a public treat and people in search of entertainment had no films or radio with which to pass their evenings and from which to extract vicarious thrills Bryan's power counted for much. Moreover his arguments genuinely appealed to those who hated or feared the big business corporations which were becoming more and more influential after the Civil War. Though McKinley's first term had been an era of prosperity, Bryan constituted a possible danger to the supremacy of the Republican party in politics and it seemed valuable to the rank-and-file of that party to have actively supporting McKinley a man like Roosevelt who had attacked the corporations in New York State and round whose head the laurel crown won in the Spanish war was still visibly green.

When Roosevelt went as a delegate to the Republican Convention at Philadelphia in June 1900, he was taken by surprise at the warm enthusiasm for him and, although the New York delegation had been instructed not to put forward his name as vice-presidential candidate, his friends from other states insisted on nominating him and he felt that he would be an ungrateful fool if he refused to accept. In this decision he was strengthened by the advice of his friend, Senator Lodge, who had long thought he should stand. 'The nomination came to me at Philadelphia', Roosevelt wrote on June 27th, 'simply because the bulk of the enormous majority of the delegates were bent upon having me whether I wished it or not, and all the more because Senator Hanna objected to it.' On the same day he wrote to Hanna offering his speaking services in the campaign: 'I am as strong as a bull moose and you can use me to the limit.' Hanna took him at his word and told him that the main burden would in fact fall upon his shoulders. Bryan's hopes were soon blasted. He had taken an unpopular line over the Spanish-American War and the American imperialism that was growing out of it and denied that it was the 'manifest destiny' of the United States to rule the world. 'The command "Go ye into all the world and preach the gospel to every creature" ', he observed, 'has no Gatling gun attachment.' Roosevelt stumped the middle west with quite a different message, while the Republican party promised 'a full dinner pail' to the electorate. McKinley beat Bryan handsomely by 292 electoral votes to 155. Roosevelt made one final mark as Governor of New York State by rebuking the Mayor and Chief of Police of New York City for attempts at intimidation and fraud in the Democratic interest. Then he sadly turned towards the light duties of Vice-President; but as it happened he was only called upon to preside over the meetings of the Senate for one week.

A former classmate of Roosevelt at Harvard had written before the election: 'I should not like to be in McKinley's shoes. He has a man of destiny behind him.' And so it proved. On September 6th, in the Temple of Music, Buffalo, New York State, McKinley was shot twice by an anarchist. Roosevelt at the time was attending an outing of the Vermont Fish and Game League in Lake Champlain. As soon as he heard the news he took a special train to Buffalo. There, despite severe wounds, the President rallied, and Roosevelt left again to join his family in the Adirondack Mountains, but on September 13th he heard that McKinley was worse. Thereupon he hired a wagon for the fifty-mile drive to the nearest station to return to Buffalo. He and the driver changed horses two or three times on the way, but by the time they reached the waiting train the President was known to be dead. The next day Roosevelt took the oath of office as his successor in a friend's house in Buffalo. He was still on the right side of forty-three and was the youngest man who had ever become President.

'It is a dreadful thing', wrote Roosevelt to Senator Lodge on September 23rd, 1901, 'to come into the Presidency this way; but

FIRST YEARS AS PRESIDENT

it would be a far worse thing to be morbid about it. Here is the task, and I have got to do it to the best of my ability; and that is all there is about it.' It must have been a little galling for those who imagined that they had sidetracked this energetic and unorthodox Republican politician by inducing him to stand for the Vice-Presidency to discover that he had now so quickly become master of them all. Senator Hanna wrote and begged him to 'go slow' and others urged him to be 'conservative and close-mouthed'. He hastened to convey appropriate assurances and announced that he would follow McKinley's policies and retain McKinley's Cabinet. The Secretary of State was his old friend, John Hay, who he described in his *Autobiography* as 'one of the most delightful of companions, one of the most charming of all men of cultivation and action'. 'Our views on foreign affairs', he added, 'coincide absolutely; but, as was natural enough, in domestic matters he felt much more conservative than he did in the days when as a young man he was private secretary to the great radical democratic leader of the 'sixties, Abraham Lincoln.' His Secretary of War was Elihu Root, an able lawyer who had been appointed to the post by McKinley when Roosevelt had coveted it for himself, while his Secretary of the Navy was that same Mr. Long to whom in the days before the Spanish war he had been Assistant. In his *Autobiography* he described his attitude to his officials:

> More than once while I was President my officials were attacked by Congress, generally because these officials did their duty well and fearlessly. In every such case I stood by the official and refused to recognize the right of Congress to interfere with me excepting by impeachment or in other Constitutional manner. On the other hand, wherever I found the officer unfit for his position I promptly removed him although the most influential men in Congress fought for his retention. The Jackson-Lincoln view is that a President who is fit to do good work should be able to form his own judgment as to his subordinates and, above all, of the subordinates standing in closest and most intimate touch with him. My Secretaries and their subordinates were responsible to me, and I accepted the responsibility for all their deeds. As long as they were satisfactory to me I stood by them against every

critic or assailant, within or without Congress; and as to getting Congress to make up my mind for me about them, the thought would have been inconceivable to me.

On the question of appointments to federal positions Roosevelt was equally clear; he recognized the right of Senators to be consulted about appointments in their states, but he refused automatically to endorse their choices; 'they may ordinarily name the men,' he announced, 'but I shall name the standard and the men have got to come up to it'. He did not care how powerful the Senator might be, he spoke his mind freely and when it came to the south he said that if he could not find suitable Republicans he would fill the vacancies with Democrats. One day a Texas Senator came to seek promotion for a certain army officer, saying that the step was favoured by the entire Texas legislature. 'But', said the President, 'it is opposed by all the man's superior officers.' 'I don't give a damn for his superior officers!' retorted the Senator. 'Well, Senator,' said Roosevelt, 'I don't give a damn for the Legislature of Texas.'

Roosevelt's first message to Congress exemplified his promise to Mark Hanna to 'go slow'. Though he wrote the whole message himself, it was a carefully balanced document such as might have emerged from departmental briefs and was designed to give as little offence as possible to anyone. Nevertheless it contained one or two positive statements: the President promised supervision of corporations, stated that he intended to create a Department of Commerce and Labour, and asked for a stronger navy. In general, however, those who scrutinized the message most closely reached the conclusion, as Mr. Pringle writes, that though 'the President might "go slow" in moving forward he objected to moving backward'.

The United States, of which Theodore Roosevelt was now chief executive, was a very different country from that over which Abraham Lincoln or his predecessors had presided. On the whole it was a tough, prosperous and dynamic community, but its prosperity was unevenly divided. On one side, there were mighty millionaires with their yachts and rare collections of paintings, their dynasties and their mistresses; on the other there were poor whites and poor Negroes, still wondering exactly what

FIRST YEARS AS PRESIDENT

emancipation had meant, there were workmen sweating long hours for low wages before they returned exhausted to their slums to sleep. A period of economic depression which hit the farmers most severely had followed the end of the Civil War while many southern towns had been damaged or devasted. Though the life of the south had recovered more rapidly than might have been expected the war had seared the souls of its men and women. Corrupt politicians — white residents of northern origin known as 'carpet baggers' — had exploited their distress, but the old rulers of the south had reasserted the supremacy of the white over the black and of the native over the intrusive northerners by a reign of terror directed through the Ku-Klux-Klan and other secret societies. Though the great estates which subsisted on slavery were broken up, cotton and tobacco were supplemented by a large fruit and vegetable growing industry and by the rise of new businesses such as iron and steel and textiles. Yet against this background of reviving prosperity there was much distress, for example among the share croppers who paid their landlords rent in kind. Both in the south and in the west debtors were injured by inflation and by the establishment of the gold standard in 1873.

During this era too the railways expanded in a haphazard fashion making fortunes for some men and ruining others. Vast crowds of alien immigrants flooded into the land — not the immigrants of old who had cleared the western forests but poor illiterate Europeans who came to seek modest livelihoods in such towns as Chicago and Pittsburgh. Great corporations arose to control the railways and the steel industry with powerful and often unscrupulous financiers at their head. Most famous of all these was J. Pierpont Morgan, whose contempt for politics only exceeded his dislike of his rivals, Harriman, Carnegie, Rockefeller, Gould. No one could plumb or has ever plumbed the depths of this strange creature's nature. As a young man he had made money out of the sale of dud carbines during the Civil War, while others fought and died. Yet he threw up his business concerns to follow the girl he loved to Paris to ask her, though she was dying of consumption, to become his wife. President Grover Cleveland had been forced to appeal to Morgan for help when in 1895 a financial crisis was draining gold out of the Treasury and threatening national bankruptcy. It was with the redoubtable Morgan that Theodore

Roosevelt broke a lance within six months of his becoming President,

On November 12th, 1901, Pierpont Morgan and James Hill, the 'railway king', had incorporated a gigantic holding company in New Jersey to control three big northern railways with the praiseworthy intention of eliminating waste and consolidating profits. Though the oppressive power and the monopolistic nature of such corporations was widely feared, hitherto they had suffered little from political control. True, the Sherman Anti-Trust Act of 1890 had declared illegal 'every contract, combination in the form of trust or otherwise, or conspiracy in restraint of trade and commerce among the several States or with foreign nations', but it was badly drawn and, partly because the Department of Justice had lacked adequate funds for its enforcement, had hitherto proved a dead letter. But in February 1902 Roosevelt asked his Attorney-General, Philander C. Knox, whether he thought the new merger violated the Sherman Act and when he said yes, decided to initiate an action against it in a federal court in Minnesota. When all qualifications have been made, this was a brave move by the new President. It is always so much easier to let sleeping dogs lie. The decision to prosecute caused a sensation in Wall Street and Morgan hurried to Washington to interview the President. 'If we have done anything wrong,' Morgan told Roosevelt, 'send your man (meaning the Attorney-General) to my man (naming one of his lawyers) and they can fix it up.' 'That can't be done', Roosevelt replied. 'We don't want to fix it up,' added the Attorney-General, 'we want to stop it.' Then Morgan asked: 'Are you going to attack my other interests, the Steel Trust and the others?' 'Certainly not,' said the President, 'unless we find out that in any case they have done something that we regard as wrong.' After Morgan left, Roosevelt said to Knox: 'That is a most illuminating illustration of the Wall Street point of view. Mr. Morgan could not help regarding me as a big rival operator, who either intended to ruin all his interests or else could be induced to come to an agreement to ruin none.' In March 1904 the Federal Supreme Court decided by 5 votes to 4 that the merger did violate the Sherman Act. Among the judges who voted in the minority was Justice Oliver Wendell Holmes, whom Roosevelt himself had just appointed.

FIRST YEARS AS PRESIDENT

In May of that same year Roosevelt had another political success in bringing to an end a big anthracite coal strike in Pennsylvania which had it not been stopped would have caused much suffering throughout the country during the winter. He had, as he knew, no real powers to interfere, but he considered that he would be shirking his responsibilities if he failed to do his utmost. First, he brought the two sides together, but when that failed to produce a settlement he threatened to send federal troops into the mines to dispossess the coal-owners and run the mines as a receiver. Under this menace the coal-owners eventually agreed to the appointment of an arbitration commission (including a labour representative whom the President nominated, to gratify the scruples of the owners, as 'an eminent sociologist'). The commission awarded the miners a ten per cent wage increase, though it denied recognition to the Union. Roosevelt's attack on corporations in the Northern Securities Case and his modest aid to the miners in the coal strike were instances of the way in which, as he claimed, he made 'an old party progressive'. Unquestionably his actions pleased many electors. For in that age of growing national wealth there was much discontent among ordinary men and women at the way things were going: the rise of a 'Populist party', the emergence of a Socialist leader in Eugene Debs, the development of trade unionism, the support given to the fantastic panaceas of Bryan in the west — all reflected a broadening trend of progressive opinion in the United States. Roosevelt sensed this — sensed the dissatisfaction lapping round the ultra-conservative policies and machine-made politics that had held command since the Civil War. Both when he was Governor of New York State and now in the wider sphere of the Presidency Roosevelt used the powers he had to promote a measure of social justice with an intelligence and an agility that exacted admiration even from his enemies. Pierpont Morgan might say of him 'the man's a lunatic — he is worse than a Socialist'; but what Morgan failed to realize was that, on the contrary, Roosevelt by recognizing that social evils existed and by trying to grapple with them, was saving his country from Socialism, which he dreaded as much as Morgan.

While at home Roosevelt was 'making an old party progressive', in matters of foreign policy he was making a new nation conscious of its imperial destiny. The treaty which ended the war with Spain had established the independence of Cuba, while permitting the United States to intervene in that country if necessary in order to maintain order; it had ceded the Philippines and Porto Rico to the United States; and thus for the first time American proconsuls bestrode the globe in the interests of reform and the development of backward peoples. What men like Lord Cromer and Lord Lugard did in Egypt and West Africa, General Leonard Wood and William Taft did in Cuba and the Philippines. 'It is a contemptible thing', wrote Roosevelt as he looked back benignly upon this period, 'for a great nation to render itself impotent in international action, whether because of cowardice or sloth or sheer inability or unwillingness to look into the future.' The United States Government had in fact moved forward since the day when Jefferson pleaded for no entanglements with Europe and had believed in keeping his toy navy of gunboats moored in the waters of the Potomac to save the pocket of the taxpayer.

In two matters, both amicably settled, in the winter of 1902-03 Roosevelt adopted a truculent attitude to European Powers. The first concerned Venezuela. This South American Republic after a customary South American revolution had refused to pay its foreign debts and Great Britain and Germany agreed to use force to exact payment for its nationals. This step, which in later times, would surely have led to war, was not openly resented by Roosevelt who told Congress that the Monroe Doctrine did not 'guarantee any State against punishment if it misconducts itself' so long as the punishers did not attempt to acquire territory. But behind the scenes Roosevelt took a firm line with the German ambassador and threatened to send an American fleet to Venezuela if arbitration were not accepted. The second case referred to the Alaskan boundary between the United States and Canada. Here it was Roosevelt who was reluctant to accept arbitration, somewhat oddly since he was convinced of the irrefragable justice of the American case. Instead he preferred to anticipate the possibility of trouble and ordered the strengthening of the border garrisons. In the end, he consented to the setting up of an arbitration tribunal by a treaty which, owing to the impartial conduct of the British Lord Chief Justice, who was one of the members of the

FIRST YEARS AS PRESIDENT

tribunal, reached a decision in favour of the American claims. But the achievement of which Roosevelt was most proud during his first term of office was taking possession of the Isthmus of Panama in order to build an American-controlled inter-oceanic canal across it.

The idea of such a canal linking Atlantic and Pacific across the Isthmus of Central America was old. In 1850 a treaty had been concluded between the United States and the British Government (the Clayton-Bulwer Treaty) whereby it was agreed that the two nations, then the greatest maritime powers in the world, should have equal privileges in such a canal and that neither should fortify it. In 1884 an independent French company, directed by the genius of Ferdinand de Lesseps, the builder of the Suez Canal, had started work on a canal across Panama, but the project had been ruined by the jungle conditions and the company had gone bankrupt. In 1894 another French company, the New Panama Canal Company, had acquired the assets of the old company, but had done nothing more. In 1899 negotiations had been begun between the United States and Great Britain to modify the Clayton-Bulwer treaty: the American Senate had been strongly opposed to any arrangement which would give a European Power any say in the military control of an isthmian canal (a view that Roosevelt heartily endorsed) and finally the Hay-Pauncefote Treaty of 1901 provided that the United States might construct, maintain and control any such canal so long as it was open to the commerce of all nations.

As soon as this treaty was ratified an American commission was appointed to investigate which was the most suitable route for an isthmian canal. The Commission reported in favour of a canal across Nicaragua, but this was mainly because the New Panama Canal Company demanded over a hundred million dollars for its assets in Panama which the Commission valued at only forty million dollars. As soon, however, as the New Panama Canal Company heard of the Commission's report it offered to sell its properties and concessions to the United States for forty million dollars — for, after all, the United States Government was the only possible buyer and unless it bought, the company's stock was worthless. In June 1902 Congress passed a Bill authorizing the President to acquire this property and to negotiate with the

Government of Colombia (to whom Panama belonged) for the acquisition of a strip of land on which to operate the canal when completed. The President offered the Colombian Government the sum of ten million dollars a year for nine years for a strip of land thirty miles long between the two oceans to come under the administrative control of the United States, though it was to remain under the nominal sovereignty of Colombia. The Colombian Congress rejected the treaty not so much because it considered the price was too low as because it objected to the virtual surrender of part of its territory to the sovereignty of the United States. Roosevelt was furious: 'Those contemptible little creatures in Bogota' [the capital of Colombia] he said, 'ought to understand how much they are jeopardizing things and imperilling their own future.' What was to be done? Roosevelt had no intention of letting the matter hang fire until the election of 1904. One plan that he considered was to seize the territory under the terms of a treaty of 1846 which laid down that 'the right of way or transit across the Isthmus of Panama should be free and open to the Government and citizens of the United States'. But this would have been naked imperialism and Roosevelt would have found it hard to defend an attack upon a small weak power in the eyes of the world. There was a better way. Supposing the people of Panama could be induced to stage a revolt against the Government of Colombia, then they could be recognized as an independent republic by the United States Government and sell to it the right to construct a canal. In October 1903 M. Bunau-Varilla, representing the New Panama Canal Company, which was now desperately anxious for its forty million dollars, saw Roosevelt and mentioned the possibility of revolution. Thus Roosevelt knew of the plot, but there is no evidence that he forwarded it. The impulse came from Bunau-Varilla and his friends who appreciated that once a revolution was started in Panama, the United States Government would use the treaty of 1846 as a justification for intervening to restore order to assist the revolutionists.

The Panama Revolution, a comic opera affair, took place on November 3rd, 1903. The only casualty was a Chinese who was killed by a shell from a Colombian gunboat. As soon as the flag of independence was hoisted at Colon in Panama, American

FIRST YEARS AS PRESIDENT

marines landed and refused to allow Colombian troops to suppress the revolt. The gallant soldiers of Panama were paid fifty dollars apiece for their trouble while the officers received ten thousand dollars. On November 6th, the Republic of Panama was formally recognized by the United States Government and by the beginning of December the independent republic ratified a treaty conceding to the United States the strip of territory which it required to complete and protect the isthmian canal. The Government of Colombia never acquiesced in the propriety of this train of events and ultimately in 1921 the Woodrow Wilson Administration paid a sum of twenty-five million dollars in compensation to Colombia.

Theodore Roosevelt had carried out nearly all the details of this tricky affair himself and compared his triumph to that of Jefferson in negotiating the Louisiana Purchase. 'If I had followed conventional, conservative methods', he said, 'I should have submitted a dignified state paper of approximately two hundred pages to the Congress and the debate would have been going on yet, but I took the canal zone and let Congress debate, and while the debate goes on the canal does also.'

The people of the United States approved this and other actions of President Roosevelt during his first term. In March 1904 he had introduced a service pension of six dollars a month for the veterans of the Civil War. In 1903 he had set up his promised Department of Commerce. The only possible opponent of his nomination as Republican presidential candidate in the next election, Mark Hanna, had died, and his Democratic antagonist, a dry lawyer named Parker, lacked the popular appeal of the fervent Bryan. Even the great corporations, like Standard Oil, who discovered, or thought they had discovered, that Roosevelt's bark was worse than his bite (for during his time in office the actual number of anti-trust cases instituted was few) were anxious to contribute to his electoral campaign chest, though he wisely gave orders that such contributions should be refused. On November 8th, 1904, he was successful by 336 electoral votes to 140. 'I am stunned by the overwhelming victory we have won', he wrote to his son, Kermit. 'I have the greatest popular majority and the greatest electoral majority ever given to a candidate for President.' On the night of the election he told the world: 'A wise custom which limits the President to two terms regards the substance and not the form, and under no circumstances will I be candidate for or accept another nomination.'

3. PRESIDENT BY ELECTION (1905-1909)

At forty-seven President Theodore Roosevelt was a man of apparently inexhaustible vitality whose interests ranged in many directions. 'While in the White House', he recorded in his *Autobiography*, 'I always tried to get a couple of hours' exercise in the afternoons — sometimes tennis, more often riding, or else a rough cross-country walk, perhaps down Rock Creek, which was then as wild as a stream in the White Mountains, or on the Virginia side of the Potomac. My companions at tennis or on these rides and walks we gradually grew to style the Tennis Cabinet.' The walks were of a most strenuous character. On several occasions in the early spring the party was called upon to swim Rock Creek when the ice was floating thick upon it or Roosevelt would lead his perspiring party of officers, politicians and diplomatists scrambling across the cliffs that lay beside the Creek. 'Once', wrote Roosevelt, 'I invited an entire class of officers who were attending lectures at the War College, to come on one of these walks. I chose a route which gave us the hardest climbing along the rocks and the deepest crossing of the creek and my army friends enjoyed it hugely — being the right sort to a man.' 'His wonderful hypnotic influence', wrote his military aide, Archie Butt, 'swept one off one's feet in a sort of whirlwind motion and, when it was over, left one exhausted.'

Physical exercise was not Roosevelt's only form of relaxation. Throughout his Presidency he was a voracious reader, while he followed with attention the latest movements in art and the theatre. To his friend and old instructor in history, Senator Lodge, he reported regularly on what he read, ranging from Aristotle's *Politics* to the latest American novels. He was on terms of intimate friendship with J. F. Rhodes, the distinguished historian, with Owen Wister, author of *The Virginians*, with Finley Peter Dunne, the humorist (better known as 'Mr. Dooley'), and would lay aside his own work to write them letters of enormous length in criticism of their latest books. His friendship extended to great English authors like John Morley, Lord Bryce and Sir George Otto Trevelyan. Morley was staying with Roosevelt during the election of 1904 and remarked to a fellow guest that Niagara Falls and the President were 'two of the greatest wonders of nature'. Roosevelt was one of the few Americans who appreciated Charles Dickens's *Martin Chuzzlewit*, a novel which causes pain to most Americans even today. There was one notable exception to the English objects of his admiration. 'I have been over Winston Churchill's life of his father', he wrote to Lodge on September 12th, 1906. 'I dislike the father and I dislike the son, so I may be prejudiced. Still, I feel that while the biographer and his subject possess some real farsightedness, especially in their appreciation of the shortcomings of that "Society" which has so long been dominant in English politics, and which produces in this country the missionary and the mugwump; yet they both possess or possessed such levity, lack of sobriety, lack of permanent principle, and inordinate thirst for that cheap form of admiration which is given to notoriety, as to make them poor public servants.' That was the pot calling the kettle black with a vengeance — and what a mistaken judgment! — more especially since Roosevelt was in many ways the American opposite number to Winston Churchill. Roosevelt's two heroes were Oliver Cromwell and Abraham Lincoln. He wrote a life of Cromwell and read and re-read the speeches of Lincoln. There was of course a puritan strain in all three of them. Yet the fact remains that Roosevelt though in his ideas he was not dissimilar from Lincoln, who influenced him deeply (as he also influenced Woodrow Wilson), was in his birth, wealth and upbringing much nearer to Thomas Jefferson than any other former President. For Roosevelt — one tends to overlook this in thinking overmuch of his youthful cowboy prancings and his gospel of strenuosity — was a highly cultivated and well-educated gentleman. In this he resembled not only Jefferson but also Woodrow Wilson, both of whom he disliked intensely.

Roosevelt's interests included the design of the coinage, simplified spelling and his boyhood love, natural history. It was at Roosevelt's suggestion that the American sculptor, Saint-Gaudens, designed a figure of Liberty wearing an Indian head-dress for the ten-dollar gold piece. His incursions into simplified spelling were soon repulsed by the orthodox officials of the Government Printing Office and by the humorous comments of the newspapers, while his criticisms of what he called 'nature faking' in an article which he helped to write for *Everybody's Magazine* in 1907 and in another essay produced a clever riposte from one of his intended victims, a Congregational clergyman who argued that Roosevelt's interest in wild life was chiefly confined to the most effective ways of ending it. Certainly Roosevelt had killed or was to kill wild animals all over the world. It was his supreme outlet for any unexpended energy.

Now that Roosevelt had become President, as it were, in his own right, he showed more clearly his determination to put an end to social abuses and to employ the big stick to give a square deal to the plain people. For this was a progressive age — the spirit of reform was in the air. Industrialism had made the rich man very rich and had given him immense powers to exploit the weak and the poor. Indeed it was claimed that the business of the United States was then in the control of twelve men. In books that commanded wide circulations writers like Upton Sinclair, Ida Tarbell, Lincoln Steffens, and Roosevelt's friend, Jacob Riis, were exposing the evils of uncontrolled capitalism, while such politicians as Bryan and 'Fighting Bob' La Follette of Wisconsin were pleading for or practising reforms. The essential truths were that the Jeffersonian type of agrarian democracy had not proved applicable to an industrialized community and a political philosophy which prided itself on a weak, because a balanced, central government made reform extremely difficult.

Roosevelt, himself an enlightened conservative, read and was moved by the revelations of the social reformers whom he dubbed 'muckrakers', but he did not consider it wise or necessary to fight for the extremist measures that they advocated. He saw the difficulties, and as he explained in his letters to his friend, Owen Wister, he did not think things were as bad as they were painted. Moreover at his right hand always stood his good friend, Senator Lodge, who thought there was little to choose between 'demagogues' and 'malefactors of great wealth'. But Roosevelt was far

PRESIDENT BY ELECTION

too intelligent and sympathetic to take a reactionary view and far too active to follow the example of his Republican predecessors by doing nothing or doing as little as possible. Hence in the Northern Securities case he had attacked Pierpont Morgan and in the anthracite strike showed his sympathy with the miners.

His second inaugural address drew attention in guarded terms to the need for workmen's compensation and the case for abolishing child labour, and he said that it was absurd to expect to eliminate abuses merely by the action of the individual states. It must always be remembered that in the United States the President can do no more than recommend legislative action to Congress and that he can only hope that his wishes will be followed when both Houses contain a majority of his own party, which is by no means always the case. All therefore depends on the strength of his prestige and the width of his personal influence. In January 1905 Roosevelt gave a clearer expression to his policy in a speech at Philadelphia. There he said that 'the great development of industrialism means that there must be an increase in the supervision exercised by the Government over business enterprise' and called specifically for the control of railway rates by 'some tribunal'; for it was common knowledge that discriminatory railway rates were a fruitful source of abuse in assisting big corporations and penalizing their weaker competitors. In 1906 the Hepburn Act, which got through a somewhat hostile Senate with help from the administration, gave the Inter-State Commerce Commission (established in 1887) the power to supervise rate regulation as well as to see that there was fair play between all parties in regard to other railway facilities, while it obliged the railway companies to sever their interests from those of other big enterprises. The Standard Oil Company of Indiana was successfully prosecuted and heavily fined for obtaining 'secret rates' from the railway companies (although the decision was later upset on appeal). 'We not only secured the stopping of rebates', wrote Roosevelt, 'but we were able to put through a measure which gave the Inter-State Commerce Commission for the first time real control over the railways.'

Other measures of reform sponsored by Roosevelt were a meat

inspection Bill, rendered urgent by the scandalous abuses that were shown in Upton Sinclair's book *The Jungle* to exist in the Chicago packing houses and were confirmed by impartial investigation, and a pure food and drugs Act suggested by the researches of the chief chemist of the Department of Agriculture. Under presidential impulse, too, Congress passed a workman's compensation act for government employees and child labour laws for the District of Columbia. Apart from these legislative achievements, administrative Acts under Roosevelt's direction put teeth into existing laws that had hitherto been dead letters, for example, the Sherman Anti-Trust Act: in particular, the Sugar Trust was indicted for fraudulent evasion of Customs duties. In general Roosevelt's deeds accorded with his view that while it was folly to try to suppress all the corporations and combinations in the business world, it was necessary to control them to prevent their abusing the public, their competitors or their workpeople.

Roosevelt's efforts to safeguard the national economy were not merely of a negative kind, for he exerted himself to protect the American forests and to reclaim the wastelands through irrigation. In this work he was advised by Gifford Pinchot, head of the Forestry Bureau, and assisted by a Democratic Senator, Francis Newlands of Nevada. Together these three planned to reclaim the arid prairies of the west and to consolidate and enlarge the federal forestry administration. In his first message to Congress the President said that 'the forest and water problems are perhaps the most vital internal problems of the United States'. In 1902 a Reclamation Act was passed by Congress; between 1902 and 1906 big reclamation projects were put into effect aiming at the irrigation of over 3,000,000 acres and the watering of more than 30,000 farms; and in 1908 a United States reclamation service was established. As to the forests Roosevelt put an end to the administrative distinction whereby all the United States forests came under one department and the foresters under another department and did his utmost to prevent the timber resources of the nation from being disposed of to private owners. By 1907 the area of these forests had been increased by presidential proclamation by more than forty-three million acres. To Roosevelt, too, the American people owe some of their finest national parks, game preserves and bird sanctuaries. The little boy who taught himself natural history had grown up to be a national benefactor not by piling up wealth and then giving it away, but by teaching the community that theirs was at least part of the earth and some of its glories.

In the year 1907 the business leaders who had smarted under the presidential big stick launched a counter-attack on Roosevelt accusing him of undermining confidence and creating unrest by his assaults on institutions that meant so much in American life. Pierpont Morgan told the President that he ought to send for the railway presidents and confer with them about the best means of soothing public anxiety. Roosevelt refused, for he naturally could not understand why there 'should be a belief in Wall Street that he was a wild-eyed revolutionist'. He explained, however, that the real reason why 'owners of predatory wealth' hated him were that hitherto they had been allowed a free hand, for no one before him had dared to take action against them in the courts or had attempted to control them by legislation as had been done under the railway rates and meat inspection Acts. But when in November 1907 the panic reached its height and trust companies and banks were threatened with failure, Roosevelt was induced to make a move which ill accorded with his principles. Representatives of Morgan's Steel Corporation came to see him and told him urgently that the only way to stop the panic was to allow the Corporation to buy the stock of the Tennessee Coal Company, but that they were afraid to do so because, if they did, they might be prosecuted under the Sherman Act. Roosevelt answered that while of course he could not advise them to take the action proposed, he felt it no public duty of his to interpose objections. Thus the Steel Corporation acquired a valuable property with impunity and though Roosevelt never doubted the wisdom of his decision (taken with proper advice) he seems to have been moved by fright rather than ratiocination. For Roosevelt's largest intellectual hiatus was an ignorance of economics.

After the Spanish-American war President Roosevelt, chief executive of a country with a population of over seventy-five million people, recognized that the United States had become a world power with world responsibilities, especially in the Far East. Consequently from the first he showed a profound concern over any events that endangered peace. On February 8th, 1904, Japan, that little group of islands that had been brought into the orbit of civilization when the American Commodore Perry had landed there in 1853, had without declaring war dispatched her fleet to attack the Russian naval force at Port Arthur, just as she was to send her torpedo aircraft against the American fleet at Pearl Harbour nearly thirty-eight years afterwards. Roosevelt was guided by two main political principles as he followed the war with the eager interest of a naval historian and a retired brigadier-general: the first was that the balance of power in the Pacific should be preserved and neither Russia nor Japan become too powerful; the second, following logically from the first, was that no Power should be strong enough to exclude American commerce from the Far East and, in particular, that there should be an 'open door' in China and Manchuria. The Russian Government had tried to exclude American trade from Manchuria, and from the beginning Roosevelt's sympathies were with Japan. The Tsar Nicholas II was regarded by him as 'a preposterous little creature' while he found that the Japanese 'always told the truth'. Shortly after the Japanese took Port Arthur in January 1905 Roosevelt intervened to propose mediation, but the Russians still had a fleet in being and it was not until this fleet was destroyed on May 27th that they felt inclined to listen to peace terms. Thenceforward Roosevelt laboured with tremendous energy and not a little tact for peace between the two belligerents.

It was all Roosevelt's own work, for his Secretary of State, John Hay, was away from duty owing to ill health (he was to die in July 1905) and even the Acting Secretary of State, Taft, who had succeeded Root as Secretary of War, was absent in the Far East while the negotiations were starting. After their naval victory the Japanese responded to Roosevelt's approaches by asking him to use his good offices as a neutral to induce the Russian Government to make peace feelers. 'I was amused', wrote the President, 'by the way in which they asked me to invite the two belligerents together directly on my own motion and initiative.' Seemingly he was not familiar with the importance that the East attached to 'face'. However, he sent an identic note to the two Powers and finally persuaded them to agree to the United States being the meeting place of the conference. Many were the difficulties,

PRESIDENT BY ELECTION

mainly arising from *amour propre*, that Roosevelt had to overcome on both sides: for example, the Russians asked for an armistice, which the Japanese refused, and each side wanted to know what the status of the other's plenipotentiaries would be before they announced their own. Ultimately in August the diplomatists gathered in New York whence they were taken by warship to call on Roosevelt at Oyster Bay before going on to Portsmouth, New Hampshire to confer. Roosevelt took the utmost trouble to show no signs of favouritism to either side and allowed his conciliatory influence to percolate upon the Japanese Government through England (which had allied herself with Japan in 1902) and upon the Russian Government through Kaiser William II who was then writing affectionate notes to his cousin, 'Nicky'. Roosevelt's friend and biographer, Bishop, states with justice that Roosevelt 'was himself the conference, for he was its guiding and controlling force'. From the beginning it was known that the Russians were willing to let Japan have Korea and Port Arthur, but the conference nearly broke down at the end of August over the Japanese demand for an indemnity and the Japanese claim to the island of Sakhalin which lies to the north of Japan proper. President Roosevelt then proposed a compromise to the Emperor of Japan, namely, that Russia should pay no indemnity but should cede to Japan the southern half of Sakhalin, in return for a payment to be determined by a mixed commission. This compromise was accepted and on September 5th the Treaty of Portsmouth was signed. Roosevelt was awarded the Nobel Peace Prize for his work. It was a little ironical that before his term of office was over the United States herself should have come to the verge of war with Japan (over anti-Japanese discrimination by California) and that within forty years mighty American armies should have been standing ready to invade the Japanese mainland in search of the unconditional surrender of the Emperor. But it is not for an Englishman to stress the irony unduly.

Before the Portsmouth Conference ended Roosevelt was involved — once more acting as his own Secretary of State — in another diplomatic effort this time not to stop a war but to prevent it from beginning. Rivalry over Morocco, forming part of the European 'scramble for Africa', was one of the features of the conflict between England and France on one side, and Germany on the other, that led in the end to the war of 1914-18. England had in 1904 concluded an *entente* with France and by secret treaties had granted her a free hand in Morocco, as England was given a free hand in Egypt. The German Government, convinced that France aimed at swallowing up Morocco, sent the Kaiser as a knight in shining armour to land at Tangier and proclaim his recognition of the freedom and independence of the Sultan. In April 1905 Von Bulow, the German Chancellor, demanded an international conference on the future of Morocco. A month earlier the Kaiser had written to Roosevelt seeking his support against France. 'Since thirty-five years', he wrote, 'Germany has been obliged to keep an armed defensive against France. As soon as France discovers that Germany meekly submits to her bullying, we feel sure that she will become more aggressive in other quarters and we do not consider that a demand for the revision of the Treaty of Frankfort (which ended the Franco-Prussian War of 1870) will be far off.' Roosevelt adopted a correct diplomatic attitude, saying that American interests were not of sufficient importance to justify interference. In this battle of prestige and power politics Germany won the first skirmish, for on June 11th, Delcassé, the French Foreign Minister, resigned because he could not induce the French Cabinet to defy Germany at the risk of war. It was at this stage that Roosevelt decided to intervene in order to try to prevent a European conflagration and he persuaded the French to agree to a conference that met at Algeciras in January 1906. The Americans at the conference proposed that the organization and maintenance of police forces in the Moroccan ports should be entrusted to the Sultan, that the police force should be trained by French and Spanish officers appointed by the Sultan, that all the Powers should share equally in the control of an international bank in Morocco, and that France and Spain should guarantee an open door to trade. The Germans, for their part, wanted the Moroccan police force officered by the Minor Powers, thus excluding France from control. But the French were backed by England, Russia, Spain and indirectly by Italy, while she received, as Professor Temperley wrote, 'concealed but no less effective support from President Roosevelt'. Germany had to climb down and to agree to a Franco-Spanish police force under a Swiss Inspector-General. Thus the peaceful penetration of Morocco by France went forward to another world-shattering crisis at Agadir in 1911.

Throughout this crisis Roosevelt toiled hard to avert a European war. In April 1905 he wrote to Taft, Acting Secretary of State: 'I am sincerely anxious to bring about a better state of feeling between England and Germany. Each nation is working itself up to a condition of desperate hatred of the other; each from fear of the other. The Kaiser is dead sure that England intends to attack him. The English people are equally sure that Germany intends to attack England. Now, in my view this action of Germany in embroiling herself with France over Morocco is proof positive that she had not the slightest intention of attacking England.' In fact, of course, had Germany attacked France, England would probably have been obliged especially in view of the close Anglo-French relations founded on the Entente of 1904 to have fought by the side of France as she did in 1914. Roosevelt by endorsing the French point of view at the Algeciras Conference virtually supported England against Germany and therefore added to the Kaiser's 'encirclement' complex which was one of the chief causes of the war of 1914-18. From the American point of view was Roosevelt right to have intervened at all? He of all men knew that moral influence by itself has its limitations in international affairs. Though the United States gained from the Act of Algeciras equal commercial rights in Morocco, the American Senate refused to assume responsibility for its enforcement. The ghosts of Washington and Jefferson were still ruling on Capitol Hill.

One other facet of Roosevelt's foreign policy remains to be mentioned. It arose out of the possibility that the island of Santo Domingo would default on its foreign debts, as Venezuela had done earlier. Roosevelt was afraid that, as was the case with Venezuela, the small republic might be intimidated by a punitive expedition sent by European Powers. He therefore produced his 'corollary' to the Monroe Doctrine, which was that in the Western Hemisphere the duty of intervention in a case of this kind belonged of right to the United States. Roosevelt in fact induced the Government of Santo Domingo to let him set up a financial receivership and this 'set a precedent for the erection of a number of virtual protectorates in the Caribbean area'. And thus the Monroe Doctrine, which had originally been aimed at defending

THEODORE ROOSEVELT

Latin America from the imperialist aspirations of European States, came to be interpreted to justify if not political at any rate financial domination by the United States.

In a message of January 31st, 1908, to Congress Roosevelt made his most outspoken attack on the evils of the capitalist system as then practised in the United States. He pleaded for the moral regeneration of the business world, condemned stock exchange gambling, criticized corporation lawyers who worked to block the enforcement of the laws affecting big business houses, and spoke in blunt terms of the 'kind of business which had tended to make the very name "high finance" a term of scandal'. The truth was that Roosevelt, who had begun his career as President with all the restrained convictions of a conservative reformer, had become less and less conservative and more and more reformist. He had enjoyed many successes and bent Congress to his will; some would have said that he had even stolen the clothes of the radicals while they went out bathing. But he had set himself no easy task in leading the Grand Old Party into the uplands of business regeneration. True, his hero, Lincoln, fountainhead of Republican doctrine, had also been a conservative reformer, but since Lincoln had died the victors of the Civil War had sunk into a lethargy from which the clarion call of the Rough Rider had aroused them with some reluctance.

Now the days of his power were approaching their end. The message of January 1908 estranged many of his former friends, such as Senator Lodge and Dr. Nicholas Murray Butler of Columbia University. As his political strength waned, so his utterances grew more daring — he even ventured to criticize an appeal court for reversing the fine levied on Standard Oil. Although he sent twenty messages to Congress in the session of 1908, ranging from a request for extended powers for the Inter-State Commerce Commission to a demand for four battleships, most of them had little result. In the session of 1908-09 (called the 'lame duck session' because it was held after the elections but before the new administration took office) a message from Roosevelt was rejected by the House of Representatives by a majority of 212 votes to 35. Unlike Jefferson and Jackson, who held the loyalty of their parties to the end, Roosevelt had driven too fast and too furiously. Yet it may be hazarded that had he chosen to stand for the Presidency

PRESIDENT BY ELECTION

of the United States again (as his namesake was to do) instead of stultifying himself by announcing as early as 1904 that he would not be a candidate, the American people would have swept him back into office in spite of the protesting voices of the party leaders. Surely it was a vast pity that this forceful man who had shown himself so nicely attuned to the spirit of his time should have been thrust out into the wilderness at an age when many men are only just realizing their political ambitions?

Roosevelt's own nominee as his successor was William Howard Taft, who had been Governor-General of the Philippines and Secretary of War, but was said to be less eager to enter the White House than was his wife. At the Republican National Convention Taft was nominated on the first ballot. 'I do not think Taft will be as aggressive as I have been', said Roosevelt complacently, 'but there will be no backward step under Taft.' The Democratic candidate for the third time was Bryan, whom Roosevelt called 'a prodigious memory with a lot of hair on it'. The chief plank in Bryan's platform was a denunciation of the trusts — hardly an effective argument against the party still led by Theodore Roosevelt: it is true that Bryan had also come out for the government ownership of the railways, but this was no part of the official Democratic programme and it must have been obvious to the electorate that there was still little to choose between the policies of the two parties. As Taft was a Unitarian, Bryan proclaimed his belief that the American people would never elect a man who did not accept the divinity of Christ and the virgin birth. However Taft was elected by a handsome majority, although he lost some ground in the middle west. Roosevelt decided that the most dignified thing he could do after his term ended was to go to Africa and hunt lions, leaving Taft to hoe his own row. 'Health to the lions!' exclaimed some impenitent Congressmen.

A not unfair appraisal of Roosevelt's work as President came from his English friend, Lord Bryce at the British Embassy two days after Taft's inauguration: 'You seem to me', wrote Bryce, 'to have done more for the advancement of good causes, more to stir the soul of the nation and rouse it to a sense of its incomparable opportunities and high mission, for the whole world as well as for this continent, than any one of your predecessors for a century save Abraham Lincoln himself . . . The bringing about peace between Russia and Japan, the construction of the Canal, the setting on foot of the Conservation of Resources Movement, all fall into their places along with and cohere with this appeal to the Nation's heart and its larger thoughts for the future which you have made.'

4. FRUSTRATION (1909-1919)

It was Theodore Roosevelt's tragedy that he had become President so young: he was only fifty when his term ended and his successor was fifty-one. Taft's tragedy — or at least his trial — was that he followed Roosevelt into office. This fat reserved man who, as his wife said, 'could not be hurried', and whose ambition was to be on the bench of the Federal Supreme Court and not in the White House, dwelt rather irritably beneath the shadow of the lively figure who had made him President. Roosevelt, he told Archie Butt, who had now become his military aide, in a revealing conversation, would always be 'the President' to him.

What could Roosevelt do now that his power had gone? Outwardly he was cheerful enough, but he handed over with reluctance. 'Of course if I had felt that I could conscientiously keep on the Presidency I should have dearly liked to try again. I shall miss a very little having my hands on the levers of the great machine', he wrote to one friend; to another he said: 'I am still looking forward and not back. I do not know any man who has had as happy a fifty years as I have had. I have had about as good a run for my money as any human being possibly could have; and whatever happens now, I am ahead of the game.' He left for Africa in March 1909 with his son, Kermit, having sold the rights in the story of his forthcoming adventures to *Scribner's Magazine*. Wild animal hunting, even in the interests of science, is a speculative pursuit in middle age. Edith Roosevelt, Kermit felt, had been left with 'her heart almost broken'. However no serious mishap befell Theodore in Africa, where his bag included nine lions, five elephants, thirteen rhinoceroses and seven hippopotamuses. He emerged cheerfully in Khartoum and civilization in March 1910 and spent the next months travelling around Europe hob-nobbing with kings and queens and delivering an occasional speech or homily. In Rome there was an 'incident' between him and the Papacy; in Germany he told the Kaiser that he considered a war between his country and England would be an 'unspeakable calamity'. 'I was brought up in England very largely', replied the All Highest, 'I feel myself partly an Englishman: I adore England.' But Roosevelt found that his welcome in Germany was chillier than in any other country. 'Excepting the university folk', he noted, 'they did not want to see me.' It was just the opposite elsewhere, for the European great jostled each other in seeking the company and wisdom of the former President of the United States. At Oxford he delivered the Romanes Lecture on the somewhat curious topic of 'Biological Analogies in History' and received an honorary degree. In London he was given the freedom of the City and represented his government at King Edward VII's funeral. When at the Guildhall he delivered a speech in which he commended British rule in Egypt — and he had already said while in Egypt that England was the guardian of civilization in the Sudan. These were rare tributes. On his return to New York on June 18th, 1910, a rapturous welcome showed that he was by no means forgotten.

In the White House there was some degree of apprehension. 'Everything is on the *qui vive* for the return of the Hunter', Archie Butt had written two months earlier. Taft felt quite nervy about what Theodore might say or do. It was not that President Taft had betrayed the policies of his predecessor — on the contrary; but he had been compelled to dismiss Gifford Pinchot, chief of the Forest Service in the Department of Agriculture, a member of Roosevelt's Tennis Cabinet, and he could not understand why Roosevelt had failed to write to him while he was away. Yet Taft asserted with an air of bravado: 'I am determined to paddle my own canoe and I do not want to say anything at first which might mislead Roosevelt into thinking that I expect or desire advice.' The truth was that there was a temperamental antipathy between the two men. 'President Roosevelt was quick, active, decisive; President Taft was deliberate. President Roosevelt believed as he himself once said, that aggressive fighting for the right is the noblest sport the world affords; pugnacity of any kind was distasteful to President Taft. President Roosevelt was born with the temperament of an advocate; President Taft with the temperament of a judge' (Lawrence F. Abbott). Roosevelt, it may be added, played tennis; Taft's game was golf. But, it must be repeated, there was no fundamental political difference between the two men. In 1909 Taft recommended and procured two radical measures, a tax on the income of corporations and a constitutional amendment permitting the federal authorities to levy income tax, while 'so many anti-trust cases were instituted and carried to completion by Taft's administration that the work of his predecessor in this field was completely overshadowed' (Swisher). Even Taft's deference to some of the party bosses, for which Roosevelt later blamed him, did not differ from Roosevelt's own practices when he first became President. At first all was outward harmony between the two men. 'I shall keep my mind as open as I keep my mouth shut', Roosevelt assured Taft and when they met Theodore said 'this is simply bully', but the conversation soon lapsed.

The trouble was that Roosevelt with the best intentions in the world could not keep his fingers out of politics. Taft after his term was over was to settle down happily into the relatively modest position of a Professor of Law at Yale. Roosevelt had been considered as successor to Charles W. Eliot as President of Harvard, but he could never have found satisfaction in the academic life. Instead he had become a contributing editor to the magazine *Outlook* and thus acquired a platform for his political opinions and at a Harvard celebration which he attended in the summer of 1910 he was musing not on academic laurels but on politics. Charles E. Hughes, who was then Governor of New York State, and was another distinguished guest at the Harvard party, persuaded Roosevelt to back his campaign for the institution of a direct primary in the state, that is to say a system in which the electors as a whole choose the party candidate instead of leaving the decision to a nominating convention. Roosevelt received a rebuff when he was rejected by the Republican State Committee as the official candidate for the post of temporary chairman of the State Convention that was to name the next Governor. It was true that when the convention itself met he was elected chairman and persuaded the delegates to introduce the direct primary into the party platform, but Roosevelt's candidate for Governor,

FRUSTRATION

Henry L. Stimpson, was defeated at the polls. Indeed the Republicans suffered a pretty general setback in the elections of 1910, for the Democrats gained eight seats in the Senate and won a majority in the House of Representatives.

Before the elections took place Roosevelt had delivered a couple of notable speeches, one in Denver, Colorado, and the other at Ossawatomie, Kansas, in which he outlined what was called the New Nationalism. Deprived of the responsibilities of office he felt that he could express more daring radical views, although he maintained that he was saying nothing of which Abraham Lincoln would not have approved. His opponents accused him of attacking property. All that he said in fact was that 'the true friend of property, the true conservative, is he who insists that property shall be the servant and not the master of the commonwealth'. This was not in itself revolutionary doctrine. However what was more to the point so far as the political future was concerned was that Roosevelt had now convinced himself that President Taft had abandoned the cause of righteousness. In October 1910 he told Elihu Root that he was 'bitterly disappointed with Taft'; just a year later he said 'Taft is utterly hopeless'; and looking back on the period in 1915 he was to write: 'Taft had thrown in his lot with the sordid machine crowd.' Roosevelt undoubtedly felt that call to reform which was everywhere becoming more insistent not merely in the American political world but also in the world of scholarship and literature, expressing a consciousness that the existing democratic machinery was incapable of coping with the evils left behind in the onrush of material progress. In particular he was deeply influenced by a book, Croly's *Promise of American Life*, as he had been earlier by Jacob Riis's *How the Other Half Lives*. Yet who was there to lead the American people towards a brave — and sane — new world? Not Taft; certainly not pacifist Democrats like Bryan and Woodrow Wilson, the Governor of New Jersey. Salvation surely could only come from the Grand Old Party employing the federal powers to secure social betterment without allowing the nation to drift into the quagmires of Socialism. And who was best suited to proclaim the new gospel? 'I am really not thinking of myself at all now,' he assured a friend, 'but as to what is right to do'. In the end, however, he realised that there could be but one answer.

THEODORE ROOSEVELT

Throughout 1911 the estrangement between Roosevelt, now preaching the gospel of the New Nationalism, and Taft, pillar, despite himself, of the Old Guard, grew more marked. The Republican party was in any case divided by quarrels over the tariff (recently revised in a moderate way) and a proposed reciprocity treaty with Canada, while several of Taft's administrative acts such as the release of a notorious swindler from prison (under the mistaken impression that he was dying) were hardly calculated to commend him to the electorate. Taft's view that 'We have a government of limited power under the Constitution and we have got to work out our problems on the basis of law', though precise enough, was scarcely a trumpet call to political victory in an age of reform. Roosevelt, whose deference for the law and the prophets had never restrained his natural ardour, came out in favour of the 'recall of the judiciary' if they interfered with social progress. Roosevelt's burning utterances chilled the President's marrow. 'I don't know what I have done to offend Theodore', he complained, but later he roused himself to say: 'I am a man of peace and I don't want to fight. But when I do fight, I want to hit hard. Even a rat in a corner will fight.' And to fight he was compelled, for as early as February 1912, Roosevelt announced: 'My hat is in the ring.' The Democrats watched the growing quarrels between these Republican bigwigs and went on their way rejoicing. In June 1912 William Jennings Bryan attended the Republican National Convention as a newspaper reporter and gazed approvingly on the scenes of strife. But poor Bryan himself was not to be the candidate of the Democratic party. Three times he had fought the good fight in vain; now he was to hand on the torch to another who, because of the Taft-Roosevelt split, was bound to win the Presidency.

The Republican Convention had met at Chicago in June. There were three possible candidates for the nomination, Taft, Roosevelt and La Follette of Wisconsin. Had Roosevelt exerted his influence on his behalf, La Follette might have won the nomination and there would have been a progressive Republican victory, for La Follette was as much a liberal in his outlook as was Woodrow Wilson. But Theodore Roosevelt was set on his fateful path. It is said that in his heart of hearts he knew he could not win; perhaps it was so, but aspirants are never without the hope

FRUSTRATION

of a miracle and Roosevelt could recollect the unquestionable evidences of his popularity during the trips he had made south and west in 1910. Even Taft had thought at one stage that if Roosevelt stood he would be elected. But now this fat perplexed President, with his 'humdrum administration' and his dubious backing from the bosses, was fighting his old patron like 'a rat in a corner'. Though Roosevelt obtained the nomination from the delegates of all the states where there was a direct primary, Taft was selected where there were State Conventions. At Chicago the party steamroller gave Taft the nomination; but Roosevelt had gone to far to recede. In the expressive American phrase, he 'bolted the party'. In August 1912 a new party, the Progressive party, held a convention in Chicago, where the delegates paid their own expenses, and nominated Roosevelt as their presidential candidate with Hiram Johnson of California as vice-presidential candidate. Roosevelt threw himself into the campaign with undimmed fervour but with little hope. In October while at a meeting in Milwaukee, Wisconsin, he was shot by a fanatic and insisted on making his speech with a bullet still lodged in his breast. The reality of his popularity was conclusively proved when it was found in November that he had polled over four million votes and beaten Taft without the aid of an effective party machine. But Woodrow Wilson was elected President. 'I did not believe we would win', Roosevelt told Sir Edward Grey; and later he explained: 'Our platform ... was rather too advanced for the average man ... The working man was not interested in social or industrial justice.' Maybe he was right. But Wilson after all was also a progressive who offered an alternative to the Roosevelt policies and to Taft's 'dissolving view'. Great men often deceive themselves and it may be doubted if the insensitiveness of the American working man was really responsible for Roosevelt's defeat in the election of 1912. The blame, Roosevelt might have recognized, lay somewhere nearer home.

In the autumn of 1912 Roosevelt's friend, Owen Wister paid him a visit at Oyster Bay and outlined to him the plots of three stories that he was proposing to write and asked him which he should begin first. One of the stories was to be the tragedy of a cowpuncher who had survived his own era and could not adjust himself to the more civilized age that succeeded it. 'Well, my dear Dan,' said Roosevelt, 'you must write all three' ... and when you come to your cowboy tragedy, why — don't leave it in such unrelieved blackness. Let in some sunlight, somehow. Leave your reader with the feeling that life, after all, does — go — on.' For Roosevelt himself life went on, with a little sunlight here and there, but after 1912 much of the zest had gone. Two libel suits, in one of which he was the prosecutor and in the other the defendant, relieved the monotony. In the first case he exposed for all time the baselessness of the slander that he was a heavy drinker. (Too many people, incapable of great exertions themselves, mistake exuberance in others for insobriety.) In the other case William Barnes, then the Republican boss of New York, brought a suit for libel against the ex-President because he had accused him of a corrupt alliance with Tammany Hall. During this trial the whole of Roosevelt's political career was subjected to the most minute re-examination: it stood up well and the jury found Roosevelt's criticism of Barnes truthful. The trial did not end until May 1915 and caused nearly as much excitement in the American press as the European war.

In 1915 Roosevelt went on a hunting trip to Arizona with his four sons, though he felt it a little absurd for 'a stout rheumatic, elderly gentleman' to sleep 'curled up in a blanket on the ground, and eating the flesh of a cougar because there is nothing else available', and in the autumn he took it into his head to explore the jungles of Brazil, where he almost died. In that year too he published his *Autobiography*, a readable, if slightly disingenuous, book, a sign that he reckoned his days of greatness were over. When he returned from Brazil, he gracefully abandoned the remnants of the Progressive party, while promising to continue to fight as long as he lived 'for the cause and platform for which we fought in 1912'. But, he added, 'when it is evident that a leader's day is past, the one service he can render is to step aside and leave the ground clear for the development of a successor'. In 1916 he re-entered the Republican fold.

Roosevelt strongly supported American neutrality in the opening months of the European war. To a friend in London he wrote: 'I am very sad over this war. I believe that, in a way, it was fatally inevitable as regards the continental nations and that each was right, from its own standpoint, under conditions as they actually were ... England could not have done other than she did ...' At the same time Roosevelt's old sympathy with militarism did not lead him to condemn at this stage German conduct over and in Belgium. The sinking of the *Lusitania*, however, roused him even from his absorption in the Barnes libel suit and he said: 'Unless we act with immediate decision and vigor we shall have failed in the duty demanded by humanity at large and even more clearly by the self-respect of the American Republic.' Of course it is always easy for politicians out of office to insist that the government of the day must take a strong line, but theirs after all will not be the responsibility for sending young men to their death. To the non-politician it is an incredible demeanour which we in England saw too much of in the nineteen-thirties. But perhaps if you are a prominent politician (or editor) you must say something about a world crisis and no doubt you can always convince yourself, as so many were to do at the time of the Munich agreement of 1938, that somehow you can attain the ends of justice by taking a firm stand without involving your own country in war. In the end Roosevelt himself appears to have recognized the danger of this attitude: 'To denounce Germany in words and not prepare to make our word good', he told Owen Wister in July 1915, 'is merely to add to our offense.' In fact while he stigmatized President Wilson in his private correspondence 'as the worst President we have had since Buchanan', he consistently upheld the administration's policy of political and moral neutrality. Although later he came out in public in condemnation of Wilson's 'supineness', 'pacifism' and unwillingness to prepare for war, Roosevelt never suggested that had he been President then, he would have acted other than in the way that Wilson acted, although of course vastly more energetically.

In February 1917 as soon as President Wilson announced to Congress the severing of diplomatic relations with Germany Roosevelt wrote eagerly to the War Department to ask permission to raise a division if war were declared and there was a call for volunteers. 'In such an event', he said, 'I and my four sons will go.' In the appeal of Theodore Roosevelt, now nearly sixty, for permission to raise and lead a volunteer division — preferably of horse riflemen — to France there was much that was pathetic; it is

THEODORE ROOSEVELT

not necessary to dwell on the story or to blame Wilson for his refusal on the ground that Roosevelt's stinging criticisms of his conduct had offended his pride. It was obviously out of the question to allow in the first totalitarian war of our democratic civilization a repetition of what had taken place in the brief war in Cuba when Theodore Roosevelt was nearly twenty years younger. His sons did more than enough to honour his name: two were severely wounded, three were decorated, and one of them, Quentin, the youngest, was killed in an air battle in the summer of 1918. 'Quentin's mother and I', he said when he heard the news, 'are very glad that he got to the front and had a chance to render some service to his country before his fate befell him.' But to others he confessed that his heart was breaking and in a moving article called 'The Great Adventure' he used the pen that he had taken up so reluctantly instead of the sword to plead the cause of service and sacrifice.

After President Wilson had seen Theodore Roosevelt when the latter was seeking permission to organize a division to send to France, he commented 'He is a great boy' and Roosevelt's biographers have stressed that Roosevelt's career in the course of which he was a cowboy, a lion hunter, a soldier who rose in double quick time to become a general, and President of the United States was of the kind best calculated to appeal to American boyhood; one of his friends indeed wrote a 'Boy's Life of Theodore Roosevelt'. Roosevelt's whole life was certainly an extraordinary triumph of mind over matter, for though in his autobiography he perhaps exaggerates the contrast between his sickly childhood and the he-man that was to emerge from it, undoubtedly he had had every temptation to become an invalid and a bookworm. Instead he taught himself to box, to ride and to shoot and to overcome bullies of every description. Yet with all his prowess he was never a bully himself. Those who worked most near to him found him the soul of charm and courtesy, even when he swept them off their feet. Furthermore he was one of those rare personalities whose attraction still impresses itself on the readers of his life long after the man himself is dead.

Yet his life was not wholly a schoolboy romance, for in real life men who make good do not usually live happily ever after. The tragic side of Roosevelt's story was not only that he became

FRUSTRATION

President too young and committed himself — at least, so it seems in the light of after-events — too rashly to not standing for another term, but that he became the leader of a party, many of whose leaders had no wish to move forward into the land of business regeneration whither Roosevelt wanted to take them. Too often he had to struggle and intrigue for the modest reforms that he advocated.

Nothing is more misleading than the often quoted phrase of Henry Adams about Theodore Roosevelt that he was 'pure act'. In fact, as any reader of his long letters can see he thought wisely and deeply about many things. He was probably a man of truer culture than many of the statesmen who rule our world today. True, he sometimes rushed to conclusions, and sometimes the conclusions were wrong. But he had a clear and consistent philosophy of life, he believed that certain values were permanent, and he practised what he preached. One could fill an album with comic strips and absurd photographs of Theodore Roosevelt, one might essay to imitate the genius of a Lytton Strachey or a Philip Guedalla and describe his eyeglasses, his prominent teeth, his cowboy hats or his cohort of Rough Riders with the band playing 'There'll be a Hot Time in the Old Town tonight', but one would not be picturing the real man who was so much loved.

Roosevelt carried forward sucessfully the tradition that the President is the real representative of American democracy. In spite of the alleged rigidity of a written constitution there had been many notable changes since George Washington had viewed his office as that of a constitutional monarch with the Senate as his advisory council. Roosevelt indeed once said: 'I do not much admire the Senate because it is such a helpless body when efficient work for good is to be done.' In a sense of course this position derived from the working of the Constitution, for the President was the only elective figure whose first duty was to the national and not a sectional interest. Yet the office was enhanced in its importance and authority through the exertions of men like Thomas Jefferson, Andrew Jackson, Abraham Lincoln and Theodore Roosevelt. By their determined actions and glamorous personalities, as Professor Swisher has written, 'presidential leadership of legislative policy was established'.

Before he died Roosevelt had several opportunities to express his opinion about the League of Nations. He did not like it. 'I hope Germany will suffer a change of heart,' he wrote to Rider Haggard on December 6th, 1918, 'but I am anything but certain. I don't put much faith in the League of Nations or any corresponding cure-all.' 'To substitute internationalism for nationalism', he said on another occasion, 'means to do away with patriotism, and is as vicious and as profoundly demoralising as to put promiscuous devotion to all other persons in the place of a steadfast devotion to a man's own family.' 'Would it not be well', he asked in an article he dictated the day before his death, 'to begin with the League which we actually have in existence, the League of the allies who have fought through this great war.' Seemingly had Theodore Roosevelt lived to this day he would have approved the idea of the United Nations Organization. But he would never have allowed the existence of an international body to be an excuse for weakening the military strength of his own country. In fact in this last article he pleaded for a democratic system of conscription similar to that of Switzerland.

Roosevelt suffered a good deal from ill health in the last years of his life. Perhaps he had tried too hard the body which he had always required to be his servant and not his master. He underwent two operations, but he was in his own much loved home at Oyster Bay when death came peacefully in his sleep on January 6th, 1919. In his article, 'The Great Adventure', which he had composed under the impulse of his son Quentin's death, he had written: 'Only those are fit to live who do not fear to die; and none are fit to die who have shrunk from the joy of life and the duty of life.'

It might have been his own epitaph. For he had lived his life to the full and had done his duty as he saw it. He indeed had 'dared the Great Adventure'.

SELECT BIBLIOGRAPHY

L. F. ABBOTT: *The Letters of Archie Butt* (1924).
J. B. BISHOP: *Theodore Roosevelt and his Times* (1920).
ARCHIE BUTT: *Taft and Roosevelt. The Intimate Letters of Archie Butt* (1930).
ANNA ROOSEVELT COWLES: *Letters from Theodore Roosevelt, 1870-1918* (1924).
H. HAGEDORN: *Roosevelt in the Bad Lands* (1930); *Boy's Life of Theodore Roosevelt.*
H. C. LODGE: *Selections from the Correspondence of Theodore Roosevelt and Henry Cabot Lodge* (1925).
HENRY F. PRINGLE: *Theodore Roosevelt* (1932); *The Life and Times of William Howard Taft* (1939).
CORINNE ROOSEVELT ROBINSON: *My Brother Theodore* (1921).
THEODORE ROOSEVELT: *Autobiography* (1913); *Works* (ed Hagedorn) (1926).
M. R. WERNER: *William Jennings Bryan* (1929).
J. K. WINKLER: *J. Pierpont Morgan* (1931).
OWEN WISTER: *Roosevelt, the Story of a Friendship* (1930).

WOODROW WILSON

THEODORE ROOSEVELT
ON
WOODROW WILSON

A conscienceless rhetorician

WOODROW WILSON

CHAPTER VII

WOODROW WILSON

'BE careful of what you wish for in your youth,' wrote Goethe, 'for you will get it in your middle age.' In his youth Woodrow Wilson produced an astonishing *tour de force*, a critical analysis of the working of the American Constitution, in which he argued that far from there being a balance of powers Congress had become the main factor in the government of the United States and pleaded for a strong man as President. Nearly thirty years later, after a distinguished but controversial career at Princeton University, Wilson himself became President of the United States and was able to realize at least in part the role that he believed ought to be played by the chief executive. As he was a man of inspiring ways, a magnificent orator, who for the first time since John Adams did not hesitate to address Congress in person, and as he had a majority of his party in both Houses, he could put into effect many of his political plans. During the war of 1914-18, into which his administration was at length reluctantly drawn, he was able by exerting — as Abraham Lincoln had done — the special powers available to the President as Commander-in-Chief to fortify the place of the President in the Constitution. Indeed, learning from Lincoln's mistakes, he was for a time even more influential than his famous predecessor. During the years 1917-18 he was the most dynamic President the United States had ever seen — with the possible exception of Andrew Jackson — until our own time.

But his methods and policies brought him enemies. His party was rebuffed in the mid-term election of 1918. Thus Congress reasserted itself after the war and Wilson found his hands tied just at the time when he hoped to shape, even to dictate, not merely the future course of his own country but the government of the whole world. Biographies of famous men are often entitled tragedies, sometimes in too facile a way. Certainly, however, if ever a statesman's career may be said to have ended on a high note of tragedy that of Wilson did. His foreign policies were repudiated by the Senate and American membership of the

League of Nations, which he had actively helped to create, was refused. While trying to appeal — as Jackson had appealed — over the heads of the politicians to the people at large he was struck down with paralysis. In the last months of his Presidency the weakness of the institution that he valued so dearly was exposed by the fact that the country was governed by an invalid whose State papers were sorted out by his second wife, a procedure that was scarcely intended by the makers of the Constitution. The man who had done so much to shape the Presidency into an effective instrument of political reform left it almost a mockery.

Yet Wilson's record — still a topic of controversy — left its mark on American history. He exemplified, as much as any man, the nature of American idealism and also the continuity of policy. In some ways he carried on the work of his political opponent, Theodore Roosevelt. And he was the first distinctive herald of the belief, now more widely held in the United States, that his country can no longer disinterest itself in world affairs, but must assume its rightful task of leadership if our civilization is to survive.

1. THE EDUCATIONIST (1856-1909)

On November 1st, 1808, two young Scots-Irish immigrants, James Wilson, aged twenty-one and Anne Adams, aged seventeen, who had crossed the Alantic in the same ship, were married in the Fourth Presbyterian Church of Philadelphia. James Wilson, ambitious and hard working, was to prosper in the professions of printer and journalist; seven years later he and his family moved to Steubenville, Ohio, where as proprietor of the local *Gazette* Wilson engaged energetically in politics, vigorously attacking, among others, another Scots-Irishman, Andrew Jackson. The tenth child of this Steubenville family, by name Joseph Ruggles Wilson, was to become a leading minister in the Presbyterian Church and the father of the future President, Thomas Woodrow Wilson.

The Woodrows were also Presbyterians. The maternal grandfather of the future President had cheerfully migrated from Carlisle, England, to the United States in 1835 when he was forty-two and had eight children. The journey proved too much for the

THE EDUCATIONIST

wife and mother who died five weeks after she arrived in New York, but the widower, Dr. Thomas Woodrow, soon won his way as a fine preacher and scholar, just as was Dr. Joseph Ruggles Wilson who married his daughter, Jane, in 1849. Dr. Joseph Ruggles Wilson who earlier had been a professor of rhetoric, chemistry and natural science, was the settled minister of the first Presbyterian Church of Staunton, Virginia, when on December 28th, 1856, his elder son, Thomas Woodrow Wilson, was born there.

A year later Dr. Wilson moved from Virginia to become minister in the sleepy little town of Augusta in the State of Georgia which was shortly afterwards to be engulfed in the Civil War. A keen believer in the right of secession, he became a chaplain in the Confederate Army and when the southern Presbyterian Church separated from the northern the Wilson home was its headquarters. Yet though the war swirled all round the manse it seems to have left little mark on Woodrow Wilson's character — as the War of Independence did upon the young Andrew Jackson. The compact Wilson family existence was relatively undisturbed. The mother was a quiet reserved well-read woman, the father with his fine presence and excellently defined sense of right and wrong both in morals and English prose style was always at home leading the family prayers, taking the children for walks, preparing his sermons, playing billiards or smoking a benevolent pipe. 'Tommy' advanced from fairy stories to Parson Weems's picturesque *Life of George Washington* and later to Scott, Dickens and Shakespeare under his parent's guidance and attended school where he was not very bright and once humanly played truant in order to follow an elephant. In 1870 the family moved on again to Columbia, South Carolina, where the father became professor in a theological seminary. 'Tommy' read his bible daily, received precise instructions on the value of words from his father, and pursued a life of high thinking and simple living. Received into membership of the Presbyterian Church in July 1873, that same year he went to Davidson College, North Carolina to study for the ministry.

Up to this point Woodrow Wilson's life had developed along a predestined plane — he was to be a Presbyterian minister like his father, his mother's father and his uncle, James Woodrow, a distinguished man who was later removed from his post as professor of science for teaching the convulsive doctrine of evolution. But at this period in his adolescence two things happened: first, at Davidson he fell in love with the arts of debating and became an enthusiastic member of a student's society which thrashed out problems of American politics and history. Secondly, after receiving a couple of excellent reports, especially for his gifts of declamation and deportment, he was taken ill, probably with some form of indigestion, and he had to leave college and return home. His home was now Wilmington, Virginia, and after a short period of his mother's cooking and his father's tuition, he left again this time for the College of Princeton, New Jersey.

Princeton College, founded in 1746, in those days was also something of a Presbytarian seminary and its president, Dr. James McCosh, who had been there since 1868 was a friend of Woodrow's father. At Princeton Woodrow read widely in the great Victorian historians and statesmen, J. R. Green and Macaulay, Bagehot, Gladstone and John Bright. All famous orators, from Demosthenes to Daniel Webster, fascinated him, and he became prominent in a literary and debating society mainly filled by young men from the south, appropriately called the Whig, of which he was elected Speaker. His interest in oratory led him to consider why American oratory had declined and he reached the conclusion that this was due to Congress's habit of settling so many of its problems in committees rather than by the cut-and-thrust of debate in open forum. As a result of his reading he came to have a preference for the British parliamentery system and actually organized a Liberal Debating Society, of which he drew up a constitution, on the lines of the House of Commons. At the same time he became managing editor of the student's magazine, the *Princetonian*, while he contributed biographical studies of Bismarck and Chatham to a students' literary magazine. Though he played baseball and became a football fan and in later life indulged in an academic game of golf Woodrow was a very serious and earnest young man. From his parents he had acquired a reserved manner and a practice of putting a high value on things of the mind. Yet he did not distinguish himself on his purely academic course and graduated in a modest way. Broadly the value of his academic life at Princeton was that it enabled him to educate himself in the subjects that he most enjoyed, such as political science and rhe-

THE EDUCATIONIST

toric, and it was here that he decided, somewhat to his father's dismay, that he did not want to enter the Church. The reason was not that he had lost his faith. On the contrary, to him religion lay outside the realm of argument and was founded on the sure conviction that there never could be any conflict between the words and the works of God. It was only that he had discovered a livelier interest in the problems of this world.

'The profession I chose', Wilson wrote to his future wife when he was twenty-five, 'was politics; the profession I entered was the law. I entered the one because I thought it would lead to the other. It was once the sure road; and Congress is still full of lawyers.' To learn the law he went from Princeton to the University of Virginia, of which Thomas Jefferson had been the founder, but he discovered that the course was boring and though he ground his way through, his favourite subjects remained politics, history and oratory and his idea of relaxation was to organize the Jefferson Society and write articles on the English Liberals. Both here and at Princeton he made congenial friends with common interests who were attracted by his southern charm, his courtesy and fine intelligence and he even fell in love for a while with a cousin of his in Ohio 'with whom he carried on an ardent correspondence'.

The law proved to be a harder taskmaster to Woodrow Wilson than it had been to Andrew Jackson and Abraham Lincoln. Clients did not hurry to the new firm of Renick and Wilson in Atlanta, Georgia, when they hung up their sign, for there were over one hundred and forty attorneys in the town from whom they could choose. Indeed though Wilson passed his bar examinations with credit, his heart was never in his work. While awaiting employment he filled in his time by reading and writing, but found the atmosphere of 'slow, ignorant, uninteresting Georgia' unconducive to study. 'History and Political Science!' he wrote enviously to a friend who was going to Germany to work for a doctorate, 'why they are of all studies my favourites; and to be allowed to fill all my time with them, instead of, as now, stealing only a chance opportunity or two for hasty perusal of those things which are most delightful to me, would be of all privileges the most valued by yours humbly.' Impatient and lonely, for him the winter of 1882-83 was a long winter of discontent, relieved only by the appearance that he made before a peripatetic Congressional

Tariff Commission to which he expounded his belief in a tariff for revenue purposes only, an exposition that he followed by founding a local Free Trade Club. But in the spring came love and hope. During a visit to the pretty town of Rome in North Georgia paid on behalf of his mother, who was virtually his only law client, he met Ellen Axson, his future wife. The romance that came to him accorded with the pattern of his life, for she was a daughter of the manse, as he was a son. Aged twenty-three with bronze gold hair and deep brown eyes and in charge of a family of five, for her mother was dead, Ellen was easily attracted by the charm and assurance of the tall young lawyer with a silky moustache and short side-whiskers (although she had the moustache off soon after they were married). Woodrow had sought an introduction to the Presbyterian Minister of Rome that he might meet the daughter. On both sides it seems to have been love at first sight. Every afternoon he called. The young couple walked and talked and discussed their plans and by the autumn, though at that time he had no job, they were officially engaged. Ellen had much to give her future husband; she was able to offer not merely a much more profound knowledge of many sides of everyday life than he had and a sympathetic understanding that could welcome and encourage all his ardent hopes, but she could introduce him to art, poetry and music and even philosophy and thus expand his narrower interests of politics, prose and prayer. In so far as Woodrow Wilson was saved from the academic priggishness towards which his upbringing had directed him, he owed — more perhaps than we shall ever know — to the wisdom and guidance of his first wife.

About the same time that he met Ellen Axson, Woodrow Wilson took a plunge and abandoned his briefless law practice, deciding to do what he most wanted by entering Johns Hopkins University, Baltimore, as a post-graduate to carry out research into history and political science. During a year in Baltimore he worked like a demon. His interests did not lie in institutional research, the normal university preoccupation, but in consideration of the practical problems of modern government. When he had been a senior at Princeton he had published an article on 'Cabinet Government in the United States' in the *International Review*. Now he developed his themes in a full-length book entitled *Congressional*

THE EDUCATIONIST

Government with the thesis that 'Our government is practically carried on by irresponsible committees'. In this book, a truly remarkable production for a young man, he argued that the neat balancing of executive, legislature and judiciary and of the federal authority against the individual states designed in the original American Constitution had not worked in practice, for the federal powers had grown both during and after the Civil War, while the power of the states had waned. At the same time, owing partly to the weakness of the Presidents since Lincoln, Congress had become predominant over the so-called 'co-ordinate branches', although

> There can be little doubt [he wrote] that had the presidential chair always been filled by men of commanding character, of acknowledged ability, and of thorough political training, it would have continued to be a seat of the highest authority and consideration, the true centre of the federal structure, the real throne of administration, and the frequent source of policies.

This was written, it must be remembered, twenty years before Theodore Roosevelt became President. Wilson went on to contrast the system of Congressional Government by standing committees working in secret with the British Cabinet system in which the executive initiated legislation and was represented in the legislature. This clever and well-written analysis was all the more remarkable in that so far as we know Wilson had never visited Washington, attended a meeting of Congress, or met any leading politicians. The whole thesis was built out of books — and therein no doubt lay its weakness. During this same year he also wrote half a book that was (happily for his reputation) never published on the history of American economic ideas, while he attended the post-graduate courses at the university and found time to organize the 'Johns Hopkins House of Commons'. His book was accepted for publication at the end of November and in the incredible space of two months he received the advance copies. Excellently reviewed, the book earned him his doctorate and assured him of an academic post. At the beginning of 1885 he had become Associate Professor in History at Bryn Mawr College, Pennsylvania, a new Quaker institution for the higher education of young ladies, at the salary of fifteen hundred dollars a year.

WOODROW WILSON

Woodrow Wilson and Ellen Axson, returned from art studies in New York, were married at Savannah in June 1885 and in September the young husband began his long career as an educationist. At that date Theodore Roosevelt was rounding up the cattle in Dakota and Bryan was a struggling lawyer in Nebraska. Wilson's road to political fame was to be a wearier one than theirs although he was as determined as they were to get there in the end. As his biographer, Ray Stannard Baker, wrote: 'Fifty-four years of his life he spent in preparation, ten in living, three in dying.' It seemed an odd way to start up the road — lecturing on ancient and modern history to a class of a few girls. But overpowering ambition knows no obstacles: though he made a mess of his first public speech in New York, though he planned but never developed a great work on political science, though he failed to supplement his family income by freelance stories and essays, though he was even unsuccessful as a teacher of women, his energy and ability soon brought him release from his initial drudgery and by 1888 he had left Bryn Mawr for Wesleyan University, Middletown, Connecticut, to undertake the more congenial task of teaching men.

After two very happy years at Wesleyan, during which he wrote a text-book on *The State* and blossomed out as a football coach, though characteristically only by demonstrating 'plays' on the blackboard, Wilson, through the influence of old friends in the Princeton class of '79, was invited to return to that college as a Professor of Public Law, on the understanding that he taught political economy for a year first. He did not hesitate to accept; it was not merely that the salary was higher than he was earning, but he was satisfied that he would have a better calibre of students who would be more appreciative of his talents as a lecturer. Mrs. Wilson and three little girls, born during the years at Bryn Mawr and Wesleyan, settled down in a comfortable house not far from the centre of college life, while her husband looked for new worlds to conquer.

Princeton was not yet a university though the number of professors and students was increasing and beautiful buildings were springing up round the campus. It was still, as it had been when Woodrow was a student there, the College of New Jersey with a

THE EDUCATIONIST

Presbyterian minister — now Dr. Patton instead of Dr. McCosh — as its president. Yet concessions were proffered to the spirit of the age and Wilson's appointment was among them. From the first Woodrow Wilson made a tremendous impression, above all by his power of oratory which he acquired by so much practice in his youth. His classes found him a spell-binder and would often cheer at the end of his lectures. Yet in education he tended to give rather than to receive, as is so often the case with the public man. The same was true of Dr. H. A. L. Fisher when he was Warden of New College, Oxford. He had been a Minister of State during the war of 1914-18 and his knowledge of public affairs and his width of experience and culture made him an extraordinarily fine lecturer — yet he seldom brought the best out of his undergraduates, as was often done by the most obscure college tutors. Wilson was cut out — he had cut himself out to be — a public man. When he found his feet he was in demand as a public lecturer and ranged as far afield as Denver to talk to a women's club on the subject of liberty. In these addresses he 'put truth and Christianity into politics' just as he put moral passion into his lectures at the university. Yet in spite of his success as an orator he was always impatient and dissatisfied with himself both over the sphere of his influence and the quality of his work. Offers of university positions were to pour in upon him, but he hankered after an opportunity in politics, which he thought would be denied him. 'I should think you would like to go to the United States Senate', his brother-in-law and friend Stockton Axson, once said to him. 'Indeed I would,' was the reply, 'but that is impossible. In this country men do not go from the academic world into politics.' As to his work he was constantly fretting over his style and was correspondingly elated at proofs of a successful speech or piece of writing. And of those proofs there was no want. Four times he was elected the most popular member of the faculty at Princeton and he swiftly became the acknowledged leader of the younger and more progressive teachers.

During the years 1895 and 1896 Professor Wilson toiled with such energy that his health broke. Articles, lectures, administrative duties overwhelmed him as he accepted everything that was offered so as to pay for the new house that he was proposing to build for himself and his growing family. In one year he earned the sum of four thousand dollars by outside work. The price paid was neuritis in his right hand and although he at once taught himself to use his left, it became necessary for him to recuperate and he spent his first holiday in Britain (without his wife) where he enjoyed himself immensely. In England he particularly loved the Lake District, but his experiences in Oxford ('enough to take one's heart by storm') and Cambridge ('rather a mean town with attractive colleges') notably influenced him. 'What do you think of England?' he was asked on his return. 'I am a better American for having been there', was his answer. In October 1896 Princeton became a university and the authorities were particularly anxious not to lose so popular and distinguished a professor. In 1898 a group of friends, the class of '79, united to subsidize his salary on condition that he stayed and so there was no longer a financial excuse for overwork.

It was during his years as professor at Princeton that the majority of Wilson's books were written, although he never wrote anything as important as his first book *Congressional Government*. His collection of essays called *Mere Literature* was excellent of its kind as was also his contribution to an historical series *Division and Reunion*. But two books into which he put a good deal of consciously turned and thoroughly bad writing were, though scarcely with intention, mere money spinners, namely his *George Washington* (1898) and his *History of the American People* (1902) for which he was paid the fabulous sum of a thousand dollars a chapter by a popular magazine. The *Washington* was far too picturesque and eulogistic a narrative, while the *History* has not stood the test of time. The trouble was, as his official biographer shrewdly wrote, that Wilson 'seemed always to be holding back his most penetrating conclusions for some greater and riper work' that was never to be written. In fact Wilson was one of those men, to be found in the universities no less than in other walks of life, who are essentially politicians and administrators and not great authors or scientists. The universities, it is recognized, need such men, a few of them at least, even though they may tread a little roughly over the nicer susceptibilities of their less worldly colleagues. The Princeton trustees realized that they had such a man, a 'sound' man, though not lacking in progressive ideas, a popular expositor, capable alike of a good article for a classy magazine and

THE EDUCATIONIST

an uplifting discourse to a ceremonial gathering, one, so at least they must have thought, fully able to combine religion and business, and for that reason, somewhat it is said, to his own surprise, in June 1902 they elected him unanimously to be the first lay president of the university. Pushing away the final proofs of his highly paid American history, laying aside with a slight twinge all thought of his unwritten masterpiece on political science, Woodrow Wilson girded his loins to use his first true chance to demonstrate his powers of leadership. Now he would show the world.

Wilson set about his new task with zest. As he prepared his inaugural speech in the summer of 1902 he wrote to his wife: 'I feel like a new prime minister getting ready to address his constituents.' The ceremonies at which the new President of Princeton was instituted that autumn were on an impressive scale and among those who attended were Speaker Reed of the House of Representatives, Pierpont Morgan, Mark Twain and Grover Cleveland, the former Democratic President of the United States who had settled in the neighbourhood of the university and had become a member of the Board of Trustees. Not only was he allowed to dismiss teachers with whom he was dissatisfied, which he sometimes did a trifle ruthlessly, but he was even empowered to bring about changes in the Board of Trustees itself.

The fact was that in spite of its popularity and prosperity — it contained one hundred and eight professors and thirteen hundred students in 1902 — the university stood in need of reform. The former president had been easy going and procrastinating in his ways: the curriculum called for urgent revision; and the growth of fraternities, rich young men's clubs and sports had tended to outweigh the importance of the university as an educational institution. Wilson set before the university a simple aim: 'I am not going to propose', he said, 'that we compel the undergraduates to work all the time, but I am going to propose that we make the undergraduates want to work all the time.' Wilson knew from his own youthful experience as a Princeton undergraduate that this was the right approach to higher education. Had he not been obliged to grind his way through a lifeless curriculum, while employing his spare time in studying those subjects that really interested him? Was not the right method of education to induce the student to read for himself and follow his own bent? Was it not the first duty of the wise teacher to stimulate his pupil to find things out for himself while guiding his reading along sound lines? That has been the essence of the system of education practised at Oxford and Cambridge over the last half century. The system of course has its disadvantages. For instance, it is expensive, for it requires a high proportion of teachers to students to ensure the frequent personal contacts necessary to bring the very best out of the youthful mind. Again, it may tend to lower the standard of lecturing, for it encourages the student to neglect lectures in order to concentrate on his own reading, while the teacher may have to devote so much of his time to individual tuition as to be unable to prepare first-class lectures. However its basic principle of using good minds to stimulate immature minds is surely wise. So at any rate Wilson thought, and after he had made an appeal for funds to put the finances of the university on a firmer and more generous footing and carried out a modernization and reorganization, he launched in 1905 what was called the preceptorial system.

This system was not exactly the same as the Oxford tutorial system. In the first place, as Wilson justly observed, 'the English . . . appoint their tutors for life and their tutors go to seed. No man can do that sort of thing for youngsters without getting tired of it'. So Wilson appointed his tutors for only five years. Secondly he had his preceptors live in dormitories in order that they might become daily companions of the young men they instructed. And thirdly the preceptors were not called on to lecture. Fifty such preceptors were selected with the rank of assistant professors, 'fifty stiffs to make us wise', as the Princeton seniors sang, and the bold and costly experiment soon proved itself a success.

The preceptorial system, though the most original part, was only one part of Wilson's plans of reform. Altogether he appealed for 12,000,000 dollars to pay among other things for a school of science, a graduate school, a school of jurisprudence and various new buildings and increases of staff. The money was to be had in that prosperous age if only the appeal were rightly directed and energetically followed up. Wilson wrote vast numbers of personal letters and delivered speeches throughout the country to old members of Princeton (the 'alumni'). The intensity of his work

THE EDUCATIONIST

and the fantastic conditions in which it began may be measured by the fact that at first he had no secretary and no properly trained financial adviser.

Wilson's uncompromising idealism attracted many excellent teachers to the university and so further raised its prestige. 'He was in many respects the greatest man I have ever known', wrote one of them in retrospect. 'He had a mind as clear and penetrating as sunlight and an incomparable grace and force of expression which had in it the quality of inspiration. His ideals were so high that to many "practical" men they seemed visionary, and yet again and again he made those visions real. He was deliberate in making up his mind and slow to begin action, but once having decided, neither the claims of friendship nor the threats of enemies could turn him from his course.' One instance of this practical idealism was his insistence that the new buildings of the university should be in Tudor Gothic and that there should be one consulting architect to co-ordinate all the plans for development. In thrusting towards his goals Wilson never had any doubts that he was right. Another colleague once said to him: 'Well, Dr. Wilson, there are two sides to every question.' 'Yes,' came the answer, 'a right side and a wrong side.' A born leader, he compelled men to follow him, but to follow him, as has well been said, as they would follow an abstract principle, for he was not a conciliator or a clever chairman, he was a Calvin and not a Ramsay MacDonald. He was not in the least introspective — he only worried if he felt he was falling below his own standards. But he never asked himself, so far as we know, 'can I be wrong?' Perhaps Tudor Gothic was not ideal for an American university? Perhaps the emphasis he placed on the development of the intellect, so natural in a man of his rigid puritan upbringing, led to a neglect of sides of life which also have their importance in the scheme of human things. But Wilson knew no uncertainties, he just pushed on, working himself to the verge of breakdown. In 1906 the neuritis that had incapacitated him before had spread across his body to an extent that induced a specialist to tell him he must give up everything and retire. Later the diagnosis was corrected, but he had to take a long vacation in the English Lakes to restore his health. Then at the end of 1906 he returned to Princeton to initiate a fresh struggle for the improvement, as he saw it, of university education.

WOODROW WILSON

The next stage in Wilson's plans for the regeneration of Princeton was based, like his preceptorial system, on the experiences of Oxford and Cambridge. During the years since he had been a student at Princeton there had been a growth in 'upper class clubs', that is to say exclusive clubs which if men were to enter in the full swing of undergraduate social life they had to join in their third year of residence. Since, however, the number of members taken into these clubs was smaller than the number of undergraduates in residence there was eager competition to obtain election to the clubs, and this competition tended to divert energies from university work; moreover men who were not elected felt that they had been left in the outer darkness, became discouraged, and sometimes left the university before their courses were completed. Thus, in Wilson's view, these clubs as they stood were inimical to the organization of the university for educational purposes. The remedy he proposed was 'to make undergraduates live together, not in clubs but in colleges'. (This would have meant the absorption, but not necessarily the elimination of the clubs.) By a college he meant an institution similar to that in Oxford and Cambridge, that is to say a group of buildings around a quadrangle (at Cambridge this is called a court) with a dining hall where resident members of the faculty could take meals with the undergraduates. The proposed system differed only from that at Oxford and Cambridge in that the colleges would have no separate autonomy — it would simply be 'a convenient residential division of the university as a social body'.

The Board of Trustees gave approval in principle to this proposal and asked Wilson to draw up detailed plans, for some of the more luxurious manifestations of the club life, which it was intended to reduce, were generally admitted evil. On the other hand, the clubs had become integral parts of the university's traditions. Old Princetonians, looking back to the hallowed traditions of their own young days, stood aghast at the notion of so radical and dictatorial a reform and many of them of course were the rich men upon whose contributions all such reforms ultimately depended. As soon as the Board realized that it had stirred up a wasps' nest it turned against the president and decided to drop the project. It was a bitter blow to Wilson who refused to take it lying down and he spent the next years writing articles and making speeches on its behalf. But it was never put into effect. The decision against the 'quad scheme', as it was called, came in October 1907. In the next three years Wilson was involved in another and more complicated university controversy, concerning the development of a graduate college. The idea of creating a graduate college, where men taking advanced courses could reside and work, had been approved for some years, among others by Wilson himself. A campaign to collect money for this purpose had actually begun under his predecessor when an able and distinguished professor, Andrew West, had been appointed dean with very wide powers. West had been opposed to the 'quad' scheme because he was afraid it would interfere with the development of his graduate college. Soon after the 'quad' scheme was dropped a friend of West's, a soap manufacturer, had offered the sum of 500,000 dollars towards the fund for the graduate college on condition that its situation should be approved by him, and the situation which he favoured was not near the centre of the university, but a mile or so away. Wilson was strongly against this proposal because he considered that the college must become an integral part of the university, in accordance with his conviction that the most valuable impulse in educational life was the mixing of men of differing years. If the graduates were to be thus physically separated from the undergraduates, then they would lose the benefit of the company and leadership of the most experienced students. Furthermore he feared that Dean West would try to run the new college independently according to his own particular views. To Wilson and his supporters too this question became the battleground of a wider issue, namely the power of money to interfere in the workings of the university. After a prolonged struggle, during which the gift was at first accepted and then withdrawn, Wilson was defeated by the surprise announcement of the enormous legacy of two million dollars to be spent chiefly on the graduate college, of which Dean West was named one of the trustees. Wilson said to his wife when he heard the news: 'We have beaten the living, but we cannot fight the dead. The game is up.' In due course the graduate college was built a mile or so from the university, as Dean West wished, but the separation of undergraduate and graduate life that Wilson feared was offset by the growth of the university as a whole and by modern means of transport. And even at that it may surely be argued that the evil was not as grave as Wilson felt. For a graduate necessarily requires a measure of isolation and comfort in which to pursue his more advanced studies or researches (had not Wilson built a tall iron fence around his own house, Prospect?) and it may be questioned whether his experience is nearly as essential to the education of the undergraduate as is that of the younger teachers. In Oxford and Cambridge the line between the graduate research student and the younger tutor is blurred.

However, so far as the wider history of the United States is concerned, the significance of Wilson's fight over the graduate college lay in the fact that he appealed (even if unfairly) to the principles of democracy against the overpowering influence of money. Newspaper readers, who knew nothing whatever of university matters, were convinced that here was a radical reformer who was indomitable and incorruptible. Wilson himself indeed had preached the doctrine of the indomitable individual, who could not be 'shamed' or 'silenced' and refused to bow to the golden calf. He had condemned too in a vigorous address to the University of Virginia the lack of leadership in politics, especially in the Democratic party, whose leader, Bryan, he privately thought 'foolish and dangerous in his theoretical beliefs'. If the nation needed a worthier political leader, he had shown that such a man was on call.

2. GOVERNOR OF NEW JERSEY AND PRESIDENTIAL CANDIDATE (1910-1913)

When a man is over fifty his character and ideas may be considered to be formed in a recognizable pattern, but this generalization when applied to a statesman requires at least two qualifications. In the first place his set principles may be modified and his aspirations chastened by the hard practical experiences of administration. Alternatively, when his term of office is over he may advocate more radical or more conservative views, views that in his days of responsibility he dared not or could not put into effect. But broadly we may detect in Wilson's career and behaviour as an educationist most of the characteristics that he was to show as a politician. To him life was always a struggle — 'for a man who has lost the sense of struggle, life has ceased', he contended — a struggle for the principles that moved him most profoundly. And yet on specific subjects he was — like Washington — slow in making up his mind. Once he had taken his decision, nothing could turn him from his purpose; he might waver and even despair but in the end he would always renew the fight with a fierce stubbornness that no one could break down. 'The older I get,' Wilson once said, 'the hotter I get.' Nor would he lightly forgive those who refused to go along with him. His attitude to Professor Hibben was a case in point. The Hibbens were among his earliest and closest friends at Princeton; but Hibben had not been on his side in the conflict over the graduate college. When he heard that Hibben had been chosen President of Princeton in his place he condemned the choice in no unmeasured terms and though he was then *ex officio* president of the Board of Trustees refused to attend the inaugural ceremonies. Yet this very stubbornness and the utter conviction he had in the righteousness of his cause gave him the power of an inspired evangelist to bring converts to bear him company. What he did for Princeton could have been achieved only by a real leader of men — though Princeton has perhaps been tardy in accepting the fact.

Wilson was one of those men who while they are insensitive to the feelings of others and find if difficult to understand how they have made enemies, are extremely sensitive themselves. To compliments he always responded graciously, but from criticism he shied. Intellectually arrogant, he left to others the tasks of conciliation so necessary in the make-up of a statesman and he sometimes had to be tactfully led to appreciate that he had given cause for offence. To cushion the sores of public life he sought comfort in the sympathy and admiration of those who had no openly pronounced opinions of their own. Hence he enjoyed corresponding with congenial women, as he did regularly for many years with the approval of his first wife, who, intelligent and understanding as she was, felt that she could not fulfil all his needs herself. Hence too, as we shall see, his friendship with Colonel House, the wealthy political amateur from Texas, who asked only to be useful to him behind the scenes. Conscious of his destiny as a political leader, as ambitious in his youth as Lincoln or Theodore Roosevelt to enter the forum, he had to wait so long that he sometimes doubted if he would ever find the way and so he had always needed those who had faith in him and could cheer him on.

Wilson knew that he was born to lead and that what his nation — and his party — needed was a leader. Surely — was it not in the logic of his Calvinist faith? — to the right man the call must come. As early as March 1897 Wilson had written of the Democrat, Cleveland: 'In him we got a President, as it were, by the immediate choice from out the body of the people.' But few are called and fewer still are rightly chosen. 'Roughly speaking', he told the Virginia Bar Association in an address that same year on 'leaderless Government' Presidents had been leaders 'until Andrew Jackson went home to the Hermitage'. Since then, he thought, there had been little leadership either in the White House or in Congress. He quoted Roger Sherman as saying in the debates of 1797 that 'he considered the executive magistracy as nothing more than an institution for carrying the will of the Legislature into effect'. That was not Wilson's idea of the Presidency, and so he could not withhold a meed of praise from the Republican President Theodore Roosevelt. (Many of Wilson's friends at Princeton were in fact admirers of Roosevelt.) But the right leader must also belong to the right party, and the leader of the Democratic party, Bryan, was not in his opinion that man. In a speech at New York in 1904 Wilson had attacked the party's domination by 'unsafe leaders'. In April 1907 in a private letter he had written: 'Would that we could do something at once dignified and effective to knock Mr. Bryan once and for all into a cocked hat!' In 1908, when it was tentatively suggested that Wilson should stand as vice-presidential candidate on the party ticket with Bryan, he refused to think of it. Bryan was much too wild.

Indeed it is a mistake to imagine that the President of Princeton was a radical — a reformer certainly, but not a radical. In accepting the prevailing opinion among the enlightened men of his time that the evils of the big business corporations — as exposed by the 'Muckrakers' — must be checked, he was careful to emphasize that he did not want to hamper 'legitimate enterprise'. Had he not many good and generous friends in the world of big business? And 'revolutionary panaceas' must be eschewed if socialism were to be averted. 'Our whole effort', he explained in a speech at Philadel-

PRESIDENTIAL CANDIDATE

phia in November 1909, 'should be not to urge reform, but to master its method.'

It was indeed because of the moderation, the conservatism almost, of his public utterances that Wilson's call to politics came. It did not come — how could it? — initially from 'the people'. Many people have claimed the title of President-maker, but there is little question that the first of them was Colonel George Harvey, sometime editor and proprietor of the *North American Review* and *Harper's Weekly* the latter a paper in which Pierpont Morgan was interested. At a dinner in February 1906 Harvey introduced Wilson as his candidate for the Democratic nomination, for in Harvey's opinion Wilson was the right man to dish Bryan. Wilson thought at the time that Harvey was joking, but the newspaper proprietor pressed forward with his campaign and finally in 1910 persuaded Senator James Smith, commonly called 'Sugar Jim', the Democratic boss of New Jersey, to support Wilson as candidate for Governor of the state but as a mere preliminary in a plan to nominate him for the Presidency in 1912. Wilson, though hesitating over the financial risk, for he was responsible for a family of four daughters, agreed to stand on condition that he was nominated unanimously by the party. This was arranged. Word went out to the local bosses. One of them was asked by a young Irishman named Joseph Tumulty if he thought Wilson would make a good governor. 'How the hell do I know whether he'll make a good governor', was the answer. 'He will make a good candidate, and that is the only thing that interests me.' Though he gave no pledges, Wilson was thus the choice of the 'machine' in a state where big business was securely in the saddle. By steamroller methods his nomination was narrowly obtained and then made unanimous. Many of the anti-machine delegates at the State Convention were resentful, but when they saw and heard the 'professor' who came to address the gathering they were converted. 'Men stood about me with tears streaming from their eyes', wrote Tumulty, who was one of the converts. In the campaign the 'trained thinker' and 'classic orator' proved a startling success. He was elected by a majority of 49,000, reversing a Republican majority in the previous election of 82,000. In October before the election took place, he was compelled to resign his office at Princeton and in January 1911 he took up his duties as Governor.

The Democratic party bosses of New Jersey who had selected Wilson had found that he was an ideal candidate except in one respect, which was that he failed to accede to their wishes or directions. During the election in the course of an exchange of open letters with a progressive Republican Wilson had pledged himself in unqualified terms that were he to become Governor it would mean the end of the 'boss system' in New Jersey. In fact though Wilson had entered the contest as the nominee of the bosses, he had been propelled by his own sense of what was fitting into the progressive camp. Soon after the election Wilson found himself obliged to engage in open conflict with the boss, James Smith. Wilson had understood that Smith had no intention of standing again for the United States Senate, although Smith had made no public pronouncement to this effect. But when Wilson's scintillating campaign had helped to win a majority for the Democratic party in the New Jersey Legislature Smith decided that he would run, for the choice of Senator rested with the legislature and the party's nominee was therefore sure of election. At the party primaries in the autumn another old but honest party man, Martine, had been chosen as the Democratic candidate for the Senate, an honorific choice as his chance was then thought hopeless. Moreover the choice of this 'preferential primary', as the party poll was called, was not of course binding on the legislature — it was only a recommendation to the party members. It was thus possible for Smith to induce his friends to choose him instead of Martine. The enlightened element were furious at Smith's revived ambitions and looked to the Governor for leadership. Wilson hesitated some time as to what he ought to do. To Tumulty it seemed as if the position of this 'amateur in politics' suddenly pitchforked into the rough-and-tumble of the real thing was 'almost pathetic'. Strictly it was not his fight, but he had claimed to be the chosen leader of his party in New Jersey and he finally acknowledged that a principle was involved. If he failed to intervene, then the world would believe that, in spite of all his promises, he was a mere 'front' put up by the 'machine'. Wilson thereupon decided to act. After he had seen Smith and vainly tried to persuade him to withdraw his name he published a statement in which he said: 'I know that the people of New Jersey do not desire Mr. James Smith, Jr., to be sent to the Senate. If he should be, he

PRESIDENTIAL CANDIDATE

will not go as their representative.' The Governor's influence and lead proved decisive and after a struggle Martine was chosen by the legislature. Smith, the man who had done as much as anyone to secure Wilson's own nomination, ultimately lost most of his influence and many of his friends; but he never ceased to admire the abilities of the professor from Princeton.

The Smith incident is far more important in Wilson's career than it might seem. For it established his sincerity in his professions and gave him the influence in New Jersey which he needed to impose 'clean government' on the state. During his term as Governor acting as Mr. A. S. Link has said as an 'unofficial Prime Minister', he was able to procure the passage through the legislature of a series of acts which cut at the root of corruption in state politics. 'I got absolutely everything I strove for and more besides', he wrote to one of his lady friends after the legislature adjourned in April 1911. 'All four of the great acts that I had set my heart on (the primaries and election law, the corrupt practices act, as stringent as the English, the working-men's compensation act, and the act giving a public commission control over the railways, the trolley lines, the water companies, and the gas and electric light and power companies) and besides them I got certain fundamental school reforms, and an act enabling any city in the State to adopt the commission form of government, which simplifies the electoral process and concentrates responsibility. Everyone, the papers included, are saying that none of it could have been done if it had not been for my influence and tact and hold upon the people. Be that as it may, the thing was done, and the result was as complete a victory as has ever been won, I venture to say, in the history of the country. I wrote the platform, I had the measures formulated in my mind, I kept the pressure of opinion constantly on the legislature, and the programme was carried out to its last detail.' Secondly his defeat of Smith won him recognition outside New Jersey. William Jennings Bryan, in spite of his ill success in three presidential elections still one of the most powerful men in the Democratic party, wrote to Champ Clark, Democratic Speaker of the House of Representatives: 'A leader must *lead*... Wilson is making friends because he *fights*. His fight against Smith was heroic. He fought for the income tax and a primary law. People like a fighter.' And Wilson, for all his expressions of distaste in his private letters, was happy fighting. Mrs. Wilson, who surely is the best witness, said that 'he positively enjoyed being Governor'. His triumphs as Governor put him on his predestined path towards the United States Presidency.

The Governorship of New Jersey had been designed by Wilson's backers as a mere 'springboard for the Presidency' in 1913 and it is plain that in his heart of hearts Wilson so regarded it too. As soon as the session of legislature closed in the spring of 1911 Wilson set off on a speaking tour in the west, starting at Kansas City, during which he made over thirty speeches in seven different states and in the first months of 1912 he spoke in eleven states. Indeed Wilson's newspaper critics dubbed the governorship his 'travelling scholarship' and rebuked him for his 'too eager chase after the nomination'. In June 1911 a Wilson propaganda organization was created in New York with the temperamental William McCombs as its amateur manager. Wilson's speeches always assured him of a large and enthusiastic audience wherever he went, but he was unduly impressed by the welcome he received, for in actual fact he did relatively little to disturb the claims of other established candidates for the Democratic nomination. In the nature of the appeal that Wilson made there was a curious evolution. When Colonel Harvey first picked him out as a possible candidate, it was because he was felt to be an ideal man to confound the radicals — indeed, it was openly asserted that he was the Wall Street candidate. Although Wilson considered himself a radical and not a conservative, there was at first little in his speeches to dash the hopes of his original sponsors. The reforms that he advocated were political rather than economic; and he was strongly opposed to revolutionary methods; he preached a 'gospel of order'. It is true that he distrusted the power of rich men and big corporations, but he believed that it was possible to distinguish between good and bad trusts and that provided the bad trusts were restrained by the ordinary methods of law the natural working of competition could be relied upon to procure social harmony. Reared on the hopeful political economy taught by the mid-Victorians Wilson did not question the beneficent operation of private enterprise. His criticisms were directed equally against capitalist and labour monopolies and indeed he was opposed to the idea of closed shops and had been taken to task by the New Jersey Federation of Labour for an incautious address in which he had appeared to describe trade unionists as 'unprofitable servants'. He sought, as Mr. Diamond has written, to steer his course between the Scylla of Socialism and the Charybdis of plutocratic power in what he called the spirit of Jefferson, that is the spirit of individualism. In sum Wilson favoured neither 'trust busting' nor the use of the federal power in the interests of labour, yet he rejected the pure *laissez-faire* doctrines on which he had been brought up: he was the 'enlightened conservative' who believed that the government should take positive action to protect the middle classes from exploitation from any quarter and give everyone his fair opportunity. On constitutional questions he was often evasive or non-committal, thus in an age when an increasing number of people in the United States were realizing the need both for political and economic reform those who advocated radical solutions did not look to Wilson for leadership but to Roosevelt, La Follette or Bryan.

Yet though it is reasonable to say that Wilson was in many respects a conservative in outlook, he was far from being a reactionary. He knew that the nation wanted to move forward and that 'progressiveness means not getting caught standing still when everything else is moving'. In a talk to a gathering of bankers before he became Governor he had informed them that there was a higher law than the law of profit; he was a consistent advocate of lowering the tariff; and he was sympathetic with the aspirations of the unprivileged south. Moreover in December 1911 Wilson broke with Harvey, as he had earlier broken with Smith, thereby repudiating the suggestion that he was the chosen representative of the moneyed interest. But the radical vote of the Democratic party, expressing in outspoken terms the traditional western fears of the Money Power, was still that of William Jennings Bryan. In his dealing with Bryan, Wilson showed himself possessed of a hitherto little disclosed diplomatic gift. When he visited Nebraska, Bryan's state, while the Great Commoner was in Wilson's own state of New Jersey, he impressed Mrs. Bryan most favourably and when at last the two eminent Presbyterian politicians met Bryan himself found Wilson 'truly captivating'. Later Bryan observed that Wilson was 'the best modern example of Saul of Tarsus'. Finally at a Jackson Day dinner in Washington at which both men spoke on January 8th, 1912, outward harmony was established, though Wilson's unfortunate letter about 'knocking Bryan into a cocked hat' had by that time been published. But in spite of this and the exhausting campaign by Wilson and his friends to gain the presidential nomination, it seemed uncertain that he would win it when in 1912 the Democratic Convention met at Baltimore.

It was the rule of the Democratic party that its candidate had to be chosen by a two-thirds majority — and although Wilson was personally opposed to the rule — in it, and the infinite opportunities it offered for negotiations behind the scenes, lay his one chance of securing the nomination. At the opening of the Convention the favourite candidate was the cautious and experienced Champ Clark of Missouri, 'a sort of elephantine smart Aleck', as Wilson privately called him, powerfully backed in the press and with many friends in the middle west. The Nebraska delegation, headed by Bryan, was pledged to Clark's support. The story of the convention was dramatic. In the early stages of the fight for the nomination the most influential single delegate was Bryan who wrote both to Clark and to Wilson suggesting that it was essential to have a 'progressive' as the temporary chairman of the conference. Clark evaded the question, but Wilson after some hesitation telegraphed his agreement from his home in New Jersey where at the end of the telephone he awaited news and advice from his sponsors. In all there were forty-six ballots before the final decision was reached. At the tenth ballot New York State, originally pledged to another candidate, swung its ninety votes to Clark and thus gave Clark a total of 566 votes against Wilson's 350, and a clear majority over all the opposing candidates. At this point McCombs despairingly advised Wilson to throw in the sponge. Another of Wilson's advisers, William McAdoo, however, gave contrary counsel and persuaded Wilson to withdraw a telegram he had written abandoning his candidature. On the fourteenth ballot William Bryan gave notice that he withdrew his vote from Clark and gave it to Wilson on the ground that the vote of New York State, representing the reactionary group of Tammany Hall, meant that Clark had become the candidate of the millionaires and the bosses. Bryan neither openly nor privately advocated the nomination of Wilson, but, in the opinion of one of Wilson's own managers, this action of his drove the 'last nails' into Clark's coffin. Some said — though Mrs. Bryan denied it — that Bryan hoped there would be a deadlock between Clark and Wilson and that he would win the nomination himself. In the end the convention slowly turned against Clark and on the forty-sixth ballot Wilson gained the nomination. It will be noticed that, even after every allowance has been made for the manœuvring of Wilson's managers, Wilson won the nomination or at least stayed the course long enough to win it, because he appeared to be a more 'progressive' candidate than Clark. Just as Roosevelt as the progressive candidate within the ranks of the Republican party was to win more votes than Taft, so in accordance with the presiding spirit of the age the Democrats swung to Wilson who found himself, almost despite himself, the focus of the reform movement in his party. It was the measure of Wilson's political wisdom that he accepted the chance given him by Bryan to associate himself with the more liberal element in his party and by so doing within two and a half years of leaving Princeton the 'cloistered professor' arrived at the White House.

Wilson's campaign managers insisted that he undertook a strenuous programme of speaking in order to show himself to the nation, for they thought it was necessary that the electorate should have the opportunity to know the sober academic figure who offered himself as a rival to the vivid Theodore Roosevelt. Wilson's speeches were filled for the most part with high-sounding though vague generalities and the only reform that he regularly touched upon was the need to revise the tariff. They showed, as one of his biographers observed, 'a thoughtful cautious mind, not sure how far his countrymen wished to go. Roosevelt seemed to be the real radical'. Roosevelt in fact advocated a number of specific proposals, whereas Wilson stuck to broad principles — 'piping a very low note', said the reformers. After all, why commit himself? The Democratic party was bound to win, if its rank and file did but do its duty and no one were alienated or offended. Except on one occasion Wilson wisely eschewed personalities and when Roosevelt was shot he cancelled his speeches until his opponent had recovered. After the campaign a selection of the speeches was published under the title of *The New Freedom*. The 'New Freedom' was not, however, really a systematic scheme of political philosophy, although Wilson intended that his appeal should lie on that level. His outlook was summarized in the sentence: 'What I am fighting for personally now is to see that the average man is not kept down and denied his opportunity.' Thus he intended that special privileges should be swept away wherever they enabled the strong to oppress the weak. But American historians are in agreement that so far as domestic affairs were concerned there was no fundamental difference between Wilson's views and those of Roosevelt. Both of them undertook to protect the 'little man'. However much Wilson may have wanted it to be, the election was in fact not a fight over principles at all; and Wilson appealed to many simply as an enlightened conservative who, while being perhaps more progressive in his outlook than Taft, would not charge at reform like a bull in a china shop as it was thought that Theodore Roosevelt might do. In the end Wilson polled only forty-two per cent of the popular vote and had a clear majority over his rivals only in the solid south which since the Civil War has always been loyal to the Democratic party. The minority vote was, however, sufficient to give him 435 votes in the Electoral College against eighty-eight to Roosevelt and only eight to Taft. Soon after the result was known Wilson left for Bermuda to take a holiday and to clear his mind on the problems that lay ahead.

Wilson's immediate problem was the choice of his Cabinet. He was the first Democratic President for twenty years and no fund of experience existed to be drawn upon, although there were faithful to be rewarded. Out of the faithful towered Bryan. Wilson was most reluctant to have him in his Cabinet and tried to fob him off with an appointment abroad, but finally accepted him as Secretary of State. Bryan solemnly explained to the President that the only objection he had to holding the office was that he felt he could not conscientiously offer intoxicating liquors when giving official entertainments. This was found not to be an insuperable objection, and diplomatists who dined with the new Secretary of State had to be affable on fruit juice. Bryan, according to Colonel House, was 'as pleased with his new place as a child with a new toy' and in the early days of the administration got on extremely well with Wilson, agreeing in the main with the lines of his foreign

PRESIDENTIAL CANDIDATE

policy. On one point only he made an independent stand; he could not agree to sending a Unitarian as a Minister to China, for he thought that this would give a bad impression in a country that was rapidly becoming Christian. McAdoo, who had distinguished himself by driving tunnels under the Hudson River and also as vice-chairman of Wilson's organization, went to the Treasury, while McCombs who had been the campaign chairman was considered to be too unstable for the Cabinet but was offered and refused the embassy to France. Burleson of Texas, an able party man, became Postmaster-General, Josephus Daniels, a newspaper man from North Carolina, another of Wilson's entourage, became Secretary of the Navy (with a brilliant young New Yorker, Franklin D. Roosevelt as his assistant) and a New Jersey lawyer, Lindley M. Garrison, obtained the War Department. A former President of Texas University, David Houston, went to the Department of Agriculture and for the first time in American history a trade unionist and former coal-miner was invited to take charge of the new Department of Labour. On the whole, the Cabinet had a good press, as consisting neither of hack politicians nor corporation lawyers. At the same time new appointments were made to the principal embassies including the dispatch of Wilson's old friend from North Carolina, the cultivated Walter Page, to London and James W. Gerard to Berlin. The clean sweep of the embassies in 1913 had very unfortunate consequences for the American Government, for when eighteen months later war broke out in Europe Wilson lacked the first-class intelligence about the situation which he might have possessed had there been continuity of tenure in these diplomatic posts.

One leading figure who was offered an office by Wilson but refused it was Colonel E. M. House of Texas. House, now the intimate friend of the President, preferred to be the power behind the throne. As early as November 1912 he had announced that although he was more interested in measures than men, he wanted to keep 'on constant watch for good materials from which to select a Cabinet and other important places' so that he might advise Wilson, should he be consulted. Clearly the self-appointed Cabinet-maker could not himself enter the Cabinet. From the beginning House had liked Wilson as being 'a man one could advise with some degree of satisfaction', a thing one could never do with Bryan. Wilson responded warmly to the approaches of this agreeable, sympathetic and resourceful friend. 'Mr. House', he explained, 'is my second personality. He is my independent self. His thoughts and mine are one.' Four days after Wilson became President, he invented a cipher in which he could write to House discussing the members of his Cabinet under pseudonyms — Bryan, for example, was 'Primus'. The world came to know the Texan Colonel as the Silent Partner in the new administration. To House, who himself described Wilson as an 'aloof man' with a 'single-track mind', the President almost alone disclosed his innermost feelings. 'At night after Mr. Wilson had wound the clock, and put out the cats and the politicians, House stayed for a further little talk' (Herbert Corey).

Just as in choosing his Cabinet Wilson had tried to avoid party obligations and had done so at least with partial success, so he planned to sweep his broom at patronage. To the amazement of his experienced Postmaster-General, he demanded to see the whole list of persons nominated as postmasters. 'Now Burleson,' he said, 'I want to say to you that my administration is not going to advise with reactionary or standpat senators or representatives in making these appointments. I am going to appoint forward-looking men and I am going to satisfy myself that they are honest and capable.' Burleson patiently explained to his chief that he could not vet thousands of appointments, that the little offices were of no significance, and that the patronage they provided oiled the wheels of the party machine, that he could only obtain the legislation that he desired by working in harmony with Congress (which had a Democratic majority in both Houses) and that if he antagonized the party leaders he would only cut off his nose to spite his face. In the end the President imbibed the lessons so lucidly taught him by his Postmaster-General.

Wilson did not resign his Governorship of New Jersey until March 1st, 1913, three days before his inauguration as President, because he was determined to complete the work of reform in his own state. During the first months of the year he pressed through the New Jersey Legislature a group of bills known as the 'Seven Sisters' designed to limit the power of trusts within the state. These bills 'too hastily drawn and poorly considered even by

Wilson himself...' were later repealed. Wilson's arrival in the federal capital introduced a more sober tone than did that of the majority of his predecessors, although the Rough Riders of Roosevelt's day had their successors in students from Princeton, for Wilson made it known that he would not hold the customary inaugural ball and refused membership of the select Chevy Chase Country Club. Simplicity and austerity too were the characteristics of his short inaugural address which concluded:

> This is not a day for triumph: it is a day of dedication. Here muster not the forces of party, but the forces of humanity. Men's hearts wait upon us; men's lives hang in the balance, men's hopes call upon us to say what we will do. Who shall live up to the great trust? Who dares fail to try? I summon all honest men, all patriotic, all forwarding-looking men, to my side. God helping me, I will not fail them, if they will counsel and sustain me.

Words apart — and how cheap such words can be — it was in a sincere spirit of self-dedication that Wilson turned to his duties. For although, as we have seen, the new President did not lack those gifts for compromising with party needs that are the hallmark of the democratic politician, his deep religion, his past academic study of the historical problems of government, and his high ambition to fashion a new freedom for the little man created a fervent idealist with fixed notions of right and wrong. His conception of his task was that of a wise social reformer. It was indeed the irony of fate, as he himself feared it might be and in the end realized, that the greater part of his work during his two terms of office was to be spent upon foreign affairs and war.

3. TOWARDS WAR (1913-1917)

The time had now come for Woodrow Wilson to put into practice the somewhat misty promises of his 'New Freedom' and he sprang off at the starter's pistol shot. For it was Wilson's habit, as exemplified both when he was President of Princeton and Governor of New Jersey, to rush his first hurdles. The Democratic party platform had included promises to reform the tariff and currency systems and to introduce anti-trust legislation, and

Wilson was determined to honour the bond. His first move electrified Washington. On April 7th he summoned a special session of Congress, but instead of sending a written message he appeared in person before the members of the two Houses (a practice no President since John Adams had followed) and asked that the tariff duties should be altered to 'meet the radical alteration in the conditions of our economic life'. Of all subjects in American political history that of the tariff was most packed with dynamite. Tariff revision had once brought the country to the edge of civil war. Every Congressman and Senator was aware that he must have his ear to the ground whenever the protection afforded to the industries of his own state was called into question; in no matter was the power of inertia so strong, in nothing was the temptation more irresistible to let sleeping dogs lie. Had not President Theodore Roosevelt, most generously sympathetic but most astute of politicians, left the tariff well alone? But Wilson felt that the tariff provided resources of privilege entirely alien to his concept of the New Freedom. In the new Tariff Bill, sponsored by Congressman Underwood in the House of Representatives and by Senator Simmons in the Senate, Wilson took an eager and active interest. The Bill passed the House without difficulty, but in the Senate its progress was obstructed by the tactics of the,'lobbyists' representing dozens of interests who swarmed into the capital to cajole and to menace. The President decided upon a bold move; on May 28th, 1913, he gave a statement to the press in which he forcibly attacked the machinations of the lobby. Though the Senate resented the implication that its members were approachable and though it was argued that the lobby was a legitimate democratic device, Wilson's statement had the effect of spurring forward the tariff reform movement and after an exhausting struggle the Senate passed the Bill by a narrow majority and Wilson signed it on October 3rd. The Tariff Act reduced duties on a fair range of commodities from an average rate of about 42 to 27 per cent, enlarged the free list to include raw wool, agricultural implements and certain other articles and made sugar free after two and a half years. To meet the expected loss of revenue the Act provided for the introduction of income tax. In September 1916 a Tariff Commission was created with Professor Taussig at its head.

TOWARDS WAR

Before the Underwood-Simmons Bill had been passed by Congress at the behest of the administration Wilson was undertaking an almost equally formidable task, the reform of the currency. History had spread its dark wings over this subject also. The Democratic party tradition, focused for all time by Andrew Jackson, had made clear that a national bank was distasteful to the American people. Yet at the same time the centring of control over national finance in effect in the hands of a group of New York bankers had proved just as unsatisfactory. For years William Bryan had been smiting hip and thigh this new manifestation of the Money Power. What was to be done? Although he had once taught political economy, Wilson made no pretence to be an expert on this prickly subject; as an enlightened conservative he was anxious to promote reform without endangering business. Many were the fervent advisers who came forward, as they come forward in all countries when this absorbing but complex question arises, with their utopias and panaceas. In the first place the idea of a central bank even if it were a Federal Government organ was not politically feasible; indeed the party platform had specifically repudiated the idea of establishing such a bank. Instead, therefore, a decentralized system had to be devised. Credit for being the inventor of the Federal Reserve Bank Scheme is claimed by many, but certainly Congressman Carter Glass of Virginia, Louis D. Brandeis of Boston and Wilson himself all have a right to a share. The problem was to draw up a Bill which would neither alienate progressives like Bryan or the moderate banking interests of the west. The opposition of the eastern bankers who wanted to retain full control had to be taken for granted. Wilson decided firmly that the bankers should not be represented on the board which was to control the currency and credit of the nation. The American Bankers Association and the United States Chamber of Commerce exerted all their influence against the proposed legislation and Wilson was freely accused of dictatorship. The Federal Reserve Act, as it finally emerged, established the principles both of public control and decentralization. The country was divided into twelve banking districts in each of which a reserve bank was set up. All national banks were compelled to become members of a Federal Reserve Bank. Reserve banks were able to rediscount the commercial paper presented to them by member banks and issue notes based on their own reserves. Co-ordination between the policies of the twelve reserve banks was secured by the creation of the Federal Reserve Board which was responsible to the Secretary of the Treasury. The provision of a flexible currency and credit structure was largely the responsibility of the reserve board, but the framers of the Act were careful to lay down conditions under which federal reserve notes could be issued.

Wilson had kept Congress in session throughout the sweating heat of a Washington summer to pass these two important Bills. But they by no means comprised the whole of the economic measures of the first year of his administration. During the following year the Clayton Anti-Trust Act, clarifying the Sherman Act, was passed and a Federal Trade Commission established — measures designed, as Wilson said, 'to destroy monopoly and maintain competition as the only effectual instrument of business liberty'. The Clayton Act prohibited interlocking directorates, defined malpractices by corporations, and held directors personally responsible for violations of the law. The Federal Trade Commission was empowered to investigate complaints of unfair methods by business concerns and order offenders to cease using such methods. One notable feature of Wilson's programme of economic reform was that he showed increasing sympathy towards the point of view of labour. Soon after he became President he approved a rider to a Supply Bill, which previously had been vetoed by President Taft, forbidding the Department of Justice to spend public money on prosecutions of persons who had entered into combinations or agreements to increase wages, reduce hours or better the conditions of labour. The Sherman Anti-Trust Act had in fact, contrary to the original intention, been largely used to prosecute trade unions. This admittedly unsatisfactory method of putting a wrong right was afterwards replaced by clauses in the Clayton Act making it clear that anti-trust legislation was not aimed at trade unions. Later, in his action over a coal strike in Colorado, Wilson employed his influence to secure an agreement rather than allow federal forces to back the cruel ways of strike breaking still commonly employed. Finally in 1916 he championed and signed the Adamson Act providing for an eight-hour day for railwaymen.

Thus Wilson had ensured that the pledges of his party were

TOWARDS WAR

redeemed and had exemplified the doctrine that he had preached since he was a young student of the need for Presidents to be the leaders of Congress in mature legislative programmes rather than mere executives. He had shown himself to be a keen, wise and a careful reformer. Maybe to a contemporary Englishman his reforms seemed far from revolutionary: for most of them had been introduced years earlier into Victorian England. But they must be judged in the light of the development of Wilson's own country, and it must be remembered that they were achieved in the teeth of vigorous and powerful opposition. Unhappily before his programme could be completed, he was swallowed up into a thousand questions of foreign affairs that were to fill his two terms of office.

Wilson's approach to foreign affairs was more academic than his attitude on domestic legislation. Although Bryan was his Secretary of State, like all strong Presidents, Wilson was in large measure his own Foreign Minister. He was reluctant to draw upon the experience of the permanent officials in the State Department — indeed his policy in China caused one of the Assistant Secretaries to resign — his replacement of all the leading ambassadors deprived him of sources of experience and intelligence, and he hamstrung the work of some of his official representatives by his habit of employing 'unofficial observers'. But his foreign policy was completely consistent with his philosophy of politics. Just as in home affairs Wilson preached the gospel of freedom, so in foreign affairs he was an opponent of imperialism and advocated American intervention only in order to ensure that freedom should prevail. Thus he was, on the whole, antagonistic to what was called 'dollar diplomacy', that is to say, to the idea that the conduct of the State Department should be influenced by American investments abroad. Soon after he became President he withdrew the approval of the administration from a plan for a Six-Power loan to China on the ground that it would involve interference with China's independence. At the same time he declared that: 'The United States had nothing to seek in Central and South America except the lasting interests of the peoples of the two continents, the security of governments intended for the people' and the development of trade. But while Wilson repudiated dollar diplomacy, he stressed his interest in the promotion of republicanism and democracy. For this reason he recognized the Chinese Republican Government while his attitude to civil war in Mexico was to bring the United States to the verge of war.

Relations between the United States and Mexico had been uneasy ever since the war in the middle of the nineteenth century, but under the long dictatorship of Porfirio Diaz, American business men and investors had become much interested in the country. Diaz had been succeeded by the liberal President Madero, but the Foreign Minister who described himself as 'the stoic of the woods, the man without a tear', General Huerta, had risen against him and Madero had been assassinated. Consistently with his outlook on foreign policy Wilson refused to recognize Huerta's government, although urged to do so by American business interests and by the American ambassador in Mexico. On the contrary, Wilson said: 'We can have no sympathy with those who seek to seize the power of government to advance their own personal interests or ambition.' Soon conditions in Mexico deteriorated and a revolution directed against Huerta headed by a certain Carranza began. Wilson dispatched in succession two personal representatives to the country and toyed with the idea of sending a message to General Huerta inviting him to hold a free general election and withdraw his candidacy as President. 'I have', he said, 'to pause and remind myself that I am President of the United States and not of a small group of Americans with vested interests in Mexico.' Following his own independent line he therefore dismissed the ambassador, who did not believe in it, and sent one of his own emissaries with his proposals for Mexico's future, to which Huerta not unnaturally failed to respond. This was an even more drastic interpretation of the United States right to interfere in the Western Hemisphere than Roosevelt's 'corollary'. On August 7th Wilson appeared before Congress to explain his Mexican policy and announced that he would request all Americans to leave the country and impose an arms embargo so that neither side in the civil war should receive any aid from American sources. Then he would exercise 'the steady pressure of moral force' for Mexico's own good and pursue a policy of 'watchful waiting'. When, however, Huerta dissolved his own Congress by force, Wilson decided to support Huerta's enemy, Carranza, leader of the 'Constitutionalists', and announced his intention of 'smoking Huerta out'. The purity of Wilson's motives in assisting Mexican self-determination was not called into question, but when in April 1914 some unarmed sailors from an American warship who had landed at Tampico in Mexico to collect supplies were put under arrest by the Huertista forces, he involved himself in some inconsistencies, for he now supported a demand by an American admiral for apologies from the very regime he had refused to recognize. He sent an ultimatum to Huerta threatening the use of force and later marines were landed at Vera Cruz to stop the delivery of German munitions to the Mexican dictator. Yet Wilson promised that under no circumstances would he levy war on the Mexican people. From this imbroglio President Wilson was finally rescued by an offer of mediation by Argentina, Brazil and Chile although between whom and over what they were mediating was not entirely clear. The South American Governments in fact suspected that the United States planned to annex Mexico, as formerly Texas had been annexed and a wave of anti-American feeling pervaded the South American Continent. Thus were maligned the motives of one who sought only peace, order and constitutionalism for others. 'Perfide Albion' had a counterpart. But victory came in the end to the right-minded, for Huerta fled the country and Carranza came into power.

Even this was not the end of the Mexican story, for Carranza proved incapable of restoring order and after the United States forces had withdrawn from Vera Cruz there were a number of incidents in 1915 and 1916 in which American lives and property were menaced, while frontier bandits even raided New Mexico. After a violent exchange of Notes between Carranza, who had proved a determined nationalist, and the State Department, Wilson was obliged to order military action on the frontier, but he was determined not to intervene in Mexican internal affairs if he could possibly avoid it, though at times he admitted he found it hard to restrain his temper. Ultimately a settlement with Carranza was patched up through the appointment of a joint Mexican-American Commission, but it was not until February 1917 that the American troops that had crossed the Mexican border to punish the bandits were finally withdrawn.

For this odd episode in American foreign policy Wilson has been praised by some and blamed by others. His admirers claim that his refusal to recognize the bloody-handed Huerta or to acquiesce in lawlessness and violence was a splendid example of moral leadership. Others represent his diplomacy as an instance of academic blundering which nearly landed his nation in an unwanted war. Certainly it cast a revealing light on the stubbornness of Wilson's character and pointed towards that policy of securing self-determination for foreign nations that Wilson pursued in Europe when the war of 1914-18 ended.

What cannot at any rate be denied is that throughout Wilson acted from the highest motives. He refused to approve wrongdoing or the use of might to attain selfish ends. From the same lofty motives he persuaded Congress to reverse an Act that had been signed by President Taft giving American coastwise shipping exemption from the Panama Canal tolls because he came to the conclusion that, whatever were the rights and wrongs from the business man's point of view, this was inconsistent with American agreements with Britain that all shipping was to be treated alike, and he was prepared to offer a general apology to Colombia because he considered that Theodore Roosevelt's method of acquiring the Canal Zone by supporting the Panama Revolution had been improper. Likewise he approved Bryan's pursuit of a series of general treaties laying down that all questions in dispute between nations which could not be adjusted by diplomacy were to be submitted to investigation and report by an international commission before war was declared. Just as from Roosevelt's day may be traced the beginnings of American imperialism, which culminated in the seeking of Pacific bases, so from Wilson's time may be traced that urge to discuss an agreed path to permanent world peace that found its most complete and innocent expression in the Briand-Kellogg Pact to outlaw war. There is indeed in recent history, as American historians themselves (among them Wilson) have pointed out, an extraordinary duality about the foreign policy of the United States. Wilson showed from the outset of his administration its altruistic side, which reflects one of the finest aspects of the American character. For to do good and be kind and generous is American second nature and often Americans will intervene to help others without being invited; indeed they do not much care to be asked.

TOWARDS WAR

Though Woodrow Wilson found the burdens of the Presidency were heavy, his first months in the White House were very happy. He and his wife and three daughters, known as the 'Three Graces', practised the simplicity and good taste that one associates with the academic life. Ellen Wilson, herself a painter, refurnished some of the rooms with well-chosen chintzes. She also had her charitable interests and particularly concerned herself with the poor living conditions of the Washington Negroes. Woodrow was dependent on his wife's good sense and sympathy — she was, he said, his 'friendly critic' — and she understood his fastidiousness and shared his ideals. In the evenings after the long day's work was done the family would gather round the fireside and the President would sometimes stand up and recite from one of his favourite Lake School poets. Two of the daughters were married in the White House: Jessie to Professor Francis Sayre on November 25th, 1913, and Eleanor to William McAdoo, Secretary of the Treasury, on May 7th, 1914. The third daughter, Margaret, who judging from her photographs, was the spit image of her father, never married. Ellen Wilson had suffered from ill health for some time, but she had not spared herself from her household duties or charitable exertions until in March 1914 a fall drew attention to the seriousness of her condition. Her case was hopeless from the first, although the facts seem to have been kept from her husband. Throughout the heat of another Washington summer as Wilson worked unremittingly, save for a game of golf to keep himself fit, Ellen Wilson's life slowly ebbed away. She died on August 6th, as war broke out in Europe, and her husband accompanied the coffin to Rome in Georgia where, a penniless student, he had found her over thirty years before. 'It seems fateful that she should go just as the world seems crashing to ruin,' Woodrow Wilson wrote to his son-in-law, Francis Sayre, shortly afterwards, 'she could hardly have stood all that. It would have broken her heart.' And so Wilson had to meet the crisis alone, even as Andrew Jackson had confronted the tasks of his first term in 1829. But, as with Jackson, the darkness of bereavement was relieved a few months later by life's perpetual renewal of itself manifested in the birth of a grandchild, the son of Mrs. Francis Sayre, over eighty years after the last child had been born in the White House, the grandson of Andrew Jackson.

WOODROW WILSON

'At the beginning of Wilson's Administration', wrote Professor Charles Seymour, 'there were few citizens of the United States who professed a knowledge of, or an interest in European politics.' It may be doubted if the President himself was especially well informed, although he had visited England several times and had been a teacher of history. For most of his studies had lain in American politics, while during the first two years of his administration he had been chiefly absorbed in American affairs. Yet the United States was a World Power both in a political and commercial sense and had perforce to be concerned over the future of Europe. Indeed Theodore Roosevelt had recognized this when he played his part in the conference of Algeciras. Wilson, however, dependent, as he was, on the view of his new and somewhat raw ambassadors and on such information as could be distilled from the State Department under the aegis of William Jennings Bryan, did not perceive the crisis looming, did not realize that the ordinary men and women in the Old World were sitting on a powder magazine. Indeed in his first inaugural address to Congress the President had forecast an age of 'settled peace and good will', while Bryan's 'cooling off treaties' as they were called, were singularly out of tune with the spirit of the age. Colonel House also had a plan of his own for decreasing armaments. But it was from his Silent Partner that Wilson was to learn the shape of things to come.

In the early summer of 1914 Colonel House had arrived in Europe on what he called his 'Great Adventure' to promote his own pet plan for international peace. He found the omens disturbing. From Berlin he wrote to Wilson: 'The situation is extraordinary. It is militarism run stark mad. Unless someone acting for you can bring about a different understanding there is some day to be an awful cataclysm.' No such atmosphere was noted by him on the other side of the Rhine: 'In France', he wrote, 'I did not find the war spirit dominant', while in London he discovered everyone of importance was thinking about the Ascot races and other society events of the season. While House was upon the high seas coming home from his self-appointed mission the Austro-Hungarian Government sent an ultimatum to Serbia because of the alleged complicity of one of her citizens in the mur der of an Austrian Archduke at Serajevo in Bosnia on July 5th.

TOWARDS WAR

Thus was set on foot the train of events that led to the first World War.

The deep lying causes of the war of 1914-18 cannot be examined here. It is sufficient to say that the 'blank cheque' of support given by the German Government to the Austro-Hungarian Government in its threatening conduct towards Serbia, the long-term preparations made by the German General Staff in concert with the Austrian General Staff for an offensive against France and England, involving the violation of Belgian neutrality, and the complete inability of the civilian government in Germany to restrain the militarists combine to give the war in retrospect the deserved title of the first German War. It did not seem like that at the time to many Americans and Wilson himself evidently thought that there was little to choose between the two sides, on one of which was ranged German Junkers and on the other the unenlightened Russian autocracy.

The last thing that the English people wanted was war. We were at the height of our prosperity — prosperity such as we have never again experienced. Immediately after the Austrian ultimatum to Serbia was known Sir Edward Grey, the British Secretary of State for Foreign Affairs, suggested a conference in London of disinterested Powers to mediate in the dispute. But Austro-Hungary proceeded blindly on a course that in the end was to cause her to vanish from the political map. It was not until three days after the German Emperor had refused to take part in Grey's proposed conference that Wilson sent a message to the American ambassador in England offering 'the good offices of the United States ... in the present crisis'. Grey had to explain that all suggestions for mediation had hitherto been refused, while he not unnaturally inquired whether the offer had been made in any other European capital besides London. Walter Page, who was the United States ambassador, felt that America's traditional policy of isolation weakened her influence as a mediator. In January 1914 he had told House in confidence: 'I see little hope of doing anything so long as we choose to be ruled by an obsolete remark made by George Washington.' Be that as it may, clearly there was nothing Wilson could have done to avert the catastrophe: 'No power on earth could have prevented it', declared Page, as he pointed the finger of guilt at German militarism.

WOODROW WILSON

On August 2nd, 1914, Germany declared war on Russia and on August 3rd declared war on France. On the following day the German army invaded Belgium in the hope (a hope repeated and realized in 1940) of smashing the French in six weeks before turning against the east. That night Great Britain declared war on Germany not because of the entanglements of the balance of power, nor, let it be said, because of the logic of capitalist economics. On the same day Grey saw Page and explained with dignity our obligations to Belgium and to our own honour. 'The principle of the sanctity of treaty rights', he observed, 'was really the test of the progress of civilization, as compared with a state of force and lawlessness; it was the foundation of all confidence between nations.' There had been two sets of people in Germany, he added, and the party of force had won. Were the German armies to sweep across Europe destroying the independence of small nations, then England would cease to be a first-class State. As Grey spoke, his eyes filled with tears. 'Thus', he murmured, 'the efforts of a lifetime go for nothing. I feel like a man who has wasted his life.' 'I came away', said the ambassador, 'with a sort of stunned sense of the impending ruin of half the world.'

In Washington Ellen Wilson lay dying and the ineffable Colonel House wrote to her husband: 'I see here and there regret that you did not use your good offices on behalf of peace.' Wilson had done all he could, for, as Page had said, Europe was not prepared to listen to the voice of sweet reasonableness from across the Atlantic. The President hastened to publish a proclamation of neutrality and to assuage the cries of panic on Wall Street. After he had returned from his wife's funeral he addressed an appeal to his fellow countrymen for steadiness of outlook and neutrality of mind. 'The United States', he said, 'must be neutral in fact as well as in name during these days that are to try men's souls. We must be impartial in thought as well as action . . .' But in this he was asking to much.

After the death of his first wife Woodrow Wilson was described as the 'loneliest man in the world'. With his hair whitening and his heart, as it seemed, broken, he carried on 'by compulsion of ne essity and duty alone'. To seek forgetfulness he read detective stories 'as a man would get drunk'. He sternly lived up to his own

TOWARDS WAR

precept of being impartial in thought and, like many other Americans, honestly regarded the war as an evil accident. In his opinion the whole conflict was worthy of moral condemnation, but his gnawing fear was that the United States might become involved; with prophetic accuracy he declared: 'I am afraid that something will happen on the high seas that will make it impossible for us to keep out of the war.'

From the beginning Wilson's policy in relation to the war in Europe had two aspects. In the first place he had to try to offset its effects on American economy. Secondly, he desired to keep his own country out of the war. These two ends were not necessarily compatible, for the United States at this time was still a debtor nation and had to export in order to live. The preservation of the export trade required the free movement of American commerce on the high seas. But it was the German objective to prevent American exports from reaching Great Britain or France to succour the Allies and it was the aim of the British and French navies to maintain a close blockade of Germany and to prevent goods useful to the Central Powers from filtering through such neutral States as Holland. If the United States Government were to insist on the maximum amount of freedom for foreign trade, then it could only do so by threats of active intervention which might lead, as they had led in 1812, to war with one or other of the belligerents. Thus Woodrow Wilson had to walk along a tricky tightrope often in an undignified manner while ardent nationalists, pacifists and Republicans watched not unhopefully to see if he would fall off. Moreover there was another facet to his policy; if he deviated a hair's breadth from neutrality, he was bound to antagonize some section of the electorate. The German-Americans were a powerful influence, particularly in certain states, such as Missouri, and, as in the second German War, the German diplomatic representatives did not hesitate to take advantage of the fact. Even the most loyal Americans of German extraction naturally had some sympathy with the Fatherland in its struggle for European domination as an alternative to utter defeat, and there was always an election not more than two years ahead. Although foreign policy does not seem to have played a major part in the mid-term elections of November 1914, the contest was sufficiently sharp to make it necessary for Wilson not to alienate any section of opinion. In spite of considerable efforts by Wilson to keep his party together, the Democrats only just retained their hold on the two Houses in 1915.

Wilson's plans for helping American industry and trade to weather the storms of war were various. His administration made a determined attempt to create a mercantile marine, for before 1914 American exporters had largely depended upon the carrying trade of other nations. The administration's scheme was to establish a government corporation to buy or build merchant ships. The scheme was opposed not only by those who disliked the idea of any form of State Socialism but also by the Allied Governments who feared that if the American Government purchased the German ships that had been tied up in the United States ports at the outbreak of war this would be of substantial if indirect benefit to their enemy. The Shipping Bill passed the House of Representatives quickly but met with determined resistence in the Senate and did not finally become law — and then not in its original form — until late in 1916. It was in connection with the opposition to this Bill that Wilson coined his famous phrase: 'You cannot fight rottenness with rosewater.'

Among other economic measures the Treasury loaned vast sums of emergency currency to steady the banks and to help the farmers government credits were forthcoming. Later the federal reserve system did much to assist in keeping down interest rates. A cotton loan fund was also started to enable southern planters to hold their crop until conditions improved and a Bureau of War Insurance was established to aid shippers. But these measures were at the best palliatives and what really helped American industry on its way was the stream of orders for goods and above all for munitions for the Allied nations — a stream that led in the end to a burst of feverish prosperity. The State Department accepted the conclusion that there was nothing in international law to prevent the export of munitions to a belligerent nation and orders from the Allied armies proved of immense benefit to American business. On the other hand, President Wilson at first resisted the lending of money to belligerent Powers to help them to maintain their flow of orders. In August 1914 he authorized an announcement to J. P. Morgan and Company: 'There is no reason why loans should not be made to the governments of neutral nations, but in the

TOWARDS WAR

judgment of this government, loans by American bankers to a foreign nation which is at war are inconsistent with the true spirit of neutrality.' However even this embargo was soon abandoned and by October of the same year the French Government had successfully negotiated a large loan in the United States. The decision not to ban the export of munitions and to allow the raising of loans inevitably aided the Allies at the expense of Germany and Austria-Hungary. For the British Government remained adamant in its determination to prevent American goods — even food and cotton — from reaching Germany. At first in order to preserve his policy of strict impartiality Wilson tried to persuade the British Government to adhere to the principles of the Declaration of London of 1909 with regard to the freedom of the seas. But neither the British nor the Americans themselves had ratified this declaration at the time and the efforts of the State Department to define principles of international law that would in fact have been of advantage to Germany were of no avail. Instead Walter Page, the American ambassador in London who was openly sympathetic with the Allied cause, protested much to Wilson's indignation at the ingenuities of the 'library lawyers'. Sir Edward Grey, who well knew how much the British cause depended on American good will, did his utmost not to hurt Wilson's susceptibilities on the subject of neutral rights. But few concessions were yielded, for, as the British ambassador in Washington expressed it: 'We each wish to defend our rights. But I am sure you will remember that the rights we are defending are our existence.' In truth Wilson's protests on the subject of neutral rights were handicapped by the fact that, as he himself confessed in 1915, 'the vast majority of the American people', were 'genuinely friendly in their attitude towards Great Britain'. And gradually under the persuasions of Page and to a lesser extent of House, it seems that Wilson's own attitude became friendly too. At least he was rigorously determined not to fight Britain in the name of international law, as President Madison had done in 1812, and thereby bestow victory on Germany.

On April 22nd, 1915, the German Embassy in Washington published a notice warning American travellers that if they sailed to the European 'war zone' on British or Allied ships, they did so at their own risk. The notice appeared in the American newspapers on May 1st and six days later the British ship *Lusitania* was sunk by a German submarine off Ireland and over a hundred American lives lost. This was the culmination of a number of such incidents provocative to American temper. Wilson and Bryan, however, kept their tempers well and sought means to avert a break with Germany. While a Note was being prepared Wilson delivered a speech in the course of which he said: 'The example of America must be a special example. The example of America must be the example not merely of peace because it will not fight, but of peace because peace is the healing and elevating influence of the world and strife is not. There is such a thing as a man being too proud to fight. There is such a thing as a nation being so right that it does not need to convince others by force that it is right.' The speech (which was much criticized) in fact contained the essence of Wilson's thought on the questions of peace and war during this trying period. Profound believer in a moral purpose in the life of nations, as of individuals, and in the strength of moral ideas to save mankind, he feared that once his government deviated from neutral thought or moved towards the arena of war it would lose its influence for good and become tainted with the evils that war itself generates. In his history books Wilson had condemned most of the wars in which his country had taken part, which he thought could have been avoided by wiser statesmanship. Though not, like the Quakers, an adherent of peace at all costs or a believer in the power of passive resistance to attain moral ends (the only logical form of pacifism) he was deeply pacific in his outlook and dreaded war as an evil thing. But his hand was on the wheel. While he managed to avert war over the *Lusitania* incident by writing a Note to the German Government which did not have the character of an ultimatum, his position was weak because in times of war nations are inclined to ignore the spectator who stands on the side lines raising his hands in horror. The United States was known by the combatants to be ill prepared to intervene and hence her advice was disregarded. More attention was of course paid to American feelings by the Allies than by the German group because the former depended on American supplies as a life-line. But certainly neither the British nor the French people could be expected, as Wilson hoped, to see all their sacrifices

TOWARDS WAR

vanish in a 'peace without victory' under the mediation of a Great Power that had taken no part in the struggle. Another inconsistency of Wilson's attitude was that at heart he and the majority of the American people sympathized with the democracies and abhorred the brutalities of German methods, exemplified not merely in the submarine warfare which directly injured them, but also in their treatment of Belgian and French civilians, foreshadowing the cruelties of a later war. On more than one accasion Wilson told his Secretary, Tumulty, 'England is fighting our fight'. Finally it must not be forgotten that the point of view of the man who is fighting is very different from that of the man who is not. It was after all an American Democratic President, a man who served in the Wilson Administration, who fastened on the United Nations in the second German War the terrible and mistaken doctrine of 'unconditional surrender'.

From the time of the sinking of the *Lusitania* events led Wilson's administration inexorably towards participation in the war. Wilson fought against events, as the hero of a Greek tragedy fights against the gods. His Note to Germany lost him the services of Bryan and his unwillingness to approve extreme measures of military preparation, on the other side, involved the resignation of his Secretary of War. In the early months of 1916, as the natural consequence of the sinking of the *Lusitania* Wilson opened a campaign for military preparedness, appealed for a big navy, and created a Council of National Defence. Again in the spring of 1916 Wilson postponed the fatal hour when the torpedoing of an unarmed French steamer, the *Sussex*, with Americans on board angered American opinion and induced Lansing, who had replaced Bryan as Secretary of State, to tell the President that the time for writing Notes had passed. However another Note was written, this time containing the menace that diplomatic relations would be broken, which exacted a promise from the German Government to modify its submarine campaign. In pursuit of the elusive practice of impartiality (elusive because it was in fact American money and American munitions that helped the Allies to sustain the fight) Wilson then used a firmer tone towards the British Government whose 'black listing' of American firms trading with the enemy 'got on his nerves'. The British Government took little notice of the protest even though a 'stronger note' was threatened. On December 18th, 1916 Wilson exerted his most powerful effort to bring about peace, partly at German instigation, for the German Chancellor seems to have hoped that a peace move at this date might weaken his enemies, by asking each side to state its terms. The President followed this by a great speech (January 22nd, 1917) in which he strove to appeal to the peoples of Europe over the heads of their rulers. This was the speech in which he introduced the phrase 'peace without victory', a phrase that was as unwelcome to the Allies as its democratic approach was to the leaders of Germany and Austria-Hungary. All Wilson's dreams of mediation — and they were never more than dreams — vanished, however, when on February 1st the Germans announced their intention of introducing unrestricted submarine warfare. When Wilson heard the news, he turned grey and said: 'This means war. The break that we have tried so hard to prevent now seems inevitable.' Diplomatic relations with Germany were at once broken off.

Even now the President delayed taking decisive action. His reluctance to order the arming of American merchant ships caused his own Cabinet to revolt against him. Yet when he appealed to Congress for approval of this step and a minority in the Senate obstructed approval, he was obliged to act. Throughout the early spring of 1917 Wilson tried hard to stem the torrent rushing him towards war. He saw America's moral strength being lost, he feared that 'war would overturn the world we had known', he hated the idea of a 'dictated peace' without bystanders 'with sufficient power to influence the terms'. Meanwhile the U-boats went their terrifying way sinking American vessels without warning while the disclosure of a German communication promising to stir up trouble for the United States in Mexico (the 'Zimmermann Note') inflamed American opinion. The March Revolution in Russia reduced scruples against fighting for the Allies, for now they would all be democracies together in a war to make the world safe for democracy. On April 2nd, 1917, on a dark and rainy evening Wilson drove to the House of Representatives to ask for a declaration of war in the name of democracy 'to make the world itself at last free'. 'God helping her,' the President said, 'the United States could do no other than dedicate herself to the task of winning right and peace through military victory.' When his speech had ended Senator Cabot Lodge, friend of Theodore Roosevelt and one of Wilson's most constant critics, shook the President's hand and said: 'You have expressed in the loftiest manner the sentiments of the American people.'

4. THE LEAGUE OF NATIONS (1917-1923)

When Wilson became war leader, he had never felt in better form or health. Once again his domestic life was tranquil, for just before Christmas 1915 he had married again. His second wife was a pleasing and educated Virginian lady, Mrs. Norman Galt (born Edith Bolling) who had been seven years a widow when she met Wilson in the spring of 1915 almost by accident. Soon the romance became public gossip, and since it was the President of the United States who was concerned it was gossip of the most repulsive kind. The two southerners exercised upon each other their characteristic charm; the widower sent the widow orchids saying: 'You are the only woman I know who can wear an orchid. Generally it is the orchid that wears the woman.' Wilson was enough of a politician to postpone his wedding until after the midterm election, but soon afterwards the ceremony took place at the bride's home; during the honeymoon Wilson celebrated his fifty-ninth birthday. It was fortunate for Wilson that his second wife was a golfer; for after their marriage they used regularly to rise early each morning to play a round of golf together and thus he was able to keep fit without meeting curious or mocking eyes. His wife was a solid and devoted worker and on occasions, like Madame de Maintenon, found that her opinions on foreign affairs were invited. Her aid was to prove invaluable to the President.

Another cause for personal satisfaction was his re-election in 1916, though only by a small majority. There was no question about his renomination — 'You are the only Democrat who can be elected', confessed one of the members of his Cabinet — but the party was less popular in the country because there were causes for irritation over domestic policy. The Underwood-Simmons Tariff, for example, was disliked in many interested quarters, while food and cotton producers resented the administration's inability to reduce the interference of the British blockade with their trade to Europe. Fortunately for Wilson his opponents were neither magnetic nor unscrupulous. Theodore Roosevelt was not a candidate and had vainly tried to force the reactionary Henry Lodge on to the Progressive party which he had created in 1912, while the official Republican candidate, Judge Charles Hughes, was so like his chief antagonist that he was dubbed a 'whiskered Wilson'. Hughes was also an honest man; the story was told that when he was asked at an election meeting whether he would have acted differently from the President over the sinking of the *Lusitania*, he simply coughed. Be that as it may, Wilson's chief claim to be re-elected rested on the slogan: 'He kept us out of war' and this slogan tended to be transmuted into the phrase: 'He will keep us out of war.' Thus the pacific and isolationist vote came his way. Wilson himself, it is true, gave no promise of peace in the future as he knew only too well the difficulties ahead. The election was so closely contested that it was not until the results from California came in that Wilson realized that he had not been beaten. Narrow though his majority was (some half million votes) it gave him content and the power to press forward into the world war.

As a war leader Wilson profited from Abraham Lincoln's example and Abraham Lincoln's mistakes. He followed his example by exerting to the full the powers conferred upon him in his capacity of Commander-in-Chief by the Constitution. On the other hand, unlike Lincoln, he refused to allow himself to be hamstrung by Congressional committees. Wilson showed — and Franklin Roosevelt was to show too — that never is the President of the United States more powerful than when a war is in progress. Wilson used his power to send an expeditionary force to France, to create a Committee of Public Information, and to establish a War Industries Board. At the same time he formed a kind of War Cabinet including a food and fuel controller, while he took over the railways and used his influence with the legislature to secure conscription or, as the system was called, 'selective service' — for men regarded as necessary in civilian work were excluded from the draft. Some pressure was exerted upon him to include Republicans in his Cabinet, but he decided against this, although he appointed a number of Republicans to important administrative posts. Wilson's drawbacks as an organizer of victory derived from the hesitant and pacific attitude he had adopted before the war

THE LEAGUE OF NATIONS

(the same applied to Neville Chamberlain). His 'preparedness campaign' of early 1916 was not much more than a gesture, as the army he proposed to create consisted of only 400,000 men to be trained over a period of three years rather sketchily by officers of the National Guard, the American citizen army. The result was, according to one of his biographers, that the American people 'entered the war almost totally unprepared so far as the army was concerned'. Again though Wilson was extremely critical of British naval policy he never appears to have understood the importance of defeating the submarine campaign and detected something Machiavellian in British insistence on the need to build destroyers. Similarly he hesitated in approving financial assistance for the Allies and when he did so he had an ulterior motive in view. 'England and France', he wrote to House in July 1917, *'have not the same views with regard to peace that we have*, by any means. When the war is over we can force them to our way of thinking, because by that time they will, among other things, be financially in our hands.' Indeed there was always a degree of distrust between the President and the leaders of the European Powers desperately engaged in resisting Germany. (He refused to call them his Allies, but only Associates.) Were they fighting, he wondered, for the *right* motives? Were they truly democratic in their outlook? Had they, as he had, 'no hate in their hearts for the German people?' Did they appreciate that they were engaged on 'a People's War'? Incorrigibly idealistic in his approach, Wilson was yet compelled by the logic of events to repudiate many of the ideals for which he had struggled so long before the United States entered the war. When the Pope proposed 'peace without victory', the President stiffly opposed any such notion; his administration joined with the British Government in 'black listing' neutrals who traded with the enemy though he himself had earlier protested with indignation against this system; and he was handicapped in the highly pitched speeches he delivered in support of the war effort by his own earlier conviction that the two sides had been fighting over nothing.

As against certain feebleness in Wilson's war administration — amounting at times almost to palsy — it is fair to say that the President trusted his generals and discouraged civilian interference with the military conduct of the war. His influence was stubbornly directed to the support of conscription, as recommended by his military advisers, and he gave unstinting backing to General Pershing, Admiral Sims and his Chief of Staff, all of whom were Republicans. His loyalty to Walter Page, his ambassador in London, whose sympathy for the Allies was often a subject of criticism, provided a valuable link with the Powers struggling for survival in Europe, and, as it came to the crux, he was not found wanting. When in March 1918 the British Ambassador in Washington appealed to him urgently for aid in staying the great German offensive he replied in a phrase that was to become famous: 'Mr. Ambassador, you need say no more. I will do my damnedest.'

To Woodrow Wilson the voice of the people was the voice of God and he was the people's spokesman. The people of the United States, he explained, had been forced into war by the Military Masters of Germany who had 'denied them the right to be neutral'. But, he reminded his fellow countrymen, 'we are not the enemies of the German people — this was a People's War against autocracy and it had to end in a People's Peace'. Such was the conception that dominated the President's thoughts and actions as his country mobilized. If his convictions did not entirely square with the facts, he overlooked the facts or refused to recognize their existence. For instance, there were those unfortunate 'secret treaties' made between the Associated Governments without any consultations with their peoples before the United States had gone to war. Balfour, the British Secretary of State for Foreign Affairs who had succeeded Grey visited Washington in 1917 and told Wilson all about them. They were, it seemed to the British, essential conditions for winning the war before the American people had been compelled by the Military Masters of Germany to abandon their neutrality. Nor was there anything fundamentally immoral from the purely historical point of view about a secret treaty — except of course that secret treaties could never be concluded by the Government of the United States for all treaties had to have the approval of the Senate, which debates them.

It was on the basis then that this was a people's war that Wilson was able to rejoice when the Russian people rose in arms and overthrew their military masters. The British, French and Italians, whatever their faults — and they were many — were at least democracies; now Russia would become one; and Japan . . .

THE LEAGUE OF NATIONS

Japan was a long way off. All the Associated Powers were thus in the same boat and beware the man who rocked it. The Russian 'people' were beginning to rock it a little, for in the winter of 1917-18 Lenin had opened negotiations with the Germans in Brest Litowsk. It was in response to the pleading voices of the Russian people 'prostrate and all but helpless' with 'their souls . . . not subservient' that President Wilson on January 1918 laid down his Fourteen Points, 'the only possible programme of the world's peace'. Wilson's thunder had been to some extent stolen by the British Prime Minister, David Lloyd George, in a speech three days earlier in which he had declared that the Allies were not fighting a war of aggression against Germany and would seek a settlement of the New Europe based 'on such grounds of reason and justice as will give some promise of stability'. Wilson, after paying lip service to the unity that prevailed among the adversaries of the Central Powers outlined his ideas of peace conditions. First of all came his advocacy of 'open covenants . . . openly arrived at . . .' Could an American President have done otherwise? But it was a blow at the Old Diplomacy and a shrewd slap at the misdeeds of his Associates. Then came the demand for 'absolute freedom of navigation on the sea' — a clear requirement that the British navy should never again be in a position to obstruct American trade in the name of belligerent rights. Next he sought the removal of all economic barriers and the reduction of national armaments. Having put Europe in its place, Wilson turned to his schemes for territorial settlement. The Fourteenth Point stated that 'a general association of nations must be formed under specific covenants for the purpose of affording mutual guarantees of political independence and territorial integrity to great and small States alike'. Except for the Ninth Point relating to the future Italian frontiers (to be drawn 'along clearly recognizable lines of nationality') Wilson's Associates did not actively object to the later points. The Fourteen Points in fact exemplified the academic mind at its best and most liberal. Perhaps it might have been more courteous to have consulted his Associates before plunging into such detail? — but still this was the American outlook and these the American ideals. The programme or 'moral offensive' was explained a little further in a speech delivered by Wilson six months later at Mount Vernon known as the 'Four Point Speech' in which he came out for the 'destruction of every arbitrary power anywhere that can separately, secretly, and of its simple choice disturb the peace of the world'. In this speech was to be seen more clearly the doctrine of self-determination which Wilson was to impress on the peace conference, just as the doctrine of legitimacy had been imposed by Metternich on another peace conference a hundred years earlier.

In time of war ideals are liable to get tipped overboard. For instance, it was all very well for Wilson to expound his peace policy for the enlightenment of the prostrate Slavs and to send wishes of warm sympathy to the Russian people (the Bolsheviks had replied to Wilson's message by expressing the hope that the American people too would 'throw off the yoke of capitalism') but the difficulty was that the terms of the treaty of Brest Litowsk (between Russia and Germany) were likely to provide aid, comfort and a useful supply of arms to the enemy that the American doughboy was about to fight. Hence Wilson was driven to approve of a military plan to intervene in Russia so long as the plan did not involve interference with the internal affairs of the Russian people. In the end his compromise pleased nobody.

From these problems, in which the spirit of sweet reasonableness and the professorial plea for self-determination struggled with the brutal realities of military facts, Wilson was rescued when on October 6th, 1918, Prince Maximilian of Baden, the new German Chancellor, sent a note inviting the President to discuss peace terms on the basis of the Fourteen Points. Colonel House advised his friend not to reply before he had consulted the Allies and noted that he had begun to appreciate that the people of his own country were against 'anything but unconditional surrender'. The truth was too — and this, under the hammering of Hitlerite propaganda, was later widely forgotten — that the Germans had in fact now been beaten on the field of battle. Yet Wilson felt that if the offer was made by 'a reputable government, it would be impossible to decline it'. Therefore without consulting anyone he sent a note asking the German Chancellor in effect to secure the abdication of the Kaiser and set up a democratic government with which other democratic governments might deal. On October 21st the reply came that the German Reichstag was to have full powers in regard to peace and war. Thereupon Wilson dispatched Colonel House to Paris with instructions to abtain the agreement of the

Big Three (Britain, France and Italy) to making peace on the foundation of his Fourteen Points. House threatened that if they did not accept the President's programme Wilson might ask Congress to withdraw from the war and even negotiate a separate peace. Under pressure of this menace the Big Three crumpled, seeking to modify but not to repudiate the Fourteen Points. Lloyd George would not accept the 'freedom of the seas'. (Wilson could not distinguish between the aggressiveness of the British navy and the German army, though the power of the British navy had long acted as a shield to his expanding nation) and the French demanded reparations. The Germans were then informed that they would be granted an armistice and three days later the guns ceased fire.

While Colonel House was bludgeoning the statesmen of the Old World with the weapons of New World diplomacy, Wilson was trying to beguile the American people. On October 25th he had appealed to his fellow countrymen (he had already promised the women the vote) to return Democratic majorities to Congress in the mid-term elections. In ordinary times, he explained, he would not have written such an appeal. But a defeat in the elections would 'certainly be interpreted on the other side of the water as a repudiation of my leadership'. The American electorate, irritated, as the most enlightened democracies can be, by the discomforts and restrictions arising out of war, did not respond, but voted so as to ensure that there was a small Republican majority in each House. It was under such somewhat discouraging circumstances — for the Senate would be required to approve the peace treaties — that Wilson at the beginning of December 1918 embarked on the liner *George Washington* to take a personal part in the Congress of Versailles that was to make the world safe for democracy.

The President's decision to go to France himself to share in the deliberations of the peace conference met with much adverse comment. He was the first American President to leave the shores of his native land during his term of office. Ought he to neglect his duties in Washington? And was it not to detract from the dignity of his position for him to descend into the hurly-burly of the diplomatic arena to argue matters as other men? True, the Prime Ministers were to be there, but is not the American President more than a Prime Minister — the formal embodiment of the Federal Union — as well as in point of his effective powers something less? But Wilson could not be dissuaded. He felt — and felt rightly — that many ordinary citizens throughout the world depended upon him to see that the ideals which he had advocated and summarized in the Fourteen Points should be realized. It was up to him to ensure that the principle of self-determination should be sanctified by the treaties and the League of Nations established as an effective organization. Though there was much to be said for his resolve to be present, it is certainly questionable if his entourage was wisely chosen. The prominent place given to his dear friend, House, was well calculated to affront his Secretary of State, Robert Lansing, while his failure to invite any prominent Republican, such as ex-President Taft, to be a peace commissioner proved to be an error. He needed more than the support of the justice of his cause and of the charming Henry White (erstwhile Republican diplomatist) to induce a Congress with a Republican majority to rubber-stamp his decisions.

The first meeting of the Council of Ten (that is to say the five leaders of the delegations of the United States, Britain, France, Italy and Japan and the Foreign Ministers of those countries) did not take place until January 12th so that Wilson had time to visit England and Italy. In London though he received a rapturous reception from the crowds he made a chilly impression by some austere observations on American moral leadership. In Italy, after he had been given the freedom of the city of Rome, he was prevented from addressing the common people because the politicians were annoyed over his known antagonism to their territorial aspirations. Back in Paris the sun shone more warmly for him and he worked with his usual concentrated energy, employing the favourite little typewriter on which he wrote all his private letters and documents of State. He himself became chairman of the commission (which included Robert Cecil and General Smuts) that drew up the Covenant of the League of Nations. Wilson, it must be understood, was not the originator of the idea of such a league nor was he even its first or most exuberant sponsor during the war. Indeed Taft and the League to Enforce Peace in the United States and the Phillimore Committee in England did most to lay the foundations of the Covenant. It was not until May 1916 that

THE LEAGUE OF NATIONS

Wilson publicly announced his adherence to the principle. But he laboured to give the Covenant shape and force. His own deepest interest was to ensure that it should contain Article X, guaranteeing the territorial integrity and political independence of the member States. The commission had to work in the evenings so as not to interfere with the plenary sessions that met in the daytime. Thus Wilson toiled incessantly and not in vain. He had to give way over one or two points — for example, he had wanted the colonial territories that were to be administered as League Mandates to be the responsibility of the small Powers — but on the whole he attained his ends. The draft of the Covenant was accepted by the plenary session of the conference and was, as he wished, to become an integral part of the peace treaty.

As soon as the Covenant had been accepted by the conference Wilson travelled back for a month to the United States. He went first to Boston where he received an enthusiastic welcome; but the atmosphere in Washington was rather difficult. It is true that he invited the members of the Senate Foreign Relations Committee to dinner and patiently discussed the Covenant with them for hours; but Senator Borah of Idaho of bushy hair and silver voice, who was to be the leader of the irreconcilable isolationists, had refused to come to the dinner and before Wilson left again for Paris thirty-seven Republican Senators had announced that they would not give their approval to the constitution of the League in the form in which it stood. Moreover the Republican majority made it clear that they were not going to allow the President to stay out of the country much longer. Thus it was in a bitter mood that Wilson made a rough crossing back to France, although he does not then seem to have recognized the strength of the opposition to the League by which he set so many hopes.

Poor Colonel House received the brunt of the President's temper for Wilson did not care for the compromises which he advocated. The French had indeed been staking high claims. They lived close to the Germans: they had fought with them twice in the last fifty years; and they had a shrewd idea of what they were like. The French Government did not fancy either the British guarantees of arbitration under the League or Wilson's guarantee under Article X as a means of stopping future German aggression. What they sought was the occupation of the Rhineland. Wilson now proposed that if the French would be content with demilitarization and temporary occupation the American Government would come to the assistance of France if the Germans should violate the terms of the treaty before the League began to function. Lloyd George had made a similar offer on behalf of Great Britain. But the British Prime Minister was sure of being able to fulfil his offer and the President was not. In fact the very suggestion stirred up a hornet's nest in Washington. Wilson clung to his belief that the voice of the people would speak for him and that the League would right every wrong. But meanwhile the Senate was demanding amendments to the Covenant — excluding the Monroe Doctrine from its sphere, permitting freedom to refuse mandates, allowing the United States Government to leave the League without notice and so on. Thus Wilson's authority at Paris was undermined and the Allied statesmen not unnaturally exploited his difficulties to achieve their own objectives. They refused to recognize that the monopoly of virtue was on the American side. They could not understand why the British navy should be weakened, the French army deprived of its security or the Italian State of its best frontiers in return for American participation in a League the effectiveness of which the American delegates themselves were now trying to reduce. So Wilson was obliged to give way over the occupation of the Saar, over German reparations and over Japanese demands in China. Only on Italy's claim to Fiume and Dalmatia Wilson refused to yield — though he sought a compromise — and he even lost confidence in House who had served him so loyally.

The Treaty of Versailles and the other treaties signed at the conclusion of the first German War were, as they had to be, when so many Allies were concerned in them, a mass of compromises. Everyone had his own fears and desires. The American interest was to settle a troublesome Europe and see that its squabbles did not again drag the United States into war. Wilson believed that the League of Nations was the right means to secure this, as against those who thought that disinterestedness and a strong navy were better ways of keeping their country out of war. Thus Wilson had to hedge over his own proposals and in hedging had to make concessions to the demands of others. Both the treaties and the League Covenant were therefore compromises, but it is mere ignorance to maintain that they were the products of greedy or stupid men. Few major injustices were to be found in the treaties and looking back from our present historical vantage point it can scarcely be said they erred on the side of harshness. As to the League it came near to success and was the first embodiment of an idea which seems to many to be the only logical method of stopping wars, if wars are ever to cease on the face of the earth.

The negotiations were completed in difficult days when, as it seemed to Colonel House, the world was crumpling and Communism was spreading across Europe. During the conference Wilson was painted by Sir William Orpen who, according to House, caught the President's 'rough-and-tumble' look as a contrast with John Sargent's early painting of the aesthetic scholar. Yet though worn and tired after the struggle Woodrow Wilson returned home in July 1919 in good spirits; he had little idea of the fierceness of the fresh struggle that awaited him. After all, he had at some cost to the other ideals in which he believed secured the amendments to the Covenant for which recalcitrant Senators had clamoured. It is true that he recognized that the Senate, emerging after the war to its full status in the Constitution, was in a critical mood. But no Senate had ever before rejected a treaty of such importance and if it was not going to reject the treaty, it could not reject the League of Nations, for had he not carefully embodied the Covenant in the treaty? The Democratic Senators could be forced to toe the line and as for the Republicans surely they would not dare to defy the will of the people, for whom Wilson believed he spoke? But the trouble was that he underestimated his critics. 'The Senate', he said, 'is going to ratify the Treaty.' But a two-thirds majority had to be obtained and the reasoned case of the critics of the League was fortified in the realm of practical politics by many forms of ignorance and prejudice. Senator Henry Lodge was not only a clever and cultivated man but a skilled politician. Senators Borah, Hiram Johnson of California and Frank L. Brandagee of Connecticut though determined bigots were less dangerous to Wilson than Lodge because Lodge understood the importance of uniting divergent forces — the reactionaries, the pacifists, the powerful anti-British groups (such as the Irish) and those who wanted only further mild amendments to the Covenant in one block. Furthermore when the fight over the League began it was only about a year to the next presidential election and since

WOODROW WILSON

Wilson was not expected to stand for a third term (although he gave no pronouncement about this) his power automatically waned. Lastly as events proved, time was against Wilson.

Wilson fought with all his skill and experience for the Versailles settlement. He was convinced that the American people were on his side and that most of the opposing Senators were men of little moment. Unfortunately for him these were complicated questions on which a democracy is ill fitted to decide. The ordinary man in the street was not going to read the large volume that comprised the treaty nor could he be expected to understand the complex legal and political arguments that ranged round Article X of the Covenant. For instance, there was the appeal to history. Ex-Professor Wilson of Princeton had one view about what George Washington and Thomas Jefferson had thought on the subject of foreign policy and ex-Professor Lodge of Harvard had another: how could one judge? Wilson, it has been said, tended to regard the Senators as a class of rather stupid students, though he did his utmost to instruct them. In an historic interview on August 19th, 1919, with the members of the Senate Foreign Relations Committee he put his case as best he knew how, giving frank answers to Lodge's searching questions and boldly defending Article X on the ground that no government could be obliged to apply force in support of the provisions of the League Covenant without its own consent. But Wilson could neither persuade the Senators that the United States had not been committed to involvement in European affairs, nor could he make headway against the diatribes of the irreconcilables among men who, he asserted, were 'poisoning the wells of public opinion'. He saw but one resource and that was to appeal to the people. In September after the session of Congress closed, he set out on a speaking tour of the middle west, far west and south to plead for the League.

Wilson had already suffered one breakdown to health when he was in Paris although its seriousness had been concealed. He had worked his nervous machine hard all his life and the attacks of neuritis in his Princeton days had been the presage of what was to come. His old friend and personal doctor, Rear Admiral Grayson, had warned him of the danger to his health in going on the speaking tour, but Wilson had replied that he could not put his health in the balance against the future peace and security of the world.

THE LEAGUE OF NATIONS

'I promised our soldiers when I asked them to take up arms that it was a war to end wars,' he told Grayson, 'and if I do not do all in my power to put the Treaty into effect I will be a slacker and never able to look those boys in the eye. I must go.' The plan was to deliver a hundred speeches before the end of September. The strain was enormous. Yet though Wilson suffered from increasingly severe headaches he never ceased to smile and be gracious and everywhere he had tremendous receptions. But he could not stay the course. On the night of September 25th after a moving speech at Pueblo (Colorado) he collapsed, and was never able to make a public speech again. 'The seal he put on his lips in that hour was never broken in all the long hard years ahead. Never once did he voice a syllable of self-pity, complaint or regret.' It was not, however, until after he returned to Washington on October 2nd that he was struck down with paralysis on the left side of his body. Some of his admirers believed that had he been able to carry on the fight a little longer he would indeed have compelled the Senate by the force of public opinion to accept the Treaty of Versailles. One cannot help but speculate how the history of the world might have been altered if Wilson had had broadcasting at his disposal.

The rest of the story is anticlimax. Senator Lodge for the more moderate group of his opponents drafted fourteen reservations to the League Covenant, one at least of which — dealing with Article X — would have undermined its whole conception. Wilson when consulted — his mind was clear in spite of his illness — refused to agree to what he regarded as wrecking proposals and indeed he rejected any reservations whatever. 'Better a thousand times', he told his wife, 'to go down fighting than to dip your colours to dishonourable compromise.' On Wilson's instructions the Democratic Senators voted against the ratification of the treaty as modified by Lodge's fourteen reservations. On the other hand, the Senate refused to ratify the treaty as it stood by the requisite two-thirds majority. Fifty-three voted for it and thirty-eight against. After prolonged and complicated manœuvres the Treaty of Versailles was finally rejected in the spring of 1920 as was also the French Security Treaty to which Wilson had given his assent, although the American Government did not waive any of its rights under the Treaty of Versailles. On May 27th, 1920, Wilson wrote a letter to the House of Representatives condemning the settlement and declaring that such a peace 'is and ought to be inconceivable, is inconsistent with the dignity of the United States, with the rights and liberties of her citizens, and with the very fundamental conditions of civilization'. Thus the chief executive had no part in his government's handling of present or future foreign policy.

In the early weeks of the President's illness virtually no one was permitted to see him except his wife and his doctor who were nicknamed the Twin Proconsuls. Bills became law without his signature, a few papers were referred to him, apparently at Mrs. Wilson's discretion, and others were passed out to members of the Cabinet. An attempt made to hold a Cabinet meeting without him resulted in his dismissing Lansing, the Secretary of State, who had summoned it. Then Wilson began to see a few visitors such as the King and Queen of the Belgians and the Prince of Wales, and there was an embarrassing visit from two Senators who had patently called to satisfy their colleagues that Wilson was of sound mind. The President, bitter and morose, greatly resented this visit from what he called 'a smelling committee'.

Wilson was determined to get well, but his case was hopeless. In the spring of 1920 he was allowed to move about in a wheel chair and was taken motor drives. He even held one or two Cabinet meetings, although he soon tired. But domestic political affairs were neglected and what he did was chiefly of a negative character: for example, he refused to agree to a soldier's bonus and vetoed a higher tariff Bill. The American democracy patiently awaited the election of 1920, which would bring a new President to office. Wilson exerted himself only to ensure that support of the League of Nations was a plank in the Democratic party platform. But the election was not fought over the treaty. To Wilson's surprise, since he knew 'a great moral issue was involved', the Republicans won easily.

Woodrow Wilson survived the ending of his term of office by three years. He settled in a house in S street, Washington and attempted to write his long projected book on political theory and to open a law office. Perforce he had to live the life of an invalid. He read a little, drove a little, and was visited by friends and distinguished guests. The world of President Harding and President Coolidge into which the United States had turned — surely

NOTE

not forward? — was one that revolted his ideals, but he kept silence. When he died on February 3rd, 1924, the obituary notices were mixed and for the most part critical. The careers of few American Presidents have been more profound objects of controversy. Wilson's intellectual arrogance, his academic prepossessions, his ruthlessness towards his colleagues, his inordinate ambition, his aloofness, laid his career open to easy and caustic comment. How satisfying it was for the lesser men in life to enjoy a vicarious pleasure from contemplating the idealist who had failed because he believed that the common people would recognize and embrace the truth if they saw it. But yet one sometimes cannot help wondering if true idealists — though they make mistakes — ever entirely fail.

NOTE

Did Bryan Procure Wilson's Nomination for the Presidency?

When the Democratic National Convention met at Baltimore in 1912 it appeared likely that Champ Clark of Missouri and not Wilson would obtain the nomination. The chosen candidate had to obtain a two-thirds majority. At the tenth ballot when the New York State delegation swung its ninety votes from Harmon of Ohio (the third candidate) to Clark, who headed the ballot, it seemed as if Wilson was doomed. However at the fourteenth ballot W. J. Bryan, one of the Nebraska delegates, explained that as the New York vote had gone to Clark and thereby made him the chosen candidate of 'Tammany Hall', his vote would be shifted from Clark to Wilson. Although the Nebraska vote thus went to Wilson, he lost several votes from other states; nevertheless Clark made no further important gains, and after a while his stock declined so that finally on the forty-sixth ballot Wilson secured the nomination.

In a recent article in the *American Historical Review* (July 1945) Mr. Arthur S. Link argued that Bryan's influence on this result has been greatly exaggerated by many American historians. He points out that Clark had gained the New York vote by the *tenth* ballot and if the anti-Clark votes had disintegrated after this,

Wilson could not possibly have been elected. But they remained steady, and therefore the danger point for Wilson had passed before Bryan made his speech at the *fourteenth* ballot. Moreover some evidence is quoted that when Bryan shifted his vote from Clark to Wilson, he was hoping that there would be a deadlock and that he himself would be called upon to stand as a 'compromise' candidate.

It is, however, fair to say, I think, that there is no substantial evidence for the view that Bryan hoped to obtain the nomination for himself. Not only did Mrs. Bryan deny this, but those who asserted that it was so — such as Colonel House, Carter Glass and Colonel Harvey were not really in a position to judge Bryan's mind or motives. As to the question whether Bryan's change of vote did help Wilson, Mr. Link has himself printed a letter from one of Wilson's managers in the course of which he said:

> As to Mr. Bryan, I will say that he was the colossal figure of the occasion and that his shadow fell across the Convention time and again and produced most astounding results ... Mr. Bryan did not dictate the nomination of Mr. Wilson, but he certainly drove the last nails into the coffin of Mr. Clark for all time and undoubtedly did a wonderful service for Mr. Wilson, and Mr. Wilson is certainly under great obligations to him and I sincerely hope that he will make him Secretary of State.

As I have pointed out, in 1912 a 'progressive' candidate was required and likely to win the presidential election. When Bryan damned Clark as the creature of the corrupt politicians of Tammany Hall, he was inviting all delegations that sought a progressive candidate to vote for Wilson — though Wilson's reputation had been largely that of an enlightened conservative. Hence it seems to me that Bryan did in fact contribute materially to Wilson's nomination.

SELECT BIBLIOGRAPHY

T. A. BAILEY: *Woodrow Wilson and the Lost Peace* (1944); *Woodrow Wilson and the Great Betrayal* (1945).
RAY STANNARD BAKER: *Woodrow Wilson and the World Settlement* (1923); *Woodrow Wilson. Life and Letters* (eight volumes) (1927-39).
RAY STANNARD BAKER and W. E. DODD: *The Public Papers of Woodrow Wilson* (1925-27).
H. C. F. BELL: *Woodrow Wilson and the People* (1945).
RUTH CRANSTON: *The Story of Woodrow Wilson* (1945).
JOSEPHUS DANIELS: *The Wilson Era, 1910-1917* (1944).
WILLIAM DIAMOND: *The Economic Thought of Woodrow Wilson* (1943),
W. E. DODD: *Woodrow Wilson and his Work* (1932).
ROBERT L. M. FOLLETTE: *Autobiography* (1913).
CARTER GLASS: *An Adventure in Constructive Finance* (1926).
B. J. HENDRICK: *Life and Letters of W. H. Page* (1924).
PAXTON HIBBER: *The Peerless Leader* (1929).
DAVID F. HOUSTON: *Eight Years with Wilson's Cabinet* (1926).
HARLEY KNOTTER: *The Origins of the Foreign Policy of Woodrow Wilson* (1937).
ARTHUR S. LINK: 'The Baltimore Convention of 1912' in *American Historical Review* (July 1945); *Wilson: the Road to the White House* (1947).
ELEANOR W. MCADOO: *The Woodrow Wilsons* (1937).
W. S. MYERS: *Woodrow Wilson. Some Princeton Memories* (1946).
EDITH G. REID: *Woodrow Wilson* (1934).
CHARLES SEYMOUR: *The Intimate Papers of Colonel House* (1926).
JOSEPH P. TUMULTY: *Woodrow Wilson as I Knew Him* (1922).
MRS. WOODROW WILSON: *My Memoir* (1939).
T. WOODROW WILSON: *Congressional Government* (1885).

CHAPTER VIII

EPILOGUE—THE UNITED STATES AND GREAT BRITAIN

NONE of the American leaders, whose stories have been told in this book, can be said to have been friendly towards England, with the exception of Theodore Roosevelt after he had ceased to be President and arrived in London to pay an unexpected compliment to his hosts on the virtues of British imperialism. George Washington, himself of genteel English blood, had been convinced as early as 1769 that the 'lordly masters' of Great Britain aimed at depriving the Americans of their freedom and had raised his sword lest the American people should fall a prey to despotism. Though Washington when he became President was often accused of being pro-British, it is clear that his foreign policy, like that of many great generals who had subsequently become statesmen, had no other object than that of keeping his country, still licking its wounds, out of another war. Thomas Jefferson did not mince his words about 'the harlot England'. Did he not visit the country and see with his own eyes that even after peace had been made and American independence established 'that nation hates us, their ministers hate us, and their King more than any man'? As President Jefferson brought his government to the edge of war with Britain and when under Madison's Presidency war came in 1812 Jefferson urged from the scene of his retirement the employment of 'hired incendiaries' to burn the city of London if New York needed avenging. President Andrew Jackson was anti-British from his early childhood. The death of his brothers at British hands in the War of Independence and his own harsh treatment as a boy by British soldiers bit deep into his soul. Not even the battle of New Orleans, won by Jackson, after the war of 1812 had ended, could put paid to the account. To him the English were cruel in war and unscrupulous in peace. Lincoln's feelings towards England during the American Civil War were often undoubtedly those of resentment. He could not be expected to appreciate the reasons why the British Government adopted a

EPILOGUE

policy of 'neutrality' and he was especially bitter over the *Trent* affair. While Theodore Roosevelt does not appear to have experienced any special animosity towards England, where he passed some happy days in his childhood, Woodrow Wilson, though his country was 'associated' with her in the first German War, was never an admirer of British policies and was always suspicious of British motives. When Germany committed her act of aggression against Belgium in 1914 and Britain went to war in fulfilment of her treaty obligations, Wilson was unable to distinguish any moral difference between one side and the other; he believed to the end that Britain and France went to war from interested motives and not, as did the United States in 1917, out of moral ardour. He thought that the British navy was as sharp a menace to the peace of the world as the German army. And he used a big stick to drive the British Prime Minister along the path that Wilson thought he ought to follow — even if the stick broke in his hands.

In these antagonisms and suspicions harboured by the American Presidents they undoubtedly represented the sentiments of the vast majority of the American people. For in every sense the Presidency, as has been argued, has been and can be a national and genuinely representative institution. There is, however, a paradox in that while the United States was still largely peopled by men and women of English descent and connections the anti-British feeling then was more pronounced than in later years when the English element became a minority. This was of course for historical reasons. It is easy to understand that memories of the War of Independence and of the war of 1812, enshrined in the school text-books, as well as in the minds of older people, long affected American feelings for England — and English feelings towards America. During the Jacksonian era much testimony was put on record of the dislike between the two nations which persisted for twenty or thirty years after those wars were over. Writing in 1833 Alexis de Tocqueville said: 'One cannot imagine any hatred more venomous than that between the Americans and the English.' Four English authors, who went to the United States at this period, Frances Trollope, Basil Hall, Harriet Martineau and Charles Dickens, all reflected in different ways in their works the attitude of moral and social superiority typical of

THE UNITED STATES AND GREAT BRITAIN

the English of their time as well as the defiant contempt of the Americans. Mrs. Trollope's book in particular was certainly not calculated to heal any wounds but rather to inflict them.

In her *Domestic Manners of the Americans* (1832) Frances Trollope emphasized the uncouth and uncultured nature of the majority of the American people, 'never ... the air of leisure or repose', no love of music, theatres few and acting indifferent, religion crude, hotel manners lacking. 'Let America give a fair portion of her attention to the arts and the graces that embellish life', she observed condescendingly, 'and I will make her another visit and write another book as unlike this as possible.' Frances Trollope made clear what she considered to be a main source of these American defects: in America 'any man's son may become the equal of any other man's son ... a spur to coarse familiarity'. The deaf, if studious, Harriet Martineau, who published her *Society in America* six years later, being herself a radical, was less illiberal in her approach. Moreover she found less to resent. Whereas Mrs. Trollope had been sent over by her husband to open a department store in Cincinnati — a project in which she failed — and found the town 'by no means of striking appearance', Miss Martineau when she toured that city in the course of her travels found it 'a glorious place'. With a grasp of the meaning of democracy, she rebutted the idea that a republic was vulgar and thought it 'absorbing to watch the process of world-making'. Nevertheless she was obsessed by the then unshaken institution of slavery and the inferiority of women's status and her long book is ill-balanced for that reason. Dickens also was outspoken about slavery in his *American Notes* which he wrote describing his visit to America in 1842. Like Mrs. Trollope too he could not resist remarking on what he considered the lack of culture and manners among Americans or on the pride that they took in 'outsmarting' each other. Neither the *Notes* nor the American episodes in *Martin Chuzzlewit* endeared this successful Victorian novelist to Americans any more than we enjoyed some of Nathaniel Hawthorne's strictures about England.

The truth is that in those formative years in American history, above all, during the democratic age of Andrew Jackson the average English visitor, let alone a pampered public pet like Dickens, could not be expected to know that they were witnessing

EPILOGUE

'a world in the making'. Many of the things that surprised and affronted English observers such as the rough-and-ready manners, the 'Jack is as good as his master' outlook, the common absorption in the accumulation of wealth and the usual contempt among men of leisure, and the almost total absence of domestic servants in the European sense were inevitable among pioneers. Today the wheel has turned almost fully. Looking at America from a new and less elevated vantage point we in England can but envy a pile of wealth that has bestowed so high a standard of living on her people, the habit of doing without domestic servants and consequent adjustments that have prevented the average woman's life from being one long drudgery, the tradition of democracy that has made most white men equals without bringing hate, malice and interminable civil war. However, broadly, it is fair to say that in the first half of the nineteenth century both in politics and society little love was lost between the two countries. We were not brothers but first cousins.

The American Civil War was a watershed in Anglo-American relations. At the time when that war began some improvement in the relationship between the two nations could be recorded. A number of long-standing political differences had been settled. The British Government had renounced its claim of a right to search foreign ships in time of peace. Minor disputes in Central America had been settled. A new generation had grown up since the war of 1812. There was a wider admiration and appreciation of the prosperity and successful social democratic experiment in the United States. On the other side, there was some recognition in America of the value of the traditions that we shared in common — the language, the common law, the puritan approach to life. But with the Civil War, unfortunately, fresh animosities were born. The north resented the British Government's proclamation of neutrality — for were not the south mere rebels? The south were hurt because the British Government did not recognize their independence as a nation struggling to be free. Yet looked at in the after-glow of events, British reactions and behaviour are understandable. When it was generally thought in England that the war was a struggle over slavery and that Lincoln would immediately proclaim the abolition of the peculiar institution of the south, British opinion as a whole was favourable to the north. In

THE UNITED STATES AND GREAT BRITAIN

July 1861, Henry Adams, son of Charles Adams, the British Minister in London, could write: 'The English are really on our side; of that I have no doubt whatever.' But when Lincoln failed to proclaim abolition in the early days of the war some British sympathies tended to veer southward. The British Government's decision to treat the southerners as belligerents was technically correct, for had not Lincoln by proclaiming a blockade of the southern ports — instead of treating his opponents as pirates — himself recognized them as belligerents? Moreover the curious behaviour of Seward, Lincoln's Secretary of State, was not calculated to endear the northern cause to the British. Seward called Britain 'the most grasping and rapacious power in the world'. He urged on Lincoln the advisability of starting a foreign war against Britain to heal the breach in American unity. It was rumoured that he had told the Duke of Newcastle before the war that if he became Secretary of State it would 'become his duty to insult England and he meant to do so'. He tried to bargain American participation in an agreement on international law against Great Britain's withdrawal of her recognition of southern belligerency. Finally towards the end of the war a scheme was again put forward for Lincoln's consideration to turn American arms against a European nation. Although this time the proposed enemy appears to have been France and not England, Charles Adams reported from London that 'the impression is now very general that peace and restoration at home are synonymous with war with this country'.

These facts are set out not because they represent a fair or complete appraisal of the relations between the United States and England during the Civil War, but because a number of contemporary American writers conveyed the impression, which still endures in some places, that there was a conspiracy on the part of the then British Whig Government and the British upper classes to destroy the United States. For example, if American readers had a right to feel disgusted over some of the observations recorded by Mrs. Trollope and Charles Dickens, British readers might resent the picture painted in Henry Adams's celebrated reminiscences (*The Education of Henry Adams*, 1905) of how Russell, Palmerston and Gladstone 'had shown power, patience and steadiness of purpose... had persisted for two years and a half in their

EPILOGUE

plan for breaking up the Union, and had yielded at last only in the jaws of war'. That it was widely thought at one time that the Union would split is true; that there was any organized conspiracy to achieve it or that the British Government violated any generally accepted code of international law is nonsense. This is proved conclusively by the American historian, E. D. Adams, in his comprehensive book on *Great Britain and the American Civil War*. Adams points out how in the eighteen-fifties there had been a positive change in British policy which had resulted in a determination to cease opposition to the expansion of American power and that a conviction had sprung up that 'the might of America would tend towards the greatness of England itself'. 'In the months preceding the outbreak of the civil war', he sums up, 'all British governmental effort was directed toward keeping clear of the quarrel and toward conciliation of the sections. No doubt there were those in Great Britain who rejoiced at the rupture between North and South, but they were not in office and had no control of British policy.' In particular the British working classes sympathized with the north as protagonists of democracy and enemies of privilege.

Such are the impartial judgments of an American historian on a subject which has too often been distorted even by so well-meaning an English author as Lord Charnwood in his life of Lincoln. After the Civil War a change for the better came in Anglo-American relations. Britain's difficulties with Ireland of course made us unpopular in those parts of the United States — and there are many — where the Irish command influence and power. But, on the other hand, after the passing of the Reform Bills of 1867 and 1885 the two countries were drawn closer together by a common democratic outlook. Writing in the eighteen-nineties the American Captain Mahan explained how British sea power had materially contributed to United States progress, an argument which has been repeated in our own times by another American, Walter Lippmann. A little earlier Lord Bryce's famous book on the American Commonwealth (first published in 1889) did much to broaden British understanding of the American political system. Except for one incident, arising out of a bonndary dispute between Venezuela and British Guiana, diplomatic relations between the two countries were most friendly as the reign

THE UNITED STATES AND GREAT BRITAIN

of Queen Victoria drew towards its close. There was co-operation over the policy of the Open Door in China and agreement over the trans-oceanic canal in Central America. In general the British press sympathized with the United States during the Cuban war.

And yet unhappily sources of misunderstanding remained, that were to be exploited during the Presidency of Woodrow Wilson and found expression in his own attitude and policies. On the British side the habit of looking down our noses at the Americans persisted — indeed it persists among the stupid and ill-informed until this day. Every provincial town still has its Mrs. Trollope. And in such country houses as have not yet been assigned to the National Trust there can still be unearthed someone like Lady Margaret Beaumont who, entertaining Americans to tea in the 'sixties, could say: 'I don't think I care for foreigners.' Such 'airs of supercilious condescension', as Lord Bryce called them, ought surely to be dropped. Yet the author encountered them among the staff of the British Embassy in Washington during the recent war. And equally he understands why (though he was taken aback at the time) on being introduced to an American colonel in an American officers' club in London he was told: 'Well, at any rate you won't be able to say that you won *this* war.'

Thus the idea that the British are arrogant, overbearing and selfish people is nurtured among Americans. How far American historical text-books, today equally sow the opinion among the rising American citizens that we have customarily been oppressors might be worth investigation. Writing at the turn of the century, Professor A. B. Hart spoke of how American writers of school histories 'have thought it necessary to provide strong food for little minds', and Professor G. B. Adams, although not regarding this as an important factor in the situation, could observe: 'It must be regarded as proved beyond all doubt that there is in the minds of a large proportion of our people, very probably the majority of them, a peculiar feeling of dislike towards England, which they cherish towards no other country. . . .'

In the more recent past, and especially during our association in the two wars against Germany, American and British men and women have come to respect the good qualities characteristic of each other's nation. No one, it seems to me, can fail to value the

EPILOGUE

individual generosity, the idealist streak, the egalitarianism, of Americans, the beauty and intelligence of their women, the tough good nature of their men. On the other hand, Americans who have visited this country have discovered beneath our many snobberies and the stand-offishness, especially of Londoners, our own forms of generosity, our love of old and beautiful things, our women's charm and grace, our men's sincerity and catholicity of interest. Much cynicism has been expended on the dangers of going abroad — and of course a risk always lies in it. You may be a Thomas Jefferson, finding relatively little to admire, a Theodore Roosevelt who speaks with a sudden but perhaps ephemeral gush of admiration to his hosts, or a Woodrow Wilson who finds much bad intermingled with little good. Or — for that matter — your visitors may themselves be poor ambassadors exhibiting either a singular gaucheness or a disagreeable superiority — like Britishers who cannot find their own type of beer abroad or Americans who hate their cocktails warm. But, on the whole, it is surely a knowledge and understanding of one another's countries and characters and cultures that contributes the most to the development of friendly relations. I hope this sketch I have written of American history and famous Americans will help a little to that end.

SELECT BIBLIOGRAPHY

E. D. ADAMS: *Great Britain and the American Civil War* (1925).
G. B. ADAMS: *Why Americans Dislike England* (1896).
HENRY ADAMS: *The Education of Henry Adams* (1905).
JAMES BRYCE: *The American Commonwealth* (1889).
CHARLES DICKENS: *American Notes* (1847).
NATHANIEL HAWTHORNE: *The English Note Books* (ed. R. Stewart, 1941).
HARRIET MARTINEAU: *Society in America* (1839).
B. A. REUTER: *Anglo-American Relations during the Spanish-American War* (1924).
G. W. SMALLEY: *Anglo-American Memories* (1911).
A. DE TOCQUEVILLE: *Democracy in America* (ed. Reeve, 1840).
FRANCES TROLLOPE: *Domestic Manners of the Americans* (ed. M. Sadleir, 1927.)

INDEX

Abbott, Lawrence F., quoted, 356
Abolitionists, 245, 255, 257, 259, 270, 285
Adams, Abigail, 147, 161
Adams, Charles, 437
Adams, E. D., quoted, 438
Adams, G. B., quoted, 439
Adams, Henry, 153, 322, 363, 437
Adams, James Truslow, quoted, 9, 311
Adams, President John, 14, 52, 54, 96, 97, 110, 114, 123 seq., 128, 134, 136, 137, 139, 140, 141, 147, 161 seq., 198, 236, 329, 398
Adams, President John Quincy, 14, 113, 141, 198, 202, 206 seq.
Adamson Act, the, 400
Agriculture, Department of, 346, 355, 395
Alabama, state of, 186, 200, 201, 274
Alabama, the, 294
Alaska, boundary dispute over, 338
Albany, 65, 67, 317, 318
Algeciras conference, 350, 351
Alien Act, the, 137, 236
Allegheny river, 38
André, John, 77
Angle, P. M., quoted, 306
Antietam creek, battle of, 283, 286, 287, 305
Appalachians, 25, 49, 50
Appomattox, 303
Argentina, 403
Arizona, state of, 325, 360
Arkansas, state of, 143, 277, 296
Arnold, Benedict, 56, 66, 67, 77, 79, 119, 120
Articles of Confederation, the, 78-9, 83, 85
Atlanta, 300, 303, 372
Audubon, John James, 314
Austria-Hungary, 406, 411, 414
Axson, Stockton, 377

Baker, Ray Stannard, 376
Balfour, A. J., 418
Baltimore, 54, 62, 198, 267, 279, 374, 392
Bank, National, and Jefferson, 130; and Jackson, 170, 211 seq., 214, 215, 218 seq.
Banks, General Nathaniel P., 296
Barbados, 37
Barnes, William, 360
Bates, Edward, 274
Belgium, 361, 408
Bell, John, 267
Belvoir, 36, 40, 83
Benton, Thomas, 185-6, 188, 222, 225, 226, 320
Berrien, John M., 208
Biddle, Nicholas, 211, 220 seq.
Bishop, J. B., 329, 349
Bissell, Colonel William H., 263
Black Hawk, 241
Blaine, James, 318, 319, 320
Blair, Francis P., 229, 275, 295
Blair, Montgomery, 275
Blennerhassett, Harman, 151, 152
Blount, William, 178, 179
Blount, Willie, 182, 187, 188
Blue Ridge, 34, 36, 107
Boone, Daniel, 237-8
Booth, John Wilkes, 304-5
Borah, William E., 423, 425
Boston, 51, 53, 55, 56, 73, 110, 423
Braddock, General John, 40 seq.
Braddock's Field, 14, 43, 94
Braddock's Road, 43, 49
Branch, John, 208
Brandagee, Frank L., 425
Brandeis, Louis D., 399
Brandywine, battle of, 65-6, 71, 100

Brazil, 403
Breckenridge, John, 267
Brest Litowsk, treaty of, 419
Briand-Kellogg pact, 404
Britain, treaty with United States, 81 seq., 90; war of 1912 with United States, 153 seq., 159, 190 seq., 269, 434; and American Civil War, 436 seq.; war with Germany, 411 seq., 439; and Jefferson, 125, 131, 134-5, 143, 433; and Jackson, 222, 433; and Lincoln, 294, 433; and Roosevelt, 349, 351, 433, 434; and Wilson, 378, 407 seq., 417 seq., 434; general relations with United States, 23 seq., 90 seq., 184, 293, 338, 339, 411 seq., 439 seq.
British Guiana, 438
Brooklyn Heights, 58
Brown, John, 266
Bryan, William Jennings, 12, 330-1, 332, 337, 341, 344, 353, 357, 358, 384, 386, 387, 391, 392 seq., 413, 429, 430; as Secretary of State, 394 seq., 406
Bryce, Lord, quoted, 14, 88, 322, 343, 353, 438, 439
Bryn Mawr College, 375, 376
Buchanan, President James, 260, 263, 271, 274
Buell, General Don Carlos, 284, 285
Buffalo, 332
Bull Run, first battle of, 280; second battle of, 283
Bunau-Varilla, M., 340
Bunker Hill, 54
Buren, President Martin Van, 22, 207-8, 209, 211, 215, 221, 222, 225, 226, 227, 228, 244, 245, 329
Burgoyne, General John, 65, 67
Burleson, Albert S., 395, 396
Burnside, General Ambrose E., 283, 298
Burr, Aaron, 137-8, 146, 151, 152-3, 176, 183, 184, 205, 224, 316
Butler, General Benjamin F., 218, 298
Butler, Nicholas Murray, 352
Butt, Archie, 342, 354, 355

Cabinet, the American, 21, 88-9, 218; the British, 21
Calhoun, John Caldwell, 197, 202, 204, 207, 210, 213 seq.
California, state of, 255, 349, 359, 416
Callender, James, 147
Cambridge University, 380, 382, 384
Camden, battle of, 76
Cameron, Simon, 272, 288
Canada, 41, 49, 56-7, 65, 66, 73, 74, 90, 160, 190, 299, 338, 358
Capitol, the, 160, 161
Caramelli, Yusuf, 143
Carleton, Sir Guy, 81, 82
Carnegie, Andrew, 335
Carranza, Venustiano, 402, 403
Carroll, Major-General William, 202
Cartwright, Peter, 250-1
Cass, General Lewis, 251
Cecil, Lord Robert, 422
Cedar Creek, battle of, 299
Chalmette, 194 seq.
Champlain lake, 66
Chancellorsville, battle of, 289, 290
Charleston, 59, 75, 81, 175, 214, 266, 276
Charnwood, Lord, 438
Chase, Salmon P., 272, 288, 300, 302
Chase, Samuel, judge, 142
Chastellux, Marquis de, 121, 123
Chatanooga, 290, 298
Chesapeake Bay, 24, 65, 79, 80, 81

442

INDEX

Chesapeake-Leopard episode, the, 155
Chicago, 243, 257, 267, 318, 335, 358, 359
Chickahominy river, 282
Chickamauga river, 290
Chile, 403
China, 348, 401, 402, 438
Chinard, Gilbert, quoted, 111, 153, 163
Churchill, Winston S., 343
Cincinnati, society of, 84, 86
Cincinnati, state of, 435
Civil Service reform, 318, 320 seq., 328
Civil War, 235, 237, 268 seq., 275 seq., 294, 297, 300, 314, 334, 436
Clark, Champ, 389, 392-3, 429
Clark, Captain William, 146
Clay, Henry, 12, 170, 198, 201 seq., 210, 212, 221, 241, 242, 248, 250, 251, 254, 255, 268, 269
Clayton Anti-Trust Act, 400
Clayton-Bulwer Treaty, 339
Cleveland, President Grover, 319, 321, 335, 379, 386
Clinton, George, 151
Clinton, Sir Henry, 71, 72, 73 seq., 78 seq.
Coal strikes, 337, 345, 400
Coffee, John, 187, 189, 192, 207, 216
Coffee, Polly, 216
Cold Harbour, battle of, 298
Colombia, 340-1, 404
Colorado, state of, 142, 357, 400, 427
Columbia, District of, 220, 245, 251, 255, 286, 346
Columbia University, 352
Columbus, 284
Commander-in-Chief, office of, 13, 52, 279, 287, 312
Commerce, Department of, 334, 341
Committee of Public Information, 416
Compromise of 1850, 255, 268
Concord Bridge, 52
Congress, the Continental, 36, 52, 55, 62, 67, 69, 70, 74, 75, 76, 79, 82, 83, 85-6
Connecticut, state of, 376, 425
Conscription, 292
Constitution, the American, 18, 87, 88, 126-7, 138, 153, 157-8, 235; formulation of, 86; amendments to, 297
Conventions, party, 266, 318, 331, 353, 356, 358, 392, 429
'Conway Cabal', 69-70, 99-100, 151
Conway, Thomas, 67 seq.
Coolidge, President Calvin, 22, 428
Cooper, Fenimore, 200
Corey, Herbert, 396
Cornwallis, Charles, 2nd Earl, 60, 61, 76, 79-81, 119
Corwin, Edward S., quoted, 14, 19, 92, 312
Cosway, Maria, 124
Cotton, 200, 244, 254, 269, 335
Council of Ten, the, 422
Craik, Dr. James, 83, 89, 98
Crawford, William H., 202, 205
Creeks the, 175, 186 seq.; see also Indians
Cresswell, Nicholas, quoted, 62
Croly, Herbert D., 357
Cuba, 273, 322 seq., 338, 362
Cuban war, see under Spain
Cumberland river, 174, 175, 177, 284
Custis, Jack, 47, 81, 82
Custis, Martha, see under Martha Washington
Custis, Nelly, 97

DAKOTAS, the, 143, 317, 319, 320, 325, 376
Dalmatia, 424
Daniels, Josephus, 395
Davidson College, 371
Davis, Henry Winter, 295
Davis, Jefferson, 274, 276, 277, 283, 289, 295, 302
Dearborn, General Henry, 140
Debs, Eugene, 337

Declaration of London, 1909, 411
Delaware river, crossing, 60 seq.
Delaware, state of, 277
Delcassé, Théophile, 350
Democratic party, the, 133, 136, 138, 287, 297, 299, 300, 357, 358, 384, 399, 410; split in 1860, 266 seq.
Denver, Colorado, 357, 377
D'Estaing, Comte Charles-Hector, 73
Detroit, 83
Dewey, Admiral George, 323
Diamond, William, 391
Diaz, Porfirio, 402
Dickens, Charles, 434, 435, 437
Dickinson, Charles, 182-3
Dickinson, John, 113, 189, 205
Dinwiddie, Robert, 38, 40, 41, 42
Donelson, Andrew J., 198, 215, 229
Donelson, Emily, 216
Donelson, John, 174
Dorchester Heights, 55
Douglas, Stephen, 16, 243, 255, 256 seq., 266, 267, 270, 273, 276
Dred Scott case, 260, 264
Duane, William, 220
Dunne, Finley Peter, 342
Duquesne, fort, 40 seq., 43; see also Pittsburgh

EARLY, GENERAL JUBAL A., 298, 299
Eaton, John Henry, 196, 208, 209, 210, 218, 229
Eaton, Margaret, 209 seq., 218
Edwards, Mrs. N. W., 306
Egypt, 350, 355
Eliot, Charles W., 356
Emancipation of the slaves, 286-7, 293; see also under Slavery
Eppes, John Wayles, 146
Eppes, John Wayles, Mrs., see Jefferson, Maria
Erie canal, 200, 326
Erie lake, 38
Erwin, Captain, 182, 183
Essex case, the, 154

FAIRFAX, ANN, 36
Fairfax, George William, 34, 37, 40, 83, 98
Fairfax, Lord, 36
Fairfax, Mrs. Sally, 40, 44, 83, 98-9
Fairfax, William, 37
Farragut, Admiral David G., 285
Fauquier, Francis, 107
Federalist, The, quoted, 13
Federal Reserve Bank, 399-400
Federal Trade Commission, 400
Ferry Farm, 33
Fillmore, President Millard, 255
Fiume, 424
Florida, 143 seq., 149, 150, 153, 185, 190, 191, 197 seq., 202, 274
Forbes, Major-General John, 43 seq., 50
Forests, American, Roosevelt and the, 346
Fort, Captain, 183
Fort Barrancas, 191
Fort Donelson, 284, 285
Fort Jackson, treaty of, 189, 196
Fort Le Bœuf, 38
Fort Mims, 186, 187
Fort Necessity, 39
Fort Strother, 188
Fort Sumter, 276-7
Fourteen Points, the, 419, 422
France, 38 seq., 49, 50, 74, 76, 91 seq., 126-7, 131, 132, 133, 135, 136, 137, 149, 150, 160, 222-3, 293, 295, 349, 350, 351, 361, 406, 409, 411, 417, 421 seq., 434
Franklin, Benjamin, 55, 113, 114, 115, 124
Franklin, state of, 174, 178
Fredericksburg, 33, 289, 290
Freedom of seas, the, 154 seq., 411, 419, 421

443

INDEX

Frémont, General John C., 285, 300
French Revolution, the, and United States, 91 seq., 125-6
Fry, Joshua, 106
Fugitive Slave Law, 255, 258, 275

GAGE, MAJOR-GENERAL THOMAS, 41, 51
Gallatin, Albert, 140, 142, 150, 151, 155, 179
Garrison, Lindley M., 395
Gates, General Horatio, 41, 53, 60, 66 seq., 71, 74, 76, 77, 79, 81, 99, 100
Gênet, Edmond C., 92, 132-3
George II, King, 39
George III, King, 112, 115, 116
George, Henry, 319
Georgia, state of, 74, 119, 197, 274, 303, 313, 373
Gerard, James W., 395
Germantown, battle of, 65-6, 100
Germany, 338, 349, 350, 351, 361, 407 seq., 417, 420, 434
Gettysburg, battle of, 289, 290, 304; dedication of national cemetery at, 291, 293
Gibbon, Edward, 34
Gibraltar, 78
Gladstone, W. E., 437
Glass, Carter, 399, 429
Gould, Jay, 335
Grant, General Ulysses, S., 22, 284, 285, 289 seq., 298 seq., 302, 303, 304; quoted, 292, 298, 304
Grasse, Admiral François, 79-82
Grayson, Admiral Cary T., 427, 428
Great Lakes, the, 200
Greeley, Horace, 287, 299
Greene, General Nathanael, 53, 58-9, 65, 75, 79, 83, 119, 120
Grey, Sir Edward, 359, 407, 408, 411, 418

HABEAS CORPUS, 288
Hahn, Michael, 296
Halifax, 55
Hall, Basil, 434
Halleck, General Henry W., 284-5, 292
Hamilton, Alexander, 64-5, 80, 84, 85, 86, 89-90, 93, 95, 97, 128, 130-1, 133, 135, 136, 137, 138, 151, 176, 200, 211; quoted, 13, 14, 46, 72, 76-7, 81, 82; appointed Secretary of Treasury, 88; comparison with Jefferson, 129; death, 146-7
Hampton Roads conference, 302
Hancock, John, 88, 116
Hanna, Mark, 330, 331, 332, 333, 334, 341
Harding, President Warren G., 22, 428
Harper's Ferry, 266
Harriman, Edward H., 335
Harrington, James, 17
Harrison, President Benjamin, 320, 321
Harrison, President William Henry, 22, 185, 225, 228, 245
Hart, A. B., quoted, 439
Harvard University, 53, 315, 320, 325
Harvey, Colonel George, 387, 390, 391, 430
Havana, 323
Hawthorne, Nathaniel, 435
Hay, John, 322, 333, 348
Hay-Pauncefote treaty, 339
Head of Elk, 65
Hearst, William R., 323
Henry, Patrick, 50, 52, 108-9, 110, 112
Hepburn Act, 345
Hermitage, the, 182, 184, 185, 189, 198, 199, 200, 206, 217, 226, 229
Herndon, William, 245, 249, 272; quoted, 245, 246, 248, 251, 252-3, 257, 272, 305
Hertz, Emanuel, 306
Hibben, John G., 385
Hill, James, 336
Hodgenville, 238
Holland, 78, 409

Holmes, Oliver Wendell, 336
Hooker, General Joe, 289
Houdon, Jean Antoine, 84
House, Colonel E. M., 385, 395-6, 406, 407, 417, 420, 421, 423, 425; quoted, 394, 395, 406
Houston, David, 394
Houston, Sam, 223 seq., 228-9, 250
Howe, Admiral Lord, 56, 73
Howe, Sir William, 55 seq., 61, 64, seq., 71
Hudson river, 58-9, 65, 66, 74, 146, 200, 395
Huerta, General Victoriano, 402 seq.
Hughes, Charles E., 356, 416
Hunter's Hill, 180, 182, 217
Hunting Creek, 33
Hutchings, Andrew Jackson, 216, 227
Hutchings, John, 180

ILLINOIS, 201, 240 seq., 245, 247, 250, 258, 259, 267, 284, 290, 311
Independence, Declaration of, 57, 105, 115 seq., 126, 258, 261
Independence, War of, 23, 57, 131, 434
Indiana, state of, 200, 238, 240, 267
Indians, 36, 38, 41, 49, 74, 174, 175, 176, 196, 224; Washington and, 74; Jefferson and, 148
Ingham, Samuel D., 208
Internal improvements, policy of, 211, 241, 242, 269
Inter-state Commerce Commission, 345, 352
Iowa, state of, 143
Italy, 350, 418, 419, 421, 422

JACKSON, PRESIDENT ANDREW, character, 175-6, 217-18; marriage, 177; elected Congressman, 178; elected Senator, 179, 203; appointed judge, 180; elected major-general, 181; duels, 183; campaign against Creeks, 186 seq.; New Orleans campaign, 191 seq.; nominated for Presidency, 202; as a Mason, 206; elected President, 207; re-elected, 215; first term, 208 seq.; second term, 215 seq.; and Nullification, 213; foreign policy, 222 seq.; farewell address, 225; religion, 226-7; death, 229-30; contribution to evolution of Presidency, 17, 169-71; quoted, 104, 179-80, 183-4, 185, 191, 196, 197, 210, 212, 213, 214, 215, 216, 219, 220, 224; mentioned, 12, 20, 22, 96, 145, 151, 152, 169, 239, 243, 244, 275, 287, 302, 311, 326, 352, 370, 371, 373, 386, 399, 405, 433, 434, 435
Jackson, Andrew, Junior, 185, 216-17
Jackson, Elizabeth, 171
Jackson, Hugh, 171
Jackson, Rachel, 175, 176, 177, 179, 181, 185, 187, 195, 198, 199; quoted, 188, 199, 202-3; death, 207
Jackson, Robert, 171
Jackson, General Thomas J. ('Stonewall'), 280, 282 seq., 289, 292, 298
James river, 34, 35, 84, 119
Jamestown, 35
Japan, 348, 349, 354, 418, 422
Jay, John, 88, 135, 154, 178; concludes treaty with Britain, 91-2
Jefferson, Maria (Polly), 125, 134
Jefferson, Martha, daughter of Thomas, 123, 124, 125, 127, 134, 161
Jefferson, Martha, wife of Thomas, 109-10, 122
Jefferson, Peter, 106
Jefferson, President Thomas, character, 121, 127-8, 139; descent and upbringing, 106-7; appointed delegate to Continental Congress, 111; and Declaration of Independence, 115-17; Governor of Virginia, 118-21; appointed Virginian delegate to Congress, 123; U.S. Minister in Paris, 124 seq.; visits England, 125; Secretary of State, 88, 90 seq., 127 seq., 153, 155-6, 158 seq., 164; Vice-President, 136; President, 139 seq.; and judiciary, 142: foreign

444

INDEX

Jefferson, President Thomas—*contd.*
  policy, 143 *seq.*, 149 *seq.*; second inaugural, 148; retirement, 157 *seq.*; religion, 146; death, 164-5; his *Anas*; and Hamilton, 128 *seq.*; and Britain, 125, 131, 134-5; contribution to evolution of Presidency, 16, 105-6, 157-8; quoted, 15, 30, 109, 113, 114, 120, 121, 122, 123, 127, 130, 132, 133, 134, 136, 138, 140, 141, 143, 145, 147; mentioned, 12, 32, 48, 84, 93, 169, 178-9, 183, 184, 196, 200, 201, 202, 217, 222, 236, 244, 254, 265, 269, 338, 341, 343, 351, 352, 391, 427, 433, 440
Johns Hopkins University, 374, 375
Johnson, Andrew, 18, 22, 96, 305
Johnson, Hiram, 359, 425
Jones, Joseph, 75

KANSAS CITY, 390
Kansas, state of, 143, 256, 259, 260, 357
Kansas-Nebraska Bill, 256 *seq.*
Keane, Major-General John, 195
Kendall, Amos, 218, 219, 224, 229
Kentucky resolutions, 137, 147
Kentucky, state of, 147, 177, 183, 194, 200, 201, 228, 239, 247, 248, 260, 277, 284, 286, 311
Kipps bay, 58, 59
'Kitchen Cabinet', the, 170, 208-9, 218, 275
'Know-Nothing' party, the, 263
Knox, Henry, 54, 55, 88, 128, 140
Knox, Philander C., 336
Knoxville, 174, 175, 181
Korea, 349
Ku-Klux-Klan, 335

LABOUR, DEPARTMENT OF, 395
Lafayette, Marquis Marie de, 64-5, 71, 73, 76, 82, 84, 93, 124, 163, 206
La Follette, Robert, 344, 358, 391
Lake Borgne, 192
Lansing, Robert, 413, 422, 428
Laski, Harold J., quoted, 14
League of Nations, the, 364, 370, 422 *seq.*
Lee, General Charles, 41, 52, 56, 59-60, 68, 69, 72
Lee, Henry, 46, 93
Lee, General Robert E., 266, 278, 282 *seq.*, 287, 289, 293, 298-9, 303
Lee, Robert Henry, 114
L'Enfant, Pierre Charles, 90
Lenin, Vladimir Ilyich, 418
Lesseps, Ferdinand de, 339
Lewis, Lawrence, 97
Lewis, Captain Merriwether, 145
Lewis, Major William B., 226, 229
Lexington, 52, 112
Lincoln, President Abraham, character, 242, 246, 252-3, 270, 301; youth and upbringing, 237 *seq.*; at New Salem, 240 *seq.*; attitude to women, 246 *seq.*; marriage, 248; as a lawyer, 243, 249, 252-3; elected Congressman, 250; and slavery, 255 *seq.*, 286 *seq.*, 297; campaigns against Stephen Douglas, 257 *seq.*; his 'House Divided' speech, 262, 267; nominated for Presidency, 266-7; elected President, 267 *seq*; and Civil War, 275 *seq.*; as war leader, 279; relations with generals, 281 *seq.*, 288 *seq.*, 292 *seq.*; Gettysburg speech, 291; and foreign policy, 293 *seq.*; re-elected President, 301; and peace, 302; assassination, 305; religion, 271; contribution to evolution of Presidency, 17-18, 236-7, 293; quoted, 104, 240, 241, 250, 251, 257, 258, 261, 265, 273, 286, 287, 290, 293, 294, 296, 298, 299, 300, 302, 303; mentioned, 12, 20, 22, 176, 311, 333, 334, 343, 352, 353, 357, 373, 375, 385, 416, 433, 436, 437
Lincoln, Benjamin, 75
Lincoln, Levi, 140
Lincoln, Mary, 247 *seq.*, 252, 301, 304, 305, 306
Lincoln, Nancy, 238-9

Lincoln, Robert Todd, 249, 301, 304
Lincoln, 'Tad', 301
Lincoln, Thomas, 238, 239, 241
Lincoln, 'Willie', 301
Link, A. S., quoted, 389, 429-30
Lippmann, Walter, quoted, 25, 438
Livingston, Robert, 115, 143, 144
Lloyd George, David, 419, 421, 424
Locke, John, 115, 126
Lodge, Henry Cabot, 320, 328, 330, 331, 332, 342, 343, 344, 352, 416, 425, 426, 427
Logan, Dr. George, 137
Logan, Stephen, 249
Long, John D., 323, 333
Long Island, 57-8
Louisiana Purchase, 16, 145, 181, 182, 183, 236, 341
Louisiana, state of, 49, 143, 147, 148, 149, 150, 151, 156, 175, 183, 192, 200, 223, 250, 269, 274, 296, 303
Louisville, Kentucky, 284
Lusitania, the, 361, 412, 413, 416
Lynchburgh, 197

MCADOO, WILLIAM, 392, 395, 405
McClellan, General George Brinton, 280 *seq.*, 289, 298, 299, 300
McCombs, William, 390, 393
McCosh, Dr. James, 372, 377
McDowell, General Irvin, 280, 282
McKinley, President William, 322, 323, 327, 330, 331, 332, 333
McLane, John, 220
McNairy, John, 174, 175
Madero, Francisco, 402
Madison, Dolly, 139, 145, 157
Madison, President James, 85, 86, 95, 118, 121, 136, 138, 139, 157 *seq.*, 179, 184, 191, 201, 202, 268, 411, 433
Mahan, Captain Alfred T., 323, 438
Maine, 190, 201, 317
Maine incident, the, 323
Manassas, 279, 280
Manchuria, 348
Manrique, Don Matteo Gonzalez, 191
Marbury *v.* Madison, case of, 141
Marshall, Chief Justice John, 93, 141, 152, 153, 182, 184, 218, 268
Martin Chuzzlewit, 171, 343, 435
Martine, James E., 388
Martineau, Harriet, 434, 435
Maryland, state of, 37, 50, 174, 274, 277, 283, 286, 297, 301
Massachusetts, 52, 88, 94, 110, 113, 201, 296, 320
Maximilian, Prince, of Baden, 421
Maysville Road Bill, 210
Mazzei, Philip, 136, 146
Meade, General George G., 289, 290
Melton's Bluff, 200
Medora, 317
Memphis, 285
'Mero', 175, 178
Mexico, 151, 152, 160, 183, 184, 203, 223, 250, 251, 252, 255, 294, 295, 402 *seq.*, 414
Mexico, Gulf of, 190
Middle Brook, 73
'Midnight Judges', the, 139
Milwaukee, 317
Minnesota, 143, 336
Mississippi river, 25, 49, 90, 92, 131, 143, 146, 148, 175, 192, 193, 195, 224, 239, 279, 284, 285, 290
Mississippi, state of, 201, 274
Missouri Compromise, 201, 245, 254, 257, 258, 268, 270, 273
Missouri river, 145, 146, 256
Missouri, state of, 143, 201, 259, 274, 277, 285, 286, 392, 409

445

INDEX

Mobile, 190, 191, 192
Monmouth Courthouse, battle of, 72-3
Monongahela river, 39, 41
Monroe Doctrine, 160, 338, 351
Monroe, President James, 92, 120, 127, 135, 145, 154, 155, 157, 160, 184, 191, 195, 196, 197, 201, 202, 205, 294, 424
Montana, state of, 143
Montgomery, Alabama, 277
Montgomery, Richard, 56
Monticello, 109, 110, 119, 120, 121, 127, 134, 158, 163, 164, 179
Montreal, 56, 66, 190
Morgan, Brigadier-General David, 194-5
Morgan, J. Pierpont, 335-6, 337, 344, 347, 379, 387, 410
Morley, Lord, 343
Morris, Gouverneur, 139
Morristown, 61, 62, 63, 75
Mount Joy, 70
Murfreesborough, battle of, 290, 304

NAPOLEON I, 93, 97, 137, 143, 144, 149, 150, 155, 159, 160, 179-80, 185, 190
Napoleon III, 294
Nashville, 174, 175, 176, 184, 284
Natchez, 175. 181, 185
Navy, American, under Jefferson, 155; under Roosevelt. 334
Nebraska, state of, 143, 256, 259, 330, 391, 429
Negroes, 38, 134, 193, 200, 217, 230, 240, 261 seq., 297, 334
Nevada, state of, 346
New Brunswick, 60, 61, 62
New England, 65, 156, 236, 245, 268
'New Freedom', the, 394, 397
New Jersey, 55, 62, 64, 65, 67, 70, 73, 79, 267, 336, 372, 376, 387 seq., 392, 396
Newlands, Francis, 346
New Mexico, 255, 325, 403
'New Nationalism', 357, 358
New Orleans, 90, 93, 131, 143, 152, 156, 182, 184, 185, 191, 196, 199, 205, 239, 259, 269, 285, 296; battle of, 192 seq.
Newport, 74, 76
New Salem, 240, 244, 246, 251
New York City, 56 seq., 65, 73, 74, 75, 78, 81, 119, 138, 198, 316, 376, 390; Washington's loss of, 58; Lincoln in, 266; Roosevelt and, 316, 319, 321, 326, 328, 332
New York, state of, 66, 200, 316 seq., 326 seq., 330, 332, 392
Niagara, 74, 251-2, 343
Non-Importation Bill, 135, 154 seq.
North Carolina, state of, 49, 106, 171, 174, 277, 303, 371, 395
North, Lord, 112, 113
Notes on Virginia, 121-2
Nullification, 213 seq.

OFFUTT, DENTON, 240, 241
Ohio, Forks of, 38, 40; see also Duquesne
Ohio, river, 38, 284
Ohio, state of, 147, 293, 322, 370
Oklahoma, state of, 143, 325
Ordinance of 1787, 123, 269
Oregon, state of, 229, 252
Orpen, Sir William, 425
Ossawatomie, 357
Overton, John, 175, 176
Owens, Mary, 247, 306
Oxford University, 378, 379, 380, 382, 384
Oyster Bay, 322, 329, 349, 359

PAGE, WALTER, 395, 407, 411, 418
Paine, Tom, 57, 140, 146
Pakenham, General Sir Edward, 192, 194
Palmerston, Lord, 437

Panama Canal, Theodore Roosevelt and, 311, 339 seq., 404
Parker, Alton B., 341
Patterson, C. Perry, quoted, 31
Patterson, General Robert, 280
Patton, Dr. Francis L., 377
Pearl Harbour, 348
Pennsylvania, state of, 37, 43, 50, 70, 79, 94, 96, 221, 222, 337, 375
Pensacola, 191, 197, 199
Peoria, 257, 259
Perry, Commodore Matthew C., 348
Pershing, General John J., 418
Petersburg, 303
Philadelphia, 43, 52, 62, 65, 66, 69, 71, 73, 139, 178, 179, 198, 331, 345, 386; Convention, 9, 18-19, 85-6
Philippines, the, 323, 330, 338, 353
Phillimore Committee, 422
Pierce, President Franklin, 256
Pinchot, Gifford, 346, 355
Pinckney, William, 155
Pinkerton, Alan, 274
Pittsburgh, 44, 49, 83, 335
Platt, Senator Tom, 326 seq., 330
Polk, James K., 221, 229, 230, 250, 251
Pope, General John, 283
Poplar's Grove, 177, 180
Port Arthur, 348, 349
Port Hudson, 290
Porto Rico, 326, 338 ?
Portsmouth, treaty of, 349
Portsmouth, Virginia, 119
Potomac river, 33, 34, 38, 49, 83, 84, 85, 90, 122, 280, 283, 285; Washington and, 83-6
Presidency, style of address, 9, 87, 139; characteristics, 12-13, 14, 19 seq., 139, 157-8, 312; constitutional clauses concerning, 13-14, 86
Priestley, Joseph, 145, 146
Princeton, 61
Princeton University, 325, 369, 372, 376 seq., 397
Pringle, Henry F., quoted, 328, 334
Progressive party, 359
Prospect, 384
Pueblo, Colorado,
Pulitzer, Joseph, 323
Putnam, Israel, 53

QUEBEC, 56, 66

RAILWAYS, AMERICAN, 335, 336, 345, 353
Randall, J. G., quoted, 276 n., 306
Randolph, Edmund, 88, 92, 93
Randolph, Jane, 106-7
Randolph, John, of Roanoake, 149, 150
Randolph, Peyton, 112
Rapahannock river, 34
Rathbone, Major, 304
Raystown, 43
Reclamation policy, 346
Reconstruction, 295 seq.
Red Sticks, 187
Redstone road, 39
Reed, Joseph, 59, 60
Reid, John, 196
Reparations, 424
Representatives, House of, 18, 19, 86, 138, 179, 254, 294, 297, 352, 357, 410, 427
Republican party, 133, 263, 270, 275, 287, 299, 318, 322, 330, 352, 358; convention of 1860, 267
Rhode Island, 73, 74, 80
Rhodes, J. F., 270, 342
Richmond, Virginia, 113, 119, 184, 279, 281, 282, 298, 303
Riis, Jacob, 318, 322, 328, 344, 357
Robards, Lewis, 175, 177

446

INDEX

Robards, Rachel, *see* Jackson, Rachel
Robertson, Captain James, 174, 175
Rochambeau, Count, 76, 77
Rockefeller, William, 335
Rockies, the, 25, 143
Rodney, Admiral George B., 78, 81
Rome, Georgia, 374
Roosevelt, Alice, 315 *seq.*
Roosevelt, Edith, 319, 354
Roosevelt, Franklin Delano, 11, 18, 19, 20, 22, 133, 313, 395, 413, 416
Roosevelt, Quentin, 362, 364
Roosevelt, Theodore, character, 319, 324, 329, 342, 362; comparison with Lincoln, 311; parents, 313; youth and education, 313 *seq.*, 316; first marriage, 315; second marriage, 319; enters politics, 316; as a cowboy, 317 *seq.*; as an author, 320, 322; character, 319, 324, 329, 342, 362; as Civil Service Commissioner, 320-1; as Police Commissioner, 321-2; Assistant Secretary of Navy, 322; takes part in South American war, 324 *seq.*; Governor of New York State, 326 *seq.*; elected Vice-President, 329 *seq.*; becomes President, 332; and trusts, 336 *seq.*, 345; foreign policy, 337 *seq.*; elected President, 341; hobbies, 342; his 'Corollary', 351; in retirement, 354 *seq.*; opinions on German war, 361 *seq.*; contribution to evolution of Presidency, 18-19, 311-12, 333-4; quoted, 168, 234, 312, 314, 318, 320, 321, 323, 324, 327, 328, 330, 331, 332, 333, 338, 341, 342, 348, 351, 353, 354, 357, 359, 360, 361, 368, 370, 391, 393, 394, 398, 404, 406, 416, 433, 440; *Autobiography*, 312, 313, 318, 319, 327, 333, 342; mentioned, 12, 17, 19, 20, 222, 237, 375, 385, 386
Root, Elihu, 333, 348, 357
Rosecrans, General William S., 285, 290
Rough Riders, 324 *seq.*, 363, 397
Rush, Benjamin, 100, 146
Russell, Lord John, 437
Russia, 78, 293, 348, 349, 354, 407, 414, 418, 419, 420
Rutledge, Anne, 246

Saar, the, 424
Saint-Gaudens, Augustus, 343
St. Louis, Missouri, 284
Sakhalin, 349
Salisbury, North Carolina, 171
Sandburg, Carl, 306
Sangamon, 240, 243
San Juan hills, battle of, 325, 326
Santiago Bay, 325
Santo Domingo, 351
Saratoga, battle of, 67, 68, 69, 100, 119
Sargent, John, 425
Savannah, 74, 303, 376
Sayre, Francis, 405
Schlesinger, A. M., quoted, 17, 209
Schulyer, Philip John, 53, 56, 66, 67
Scott, General Winfield, 273, 279, 280
Secession, right of, 236
Security treaty, proposed with, 424, 427
Sedition act, 137, 236
Senate, the, 21, 86, 93, 138, 157, 169, 254, 332, 351, 363, 369; treaty-making powers, 93; and Jackson, 218 *seq.*; and Roosevelt, 334, 339; and Wilson, 398, 410, 423 *seq.*
Serajevo, 406
Serbia, 406, 407
'Seven Sisters', the, 396-7
Sevier, John, 174, 176, 178, 181, 182
Seward, William H., 261, 267, 272, 273, 286, 288, 293, 295, 305, 437
Seymour, Charles, quoted, 406
Shadwell, 107
Share croppers, 335

Shays rebellion, 94, 126
Shenandoah valley, 34, 37, 279, 280, 282, 283, 292, 298, 299
Sheridan, General Philip H., 299
Sherman Anti-Trust Act, 336, 346, 400
Sherman, Roger, 114, 386
Sherman, William T., 280, 289, 290, 298, 300, 303
Shiloh, battle of, 285
Shipping Bill, 1916, 410
Sigel, General Franz, 298
Sims, Admiral W. S., 418
Sinclair, Upton, 344, 346
Sinking Spring, 238
Skelton, Martha Wayles, *see* Martha Jefferson
Slavery, 244 *seq.*, 254 *seq.*, 269 *seq.*, 436, 437
Small, Dr. William, 107
Smith, Caleb B., 275
Smith, Senator James, 387, 388-98, 391
Smith, Captain John, 35
Smith, Robert, 140
Smuts, General Jan C., 422
Soldiers' Home, the, 301
South Carolina, state of, 75, 76, 119, 213 *seq.*, 236, 268, 270, 271, 274, 303, 313, 371
Spain, 49, 50, 78, 92, 93, 131, 143, 149, 150, 154, 160, 182, 183, 184, 186, 190, 198, 199, 223, 294, 322, 350; American war against, 25, 322 *seq.*, 332, 338, 439
'Specie Circular', 224, 227
Speed, Joshua, 244, 255, 258, 271, 272; quoted, 244
'Spot Resolutions', 251
Spotsylvania Courthouse, battle of, 298
Springfield, Illinois, 242, 243, 244, 245, 249, 251, 257, 267, 271, 272, 305
Spring Rice, Cecil, 322
Stamp Act, 50
Stamp Act Congress, 50-1
Standard Oil Company, 341, 345, 352
Stanton, Edwin M., 288
State Department, 401, 403
Staunton, 370
Steel, 335, 347
Steele, General Frederick, 297
Steffens, Lincoln, 344
Stephens, Alexander H., 273, 303
Steuben, Baron von, 71, 72
Steubenville, 370
Stirling, General, 67-8
Stuart, John T., 243, 246, 249, 255
Styles, Ezra, quoted, 13
Submarine campaign, 412 *seq.*
Sub-treasury scheme, 227, 245
Sullivan, Major-General John, 60, 61, 74
A Summary View of the Rights of British America, 112, 115,
Supreme Court, the, mentioned, 21, 22, 170, 219, 260, 266, 336
Sussex, the, 413
Swann, Thomas, 183, 186
Sweden, 78
Swisher, C. B., quoted, 14, 363

Taft, President William, mentioned, 14, 338, 348, 351, 353, 354 *seq.*, 394, 400, 403, 404, 422
Talladega, battle of, 187-8
Tallushatchee, 187
Tammany Hall, 138, 316, 328, 360, 392, 429
Tampico, 403
Taney, Roger, 218, 220-1, 302
Tangier, 350
Tarbell, Ida, 344
Tariffs, 203, 206, 213, 241, 269, 270, 374, ⁀⁀8
Taussig, F. W., 398
Taylor, President Zachary, 250, 251, 255
Tea Act, 51
Tecumseh, 185, 186
Temperley, H. W. V., quoted, 350

INDEX

Tennessee, 147, 174, 178, 181, 182, 187, 194, 195, 200, 202, 205, 216, 225, 227, 277, 284, 285, 290, 298, 303
'Tennis Cabinet', 342, 355
Texas, state of, 223, 228, 250, 251, 254, 277, 325, 334, 395
Thacher, James, quoted, 77-8, 80
Thomas, General George, 290, 303
Thornton, Dr. William, 90
Ticonderoga, 66, 67
Tilghman, Colonel, 83
Timberlake, *see* Eaton
Tobacco, 35, 269, 335
Tocqueville, Alexis de, quoted, 434
Tohopeka (or Horseshoe Bend), 189
Toronto (York), 160, 190
Townshend duties, 51, 109, 110
Trent, the, 294
Trenton, battle of, 60 *seq.*, 66
Trevelyan, Sir George Otto, 343
Trollope, Frances, 434, 435, 437, 439
Truman, President Harry, 23
Trusts, 336 *seq.*, 341, 346, 352
Tumulty, Joseph, 387, 413
Turner, F. J., quoted, 145
Twain, Mark, 379
Tyler, President John, 228

Uncle Tom's Cabin, 255
Underwood-Simmons Tariff, 398-9, 415
Utah, state of, 255

VALCOUR ISLAND, BATTLE OF, 66
Valley Forge, 66, 70-1, 75
Vallindigham, Clement L., 293
Vandalia, 242
Venezuela, 338, 351, 438
Vera Cruz, 403
Vergennes, Charles, Comte de, 124
Vermont, state of, 66, 147
Vernon, Mount, 33, 36, 37, 40, 42, 47, 79, 82 *seq.*, 84, 87, 96-8, 419
Versailles, treaty of, 421 *seq.*, 421
Vice-Presidency, 138
Vicksburg, 285, 290, 303, 304
Vidal, Mercedes, 199
Virginia, 32, 34 *seq.*, 42 *seq.*, 49, 50, 52, 65, 76, 78, 83, 85, 105-7, 109, 110, 111, 114, 118 *seq.*, 158 *seq.*, 177, 201, 238, 276 *seq.*, 283, 284, 298; society in, 35; Jefferson's reforms, 117 *seq.*
Virginia, university of, 163, 373, 384
Voltaire, François-Marie Arouet de, 125

WAKEFIELD, 33
Walker, Robert J., 228
Wall Street, 336, 347, 390, 408
War, Board of, 69, 71
War Industries Board, 416
Ward, General Artemas, 52 *seq.*
Washington D.C., 139, 181, 251, 283, 298, 299, 327, 275, 298, 423; foundation, 90; sack of, 190
Washington, Augustine, 32, 42
Washington, President George, character, 31 *seq.*, 40, 44, 45-6, 59, 78, 97-8; descent and upbringing, 32-4; youth, 36; fights against French, 38 *seq.*; as disciplinarian, 42, 54, 79; marriage, 44; elected to Virginian House of Burgesses, 45; and slavery, 46-7; finances, 48-9; chosen Commander-in-Chief, 52; as general, 53, 62 *seq.*, 79 *seq.*; favours independence, 57; temper, 69; and Indians, 74; views on Constitution, 82; elected President, 87; as President, 87 *seq.*; foreign policy, 92 *seq.*; farewell address, 95-6; daily round, 48, 82, 98; called from retirement as Lieutenant-General, 97; religion, 47-8; death, 98; contribution to evolution of Presidency, 15-16, 31, 93-5; quoted, 34, 36, 39, 40, 42, 51, 58, 62, 63, 64, 65, 67, 70, 72, 73, 75, 76, 77, 84, 85, 86, 87, 93, 94, 95; mentioned, 9, 12, 15, 20, 25, 105, 109, 116, 119, 130, 133, 134, 135, 145, 148, 152, 169, 163, 178, 211, 217, 222, 254, 278, 288, 351, 363, 407, 427, 433
Washington, Colonel John, 32
Washington, John Augustus, 83
Washington, Lawrence, 33, 36, 40
Washington, Lund, 81
Washington, Martha, 44, 47, 55, 70, 75, 81, 83, 87, 97, 98, 99, 185
Washington, Mary, 33, 81
Washington Turnpike Bill, 211
Waxhaw river, 171
Weatherford, Bill or 'Red Eagle', 187, 189
Webster, Daniel, 207, 255, 372
Weightman, Roger, 164
Welles, Gideon, 274
Wesleyan University, 376
West, Andrew, 383
West Indies, 73, 78, 81, 132, 154, 190, 222
West Point, 77
Whigs, 250, 263
White, Henry, 422
White Plains, battle of, 58, 60
Whitney, Eli, 254
Wilkinson, General James, 67-8, 151, 153, 183, 184, 185
William II, Kaiser, 349, 350, 315, 355, 420
William and Mary College, 107, 117, 163
Williams, Colonel John, 203
Williamsburg, 45, 107, 108, 111
Wilmington, 65, 70, 372
Wilmot, David, his proviso, 251
Wilson, Edith, 415, 428
Wilson, Eleanor, 405
Wilson, Ellen, 374, 376, 390, 405, 408
Wilson, James, 370
Wilson, Jessie, 405
Wilson, Joseph Ruggles, 370
Wilson, President Thomas Woodrow, character, 374, 377, 381, 384-5, 397, 408; upbringing and education, 370 *seq.*; as an orator, 372; as a writer, 372, 374, 378; first marriage, 376; second marriage, 415; teacher of history, 375 *seq.*; appointed president of Princeton, 379; educational theories, 379 *seq.*; elected Governor of New Jersey, 387 *seq.*, 396; campaign for Presidency, 390 *seq.*; relations with labour, 390-1; choice of Cabinet, 394; first term 398 *seq.*; foreign policy, 401 *seq.*; policy of neutrality in first German war, 408 *seq.*; declaration of war on Germany, 414 *seq.*; re-elected, 416; as a war minister, 416 *seq.*; as peacemaker, 419 *seq.*; and League of Nations, 422 *seq.*; religion, 373; paralysis and death, 428-9; contribution to evolution of Presidency, 20-1, 369, 375; quoted, 14, 234, 270, 310, 386, 388, 389, 397, 400, 402, 408, 412, 413, 414, 418, 427; mentioned, 12, 18, 19, 22, 133, 222, 237, 313, 341, 343, 357, 359, 362, 434, 439, 440
Wisconsin, state of, 254, 344, 359
Wister, Owen, 342, 344, 359, 361
Wolcott, Oliver, 96
Wood, Private John, 189, 205
Wood, General Leonard, 325, 326, 338
Woodrow, Dr. Thomas, 371
Wyoming, state of, 143
Wythe, George, 107, 108, 201

'X. Y. Z. AFFAIR', 137, 138, 140

YALE UNIVERSITY, 325, 356
York river, 34, 281
Yorktown, siege of, 80, 126

ZIMMERMANN NOTE, 414

448

MR. PRESIDENT